M000083991

SUDDENLY SENIOR

The Funny Thing About Getting Older

TOM HAY

ILLUSTRATIONS BY IAN BAKER

summersdale

SUDDENLY SENIOR

Summersdale Publishers Ltd
46 West Street
Chichester
West Sussex
PO19 1RP
UK

www.summersdale.com

Printed and bound in Great Britain

ISBN: 978-1-84953-076-7

Contents

Editor's Note

We're old enough to have seen life begin at forty. Perhaps we've faced the big five-O with a frolic and seen in our sixtieth with a smile. Officially attaining senior citizen status and being awarded a free bus pass might seem to some the last landmark celebration to be enjoyed in later life.

But, having wrestled with middle age, we must remember that from here on in it's all downhill in the nicest possible way; a time to kick back, relax and, in the words of William Shakespeare, 'With mirth and laughter let old wrinkles come.'

This book, a hearty tonic of wit, wisdom and wisecracks, will help you keep a spring in your step and a song in your heart (albeit a golden oldie), giving you a (somewhat creaky) leg-up to enjoying the brighter side of feeling suddenly senior. So read on and, as you do, don't be too alarmed when you start to feel a twinkle in your wrinkle!

ACHY BREAKY PARTS

I'm at an age where my back
goes out more than I do.

Phyllis Diller

One morning, while lying in bed, an elderly man leans over to kiss his wife when all of a sudden she shouts, 'Don't touch me – I'm dead!'

'What are you talking about?' says the husband.

'I'm definitely dead,' replies the wife.

'What in the world makes you think you're dead?'

'I woke up this morning and nothing hurts!'

I don't need you to remind me of my age. I have a bladder to do that for me.

Stephen Fry

As for me, except for an occasional heart attack, I feel as young as I ever did.

Robert Benchley

Like a lot of fellows around here, I have a
furniture problem. My chest has fallen into
my drawers.

Billy Casper

An old fellow meets the woman of his
dreams. When he plucks up the courage
to propose, he gets down on one knee and
tells her there are two things he would like
to ask. 'First,' he says, 'will you marry me?'
The woman replies, 'Yes! Yes, I will!' and
awaits his second question eagerly. 'That's
wonderful!' he cries. 'Now for my second
question: will you help me up?'

An aging gent visits his doctor for a check up. A few days later the doctor sees him walking along the street with a stunning young lady on his arm. A week passes and, on his follow-up visit, the doctor says to the man, 'You're doing well, aren't you?'

'Just doing what you told me to, doc,' the patient replies. 'Get a hot mama and be cheerful.'

'Actually, I said, "You've got a heart murmur, be careful".'

A recently retired gentleman applies for his state pension. After waiting in line for quite a long time, he arrives at the counter. The clerk asks him for his identification to verify his age. The man looks in his pockets and realises he has left his wallet at home. 'Will I have to go home and come back?' he asks. The woman pauses and then says, 'Unbutton your shirt please, sir.' The man opens his shirt, revealing lots of curly silver hair. The woman says, 'That silver hair on your chest is proof enough for me,' and processes his application. When he gets home, the man excitedly tells his wife about his experience, to which she replies, 'It's a good job you didn't take one of your blue pills before you went – if she'd asked to see any more of you she'd never have believed you're sixty-five!'

They say that age is all in your mind. The trick is keeping it from creeping down into your body.

Anonymous

I don't deserve this award, but I have arthritis
and I don't deserve that either.

Jack Benny

An irate customer calls up her local
newsagent and demands to know why her
Sunday paper hasn't arrived. 'I'm sorry,
madam,' the newsagent calmly informs her,
'but I'm afraid today is Saturday. The Sunday
paper is not delivered until Sunday.' There is
a long pause on the other end of the phone,
before the lady replies, 'And I'll bet that's why
no one was in church today.'

I complain that the years fly past, but then
I look in a mirror and see that very few of
them actually got past.

Robert Brault

The problem with beauty is that it's like being
born rich and getting poorer.

Joan Collins

A senior lady goes to the doctor complaining
of a range of aches and pains. After
examining her, the doctor feels he should be
frank: 'Well, Mrs Smith, I'm sorry to say that
the aches and pains you're getting are all part
of the natural aging process. I'm afraid I can't
prescribe anything to make you younger.'
'Well, doctor,' she replies, 'I'm not so worried
about getting younger, I'd just like you to
help make sure I get a little bit older!'

You know you're getting old when you can
pinch an inch on your forehead.

John Mendoza

An aging playboy visits his doctor after a lifetime of wine, women and song. 'Well,' says the doctor. 'The good news is you don't have to give up singing'.

A senior man walks awkwardly into an ice cream shop and pulls himself slowly, painfully, up onto a stool. After catching his breath, he orders a banana split. The waitress asks kindly, 'Crushed nuts today?'
'No,' he replies, 'Arthritis.'

After thirty, a body has a mind of its own.
Bette Midler

I was getting dressed and a peeping tom looked in the window, took a look and pulled down the shade.

Joan Rivers on getting old

A retired woman is complaining to her friend about the amount of housework she has to do: 'I spend all day washing, ironing, cleaning, doing the dishes…' she says. 'But what about your husband?' asks her friend. 'My husband? No – I make him wash himself.'

I don't feel old. I don't feel anything until noon. Then it's time for my nap.

Bob Hope

Alf and Vera, a couple in their sixties, are holidaying in America. Alf has always wanted some authentic American cowboy boots, so he treats himself to a pair. Back at the hotel, he puts them on and walks into the bedroom and says to his wife, 'Notice anything different about me?'

'No,' she replies, after looking him up and down. Frustrated, Alf storms off into the bathroom, undresses, and walks back into the room completely naked except for his beloved boots. Again he asks, a little louder this time, 'Notice anything different about me *now*?'

Vera looks him up and down and says, 'Alf, what's different? It's hanging down today, it was hanging down yesterday, it'll be hanging down again tomorrow!'

As you get older, the pickings get slimmer, but the people don't.

Carrie Fisher

I refuse to think of them as chin
hairs. I think of them as
stray eyebrows.

Janette Barber

I guess I don't mind so much being old, as I mind being fat and old.

Peter Gabriel

Early one evening, a police car pulls up in front of Grandma Rose's house. She looks out of her window and is shocked to see her husband being escorted out of the car by a police officer. She meets them at the door and is soon relieved to hear that her husband hasn't been up to mischief but had become lost while trying to find his way home from the pub.

'Oh, Stanley,' says Rose. 'You've been going to that pub for over thirty years! How could you get lost?' Leaning close to his wife, so that the policeman can't hear him, Stanley whispers, 'I wasn't lost. I was just too tired to walk home!'

A lady wearing a flowing dress and wide-brimmed hat quickly realises that she could have made a better choice of clothes for such a windy day.

As she's walking past a couple of policemen on the corner of her street, a gust of wind blows her hat off and catches her skirt, blowing it up to reveal she has no underwear on. The woman is promptly arrested for indecent exposure.

At the police station the chief constable says, 'Madam, what on earth were you thinking letting your skirt blow up, exposing yourself just to catch your hat?' To which the lady replies: 'That's easy. Everything under my skirt is seventy years old; that hat was brand new!'

As we grow older, our bodies get shorter and our anecdotes longer.

Robert Quillen

Time wounds all heels.

Dorothy Parker

Wrinkled was not one of the things I wanted
to be when I grew up.

Robert Frost

In a man's middle years there is scarcely a
part of the body he would hesitate to turn
over to the proper authorities.

E. B. White

A woman walks into a bar and orders a Scotch and two drops of water, 'It's my sixtieth birthday today,' she explains. The barman says, 'Well, since it's your birthday I'll buy you a drink.'

As the woman finishes her drink a woman to her right says, 'I guess I should buy you a drink too.' The birthday girl says, 'All right. I'll have a Scotch and two drops of water.'

As she finishes her drink, the man to her left says, 'Since I'm the only one that hasn't bought you a drink I guess I might as well buy you one too.' The woman says, 'OK, well make it another Scotch with two drops of water.' As the bartender gives her the drink he says, 'Madam, I'm dying of curiosity. Why the Scotch and only two drops of water?'

The woman replies, 'Well, when you're my age, you realise that you can hold your liquor but you certainly can't hold your water!'

HAIR-UM SCARE 'EM

I love bald men. Just because
you've lost your fuzz don't
mean you ain't a peach.

Dolly Parton

A man consults his friend about his increasing hair loss: 'I'm having to find more and more extravagant ways of combing my hair to make it look as if I have any left,' says one man. 'I know what you mean,' says a similarly balding man. 'I've seen men down-comb, up-comb and cross-comb. The thing is, you get to a stage where you only have three options left: parted, not parted, and departed.'

There's one thing about baldness; it's neat.

Don Herald

It's great to have a grey hair. Ask anyone who's bald.

Rodney Dangerfield

A balding gent walks into a barber shop and says, 'I'd like a haircut, please,' to which the hairdresser replies, 'Certainly, which one?'

There is more felicity on the far side of baldness
than young men can possibly imagine.

Logan Pearsall Smith

Two ladies in their sixties are discussing
an upcoming dance at their country club.
'I've been told that the dress code is to wear
something that matches our husband's hair,
so I'll be wearing my black, silky dress with
the silvery flecks!' says Mrs Smith with a
chortle. 'Oh my goodness,' says Mrs Jones,
thinking of her husband's bare noggin, 'I'd
better not go in that case; I don't want to
reveal *that* much!'

The whiter my hair becomes, the more ready
people are to believe what I say.

Bertrand Russell

There is only one cure for grey hair. It was
invented by a Frenchman. It is called
the guillotine.

P. G. Wodehouse

What should you buy if your hair begins
falling out?
A good vacuum cleaner.

Grey hair is God's graffiti.

Bill Cosby

A man whose hair has long since departed the top of his head sits down in the barber's chair, feeling despondent.

He begins telling the barber about his bad experience at the hair transplant clinic: 'I thought, if it's good enough for Elton then it's good enough for me, but I couldn't stand the pain.' The man then brightens up when he comes up with a wager for the barber: 'If you can make my hair look like yours without causing me any discomfort, I'll pay you a thousand pounds.' The barber thinks about this for a moment, picks up his clippers and shaves his own head completely bare. 'That'll be one thousand pounds please, sir.'

I have a better head of hair than Rick Perry; it's just not in a place I can show you.

Kinky Friedman

My daughter teases me once in a while
saying, 'Remember when you used to be my
mother and you had black hair?'

Loni Anderson

They talk about the economy this year...
my hairline is in recession, my waistline is in
inflation. Altogether, I'm in a depression.

Rick Majerus

A hair in the head is worth two in the brush.

William Hazlitt

THE SOUNDS OF SILENCE

He needs to read lips. I don't mind him reading lips, but he uses one of those yellow highlighters.

Brian Kiley on his grandfather's hearing problems

A man goes to his doctor and says, 'I don't think my wife's hearing is as good as it used to be. What should I do?' The doctor replies, 'Try this test to find out for sure. When your wife is in the kitchen doing dishes, stand fifteen feet behind her and ask her a question, if she doesn't respond keep moving closer, asking the question until she hears you.'

The man goes home and sees his wife preparing dinner. He stands fifteen feet behind her and says, 'What's for dinner, honey?' He gets no response, so he moves to ten feet behind her and asks again. Still no response, so he moves to five feet. Again, no answer. Finally he stands directly behind her and says, 'Honey, what's for supper?' She replies, 'For the fourth time, I SAID CHICKEN!'

Gloria and her lifelong friends Sally and Janice are discussing their increasing memory loss over a cup of tea: 'I think I must be getting old,' confides Sally. 'I sometimes find myself at the foot of the stairs, and I can't remember if I was going up to get something or coming back down.'

'I know what you mean,' says Janice. 'The other day I was in front of the fridge and I couldn't remember if I was taking something out, or if I had just put something in.' Gloria sits up and reaches for a biscuit. 'Well,' she says, 'I haven't had any problems like that so far, knock on wood', rapping three times on the table. Suddenly, looking a little startled, she stands up. 'Excuse me,' she says, 'Was that someone knocking at the door?'

An aging gentleman is on the bus home from town, telling his friend about his new hearing aid: 'I've had hearing problems for years, as you know, so I thought it was about time I treated myself to a top-of-the-range hearing aid,' he says, pointing to the neat device in his ear. He continues, 'Eight hundred pounds it cost me... but it's worth it, it's absolutely perfect; I can hear the birds singing in the trees!'

'What kind is it?' his friend asks, looking suitably impressed.

'Oh, er... twelve thirty,' the man replies.

An older couple go to church one Sunday. Halfway through the service, the wife leans over and whispers in her husband's ear, 'I've just let out a silent fart. What do you think I should do?' Her husband replies, 'Put a new battery in your hearing aid, dear.'

Two young boys are spending the night
at their grandparents' house. At bedtime,
the two boys kneel beside their beds to
say their prayers. The youngest one begins
praying at the top of his lungs: 'I PRAY
FOR A BICYCLE... I PRAY FOR A NEW
COMPUTER... I PRAY FOR A NEW DVD
PLAYER...' His older brother leans over,
nudges him and says, 'Why are you shouting
your prayers? God isn't deaf.' To which the
little brother replies, 'No, but grandma is!'

One of the best hearing aids a man can have
is an attentive wife.

Groucho Marx

An aging man decides it's time he invested in a hearing aid, but he feels a little reluctant to spend lots of money.

While investigating his options at the local hearing centre, the man asks, 'What price do your hearing aids start at?' To which the assistant replies, 'Our entry-level model is one hundred pounds, and our top of the line is five hundred.' The man considers this and still thinks the price is too much. 'Is there absolutely nothing cheaper?' he asks. 'Well,' the assistant says, 'I shouldn't really tell you this, but we do have some recovered models we could let you have for a small charge.' At this the man requests to see the cut-price model. 'You simply put this earpiece in and attach the wire to the inside of your pocket.' 'It seems a bit basic,' the man says, 'How does it work?'

'Well,' the assistant replies, 'for twenty pounds it doesn't work; but when people see you wearing it they'll start shouting at you anyway!'

Since I came to the White House, I got two hearing aids, a colon operation… and I was shot. The damn thing is I've never felt better in my life.

Ronald Reagan

Three old friends are out for an amble:
'Windy today, isn't it?' Geoff says.
No,' Cyril says, 'it's Thursday!'
Jim says, 'So am I. Let's go and get a pint.'

By deafness one gains in one respect more than one loses; one misses more nonsense than sense.

Horace Walpole

A senior lady is driving along the motorway, being careful to adhere to the speed limit and keep a safe distance from other cars. After a while she can see that a police car is behind her in the same lane. Feeling slightly self-conscious, she checks her speed and sees that she is well within the limit.

However, the policeman continues to follow her and after a while she notices he's switched his flashing lights on. The lady decides to pull over. The policeman walks up to her window and begins speaking. As he does this, the lady points to her ear and shakes her head, indicating that she is deaf. The policeman smiles and, knowing sign language, signs back, 'That's no problem, madam. I'm here to tell you that your horn is stuck!'

I would write plays for my grandmother, who was stone deaf, my mother and the dog; that was our audience.

Jayne Meadows

An elderly man decides that it has become necessary to invest in a hearing aid, and so visits a specialist, who gives him a device that restores his hearing completely.

After a month, the man goes back for a check-up: 'Your hearing is perfect,' the specialist says, 'your family must be really pleased that you can hear again.' To which the man replies, 'Well, I haven't actually told my family yet. I've just been sitting around and listening to their conversations... and considering what they've been saying about me I can see I've got some big changes to make to my will!'

SIGHT, FOR SORE EYES

The easiest way to diminish the appearance of wrinkles is to keep your glasses off when you look in the mirror.

Joan Rivers

David and Paula, a couple in their late sixties, are getting ready for bed. Paula is undressing in front of her full-length mirror, taking a long, hard look at herself.

'You know, David,' she comments, 'I stare into this mirror and I see an ancient creature. My face has more crows feet than a bird sanctuary, my boobs have gone south, my bingo wings are big enough for me to take off and my bum is starting to look like a hundred-year-old saddle bag. Darling, please tell me just one positive thing about my body so I can feel better about myself.'

David studies Paula critically for a moment and then says in a soft, thoughtful voice, 'Well, dear, there is at least one thing that's in good nick – there is absolutely nothing wrong with your eyesight!'

I was walking down the street wearing glasses when the prescription ran out.

Steven Wright

My face in the mirror isn't wrinkled
or drawn.
My house isn't dirty. The cobwebs are gone.
My garden looks lovely and so does my lawn.
I think I might never put my glasses back on.

Anonymous

I don't read anything any more. I don't have
the eyesight… I think I've read everything
that's worth reading.

John Gould

It's not what you look at that matters, it's
what you see.

Henry David Thoreau

43

I am getting to an age when I can only enjoy the last sport left. It is called hunting for your spectacles.

Edward Grey

Jack, a senior man, is giving his testimony in court. The defence lawyer asks Jack, 'Did you see my client commit this burglary?'
'Yes,' says Jack, 'I have no doubt it was him.'
The lawyer, pressing Jack further, asks again: 'Now, Jack, this happened at night. Can you be entirely sure that it was my client you saw?'
'Yes,' says Jack, 'I saw him as plain as day.'
Then the lawyer asks, 'Jack, with all due respect, at your age a man's eyesight isn't all that it used to be. Just how far can you see at night?' Jack says, 'Well, I can see the moon, how far is that?'

The grey-framed spectacles magnified the grey hazel eyes, but there was no greyness in the mind.

John Gunther

One day, Harry, a sporty man in his sixties,
arrives home from an afternoon of golf,
feeling depressed.
'I've decided I'm giving up golf. My eyesight
has become so bad that once I've hit the ball,
I can't see where it went.' His wife consoles
him, makes him a nice cup of tea and says,
'Why don't you take our Arthur along next
weekend and give it one more try?'
'That's no good,' sighs Harry. Your brother's
ten years older than I am. He can't help.'
'He may be a bit older than you,' says the
wife, 'but his eyesight has never been better.'
So the next weekend, Harry heads off to
the golf course with his brother-in-law. He
tees up, makes his shot, and looks down the
fairway, squinting.
He turns to his brother-in-law and asks, 'Did
you see the ball?'
'Of course!' replies Arthur. 'I have
perfect eyesight.'
'Right – where did it go?' asks Harry.
'Oh, er, sorry… I don't remember.'

If you ever find happiness by hunting for it, you will find it, as the old woman did her lost spectacles, safe on her own nose all the time.

Josh Billings

To see what is in front of one's nose needs a constant struggle.

George Orwell

A senior woman pays a visit to her local pharmacy to complain about a product she's been using regularly.

'I've been applying this every day for a month and it's just not working,' the woman says, presenting the tube to the pharmacist. The pharmacist takes the product and examines it. 'Well,' the pharmacist says, 'to my knowledge this is a very effective and reliable treatment.'

'I've been brushing with it twice a day,' the woman insists, 'once in the morning and once at night, and I can honestly say it has done me no good.'

'Well madam, there shouldn't really be any need to use a brush – haemorrhoid cream can be applied quite easily without one,' says the pharmacist, looking slightly alarmed. 'Ah…' the woman replies, 'I see. Could you do me a favour and check your records? I think I might be due for an eye examination.'

BITING BACK

I don't have false teeth. Do you
think I'd buy teeth like these?

Carol Burnett

A senior couple are enjoying a meal at a fine restaurant when all of a sudden the old man sneezes: 'I'm so proud of you,' his wife says, 'You've finally learned to put your hand in front of your mouth!'
'Of course I have,' her husband replies crossly, 'How the hell else am I going to catch my teeth?'

A boy visits his grandma with his mate. While the boy is talking to his grandma in the kitchen, his friend helps himself to some peanuts from a bowl. When it's time to go his friend calls out: 'Thanks for the peanuts!'
'That's all right,' the grandma replies. 'Since I lost my dentures I can only suck the chocolate off them!'

Laughter doesn't require teeth.

Bill Newton

A care home nurse brings her six-year-old daughter to work one day to have a look around. The little girl is fascinated by all the paraphernalia, such as the walkers, wheelchairs and gripping devices. They pay one lady a special visit, she has just got up and is yet to put her teeth in. The little girl's eyes widen in shock on seeing the full set of false teeth floating in a glass. She turns to her mum and whispers, 'The tooth fairy will never believe this!'

I told my dentist my teeth are going yellow. He told me to wear a brown tie.

Rodney Dangerfield

What's one thing that an old person can do
that a younger person can't?
Sing aloud whilst brushing their teeth!

An old couple are sitting down at a table in
a restaurant, waiting for their food to arrive.
The waiter sets down their meals and notices
a short while later that they are meticulously
splitting the food between the two of them.
Fair enough, he thinks, but then he notices
that the wife is just sitting there while the
husband is busily tucking in. He then asks
them if there's any problem with the food.
'Oh, no,' the old man says, 'it's just that
after fifty years of marriage we always split
everything down the middle.' Still a little
confused, the waiter then asks the lady if she's
going to eat, and she replies, 'Not yet. You
see, it's *his* turn with the teeth!'

After eating his dinner, an old man coughs violently, sending his false teeth flying across the room. 'Oh dear,' he says, 'they're ruined… smashed to bits. There's no way I can afford another set.'

'Don't worry, Dad,' says his son, 'I'll get a pair from my pal at work. Just give me what's left of your set so I can give him an idea of the size.' The next day the son comes back with the teeth, which fit perfectly. 'This is wonderful, son' says the man. 'Your friend must be a very good dentist.'

'Oh,' says the son, 'he's not a dentist, he's an undertaker.'

We idolised the Beatles [and] the Rolling Stones, who in those days still had many of their original teeth.

Dave Barry

The first thing I do in the morning is brush my teeth and sharpen my tongue.

Dorothy Parker

While watching a movie at the cinema, an elderly man begins rummaging around at the feet of the people sitting next to him. Becoming slightly annoyed at him, the lady in the neighbouring seat whispers crossly, 'Just what is it that you're doing down there?'
'I've lost a toffee,' the old man replies.
'You're going through all that bother just for a toffee?' the woman asks.
'Yes,' says the old man, 'you see, my teeth are in it.'

Two ladies, fiercely competitive in their latter years, are attending a dinner at their favourite country club. 'Well, Margaret,' one says, 'you're looking absolutely splendid tonight. And what's this?' she asks, noticing her necklace, 'Real pearls, I suppose?'
'Why yes, dear,' Margaret replies. 'Of course,' the other retorts, 'in order to tell for sure, I'd have to bite them, what?'
'I'd be perfectly happy for you to do that, dear,' Margaret says, 'except, you'd need real teeth for that, wouldn't you?'

She had so many gold teeth… she used to have to sleep with her head in a safe.

W. C. Fields

MEDICATION'S WHATCHA NEED

Every time I hear it, I think I'm supposed to put my breast in an envelope and send it to someone.

Jan King on the word 'mammogram'

A man in his sixties with a much younger wife decides to try Viagra so that he can keep up with her demands in the bedroom. They go to pick up his Viagra prescription, but the man baulks upon seeing the £5-per-pill price. His wife, on the other hand, looks indifferent… 'I don't know,' she says, 'thirty pounds a year isn't so bad.'

A hospital bed is a parked taxi with the meter running.

Groucho Marx

I'm taking Viagra and drinking prune juice – I don't know if I'm coming or going.

Rodney Dangerfield

An aging woman goes to her doctor to see what he can recommend for her troublesome constipation. 'It's terrible,' she says to the doctor. 'I haven't had a bowel movement in more than a week.'

'I see. Have you done anything about it?' asks the doctor.

'Oh, yes,' she replies, 'I sit in the bathroom for a good half an hour in the morning and then again at night.'

'No,' the doctor says, 'I mean do you take anything?'

'Of course I do,' she answers, 'I take the crossword book.'

A senior man is recovering from surgery when a nurse asks him how he is feeling. 'I'm OK but I didn't like the four-letter-word the doctor used in surgery,' he replies.

'What did he say?' asks the nurse, looking concerned.

'OOPS!' He exclaims.

A man comes home from work and notices his father has hidden himself behind the sofa. 'What's the problem?' he asks his dad. 'Are the children getting a bit too rowdy today?' The old man shakes his head and reaches into his trouser pocket for his prescription and points to the small print, 'Read the label,' he says, 'Take two pills a day. KEEP AWAY FROM CHILDREN.'

A retired gentleman goes to the doctor and tells him that he hasn't been feeling well. The doctor examines him, leaves the room, and comes back with three different bottles of pills. The doctor says, 'Take the green pill with a big glass of water when you get up. Take the blue pill with a big glass of water after lunch. Then just before going to bed, take the red pill with another big glass of water.' Startled to be put on so much medicine, the elderly man stammers, 'My goodness, exactly what's my problem?' The doctor says, 'You're not drinking enough water.'

A senior man is nervously awaiting the results of his medical when the doctor returns with his results. 'Well, doctor,' he says, 'how do I stand?'
'To be honest,' the doctor replies, 'that's what's puzzling me.'

An old man goes to the pharmacy for some cough syrup. The assistant can't find any so he recommends a strong laxative. The old man asks, 'How will a laxative help my congestion?'
'It won't,' replies the assistant, 'but you'll be too scared to cough.'

A woman is waiting at the pharmacy for her HRT prescription. As the pharmacist hands over her medicine, he makes a point of explaining the dosage directions: 'Now, Mrs Smith, it's important that you take no more than one tablet every four hours.' To which Mrs Smith replies, 'There'll be no problems there, I can assure you. It usually takes me at least two hours to find the bottle, and another two to get the damn lid off!'

Now I'm getting older I don't need to do drugs any more. I can get the same effect just by standing up real fast.

Jonathan Katz

You don't really know the meaning of embarrassment until your hip replacement sets off a metal detector at the airport.

Anonymous

STAYIN' ALIVE

I exercise every morning
without fail. One eyelid goes up
and the other follows.

Pete Postlethwaite

A gentleman is telling his friend about his new exercise regime: 'I think I'm a little old for all this gym stuff, but I'm building up some equipment at home. I got one of those Ab Roller contraptions recently. Thing is, I've been rolling it up and down my stomach for the past six weeks, and all I've got to show for it is this unsightly red line down my middle!'

Muscles come and go; flab lasts.

Bill Vaughan

It is better to wear out than to rust out.

Bishop Richard Cumberland

The best, the most exquisite automobile is a walking stick; and one of the finest things in life is going on a journey with it.

Robert Coates Holliday

'My doctor told me if I took up jogging it could add ten years to my life,' a middle-aged man was telling his friend. 'He was absolutely right – I now feel ten years older.'

... the dead centre of middle age... occurs when you are too young to take up golf and too old to rush to the net.

Franklin Adams

A determined lady of a certain age is telling a friend about her new aerobics class: 'I felt as if I was completely out of shape, so I just went for it. I stretched, twisted, jumped up and down and wiggled... Of course, by the time I'd got my leotard on, the class had finished.'

A man is standing on the bathroom scales desperately sucking his stomach in. 'That's not going to help,' says his wife. 'Yes it will,' replies the man. 'It's the only way I can see the numbers.'

A health specialist is giving a talk on well-being to an over-fifties club in the local village hall. 'The best way to start the day is to do five minutes of light exercise, and five minutes of deep breathing,' says the specialist. 'Then I take a hot shower, and feel rosy all over.' There are nods of agreement from the group until one wisecrack at the back pipes up: 'Tell us more about Rosie!'

Health nuts are going to feel stupid someday,
lying in hospitals dying of nothing.

Redd Foxx

How pleasant is the day when we give up
striving to be young – or slender.

William James

My doctor told me to do something that puts
me out of breath, so I've taken up
smoking again.

Jo Brand

It's no longer a question of staying healthy.
It's a question of finding a sickness you like.

Jackie Mason

An older woman goes to a leisure centre
and asks if she can join a gym class. 'I'm not
sure if that's a good idea,' says the instructor.
'How flexible are you?'
'Oh, very,' replies the woman. 'But I can't
make Tuesdays.'

HOLDING BACK THE YEARS

I don't plan to grow old gracefully. I plan to have face-lifts until my ears meet.

Rita Rudner

A sixty-year-old woman decides it's high time she had a facelift, so she goes for a consultation at a smart clinic. 'We have a new procedure,' the surgeon explains. 'We put a small screw in the top of your head, so that any time you see wrinkles reappearing, you simply turn the screw to tighten and lift the skin.' She thinks this sounds marvellous and signs up to the procedure that very day. However, the woman soon starts to experience problems and returns a few months later to give the surgeon a piece of her mind, 'This is the biggest mistake I've ever made! Just look at these terrible bags under my eyes!'

'Madam,' the surgeon replies, 'those are not bags, those are your breasts.'

There is still no cure for the common birthday.

John Glenn

I'm sixty-three now, but that's just
seventeen Celsius.

George Carlin

Age is not a particularly interesting subject.
Anyone can get old. All you have to do is live
long enough.

Groucho Marx

Looking fifty is great – if you're sixty.

Joan Rivers

I've found the secret of eternal youth. I lie about my age.

Bob Hope

Beautiful young people are accidents of nature, but beautiful old people are works of art.

Eleanor Roosevelt

I refuse to admit I'm more than fifty-two, even if that does make my sons illegitimate.

Nancy Astor

A traffic policeman stops a female motorist for speeding. 'Madam,' he begins, 'I'm sure you know exactly why I stopped you. As you came down the street I had you at sixty-five, minimum.'

'Outrageous!' the woman replies. 'I'm not a day over fifty-five. And besides, there's no way you could have made an accurate estimate – I was driving far too fast for that.'

The woman who tells her age is either too young to have anything to lose or too old to have anything to gain.

Chinese proverb

A diplomat is a man who always remembers a woman's birthday but never remembers her age.

Robert Frost

In dog years, I'm dead.

Anonymous

A woman's always younger than a man of
equal years.

Elizabeth Barrett Browning

I do wish I could tell you my age but it's
impossible. It keeps changing all the time.

Greer Garson

A lady goes into a cosmetics store and asks for a new anti-aging cream she has seen on TV. She spends the next month applying it day and night, but isn't sure if it's working or not. She decides to ask her husband: 'Darling, be honest, what age would you say I am?'

'Well,' he says, 'judging from your skin, I would say twenty; your hair, eighteen; your body, twenty-five.'

'Oh! You say all the right things,' she cries, covering him in kisses.

'Hang on,' the husband says, 'you didn't give me a chance to add them up!'

How old would you be if you didn't know how old you were?

Satchel Paige

There are three ages of man – youth, age, and 'You're looking wonderful.'

Francis Spellman

No man is ever old enough to know better.

Holbrook Jackson

No woman should ever be quite accurate about her age. It looks so calculating.

Oscar Wilde

Jewellery takes people's minds off
your wrinkles.

Sonja Henie

A man who correctly guesses a woman's age
may be smart, but he's not very bright.

Lucille Ball

Men become much more attractive when they
start looking older. But it doesn't do much
for women, though we do have an advantage:
make-up.

Bette Davis

I must confess, I was born at a very early age.

Groucho Marx

I have never known a person to live to be one hundred and be remarkable for anything else.

Josh Billings

Whenever the talk turns to age, I say I am forty-nine plus VAT.

Lionel Blair

Old age is fifteen years older than I am.

Oliver Wendell Holmes

Time and tide wait for no man, but time always stands still for a woman of thirty.

Robert Frost

As a graduate of the Zsa Zsa Gabor School of creative mathematics, I honestly do not know how old I am.

Erma Bombeck

Age to women is like Kryptonite
to Superman.

Kathy Lette

Please don't retouch my wrinkles. It took me
so long to earn them.

Anna Magnani

I don't believe in aging. I believe in forever
altering one's aspect to the sun.

Virginia Woolf

Time may be a great healer, but it's a
lousy beautician.

Anonymous

LOVE ME TENDER

An archaeologist is the best
husband any woman can have:
the older she gets, the more
interested he is in her.

Agatha Christie

After thirty years of marriage, a man looks at his wife one day and says, 'You know, thirty years ago we lived in a cheap apartment, drove a rusty old car and made do with a tiny twelve-inch TV set. Yet, every night I got to sleep with a hot twenty-five-year-old blonde.'

'Now,' he continues, 'we have a beautiful house, an expensive car, a big flat-screen TV, but I have to sleep with a fifty-five-year-old woman. It doesn't seem fair.'

'Well,' she snaps, 'why don't you go out and get yourself a hot twenty-five-year-old blonde? Then, once the divorce papers have gone through, you will be living in a cheap apartment, driving a rusty old car and watching a tiny twelve-inch TV set.'

A wedding anniversary is the celebration of love, trust, partnership, tolerance and tenacity. The order varies for any given year.

Paul Sweeney

A senior couple are sitting together watching television. During an advert showing a young, passionate couple the husband turns to his wife and asks, 'Whatever happened to our sexual relations?' After a long, thoughtful silence, the wife replies, 'You know, I'm not sure. Gordon completely forgot your birthday and we didn't even get a Christmas card from your sister this year!'

An older couple are planning their wedding, and before the big day they have a long conversation about how their marriage might work. They discuss the usual things like finances, living arrangements and so on. After some hesitation, the old man broaches the subject of sex. 'How do you feel about sex?' he asks hopefully. 'Well, I have to admit, at my age I like it infrequently,' she replies. The old man is silent for a moment and then asks, 'Sorry – was that one word or two?'

Two senior newly-weds are trying to get things started in the love-making department but they're not getting anywhere. 'You'll have to do something,' says the man. 'Like what?' asks his wife. 'You know,' he says, 'like moaning and stuff.' Thinking this is a reasonable idea, the woman begins: 'Would you look at the state of those curtains, they're hideous! And the dust on that dressing table! Didn't your mother teach you how to fold your trousers properly?'

I'd marry again if I found a man who had fifteen million dollars, would sign over half to me, and guarantee that he'd be dead within a year.

Bette Davis

Two men are pushing their trolleys around a hardware store when they collide. The older man says to the younger one, 'Sorry about that. I'm a little preoccupied – I can't find my wife, you see.' The young man says, 'That's OK. I'm looking for my wife too, actually. I can't find her and I'm getting a little desperate.'

'Well,' says the old man, 'two heads are better than one – let's help each other. What does your wife look like?'

'Well, she's twenty-four years old; blonde hair; blue eyes; she's wearing a short blue skirt… What does your wife look like?'

'Never mind,' the old man says excitedly, 'let's look for yours first!'

94

Never feel remorse for what you have thought about your wife; she has thought much worse things about you.

Jean Rostand

The concept of two people living together for twenty-five years without a serious dispute suggests a lack of spirit only to be admired in sheep.

A. P. Herbert

A husband and wife are having a bitter quarrel on the day of their ruby wedding anniversary. The husband yells, 'When you die, I'm getting you a headstone that reads, "Here Lies My Wife – Cold as Ever".' 'Well,' the wife replies, 'When you die, I'm getting you a headstone that reads, "Here Lies My Husband – Stiff at Last".'

A man blows his retirement pay-out on a brand new BMW Z3 convertible. Turning on to the motorway, he decides to find out what his new toy can do. Just as he is pushing 120 mph, he sees the blue flashing lights of a police car behind him.

Rather than push his luck any further, he decides to pull over and take the wrap. 'Sir,' the policeman begins, 'my shift ends in ten minutes. Today is Friday and I'm going away for the weekend. If you can give me a reason why you were speeding that I've never heard before, I'll let you off with a warning.' The man looks very seriously at the policeman, and replies, 'Years ago, my wife ran off with a policeman. I thought you were bringing her back!'

I have learned that only two things are necessary to keep one's wife happy. First, let her think she's having her own way. And second, let her have it.

Lyndon B. Johnson

It used to be wine, women and song. Now, it's beer, the old lady and TV!

Anonymous

An old professor visits his doctor for a routine check-up and everything seems fine. The doctor proceeds to ask him about his sex life. 'Well,' the professor drawls, 'not bad at all, to be honest. The wife isn't all that interested any more, so I just cruise around. In the past week I have been able to pick up and bed at least three girls, none of whom were over thirty years old.'

'My goodness, and at your age too!' the doctor says with surprise. 'I hope you at least took some precautions.'

'Yep. I may be old, but I'm not senile yet. I gave them all a fake name.'

Tony is trying to persuade his wife, Alison, to go up in a plane at the local air show: 'But the ride is fifty pounds, and fifty pounds is fifty pounds,' argues Alison. Luckily for Tony, a pilot is walking past and overhears their argument.

He walks up to them and says, 'Listen, folks, I'll make you a deal. I'll take you both up for a ride. If you can stay quiet for the entire ride I won't charge you, but if you say one word it's fifty pounds!'

The couple agree to his terms and up they go. The pilot performs all kinds of rolls, twists and dives, and the couple remain absolutely silent. After a perfect landing, the pilot turns round to Tony and says, 'I'm impressed. I did everything I could think of to get you to yell out, but you didn't.' To which Tony replies, 'Well, I was going to say something when Alison fell out, but, after all, fifty pounds is fifty pounds!'

RELIGHT MY FIRE

At my age I'm envious of a
stiff wind.

Rodney Dangerfield

Two elderly men are talking about Viagra.
One has never heard of it and asks the other
what it is for. 'It's the greatest invention ever,'
he says. 'It makes you feel like a man of thirty.'
'Can you get it over the counter?'
'Probably – if you took four.'

A sixty-year-old man goes to the doctor's and
says: 'Doc, my sex drive is too high – I want it
lowered.' The doctor can't believe what he is
hearing. 'You're sixty and you want your sex
drive lowered?'
'That's right,' says the man pointing to his
head. 'It's all up here. I want it lowered.'

I once saw my grandparents have sex, and
that's why I don't eat raisins.

Zach Galifianakis

Everything that goes up must come down.
But there comes a time when not everything
that's down can come up.

George Burns

An old man goes to church to make a
confession. 'Father,' he begins, 'I'm sixty-
two years old. I've been married for forty
years. Until recently I had been faithful to my
wife, but yesterday I was intimate with an
eighteen-year-old model.' The priest replies,
'I see. And when was your last confession?'
The old man says, 'Actually, I've never been to
confession. I'm Jewish.'
'So, why are you telling me about this young
girl?' asks the priest.
'I'm not just telling you,' says the old man
excitedly, 'I'm telling everybody!'

An old lady is feeling lonely living on her own, so she decides to buy a pet to keep her company.

At the pet shop she stops to take a closer look at a frog, and to her surprise he whispers, 'Take me home and you won't be sorry.' So the old lady picks him up and gets into her car.

Driving down the road the frog whispers again to her, 'Kiss me and you won't be sorry.' The old lady thinks about this and says, 'Well, why not?'

So she stops the car and stoops down to kiss the frog. All of a sudden, in a blaze of fireworks and coloured smoke, the frog transforms into a handsome young man. The young man kisses the old lady in return, and you know what the old lady turned into? The first B & B she could find!

A man, getting on a bit, begins to find that he is unable to perform sexually. After trying everything conventional medicine has to offer, he decides to take a chance on a medicine man, who gives him a vial of blue liquid. 'This is powerful stuff,' the medicine man says. 'All you have to do is say "one-two-three" and you'll instantly rise to the occasion. When your partner is completely satisfied, all she has to say is "one-two-three-four", and the liquid will wear off.' The old gent rushes home, anxious to try out this new wonder potion. That night, he drinks the liquid, cuddles up to his wife and says 'one-two-three' and suddenly he's ready for action, just as the medicine man promised. Just then, his wife turns to him and asks, 'What did you say "one-two-three" for?'

When did my wild oats turn into shredded wheat?

Anonymous

A terrible thing happened to me last night
again – nothing.

Phyllis Diller

Two senior singles, Jack and Audrey, meet
at a dance one evening, and after several
weeks of going for coffees, decide to go out
for dinner on a proper date. They have a
lovely evening dining at the most romantic
restaurant in town, after which they go to his
place for a nightcap. Things continue along
a natural course and, age being no inhibitor,
Audrey soon joins Jack for a bit of rough and
tumble. Afterwards, as they both lie smiling,
they quietly ponder this special moment:
Jack thinks to himself: 'If I'd known she was
a virgin, I'd have been gentler.'
Audrey thinks: 'If I'd known he could still do
it, I'd have taken my tights off.'

A man is surprised to find his elderly father sitting on his deck chair in the garden, with no trousers on. 'What on earth are you doing sitting out here with no trousers on?' he asks. The old man looks at him slyly and says, 'Well, last week I sat out here with no shirt on and I got a stiff neck. This was your mother's idea!'

I can still enjoy sex at seventy-four. I live at seventy-five, so it's no distance.

Bob Monkhouse

Continental people have sex lives; the English have hot-water bottles.

George Mikes, *How to Be an Alien*

Two senior men are discussing the ups and downs of their sex lives: 'Did you know,' one says, 'that scientists have recently developed a soluble form of Viagra? I dropped one into my cuppa the other day.'

'Did it work?' the other man asks.

'Well,' the first man says, 'it didn't enhance my sexual performance, but it did stop my biscuit going soft!'

Two mature women are in a cafe talking. One says to the other, 'How's your husband holding up in bed these days?' The woman replies, 'To be honest, he makes me feel like an exercise bike. Each day he climbs on and starts puffing and panting, but we never seem to get anywhere.'

A noted sex therapist comes to the conclusion that people often lie about the frequency of their encounters, so he devises a test to tell how often someone has sex.

To prove his theory, he fills an auditorium with people, and asks each person in turn to smile. Using the size of the person's smile, the therapist is able to guess accurately until he comes to the last man in line, an elderly gentleman, who is grinning from ear to ear. 'Twice a day,' the therapist guesses. But the therapist is surprised when the man says no. 'Once a day, then?' Again the answer is no. 'Twice a week?' 'No.' 'Twice a month?' 'No.' The man finally says yes when the therapist asks 'Once a year?' Annoyed that his theory has been disproved, the therapist snaps, 'Then what on earth are you so happy about?'

The gent answers, 'Tonight's the night!'

My best birth control now is to leave the lights on.

Joan Rivers

I only take Viagra when I'm with more than one woman.

Jack Nicholson

An old man goes to the doctor for his annual check-up. The doctor listens to his heart and pronounces: 'I'm afraid you have a serious heart murmur. Do you smoke at all?'
The man says no. 'Do you drink to excess?' Again, the man says no. 'Do you still have a sex life?' the doctor asks. 'Yes,' the man replies. 'Well, I'm sorry to have to tell you,' the doctor says, 'but with this heart murmur, you'll have to give up half of your sex life.' Looking a bit perplexed, the old man answers, 'Which half – the looking or the thinking?'

OLD-FASHIONED ROMANCE

I'll see a beautiful girl walking up to me... I can't believe my good luck. But then she'll say, 'Where's your son?' or 'My mother loves you.'

James Caan

A mature man decides to throw caution
to the wind and approach a young female
library clerk he has taken a shine to. He goes
up to the counter and with a sly wink says,
'You know, some people say that when a
man reaches a certain maturity he becomes
attractive even to someone half his age…
have you ever heard that?'
'Yes,' she says, smiling brightly, 'as a matter of
fact I have. Fictional Romance, aisle four.'

You know you're over the hill when the only
whistles you get are from the tea kettle.

Raquel Welch

One of the best parts of
growing older? You can flirt all
you like since you've
become harmless.

Liz Smith

Reg, a sixty-three-year-old postman, has worked hard all his life, never finding the time to get married. But one day a beautiful nineteen-year-old girl walks into his office and it is love at first sight. Within a month, Reg and Rachel get married and go to Butlins for their honeymoon. 'So how was it?' asks Bill, one of Reg's colleagues back at the post office. 'Oh, just beautiful,' replies a starry-eyed Reg. 'The cream teas, the karaoke... and we made love almost every night, we –'
'Just a minute,' interrupts Bill. 'At your age, forgive me for asking, you made love almost every night?'
'Oh yes,' says Reg, 'we almost made love Saturday, we almost made love Sunday...'

Old age is when a guy keeps turning off lights for economical rather than romantic reasons.

Anonymous

A senior couple are in a romantic mood. While the pair are wrapped up in bed the wife says, 'I remember when you used to kiss me every chance you could get.' So the husband leans over and gives her a little peck on the cheek. Then she says, 'I also remember how you used to hold my hand all the time.' So he reaches over and gently squeezes her hand. 'I can also remember when you used to nibble on my ear,' the wife says. The husband sighs, stands up, and starts to make his way out of the room. 'Where are you going?' asks the wife. 'To find my teeth,' says the husband.

An aging woman is telling her daughter about a date she has been on with a retired gentleman that she recently met. 'Can you believe I had to slap his face three times?' she says. 'What do you mean,' the daughter asks, 'did he get a little frisky?'

'Oh, no!' her mother explains, 'I had to slap him three times to keep the old bugger awake!'

Love is not a matter of counting the years...
but making the years count.

Michelle Amand

A widow and widower have been dating for about two years. After a happy courtship, the man decides to ask for the lady's hand in marriage. When he asks her, the lady is overjoyed and immediately says yes.
The next morning, he struggles to remember what her answer had been! He thinks to himself: 'Was she happy when I asked? I think so... but she did look at me funny.' After about an hour of trying to remember to no avail, he decides to give her a call. Embarrassed, he admits that he can't remember her answer to the marriage proposal. 'Oh,' she says, 'I'm so glad you called. You see, I remembered saying yes to someone, but I couldn't remember who I said it to!'

Men always want to be a woman's first love. Women have a more subtle instinct: what they like is to be a man's last romance.

Oscar Wilde

To keep the heart unwrinkled, to be hopeful, kindly, cheerful, reverent that is to triumph over old age.

Thomas B. Aldrich

[F]ood has taken the place of sex in my life... I've just had a mirror put over my kitchen table.

Rodney Dangerfield

A retired lady goes to visit her daughter and finds her naked, waiting for her husband Tim to return from work. The mother asks: 'What on earth are you doing with no clothes on?' To which the daughter replies shyly, 'Well, this is my "love dress" – I'm waiting for Tim to come home.' After the mother gets home she decides to strip naked and surprise her husband when he gets home. Upon arriving home, her husband asks, 'Dear, what are you doing with no clothes on?' With a smile she says, 'This is my "love dress" of course!' To which he replies, 'Well dear, I suggest you go and iron it.'

Two older women are watching their husbands from a bench as they wander through the park. 'Looks like your Edward still likes to chase the ladies,' one says, as she sees him greet a young girl he passes. 'It doesn't worry me,' the other says. 'Even if he could catch one he wouldn't be able to remember what he wanted them for!'

A couple of old chaps are taking a quiet stroll when they see a group of teenage girls. One says, 'You know, when I see pretty girls like that it makes me want to be thirty years older.'
'What?! Don't be daft,' says the other. You're sixty years old. If anything you should be wishing you were thirty years *younger*.'
'Maybe,' the other replies. 'But if I were thirty years older, I'd be past caring.'

A retired divorcee decides he needs a little romance in his life, and so goes out to try and find himself a girl.

After trying his luck at several of the seniors' dances and bingo nights, one evening he decides to stop off at a local pub. As he's commiserating with a pint he notices a young, shy-looking woman in the corner smiling at him. He decides to throw caution to the wind and ask if she'd like some company, to which she replies, yes. The man can't believe his luck, and as the night progresses they seem to be getting on like a house on fire.

As the pub is about to close, the woman invites him back to her place. They end up in the bedroom, when the man asks, 'So, did your mother tell you everything you need to know about spending the night with a man?'

'Oh, yes,' she replies. 'That's lucky,' the man says, 'because at my age you tend to forget these things!'

LAST INNINGS

I intend to live forever, or
die trying.

Groucho Marx

A senior lady is at her husband's funeral. She tells her daughter that throughout their married life they had enjoyed physical relations each and every Sunday morning in time to the church bells. 'Maybe he was getting a bit old for that sort of thing,' says the daughter. 'Nonsense,' replies the old lady. 'If it hadn't been for that ice cream van, he'd still be alive today.'

He is alive, but only in the sense that he can't be legally buried.

Geoffrey Madan

When doctors and undertakers meet, they always wink at each other.

W. C. Fields

The idea is to die young as late as possible.

Ashley Montagu

How young can you die of old age?

Steven Wright

George visits his solicitor to make a will. 'So what exactly do I do?' he asks.
'I'll just need you to answer a few questions, then you can leave it all to me,' says the solicitor. 'Well,' says George, 'I do thoroughly appreciate what you're doing for me, but I was hoping to leave at least some of it to my wife.'

My grandmother was a very
tough woman. She buried three
husbands and two of them were
just napping.

Rita Rudner

Three elderly gentlemen are talking about what their grandchildren might say about them after they've passed on. 'I would like my grandchildren to say, "He was successful in business",' declares the first man. 'I want them to say, "He was a loyal family man",' says the second. Turning to the third gent, the first gent asks, 'So what do you want them to say about you in fifty years?'

'Me?' the third man replies. 'I want them all to say, "He certainly looks good for his age"!'

No one is so old as to think he cannot live one more year.

Marcus T. Cicero

I hope I never get so old I get religious.

Ingmar Bergman

I look at the obituary page. If my name is not on it, I get up.

Harry Hershfield on his morning routine

I don't think anyone should write their autobiography until after they're dead.

Samuel Goldwyn

DRIVING MISS DAISY

That's a good thing. He's getting old. He ran his entire last race with his left blinker on.

Jon Stewart on Mario Andretti's retirement from car racing

A group of ladies are chatting about their ailments over a cuppa. 'My arm is so weak I can hardly hold this teacup,' one complains. 'Yes, I know what you mean,' says another. 'My cataracts are so bad I can't see to pour the tea.'
'I can't turn my head because of the arthritis in my neck,' another friend says. 'My blood pressure pills make me feel faint.'
'I guess that's the price we pay for reaching our seventies,' one suggests.
'Well, it's not all bad... at least we're all still allowed to drive!'

If God wanted us to walk, he'd have given us pogo sticks instead of feet. Feet are made to fit car pedals.

Stirling Moss

The elderly don't drive that badly; they're just the only ones with time to do the speed limit.

Jason Love

A man is driving down the motorway when his mobile rings. It's his wife.

'Jack, drive carefully, I just heard on the news that there's a car going the wrong way on the motorway.'

'Tell me about it,' he replies. 'It's not just one, there are hundreds of them.'

While on a car trip, an elderly couple stop at the services for lunch. After finishing their meal, the woman absentmindedly leaves her glasses on the table, but she doesn't miss them until they are well into their journey.

'I'm sorry, Jim,' the wife says, 'but I've left my glasses at the service station. We'll have to go back for them.' The man fusses and complains all the way back to the restaurant, cursing his wife under his breath.

When they finally arrive at the restaurant, as the woman gets out of the car to retrieve her glasses, her husband says sheepishly, 'While you're in there, dear, you might as well get my hat, too.'

Oddly enough, all the bad drivers I've known
died peacefully in their beds.

Paul Johnson

I'm the worst driver... I should drive a hearse
and cut out the middleman.

Wendy Liebman

If you don't like the way I drive, stay off
the sidewalk!

Joan Rivers

An old lady is walking back to her car after doing the weekly shop at the supermarket. As she nears her car, she is shocked to find four strange-looking men sitting in it. She drops her shopping and draws a handgun from her bag and screams, 'Get out of my car this instant you scoundrels. I've got a gun!' The four men jump out of the car and run as fast as they can out of the car park.

After a few minutes of trying the key she realises that it doesn't fit... she gets out to see her own car parked five spaces down the row. Feeling overwhelmed with guilt, she drives to the nearest police station. As she's explaining her story to the sergeant at the station, he beings to giggle uncontrollably and points to the desk opposite, where four petrified men are telling another officer how they were car-jacked half an hour ago by a crazed old lady with a bobble hat and a .44 Magnum!

As you get older you need to sleep more. My favourite time is on the motorway, during rush hour.

Bob Hope

It finally happened. I got the GPS lady so confused, she said, 'In one-quarter mile, make a legal stop and ask directions.'

Robert Brault

I saw a second-hand car last week that was so old it had bifocal headlights.

Edward Philips

PARTIAL RECALL

Sometimes it's fun to sit in your garden and try to remember your dog's name.

Steve Martin

Two dear old friends of many years are playing cards, when one says: 'My friend, this is terrible, but can you remind me what your name is?'
Her friend gives her a long, hard stare, then replies: 'How soon do you need to know?'

First you forget names… Next you forget to pull your zipper up and finally, you forget to pull it down.

George Burns

Three things happen when you get to my age. First your memory starts to go and I've forgotten the other two.

Denis Healey

Those who cannot remember
the past will spend a lot of time
looking for their cars in mall
parking lots.

Jay Trachman

It is lovely, when I forget all birthdays, including my own, to find that somebody remembers me.

Ellen Glasgow

The advantage of a bad memory is that one enjoys several times the same good things for the first time.

Friedrich Nietzsche

A well-dressed, debonair man in his eighties enters a swanky cocktail bar and finds a seat next to a good-looking, younger woman in her mid sixties, at the most. Trying to remember his best chat-up line, he says, 'So tell me, do I come here often?'

A senior lady calls 999 on her mobile phone to report that her car has been broken into. In a hysterical state, she describes the situation to the operator: 'They've stolen the steering wheel, the brake pedal and even the accelerator!' she cries. The operator tells her to keep calm, and that a police officer is on his way. A few minutes later, the officer reports back to the station. 'Disregard,' he says, 'She got in the back seat by mistake.'

Perhaps being old is having lighted rooms inside your head, and people in them, acting. People you know, yet can't quite name.

Philip Larkin

I have a photographic memory. Unfortunately, it no longer offers same-day service.

Anonymous

A retired couple go to dinner at the home of some old friends. After dinner, the two men get talking. One says, 'Last week we ate at a marvellous restaurant. I highly recommend it.' The second man says, 'Well, I'll take your word for it. What was it called?' The first man pauses, thinking intently, then says, 'What's the name of that flower you give to someone to be romantic, the one that is usually red that has thorns?'

'Oh, you mean a rose?' asks the second man. 'Yes, that's it,' says the first man. Then he calls into the kitchen, 'Rose, what's the name of that restaurant we went to last week?'

Old age puts more wrinkles in our minds than on our faces.

Michel de Montaigne

I'm a senior citizen and I think I am having
the time of my life… Aren't I?

Anonymous

When you're getting old, there's no question
in your mind that there's no question in
your mind.

Anonymous

When it comes to staying young, a mind-lift
beats a facelift any day.

Marty Bucella

A travel agent looks up from his desk to see an older couple at the window, peering inside at the posters showing the glamorous destinations around the world.

The agent, having reached his sales targets for the week and feeling a sudden wave of generosity come over him, decides to call the couple into the shop and says to them, 'I know that on your pension you could never hope to go on a luxury holiday, so I am sending you away at my expense – and I won't take no for an answer!' The couple are overjoyed, and within a week are on their way to an exotic, five-star resort.

About a month later, the lady returns to the shop. 'And how did you like your holiday?' he asks eagerly. 'The flight was exciting and the room was lovely,' she says. 'I've come to thank you. But, one thing is still puzzling me. Who was that old guy I had to share the room with?'

As you get older three things happen.
The first is your memory goes, and I can't
remember the other two...

Norman Wisdom

A man goes to his friends' home for
dinner. During the meal, he notices his
friend addressing his wife with endearing
nicknames, calling her 'honey', 'my love',
'sweetheart' and so on. While the wife is off
in the kitchen, the man says to his friend, 'I
think it's wonderful that after all these years
you still love your wife enough to call her
those pet names.' His friend hangs his head
and replies, 'To tell you the truth, it's because
I forgot her name about ten years ago.'

OLD FOLKS, AT HOME

We spend our lives on the run…
and then we retire. And what do
they give us? A bloody clock.

Dave Allen

Two retired professors are sitting on the
patio one fine evening, watching the sun set.
The history professor asks the psychology
professor, 'Have you read Marx?'
To which the professor of psychology replies,
'Yes, and I think it's these blasted
wicker chairs!'

As I get older, I just prefer to knit.

Tracey Ullman

Preparation for old age should begin not
later than one's teens. A life which is empty
of purpose until sixty-five will not suddenly
become filled on retirement.

Dwight L. Moody

The first sign of maturity is the discovery that the volume knob also turns to the left.

Jerry M. Wright

When you're a young man, Macbeth is a character part. When you're older, it's a straight part.

Laurence Olivier

I've got to watch myself these days. It's too exciting watching anyone else.

Bob Hope

When men reach their sixties and retire they go to pieces. Women just go right on cooking.

Gail Sheehy

At sixty-five, Jill decides she's ready to retire. At her leaving party at work her boss makes a speech: 'Well, Jill, there's no doubt that after you've left we'll find it hard to replace you… You could even say you are irreplaceable. Of course, that's mainly down to the fact that, for the past ten years, we're not entirely sure what it was you did around here!'

Getting old is a fascinating thing. The older you get, the older you want to get.

Keith Richards

People are living longer than ever before, a phenomenon undoubtedly made necessary by the thirty-year mortgage.

Doug Larson

A man of sixty has spent twenty years in bed
and over three years in eating.

Arnold Bennett

I can still cut the mustard... I just need help
opening the jar!

Anonymous

My parents didn't want to move to Florida,
but they turned sixty and that's the law.

Jerry Seinfeld

At his retirement presentation, Tom's boss decides to say a few words. 'We'd like to thank Tom for his many years of service to the company... I can say with absolute certainty that he's a man who, while at work, didn't know the meaning of "impossible task", who never took the words "lunch break" to heart, and who has shown professional contempt for the command "no". So, Tom, we've all clubbed together and bought you... a dictionary.'

Retirement at sixty-five is ridiculous. When I was sixty-five I still had pimples.

George Burns

I still have a full deck; I just
shuffle slower now.

Anonymous

THE GIFT OF GRANDKIDS

Grandchildren don't make a man feel old; it's the knowledge that he's married to a grandmother.

Agatha Christie

THE GIFT OF GRANDKIDS

A young mother's three-year-old son opens a birthday gift from his grandmother, and is delighted to discover that it's a water pistol. He heads straight for the nearest sink so he can fill it up. His mother, looking displeased, turns to her mother and says, 'I'm surprised at you getting him something like that. Don't you remember how we used to drive you up the wall with water guns?' At which the older lady smiles and then replies, 'Oh yes, I remember!'

Children are a great comfort in your old age – and they help you reach it faster, too.

Lionel Kauffman

Wrinkles are hereditary. Parents get them from their children.

Doris Day

An old lady visits her doctor and asks for some birth control pills. 'Why do you want them at your age?' asks the doctor. 'They help me sleep better,' replies the old lady. 'Oh, really? How?' asks the doctor. 'I put them in my teenage granddaughter's orange juice.'

'Nanny, nanny, I'm so glad to see you!' the little boy says to his grandmother 'Now Daddy will do the trick he's been promising us!'
'Oh?' His grandmother says, 'What trick is that?'
'He told mummy that he'd climb the walls the next time you came to visit,' says the little boy, grinning.

Blessed are the young, for they shall inherit the national debt.

Herbert Hoover

A young grandson decides to call his grandma and wish her happy birthday. While on the phone he asks, 'Grandma, how old are you now?' His grandma replies, 'I'm sixty-two years old now, son. It's been a long time coming.' After a slight pause, the grandson replies, 'Wow, Nan, that's a lot of years – did you start at one?'

What a bargain grandchildren are! I give them my loose change, and they give me a million dollars' worth of pleasure.

Gene Perret

The reason grandparents and grandchildren get along so well is that they have a common enemy!

Margaret Mead

A young girl is at the deli counter buying some food for her dinner party. 'I'd like five hundred grams of that cheese,' she says, 'two hundred grams of the smoked ham and – how much is the caviar, please?'

'It's quite expensive I'm afraid – fifty pounds an ounce,' says the smooth-looking male server, 'but from a gorgeous girl like you I'd accept a kiss for each ounce you buy.'

'OK,' the girl says after a little thought, 'I'll take five ounces.' With an excited look the male server quickly measures out the caviar, wraps it up and holds it out suggestively for the girl. As he does, the girl quickly snatches the food. 'Thanks,' she says, and points to an elderly man beside her. 'My granddad said he'd pay.'

AND ANOTHER THING...

Old age is an excellent time for outrage. My goal is to say or do at least one outrageous thing every week.

Maggie Kuhn

I have a problem about being nearly sixty: I keep waking up in the morning and thinking I'm thirty-one.

Elizabeth Janeway

If God had to give a woman wrinkles, He might at least have put them on the soles of her feet.

Ninon de L'Enclos

With sixty staring me in the face, I have developed inflammation of the sentence structure and a definite hardening of the paragraphs.

James Thurber

Audrey and Annabel are walking along the beachfront on a quiet Sunday afternoon, when all of a sudden a large seagull dropping lands on Audrey's shoulder. 'You see, Annabel,' she says angrily, 'this is why I don't come to the beach – too many undisciplined animals about! Do you have a tissue there dear, so I can sort this out?'

'Well, Audrey,' Annabel says, 'there doesn't seem to be much point – there's no way you'll get him to wipe his bum now, he's long gone!'

Inside every older person is a younger person – wondering what the hell happened.

Cora Harvey Armstrong

The surprising thing about young fools is how many survive to become old fools.

Doug Larson

By the time man is old enough
to read a woman like a book,
he's too old to start a library.

Anonymous

You can judge your age by the amount of
pain you feel when you come in contact with
a new idea.

Pearl S. Buck

Growing old is like being increasingly
penalised for a crime you have
not committed.

Anthony Powell

Women are not forgiven for aging. Bob
Redford's lines of distinction are my
old age wrinkles.

Jane Fonda

... at forty we don't care about what others think of us; at sixty we discover they haven't been thinking about us at all.

Anonymous

Nobody is forgotten when it is convenient to remember him.

Benjamin Disraeli

When you are younger you get blamed for crimes you never committed, and when you're older you begin to get credit for virtues you never possessed.

I. F. Stone

I've travelled a long way, and some of the
roads weren't paved.

Anonymous

There's nothing worse than being an aging
young person.

Richard Pryor

I would like to find a stew that will give me
heartburn immediately, instead of at three
o'clock in the morning.

John Barrymore

If I'd known how old I was going to be I'd have taken better care of myself.

Adolph Zukor

I'm fifty-nine and people call me middle-aged. How many 118-year-old men do you know?

Barry Cryer

Whatever poet, orator or sage may say of it, old age is still old age.

Sinclair Lewis

There was no respect for youth when I was young, and now that I am old, there is no respect for age – I missed it coming and going.

J. B. Priestley

A senior man and his wife are having an anniversary meal at Chez Trevor, a supposedly top-notch restaurant. As they're finishing their final course, the waiter comes over to ask them if they've enjoyed their evening. 'We would have enjoyed the evening,' the senior man begins, 'if the melon had been as cold as the soup, the soup as warm as the wine, the wine had been as old as the chicken.'

I'm so sorry, sir,' the waiter replies, 'is there anything I can do to make up for this?'

'As a matter of fact there is,' says the man. 'You can make the bill as cheap as the god-awful wallpaper you've got on the walls!'

The time to begin most things is ten
years ago.

Mignon McLaughlin

By the time I have money to burn, my fire will
have burnt out.

Anonymous

The first half of life consists of the capacity
to enjoy without the chance; the last half
consists of the chance without the capacity.

Mark Twain

You know you are getting old
when the candles cost more
than the cake.

Bob Hope

There is absolutely nothing to be said in favour of growing old. There ought to be legislation against it.

Patrick Moore

The older I get the better I used to be!

Lee Trevino

Youth would be an ideal state if it came a little later in life.

Herbert Asquith

The years between fifty and seventy are the
hardest. You are always being asked to do
more, and you are not yet decrepit enough to
turn them down.

T. S. Eliot

Everything slows down with age, except the
time it takes cake and ice cream to reach
your hips.

John Wagner

... the sign of old age is that I begin to
philosophise and ponder over problems
which should not be my concern at all.

Jawaharlal Nehru

When our vices desert us, we flatter ourselves
that we are deserting our vices.

Francois Duc de La Rochefoucauld

I am old enough to see how little I have done
in so much time, and how much I have to do
in so little.

Sheila Kaye-Smith

The more you complain, the longer God lets
you live.

Anonymous

An old couple, bored of having tea at their regular restaurant, decide they'd like to experience a bit of modern cuisine.

So one night they head into the city and come across a trendy-looking restaurant – they walk in but are turned away as it's fully booked. 'I suggest, sir, that you call tomorrow to check if we've had any cancellations. You see, we're booked up for the next three weeks,' a haughty maître d' says. Feeling a little bemused, the couple return home.

The next evening they call the restaurant, but are told there have been no cancellations, and to try again another night.

After a week of calls, the old man has had enough and calls to complain: 'And let me give *you* some advice, sonny: trendy or not, you'd do a darn sight more business if you weren't so damn full all the time!'

KEEPING A TWINKLE
IN YOUR WRINKLE

It's sad to grow old, but nice
to ripen.

Brigitte Bardot

I love everything that's old: old friends, old times, old manners, old books, old wines.

Oliver Goldsmith

With mirth and laughter let old wrinkles come.

William Shakespeare, *The Merchant of Venice*

None are so old as those who have outlived enthusiasm.

Henry David Thoreau

The best thing about getting old is that all
those things you couldn't have when you
were young you no longer want.

L. S. McCandless

One of the good things about getting older is
you find you're more interesting than most of
the people you meet.

Lee Marvin

Another belief of mine: that everyone else my
age is an adult, whereas I am merely
in disguise.

Margaret Atwood

Two senior men, both dragging their legs slightly, pass each other in the street. One says to the other, 'I can see we've both discovered the perils of old age… what happened to you?' 'Well,' the other man replies, 'this is an old war wound coming back to haunt me. Took some shrapnel in the leg at Normandy, 'forty-four. What's your story?' 'Me?' says the other man, 'Got a problem with my foot. I trod in some dog muck a couple of streets back.'

You can't turn back the clock. But you can wind it up again.

Bonnie Prudden

I'll have a lot of wrinkles on my face, but I feel like my heart will be fat and full.

Goldie Hawn

I'm not denying my age, I'm embellishing
my youth.

Tamara Reynolds

It's important to have a twinkle in
your wrinkle.

Anonymous

I've only got one wrinkle and I'm sitting
on it.

Jeanne Calment

I'm saving that rocker for the day when I feel
as old as I really am.

Dwight D. Eisenhower

You're never too old to become younger.

Mae West

I was always taught to respect my elders and
I've now reached the age when I don't have
anybody to respect.

George Burns

Growing old is mandatory;
growing up is optional.

Chili Davis

Age is something that doesn't matter, unless
you are a cheese.

Billie Burke

To get back my youth I would do anything in
the world, except take exercise, get up early,
or be respectable.

Oscar Wilde

You're not old. You're classic.

Anonymous

A man's only as old as the woman he feels.

Groucho Marx

Age is an issue of mind over matter. If you don't mind, it doesn't matter.

Mark Twain

There is no pleasure worth forgoing just for an extra three years in the geriatric ward.

John Mortimer

There is always a lot to be thankful for...
I'm sitting here thinking how nice it is that
wrinkles don't hurt.

Anonymous

A reporter is interviewing a group of senior
citizens for a newspaper feature entitled
'Super Seniors'. The reporter asks one lady
what the secret to her youthful appearance
is, to which she replies, 'I think a little bit of
everything is the best way to stay healthy and
happy. If you do things in moderation, you
can't go far wrong.'
'But madam,' the reporter replies, 'Your
daughter told us earlier that you have, on
several occasions, been seriously ill as a result
of your lifestyle.'
'Well, yes,' the woman replies. 'But you can't
very well put that in the article can you?'

Grow old with me! The best is yet to be.

Robert Browning

I don't want my wrinkles taken away – I don't want to look like everyone else.

Jane Fonda

I'm not interested in age. People who tell me their age are silly. You're as old as you feel.

Elizabeth Arden

The aging process has you
firmly in its grasp if you never
get the urge to throw
a snowball.

Doug Larson

Sometimes age succeeds, sometimes it fails. It depends on you.

Ravensara Noite

To be seventy years young is sometimes far more cheerful and hopeful than to be forty years old.

Oliver Wendell Holmes

I didn't get old on purpose, it just happened. If you're lucky, it could happen to you.

Andy Rooney

A man is not old as long as he is
seeking something.

Jean Rostand

Live your life and forget your age.

Norman Vincent Peale

He has a profound respect for old age.
Especially when it's bottled.

Gene Fowler

The trick is growing up without growing old.

Casey Stengel

After avoiding it for several years, a retired man decides to bring himself into the modern age and get a computer. His young grandson, a dab hand at using the Internet, decides to help him get to grips with surfing the World Wide Web. 'What's this search engine thing, then?' the old man asks. 'It's great, Granddad,' the grandson replies, 'you just ask it a question and it gives you the answer. You can find out anything!' 'Anything, eh?' the old man says, types 'What will next week's winning lottery numbers be?' and hits 'SEARCH'.

You're not over the hill until you hear your favourite songs in an elevator!

Anonymous

While there's snow on the roof, it doesn't mean the fire has gone out in the furnace.

John G. Diefenbaker

I've got it two ways: I'm still making movies, and I'm a senior citizen, so I can see myself at half price.

George Burns

Don't act your age. Act like the inner young person you have always been.

J. A. West

Cherish all your happy moments: they make a fine cushion for old age.

Christopher Marley

As a senior citizen, you may as well learn to laugh at yourself. Everyone else is.

Judy Huffman

Aging is a privilege, not a predicament.

Anonymous

There is no danger of developing eyestrain
from looking on the bright side of things.

Anonymous

A legend is an old man with a cane known
for what he used to do. I'm still doing it.

Miles Davis

There is no old age. There is, as there always
was, just you.

Carol Matthau

A WORD TO THE WIZENED

Wisdom doesn't necessarily come with age. Sometimes age just shows up all by itself.

Tom Wilson

Don't let aging get you down. It's too hard to get back up.

John Wagner

At a local cafe, a young woman is telling her friends about her idea of the perfect partner. 'The man I marry should be a shining light in company. He must be musical. Tell jokes. Entertain. And stay at home with me at night!' An old lady overhears and decides to speak up: 'Pardon me for saying so, but after a lifetime's experience I can say with confidence that if that's all you want, I would advise getting a TV!'

Old age is like everything else. To make a success of it, you've got to start young.

Fred Astaire

The gardener's rule applies to youth and age:
when young sow wild oats, but when old,
grow sage.

H. J. Byron

What is the most common remark made
by sixty-year-olds when they browse in an
antiques shop?
I remember these.

Old age... It is true you are gently shouldered
off the stage, but then you are given such a
comfortable front stall as spectator.

Jane Harrison

Age does not diminish the extreme
disappointment of having a scoop of ice
cream fall from the cone.

Jim Fiebig

A word to the wise ain't necessary – it's the
stupid ones that need the advice.

Bill Cosby

A woman past forty should make up her
mind to be young; not her face.

Billie Burke

Old age comes on suddenly, and not
gradually as is thought.

Emily Dickinson

An old man is walking past a group
of teenagers who are all laughing
uncontrollably. The man is intrigued and
so asks what the joke is. 'Well, if you must
know,' one boy explains, 'we're seeing who
can tell the biggest lie about their sex life.'
With a look of disgust the old man says, 'You
lot should be ashamed of yourselves! When I
was your age the thought of sex hadn't even
crossed my mind!' To which the boy replies,
'OK old timer, you win!'

The secret of staying young is to live honestly,
eat slowly and lie about your age.

Lucille Ball

Don't worry about avoiding temptation – as you grow older, it starts avoiding you.

Anonymous

Middle age is when you go to bed at night and hope you feel better in the morning. Old age is when you go to bed at night and hope you wake up in the morning.

Groucho Marx

Of course I have regrets, but if you are sixty years old and you have no regrets then you haven't lived.

Christy Moore

Anyone who stops learning is old, whether at twenty or eighty.

Henry Ford

Old age isn't so bad when you consider the alternative.

Maurice Chevalier

We are only young once. That is all society can stand.

Bob Bowen

An old-timer is someone who can remember when a naughty child was taken to the woodshed instead of to a psychiatrist.

David Greenberg

The key to successful aging is to pay as little attention to it as possible.

Judith Regan

In spite of the cost of living, it's still popular.

Kathleen Norris

An old gent is backing his Rolls Royce into the last available parking space, when a young guy in a brand new sports car zips into the spot. The young driver jumps out and says, 'Sorry old boy, but you've got to be young and smart to do that.' The old man ignores the snide remark and keeps reversing until his Rolls crushes the back of the sports car into an unrecognisable mess. 'Sorry son, you've got to be old and rich to do that!'

You know you're getting old when you get to that one candle on the cake. It's like, 'See if you can blow this out.'

Jerry Seinfeld

... behave in a manner befitting one's age. If you are sixteen... try not to go bald.

Woody Allen

A person is always startled when he hears himself seriously called an old man for the first time.

Oliver Wendell Holmes

The best way to get most husbands to do something is to suggest that perhaps they're too old to do it.

Anne Bancroft

A man asks his father how he feels about reaching his sixty-fifth birthday. 'Well son, I've worked hard all my life, and to be honest, I don't feel like I've got much to show for it.' Seeing that his question had saddened the old man, the son decides to lighten the mood: 'But dad, what with the silver in your hair, the gold in your teeth and the gas in your stomach, you're worth a small fortune!'

Old age is like a plane flying through a storm. Once you're abroad, there's nothing you can do.

Golda Meir

True terror is to wake up one morning
and discover that your high school class is
running the country.

Kurt Vonnegut

Age is whatever you think it is. You are as old
as you think you are.

Muhammad Ali

There are people whose watch stops at a certain
hour and who remain permanently at that age.

Charles Augustin Sainte-Beuve

It takes a long time to become young.

Pablo Picasso

It's all that the young can do for the old, to
shock them and keep them up to date.

George Bernard Shaw

They only name things after you when you're
dead or really old.

George H. W. Bush

If you survive long enough,
you're revered – rather like an
old building.

Katherine Hepburn

Old men are fond of giving good advice, to console themselves for being no longer in a position to give bad examples.

Francois Duc de La Rochefoucauld

You must become an old man soon if you would be an old man long.

Roman proverb

The older I grow the more I distrust the familiar doctrine that age brings wisdom.

H. L. Mencken

I'm going to be eighty soon, and I guess the
one thing that puzzles me most is how quick
it got here.

Roy Acuff

Age is not different from earlier life as long as
you're sitting down.

Malcolm Cowley

Old age is ready to undertake tasks that
youth shirked because they would take
too long.

W. Somerset Maugham

An inordinate passion for
pleasure is the secret of
remaining young.

Oscar Wilde

Forty is the old age of youth; fifty the youth of old age.

Victor Hugo

We are always the same age inside.

Gertrude Stein

It is not how old you are, but how you are old.

Marie Dressler

A concerned senior lady visits her doctor
to check her health. After her examination,
the doctor tells her that she's in good health.
'Good enough to live till a hundred?' she
asks. 'Well,' says the doctor, 'you don't smoke,
do you?'
'No,' she says. 'And you don't drink?' Again
the answer is no. 'And you don't have a
frivolous and excessive lifestyle, taking
advantage of every moment to
enjoy yourself?'
'Not at all,' the lady says. 'In that case,' the
doctor says, 'why on earth would you want to
live to a hundred?!'

The older you get, the more you tell it like it
used to be.

Anonymous

Old age ain't no place for sissies.

Bette Davis

You're only as young as the last time you changed your mind.

Timothy Leary

If you think nobody cares if you're alive, try missing a couple of car payments.

Flip Wilson

In three words I can sum up
everything I've learned about
life: it goes on.

Robert Frost

Have you enjoyed this book? If so, why not write a review on your favourite website?

Thanks very much for buying this Summersdale book.

www.summersdale.com

Nepal Trekking

AND THE

GREAT HIMALAYA TRAIL

A ROUTE & PLANNING GUIDE

ROBIN BOUSTEAD

TRAILBLAZER PUBLICATIONS

Contents

ROBIN BOUSTEAD (above, right) first fell in love with the Himalaya in 1993 and has returned every year since. With a group of friends he conceived the idea of developing the most challenging trek in the world along a route which encompassed the entire Himalaya from one end to the other. This became known as the Great Himalaya Trail (GHT).

Robin began researching new trekking routes that link each of the *himals* in 2002 and has now completed high traverses of the Indian, Bhutanese and Nepal Himalayan ranges as well as dozens of shorter treks. He completed a full traverse of the Great Himalaya Trail over two seasons, an epic journey which took six months and during which he lost over twenty percent of his body weight.

Nepal Trekking & The Great Himalaya Trail
First edition 2011, this **second edition 2015**

Publisher Trailblazer Publications
🖳 www.trailblazer-guides.com
The Old Manse, Tower Rd, Hindhead, Surrey, GU26 6SU, UK

British Library Cataloguing in Publication Data
A catalogue record for this book is available from the British Library

ISBN 978-1-905864-60-7

Editor: Anna Jacomb-Hood
Series editor: Bryn Thomas
Typesetting: Nicky Slade
Layout: Anna Jacomb-Hood & Bryn Thomas
Proofreading: Nicky Slade & Anna Jacomb-Hood
Colour cartography: Himalaya Map House
B&W cartography: Himalaya Map House & Nick Hill
Photographs: © Robin Boustead unless credited – RR: © Robert Rosenbaum,
YP: © Yann Piron, SB & TR: © Sandra Butler & Tim Reynolds
Index: Anna Jacomb-Hood

Photos – Front cover and opposite this page: Dolpo – The nunnery of Ribum Gompa
(see p229) and Regu Chorten above Dho Tarap. **Overleaf**: West Barun Glacier © RR

WARNING: mountain walking can be dangerous
Please read the notes on risks (p6), when to go (pp17-23), trekking grades (p30), safety
(p59 & pp63-4) and health (pp66-70). Every effort has been made by the authors and
publisher to ensure that the information contained herein is as accurate and up to date as
possible. However, they are unable to accept responsibility for any inconvenience, loss or
injury sustained by anyone as a result of the advice and information given in this guide.

A REQUEST – The author and publisher have tried to ensure that this guide is as accurate as possible. Nevertheless, things change. If you notice any changes or omissions,
please write to Trailblazer (address above) or email us at 🖳 info@trailblazer-guides.com.
A free copy of the next edition will be sent to persons making a significant contribution.

Updated information will be available on: 🖳 **www.trailblazer-guides.com**

Print production by D'Print (☎ +65-6581 3832), Singapore; printed in China

ACKNOWLEDGEMENTS

Nepal is a wonderful country to explore and is made even more special thanks to the people you meet along the trail. There is no chance the Great Himalaya Trail would have been completed without the help, patience and support of local porters and guides. Communities throughout the mountains have welcomed us for many years and their natural hospitality has only deepened my love of the Himalaya. To all those who have trekked with me as porter, cook or guide and to everyone who has offered shelter or food, I offer a thousand thank yous. I sincerely hope that the Great Himalaya Trail will grow in the years ahead and help provide income across the Himalaya.

A special thank you goes to those friends who have accompanied me along the trail and helped me with logistics and supplies, especially Mr Puru Dhakal. Big thank yous also go to text contributors: Ade Summers (🖳 www.ade-summers-photography.com), Jamie McGuinness (🖳 www.project-himalaya.com), Robert Rosenbaum, Dhendup Lama, Justin Lichter and Judy Smith.

I'm also grateful to the team at Himalayan Map House, including Udyog, Pawan, Era and Santosh for producing the map at the end of this book, as well as the range of topographic GHT maps.

Thanks also to Bryn Thomas at Trailblazer for taking on this project, Nicky Slade for typesetting, Nick Hill for the B&W maps and Anna Jacomb-Hood for editing, for additional research and for compiling the index.

❏ **Warning**

All outdoor activities involve an element of risk, which could endanger you and those with you. It is impossible for any guidebook to alert you to every possible danger or hazard, or to anticipate the limitations of your party. The descriptions of trails, passes, routes and geographical features in this guide are therefore not in any way a guarantee that they will be safe for you or your party. When you follow the advice and/or route information in this book you do so at your own risk and assume responsibility for your own safety.

Ensuring that you are aware of all relevant factors and exercising good field-craft combined with common sense is the best way to enjoy the mountains. If you feel unsure about your skill level, experience or knowledge base you should not assume responsibility for yourself or a party.

The political situation in Nepal will change and could affect your plans. It is wise to keep abreast of all developments and check government and relevant agency websites for your own safety. You assume the risk of your travels and the responsibility for those with you. Be safe, be prepared, be informed.

INTRODUCTION

The Nepal Himalaya is amazing; a place where you can immerse yourself in cultures little changed by the modern world and be inspired by the greatest mountain scenery on the planet. Since the early 1950s, trekkers have been exploring the countless valleys and peaks of the mid-

> **You can immerse yourself in cultures little changed by the modern world and be inspired by the greatest mountain scenery on the planet.**

hills, *pahar*, and high ranges, *himal*, throughout Nepal. Recent elections and relative political stability have led to a surge in visitors and the mountains once again offer unhindered trails for anyone to explore.

The three main trekking regions, Everest (Solu-Khumbu), Annapurna and Langtang attract over 160,000 trekkers every year but represent less than a quarter of Nepal's *himals*. If you want a little luxury, facilities have never been better along these major trekking routes, sometimes rivalling those found in Europe or elsewhere. Trails are well maintained and safe, and locals will welcome you with a genuine friendliness that will make your heart melt.

The other three-quarters of Nepal's mountain terrain is considered 'off-the-beaten-track' and often counts visitors in mere dozens. From the lush rhododendron forests of the east to the dense woodlands of

(**Above**): 'Namaste!' Rai children in the Makalu region greeting trekkers in the traditional way.

the west the himals form a wilderness interspersed with remote communities that have remained relatively untouched. In these regions, a small trekking group can make a real difference to lives that often barely subsist. Although the mountains are beyond compare, it is the people you meet along the trail who linger in your memory. You can't help but admire their indefatigable boldness and energy, their independence, strength and resilience when times are bad, and their fun, open-hearted, generous nature towards strangers who may never return. It's impossible to make a comparison, but surely the people of the Himalaya are the very best of mankind?

> Although the mountains are beyond compare, it is the people you meet who will linger in your memory.

In 2002, the Nepali government reconciled all border disputes with its northern neighbour China. This de-militarised seven border areas and for the first time in over fifty years tourists were allowed to explore them. All these areas offer unique trekking opportunities, with many resembling the now popular regions as they were thirty or more years ago. They also tend to be next to

(**Below**): One of the best viewpoints for Everest (on the left directly above the lake in this photo) is from the Renjo La (5306m, see p136) to the west of Gokyo.

the major trekking routes so it's possible to design itineraries combining old and new routes thus making your holiday a more 'complete' Nepali experience.

For many years, one of the great trekking 'holy grails' has been a route through the remotest peaks of the entire Himalaya, linking all the major trekking regions. The author is the first person to survey, plot and describe such a route: the Great Himalaya Trail (GHT). The Nepal section of the GHT can take 90 to 160 days of walking, so for convenience it is broken into sections, all of which have easy access and lower route alternatives through the pahar.

The Nepal section of the Great Himalayan Trail (GHT) can take 90 to 160 days of walking

The introduction of new trekking routes through remote communities will encourage micro-tourism projects in places that are too remote for intensive infrastructure development. By creating value in regions that previously had little to offer for tourism, it is hoped that the relevant government departments will establish a network of National Parks and Conservation Areas as a transboundary corridor for animal migration, which could reduce illegal hunting and help save many endangered species. The snow-covered crown of Asia may then become one of its greatest assets.

INTRODUCTION

Background to the GHT

The Great Himalaya Trail runs through regions and countries that have cultures dating back thousands of years, and for much of the time they have been trading with each other across the mountains. Salt, wood, grains, wool and livestock, gold and gems are just a few of the products that helped to establish a network of trails from Indochina to Afghanistan, including sections of the famous Silk Route.

It is easy to imagine local traders plying trails with their yak or donkey trains throughout the region. Over centuries, they explored remote valleys trying to find the easiest trails over the never-ending 'Abode of Snow', the Himalaya. In the larger valleys small communities sprang up and developed their own unique languages and traditions. For over a thousand years the people of the Himalaya were cut off from the rest of the world as Ladakh, Nepal, Sikkim, Bhutan and

Tibet all kept their borders closed from prying, colonial eyes.

Jesuit missionaries were the first Europeans to penetrate deep into the Himalaya, in the early seventeenth century. The first was Father Antonio Andrade, in 1626, who crossed from India to western Tibet and then enjoyed the local Tibetans' open-minded hospitality that still exists today. However, it is William Moorcroft who is considered the father of modern Himalayan exploration. His first trip, in 1812, was in search of Tibetan goats to trade cashmere; another followed this in 1819-25, when he disappeared without a trace. In his wake came a long succession of missionaries, botanists, geographers and traders who criss-crossed the mountain ranges from east to west and began mapping the himals. Exploration activity increased from the 1850s with the Great Game, a period when the British Raj, Russian Tsar and Chinese Qing empires all vied for ascendancy in the region.

The then new sport of mountain-climbing arrived in the Himalaya in the 1880s with WW Graham, Sir Martin Conway and Douglas William Freshfield

> Jesuit missionaries were the first Europeans to penetrate deep into the Himalaya, in the early seventeenth century.

INTRODUCTION

(**Below**): Lama musicians at the Teeji Festival (see p211) in Lo Manthang, Mustang.

INTRODUCTION

❑ GREAT HIMALAYA TRAIL CODE

Community
● **Respect cultures and traditions** – be a considerate guest, understand protocol, offer appropriate gifts when necessary, ask before taking a photo, do not show affection in public, and donations to gompas or shrines are appreciated.
● **Benefit local communities, commercially and socially** – share skills and experience, teach when you can, offer a fair pay for services, participate in activities. Do not encourage begging, publicly argue, drink excessively or fight.
● **Adopt new customs** – do not wear tight or revealing clothing, do not enter someone's home unless invited, avoid touching people of the opposite sex, do not use your left hand to eat or pass objects and try to learn as much Nepali as possible.

Environment
● **Tread softly** – stick to trails and recognised camping areas. Avoid creating new tracks, or damaging the environment in any way. Follow the adage: take only photos and leave only footprints.
● **Pack it in, pack it out** – avoid taking tins, glass, or plastic containers and bags unless you plan to carry them back to Kathmandu or Pokhara. Wash away from water sources and always use local toilet facilities when available. Bury all organic waste at least 30cm below the ground and ideally 50m away from water sources.
● **Conserve natural resources** – what few resources there are belong by right to the locals. Always ask permission before using anything along the trail. It is illegal to disturb wildlife, to remove animals or plants, or to buy wildlife products.

Safety
● **Beware of altitude sickness** – use the buddy system to watch for symptoms of altitude sickness. Make sure everyone remains fully hydrated by drinking water throughout the day, every day. Stay together along the trail, and communicate frequently with everyone.
● **Be safe** – carry an extensive first-aid kit and know how to use it. Have multiple plans for emergency evacuation and designate decision-makers. Leave your itinerary details with someone responsible at home. Beware of yaks and other animals on narrow trails!
● **Be self-reliant** – don't assume you will receive help or assistance. Ensure your group has extensive field-craft and navigation skills. Research thoroughly, is your route appropriate for your party? Do you have the necessary skills, experience, resources and equipment?

(Opposite): Nepal's many rivers are sometimes crossed by suspension bridges, some in better condition than others. This one is on the Manaslu trail. (Photo © SB & TR).

who pushed deep into the unexplored valleys of Sikkim and the Karakorum. However, most of the Himalayan Kingdoms still discouraged visitors, leaving many areas 'blanks on the map'. After the First World War, a number of expeditions were organised to reconnoitre and climb significant peaks. However, it was the mysterious disappearance of Mallory and Irvine on Mt Everest in 1924 that really ignited the world's imagination for Himalayan exploration, and was a precursor to the successful expedition led by Lord Hunt that placed Sir Edmund Hillary and Tenzing Norgay on the summit on 29th May 1953.

It was the research expeditions to identify new peaks and climbing routes that began what we now call 'trekking'. In 1949, WH (Bill) Tilman visited the Helambu, Langtang, Kali Gandaki valley and Everest regions intent on walking through valleys rather than climbing any specific peak, and so became the first Himalayan 'trekker'. In 1965, Colonel Jimmy Roberts introduced the world to organised trekking holidays and began a revolution in adventure holidays that made regions of the Himalaya accessible to anyone.

> In 1949, Bill Tilman visited ... intent on walking through valleys rather than climbing any specific peak and so became the first Himalayan 'trekker'.

INTRODUCTION

All of the activity to date was largely north to south across the Himalayan ranges, so when an east to west route along the entire range was suggested in the 1970s it was considered a radical idea. Yet the challenge had been set: who could be the first to traverse the entire range?

At the time, the eastern ranges through Bhutan and Tibet were closed so the first attempts could only start in Sikkim, an autonomous region of India. The first attempted Himalaya traverse was in 1980 with Harish Kohli leading an Indian Army team who operated in relay. However, the first unbroken traverse was by Peter Hillary (son of Sir Edmund), Graeme Dingle and SP Chamoli in 1981 (they told their story in *First Across the Roof of the World*). Both treks began at Kanchenjunga, on the border of Nepal and Sikkim and ended in or near Concordia at the base of K2 (Pakistan border).

A nine-month trek over 1981-82 saw Hugh Swift and Arlene Blum complete a traverse from Bhutan to Ladakh in India (Blum documented her story in *Breaking Trail*). In 1983, the Crane brothers (Adrian and Richard) ran 3200km (2000 miles) from Darjeeling (Sikkim) to Pakistan, thus setting a record, which has yet to be broken (the Crane's story is told in *Running the Himalayas*). This was to remain the longest attempt until 1990, when Sorrell

Wilby and her husband, Chris Ciantar, made a traverse from Pakistan to Arunchal Pradesh (northern Assam in India), which included nearly every Himalayan region (documented in Wilby's book, *Across the Top*). In 1994, the French duo of Paul-Eric Bonneau and Bruno Poirier crossed the Nepal Himalaya in 42 days (October 21 to December 1, 1994) from Pashupatinagar to Mahakali (see their book, *Trans-Nepal-Himalaya*). Then, in 1997, two Frenchmen, Alexandre Poussin and Sylvain Tesson, embarked on an epic adventure along the Himalaya (Bhutan to Tajikistan) that involved getting arrested in three countries – Tibet, Pakistan and Tajikistan. Their journey (published as *La Marche dans le Ciel*) really pushed the boundaries of what was considered to be 'Himalayan'.

Since 1997, there have been many attempts traversing the Himalaya by walking, running and biking, but all these expeditions suffered from restrictions on where they could visit. Closed and restricted areas meant trekkers often had to detour to the pahar, away from the Great Himalaya Range. Even Nepal, perhaps the most accessible of the countries, had strict 'no-go' areas along the border with Tibet. In 2002, things changed and Nepal opened every one of its

(**Below**): Makalu from Sherpani Col (see p134).

INTRODUCTION

himals to permit-based trekking. Along with new trekking areas in Bhutan and India, the Great Himalaya Range was completely open to trekkers for the first time in history.

The first person to take advantage of the newly-opened regions of Nepal was Rosie Swale-Pope, who ran the length of Nepal in 2003. Her 1700km route from Taplejung to Simikot was an early precursor to the current Great Himalaya Trail concept. Dr Gillian Holdsworth walked a similar route in 2007, which is documented on the British Nepal Medical Trust website. From early 2004, Robin Boustead (the author of this guide, 🖥 www.greathimalayatrail.com) systematically researched and documented each of the newly opened trekking regions over four years, culminating in a 162-day Great Himalaya Trail high traverse of Nepal's himals from September 2008 to July 2009. Between 2008 and 2011 Jean-Claude Latombe walked across Nepal in two sections of 56 and 53 days and his website (🖥 http://ai.stanford.edu/~latombe) has a wonderful collage of images of the people and landscapes he encountered. In 2010 another adventurer, Sean Burch, completed a route across Nepal in 49 days with the support of the Nepal Trust, and in 2011 Shawn Forry and Justin Lichter walked and ran an unsupported trek of 57 days across Nepal.

Each of these documented journeys was different, a clear example of how the Great Himalaya Trail is a personal challenge along a trail system that allows you to develop your own route priorities and set your own goals. Treks can be as short as just 5 or 6 days at low elevation through to extreme journeys of months at high altitude. For some, the ultimate Great Himalaya Trail challenge follows a trail network that links the 'highest feasible route' along the length of the various himals. However, weather and time restrictions mean that trekkers often choose sections that bypass technical passes or navigation-problem areas. So linking village trails with higher routes has become the accepted norm when designing itineraries.

The GHT has become a way to immerse yourself in Himalayan cultures and challenge your boundaries – there truly is a trail for everyone!

Following pages
● **C1 (opposite) Top**: Amphu Labsta (photo © RR, see p125). **Bottom**: Thyangbo Kharka (p152) above Thame.
● **C2 Faces of Nepal (clockwise from top left)**: Children in Hongon; young girl in Sipti; Humla man with pipe; local woman from Tak Bazaar; farmer from Bhulbule and Sipti man with dried fish; woman in Bhijer preparing wool for weaving and old lady in Chharka Bhot; making dhal bhat, Dailekh.
● **C3 Top**: The panorama from Poon Hill (see p199), near Pokhara – looking north up the Kali Gandaki valley with the Annapurnas on the right. **Left**: The village of Braga (p193) clings to the side of the Manang valley. **Right (middle)**: One of the five glacial lakes (Panch Pokhari, p154) in the Honku Basin, near the Amphu Labsta. **Right (bottom)**: The impressive kani gateway (**left**) of Samdo village (p168), Manaslu; purification dance (**right**) at the Teeji Festival (p211) in Lo Manthang.
● **C4 Top**: The remote and spectacular 'new' Yala La (see p232), Upper Dolpo. **Left**: Phoksundo Tal (p216) really is this stunning cobalt-blue colour; Upper Dolpo. **Right (middle)**: Perhaps one of the best campsites in Nepal at Danigar (p229), between the Bagala La and Numala La, Upper Dolpo. **Right (bottom)**: Rara (p241), Nepal's largest freshwater lake, is in the Far West of the country.

C2

C3

❏ Important notes

● **Walking times**, both of total trek duration and daily walking times are for the average trekker of good fitness and you will probably not walk exactly the same time. Measure your walking pace against those stated and you should find that it is consistently different. You can then calculate your relative walking time for each day.

Note that the walking times quoted **do not include** any rest breaks.

● **Total trek durations** are for itineraries that begin and end in Kathmandu or Pokhara.

● **Quoted altitudes** have an average accuracy of + or -15m; however, considering trail and demographic changes, it is wise to assume a general accuracy of + or -50m.

● **Place names** are given in their most common form but pronunciation may vary considerably.

● **Directions** are given as you look ahead, or in the direction of movement along the trail. When referenced to a water course, directions are given as the 'true' direction (facing downstream) so, 'true left' is the left bank of a river while facing downstream.

● **Make sure you are not over committing yourself**. Your mental and physical health combined with environmental factors can affect your trekking speed on a daily basis.

(Photo above): Looking down into the Chilime valley, Langtang region.

PLANNING YOUR TREK

First decisions

Nepal has become one of the world's best trekking destinations with thousands of trails and endless mountain views. Choosing the right trek to suit your holiday has become a challenge in itself as the Nepal Himalaya offers a path for everyone, regardless of fitness level, experience or time available. This book is designed to help you first identify when to trek and what style of trek best suits your needs, and then which destination matches your expectations of the Himalaya. In taking the time to carefully consider these things there is a much greater chance of returning home having had a memorable experience. You never know, you may end up wanting to trek every region by doing the Great Himalaya Trail (about 150 days) and immerse yourself entirely in the various cultures of the high Himalaya!

WHEN TO TREK?

The most important factor in deciding when to trek in Nepal is the weather (see pp18-19). Nepal has a monsoonal climate; heavy rains driven north from the Bay of Bengal engulf the country from June/July to September/October. This means that regions in the east, like Kanchenjunga and Makalu, receive heavier amounts of rain than in the west. The result is that the eastern ranges of Kanchenjunga and Makalu tend to have slightly shorter trekking seasons than the west of Nepal, which is drier. However, Far West Nepal tends to have longer, more severe winters due to its more northerly latitude.

The monsoon season is not a very popular time for general trekking as the valleys that approach the mountains suffer from sporadic and sometimes intense rainfall, leeches along the trail, transport delays and limited views. However, the Annapurna and Dhaulagiri massifs block the northerly push of the monsoon clouds and create a partial 'rain-shadow' along the border with Tibet. So Naar, Phu, Mustang and Dolpo only receive brief showers each day during the rainy season which transforms their arid landscapes into fields of wild-flowers and the locals get busy planting crops.

After the monsoon has finished, stable dry conditions predominate throughout the Himalaya for two or three weeks until a storm front of unpredictable intensity affects some areas, usually in the third or fourth week of October. (continued on p20)

PLANNING YOUR TREK

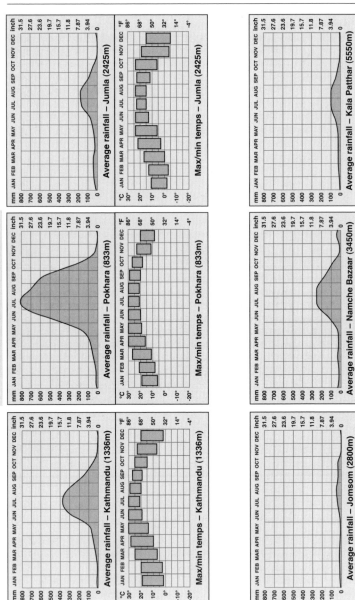

Average rainfall – Kathmandu (1336m)

Max/min temps – Kathmandu (1336m)

Average rainfall – Pokhara (833m)

Max/min temps – Pokhara (833m)

Average rainfall – Jumla (2425m)

Max/min temps – Jumla (2425m)

Average rainfall – Jomsom (2800m)

Average rainfall – Namche Bazaar (3450m)

Average rainfall – Kala Patthar (5550m)

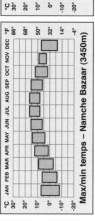

Max/min temps – Jomsom (2800m)

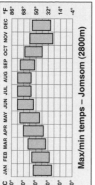

Max/min temps – Namche Bazaar (3450m)

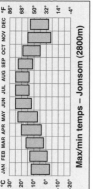

Max/min temps – Kala Patthar (5550m)

● **October to November** is a very popular trekking season as the entire country has long spells of fine weather with relatively clear air for photography. Occasional storms can dump large amounts of snow at higher altitudes, and the night-time temperature frequently falls below freezing above 4000m (13,123ft).

● **December to January** boasts the clearest skies for photography and the coldest temperatures, frequently falling below -5°C above 4000m. Many of the locals who live above 4000m in the warmer months begin to move down during December, so it is important to check that you'll be able to re-stock or find shelter prior to departure.

● **February to March** is warmer than January but occasional heavy rain and blizzards sweep over the mountains, sometimes closing passes for weeks. In March, early spring rain brings the first rhododendron blooms at lower elevations. Dust from India begins to obscure views towards the end of March and temperatures climb considerably in the lower valleys.

● **April to May** is renowned for the progressive blooming of rhododendron up to the tree line (some sheltered flowers will continue into June). In May, temperatures start to get very high at lower elevations and haze obscures views of distant mountains. This is a good time to spot migratory birds.

Note: The introduction to each trekking region states the ideal times to visit.

Climate change

In recent years locals throughout the Himalaya have begun believing that the traditional weather patterns are becoming more unpredictable; this they attribute to climate change. There are obvious examples of glacial recession and while there may be insufficient scientific data to prove their theory at present, it is obvious that things are changing. Be careful with Himalayan weather, it can be very severe and unpredictable.

For more information see: Himalayan Climate Initiative, ▢ www.himalayanclimate.org and International Centre for Integrated Mountain Development, ▢ www.icimod.org.

(continued from p17) The weather then stabilises again, probably until late November when the chance of occasional showers coincides with the beginning of a colder weather pattern. The clear skies and cold nights of December and January are in turn replaced by winter storms in mid to late February.

The beginning of March sees the sun regain intensity and the weather becomes unstable for alternating periods of three to five days. By the end of March dry, warm weather is the norm but haze begins to build in the lower valleys. As temperatures rise through April the remaining rain clouds disperse to be replaced by hot, hazy conditions largely produced by dust blowing up from the plains of India, and local fires.

May to June is the hottest period of the year, only cooled by occasional pre-monsoon storms, which gradually gain in intensity until the monsoon begins with vigour, usually at some point from mid June to mid July.

Festivals and faiths

The other major factor to consider when deciding to visit Nepal is the festival calendar. There are more than 365 festival days in Nepal, so there is always

❏ **Festival locations throughout the year**

MONTH	FESTIVAL	LOCATION
January	Maghe Sankranti	all Nepal
	Shree Panchami	all Nepal
February	Lhosar, Tibetan New Year	all Nepal
	Maha Shivaratri	mainly in Kathmandu, central Nepal
March	Holi	all Nepal
March or April	Gatunath*	most Magar villages, west Nepal
April (usually 14th)	Nepali New Year	all Nepal
May	Mani Rimdu	Thame, Everest Region, east Nepal
	Teeji	Mustang, central Nepal
	Buddha Jayanti	all Nepal
July	Gunla	Sherpa & Tibetan communities in all Nepal
	Bhairav Kumari Jatra	Dolkha, central Nepal
August	Gai Gatra	all Nepal
	Tamu Dhee	Gurung villages, central Nepal
September	Krishna Janmastami	all Nepal
	Gaura Parva	west Nepal
	Teej	all Nepal
October	Mani Rimdu	Tengboche, Everest Region, East Nepal
	Horse-riding Festival#	Manang, Annapurna region, central Nepal
November	Dashain, Tihar & Bhai Tikka	all Nepal
December	Bibah Panchami	all Nepal

Notes
* Gatunath is a spring festival and held for three days in March or April.
# Horse-riding festival, held for one day

something happening somewhere! Almost all festivals are related to phases of the moon and do not occur on specific Gregorian calendar dates.

It is a good idea to avoid travelling on some of the main festival days such as Dashain (aka Dasain, Dussehra) or Tihar, as transport systems tend to suffer from overcrowding and delays throughout Nepal. You should also be aware that some festivals traditionally require the slaughter of a goat and/or payment of a cash amount, and that visitors are expected to contribute. If you are unsure of the potential impact of a festival to your plans it's a good idea to consult with locals and be prepared for your plans to change a little.

Below is a summary of the most popular festivals; for further information see ⌨ www.visitnepal.com, ⌨ www.nepalvista.com or ⌨ www.qppstudio.net (navigate to the Nepal page).

Hindu festivals
● **Maghe Sankranti** is to worship the god Vishnu. It is held for one day in all Hindu communities during mid January.
● **Shree Panchami** celebrates the birthday of Saraswati, the Goddess of Learning and is combined with Martyr's Day all over Nepal; held on one day in late January/early February.
● **Maha Shivaratri** celebrates the god Shiva. The focus of celebrations is Pashupati Temple in Kathmandu where very large crowds pack the temple for days. It is also celebrated at most Shiva shrines in Nepal during February.
● **Holi**, or **Fagun Purnima**, is a week-long festival culminating in a spectacular day of coloured water and paint fights. One of the most popular festivals for locals and tourists alike and celebrated in all Hindu communities in late February or early March.
● **Bhairav Kumari Jatra** celebrates the gods Bhairav and Kumari at Dolka and Bhairav Kund. Held for five days in late July/early August.

❏ Hinduism
Over 85% of Nepali people are Hindu, a religion that dates back to 1500BC. Hinduism has thousands of deities, but there are three main gods: Brahma the creator, Vishnu the preserver and Shiva the destroyer. Most Hindus are Vaishnavites (followers of Vishnu) or Shaivites (followers of Shiva). Popular gods/goddesses are also Ganesha (the elephant-headed god who is the remover of obstacles), Laxmi (goddess of wealth), Saraswati (Brahma's consort and goddess of wisdom), Hanuman (the monkey god who symbolises strength and protects against accidents), Kali or Durga (the blood-drinking consort of Shiva and goddess of change and death), and Krishna (an avatar of Vishnu), the blue-skinned cowherd who had a penchant for milkmaids and is usually depicted with his flute.

Hindus believe in reincarnation and that the circumstances of your rebirth are determined by your deeds in the present life. The caste system is an important part of Hindu culture in Nepal, but its influence is less noticeable in the major cities. The highest caste is Brahmin (usually priests or civil servants), followed by Chhetri (warriors and rulers), Vaisyas (traders and farmers) and Shudras (artisans). Below this are the Dalits (untouchables) who traditionally have performed menial tasks such as sweeping, butchering and tailoring.

● **Gai Gatra (Cow Festival)** allows any sort of joke, or prank, to be played on someone, but is traditionally in honour of Yamaraj, the god of death. Held for one day in all Hindu communities during August/September.

● **Krishna Janmastami** celebrates the birth of the god Vishnu. Held for one day during August/September in all Hindu communities that have a Vishnu shrine. This festival is also celebrated as **Gaura Parva** for two days in west Nepal at about the same time.

● **Teej** is a married women's festival to honour the god Shiva. Held at all Shiva and Parvati shrines across Nepal during September.

❏ BUDDHISM AND BON

Buddhism

Buddhism is the second most popular belief system in Nepal and is dominated by Tibetan monasteries, or *gompas*, of four major sects called Nyingmapa, Kagyupa, Sakyapa and Gelugpa. The Dalai Lama is the head of the Gelugpa sect and their gompas normally boast a large statue of the sage Tsong Khapa who re-introduced Buddhism to Tibet in the 14th century. The Buddha was born in Lumbini in the Nepal *terai*, the plains along the southern India–Nepal border, in 560BC as a prince, and renounced his worldly possessions to find the 'middle path' – the way to enlightenment not through suffering or excess, but by realising that desires lock people into the cycle of suffering and rebirth.

Although Buddhism does not have gods as such, their gompas are decorated with figures depicting certain good or bad characteristics, such as hungry ghosts with tiny necks who were greedy people in a former life, or Buddhas with particular characteristics, or scary-looking temple protectors to keep away evil spirits. Each sect has its own practices and traditions, and the Newar people have combined Hindu and Buddhist beliefs to form a complex religion called Newar Vajrayana Buddhism. The World Heritage listed temples of Boudhanath and Swayambunath are the main Buddhist sites in the Kathmandu valley.

You will frequently hear Buddhists chanting throughout the day, and especially while walking clockwise around a place of worship. The most popular chant is *Om MaNi PadMe Hum*, a common translation being, 'Hail! The Jewel in the Lotus.'

Bon

The Bon religion was historically confined to Tibet and surrounding areas such as Dolpo, Sichuan, Yunnan, Bhutan and Assam, and is a combination of Buddhism with older animistic and shamanistic beliefs. Although many of its tenets melded with Buddhism, Bon is distinctly different in its day-to-day practices. There are very few Bon gompas remaining in Nepal; most of them are in Upper Dolpo. People who follow Bon are called Bon Po.

The most obvious differences between Bon and Buddhism are: Bon followers go around *chorten* (memorial or decorated cairns built on passes, ridges, or other significant spots) and monasteries counter-clockwise (keeping the object on their left side) whereas Buddhists keep the building on their right and go clockwise, the power symbol of Bon is a left-facing swastika (Hindus use a right-facing swastika), whereas Buddhists use the *dorje* (thunderbolt). The original Bon religion was mostly based on magic, spirits and blood sacrifice to propitiate the gods, who lived in all natural things. Bon followers also chant throughout the day, the most common being, *Om Matri MuYe SaLe Dhu*, which means much the same as the Buddhist mantra.

• **Dashain**, or **Dasain**, is the largest festival in the Nepali calendar and celebrates the goddess Durga. Held for 15 days in all Hindu communities during October/November.

• **Tihar**, **Diwali** or **Deepawali**, is the festival of lights to honour the goddess Laxmi (the Goddess of Wealth). It is held for five days and ends with Bhai Tikka (the brother/sister festival) in all Hindu communities during October or November.

• **Bibah Panchami** celebrates the marriage of the god Ram to Sita and is held for seven days all over Nepal during December.

Buddhist festivals

• **Lhosar**, **Buddhist New Year**, is held for one day in all Buddhist communities the day after the new moon appears during February.

• **Teeji** is a spring festival and a ritual-cleansing ceremony. Held for four days in Lo Monthang, Mustang during late April to mid May.

• **Buddha Jayanti (Buddha's Birthday)** is focused at Lumbini and all major Buddhist places of worship. Held for one day in all Buddhist communities on the full moon night in May/June.

• **Tamu Dhee** is a ritual cleansing festival to protect homes and fields owned by Gurung communities. Held for one day during August.

• **Gunla** is a month-long festival to celebrate the beginning of the monsoon and when Buddha led his disciples into a month-long teaching retreat. Held in most Buddhist communities during July/August.

• **Mani Rimdu** is held for four days in the Everest region. The festival at Tengboche is held in mid October, and at Thame in May.

TREKKING STYLES

There are three main 'styles' of trekking, each of which has pros and cons, but your choice will depend on your destination, budget, time available and personal preferences. There is no better or worse style, in fact you might find yourself combining styles in some destinations to provide a broader experience.

Independent trekking without a guide

For many, the idea of finding one's own way and living off the land is what trekking is all about. To be completely free to plan your day, to have all your gear on your back, and to interact one-on-one with locals is a liberating experience. Due to the nature of independent trekking it is normally a good idea to trek with a friend or in a small group of up to four for safety – larger groups tend to find it difficult to find accommodation.

Being an independent trekker doesn't mean to say that you cannot have a porter or a porter/guide. The introduction of the TIMS (Trekkers Information Management System) has made this option a little more complicated, but it is still possible to employ a local for almost any period of time, which can make tricky navigation and strenuous sections considerably easier.

Most independent trekkers prefer to trek the main routes of the Annapurna, Everest, Langtang, Makalu, Manaslu, Mustang, Rolwaling and Tamang

Heritage Trail areas as they offer teahouse accommodation and a standardised menu. Trails in these areas are well marked and some of the local people speak enough of a range of languages that the individual trekker can get along with the most basic Nepali. Even though you may walk on your own, or with a local porter, it is in fact very rare that you will find yourself without company, especially in the evenings when you sit in the teahouse communal dining room. The main trails are normally busy with local traffic so if you carry a pocket guide and map it is unlikely that you'll take a serious wrong turn, although getting a little lost is almost inevitable.

Independent trekking is also the cheapest way to explore the mountains so it is popular with budget-conscious travellers. Expect to pay anything from US$1.50 to US$15 a night for a bed depending on room type, teahouse location, and season demand (in extreme cases teahouse owners have been known to auction beds!). Food per day will average US$5-12 for Nepali fare, which is normally *dhal bhat* (rice, vegetable curry and lentil soup), to US$10-20 for three Western meals. You should probably also budget for the occasional hot shower (US$1-2) and battery re-charge (roughly US$4 per hour). If you employ a local porter or porter/guide, you will probably have to pay US$8-20 (plus meals) a day depending on the region, amount they carry and trail difficulty (see p59).

There are a few drawbacks to independent trekking: coping with altitude and health problems on your own, logistical challenges, communication issues and safety concerns. None of these is insurmountable but they do need to be taken seriously both before and during your trek. Altitude and health problems are best monitored and dealt with as part of a 'buddy system' – that is, you and your trekking companion look after each other (for more details, see *Altitude Sickness*, pp67-8).

There are also some potential logistical issues in high season: the most common is that many teahouses are booked in advance by organised trekking groups and you may find getting a room, or even floor space to sleep on, difficult and/or expensive. It is therefore a good idea to start trekking before or just after the main rush of tourists (see *When to Trek,* pp17-23 and the introduction of each trek for more information). It's very useful to be able to speak basic Nepali on the trail to find your way, order food and drinks, and get to know the locals, which is after all one of the main advantages to independent trekking!

If this is going to be your first visit to the Himalaya the independent option probably isn't the best style to kick off your adventures, unless you are the ultimate intrepid traveller and you stay on the main trails. Independent trekking in

---

❏ **Top tip**
There is always the risk of being robbed anywhere you travel in the world, and Nepal is no exception. Ironically, there is probably more chance of having something stolen by a fellow trekker than by a local, so always lock away your belongings when in shared accommodation and lock your bag to an immovable object at night or when unattended. You should also carry a spare lock to secure your bedroom door when staying in a teahouse.

remote wilderness areas is only suited to trekkers who have already learnt how their body deals with altitude, developed some familiarity with Nepali and the various customs of mountain communities, and have a good knowledge of Himalayan terrain and navigation.

Teahouse trekking with a guide

Recent years have seen a dramatic increase in both the number and the standard of facilities in villages on the main trails. For example, Namche in the Everest Region now boasts 24-hour electricity, a laundrette, multiple internet cafés, bakeries, and all the trappings of Thamel (the tourist district in Kathmandu) but at 3500m! It is no surprise therefore that teahouse trekking with a guide has become incredibly popular.

The convenience of teahouse trekking in the Everest, Annapurna and Langtang areas is a major drawcard for tens of thousands of trekkers every year. The subsequent level of investment by local communities in these regions is extraordinary compared to the level of poverty elsewhere in the Himalaya. Large teahouses with comfortable communal dining rooms, private bedrooms (some with en suite bathrooms) with mattresses and bedding, extensive menus or specialty restaurants and bakeries can make your trek a very comfortable experience. Commercial trekking companies from all over the world sell organised walking holidays using these teahouses and a local guide agency, and they're flexible enough to suit almost any fitness and experience level. Recent years have also seen the development of more basic teahouse facilities in Kanchenjunga, Makalu, Rolwaling, Manaslu, Tamang Heritage Trail and Mustang regions, all of which offer an authentic Nepali trekking experience.

Guides are normally hired through a trekking agency in Kathmandu or Pokhara, as professional registration is a necessary qualification to lead groups within National Parks. It is important to make sure your guide has been to, or preferably comes from, the area where you want to trek – it is surprising how many guides have only trekked a few trails. The role of a guide can encompass a great many activities. Apart from being the person who escorts you along the trail, they can often explain customs, culture, history, flora and fauna. A guide may also manage any porters (should you only want to carry a small pack), ensure your accommodation is booked, transport is confirmed, and that the food is well prepared; in fact your guide will probably become your personal assistant, man-Friday, guardian, and best friend. For this reason most good guides are normally snapped up by the bigger agencies and accompany groups booked by overseas trekking companies.

There are no major drawbacks to this style of trekking. However, there are a few issues that people regularly complain about. One is that teahouses that accept larger groups can be very noisy at night; for most people it's tougher to sleep at altitude, so anything that disrupts sleep is irritating. Another involves the decisions that your guide makes without consultation, like where to stay, or route options. Make sure you have a clear understanding of who makes which decisions. Small groups trekking with a guide may find it difficult to secure rooms or even meals in some teahouses that devote themselves to larger, more profitable parties. If you are a woman trekking alone with a guide be aware that even simple acts can be misconstrued as a proposition (see *Trekking as a Single Female*, p54).

Booking a trek through an overseas operator means you don't get to have any choice of guide, but you do have the reassurance that they are probably going to be excellent and if not, you have recourse to complain. The size of group you will be trekking with becomes important when you choose a 'packaged trek'. Some companies are still in the habit of sending over twenty trekkers into the hills with a single guide and a few porters, which is irresponsible and doesn't make for a good holiday. A group size of twelve to fourteen is normally considered a manageable maximum and you'll still get the opportunity to chat with your guide and spend time with any crew that they might hire.

One main advantage of hiring your own guide and teahouse trekking is that you can control your costs and stay within a budget that would be considerably less than booking with a big travel company. The logistical convenience of having someone with local knowledge handling routine details such as where to stay, negotiating prices, and giving route directions is a great peace of mind. The safety and security of local knowledge should not be underestimated, nor should the ability to communicate to your heart's content through your guide's interpreting. Finally, the chance to build a friendship with someone is perhaps the most remembered feature of any trekking holiday. You might forget the name of the mountains you'll photograph, but you'll never forget your guide!

Trekking with a camping crew

The most flexible, comfortable and hygienic way to explore the Himalaya is on a camping trek. To have unrestricted access to trails, viewpoints, and passes you need to be self-sufficient, with the support of a team of experienced staff. For many trekkers their first trip to Nepal will be teahouse based, but the lure of what lies beyond the main trails is so strong they return for a camping trek, often to the more remote areas.

Trekking in Nepal was initially exclusively camping based so there is a substantial experience pool that means even the first-time camper will be comfortable and well looked after. Each morning you will be woken with a mug of tea delivered by a smiling sherpa (as opposed to Sherpas, the famous ethnic group from the Everest Region, see box p135), followed by a bowl of water to wash your face. Breakfast is preferably served al fresco in the morning sun as your crew packs up the camp. At some point along the day's trail your cook will have prepared a lunch for you at a scenic spot before you complete your journey to the next campsite and an extensive dinner menu. Shower, toilet and dining tents with tables and chairs complete your campsite and comfort comes courtesy of a foam mattress and pillow (usually an optional extra). In fact, camping in Nepal is frequently more comfortable and less crowded than teahouses!

Nearly all remote or exploratory treks will be camping based as a group needs to have sherpas and crew available to help cross passes and break trail. The roles of various crew members is normally well defined: the guide (or *sirdar*) is in charge; the sherpas look after clients on the trail, serve meals and make/break camp; the cook and kitchen staff prepare meals and wash dishes for the group, while the porters carry everything. Normally, a guide discourages trekkers from becoming too friendly with the crew as companies are paranoid they might lose your future business to prospecting staff.

With the increasing popularity of teahouse trekking, companies that specialise in camping treks are becoming more competitive so it is important to check the details of your trek before you depart. The two most common ways companies cut costs are: firstly, increasing the amount of load the porters carry and not providing them with necessary clothing and equipment (see the International Porter Protection Group, 🖳 www.ippg.net for how you should care for your porters and your obligations towards them); secondly, either the agency or the cook reduces the money dedicated to your food and fuel allowance. It is important that the group leader should keep an eye on the quantity and quality of stocks.

The obvious drawbacks to camping-style treks are perceived inconvenience and potentially having to share a tent with someone you would rather not sleep next to. To resolve both issues research is necessary. Camping really is more convenient than teahouses on the condition that you have a slightly flexible itinerary, so you can ensure washing and relaxing time for all, especially when the weather is good. Almost all camping groups offer single occupancy tents but you normally have to specify when you book, and you should always check the terms and conditions.

For many, these drawbacks are easily mitigated and, in fact, are overwhelmed by the advantages of camping-style treks. Choosing your own path and rest spots offers a level of itinerary customisation that not even teahouses in the most popular regions can compete with. The main benefit, however, is being able to explore remoter regions away from the main trails and meet some of the inhabitants of the wild Himalaya. It is hard to believe that there are still many villagers who have never seen a tourist, where communities greet you as an honoured guest and not as an opportunity to make another buck. Away from the main routes is where you'll most likely see many of the species for which the Himalaya is famous: red panda, black bear, musk deer, snow leopard and a multitude of birds.

For many trekkers and trek leaders, camping-style treks are their favourite method of exploring Nepal; they often say that their experience feels more genuine. Camping brings you closer to nature, and the camaraderie built around a campfire often outlasts that of a teahouse trek.

WHICH STYLE OF TREK IS RIGHT FOR YOU?

The desire to make the most of what may be a once-in-a-lifetime trip to Nepal means that there is a temptation to choose itineraries that are too hard or long for your group's level of walking experience or fitness. Surprisingly, many trekkers choose teahouse treks with tough itineraries believing that by staying in a room they will recover faster from the day's walk. This doesn't actually make sense and the number of rescue helicopters taking overstressed or injured bodies back to Kathmandu grows each year. However, it is easy to understand that trekkers want to tackle a route that leaves them feeling they have achieved the most from their holiday. Perhaps the most important things you need to consider before choosing a trek are:

● **Fitness level** Join a walking club or a gym to get a comparative assessment of your fitness level. How long does it take you to climb 500 metres? Test your stamina: can you walk for four or five hours a day? Try to find people who have done the trek before and ask them what it was like and how fit they were.

● **Walking experience** How easily and confidently can you cross rough trails? Do you have a good sense of balance? Can you cope with slippery surfaces or exposed trails? Try to find some walks near to your home with steep up and down sections. Does the trek operator offer training walks or suggested programmes?

● **Have you been to altitude before?** If not, then choosing an extreme altitude trek (over 5500m), or a trek that stays at high altitude for long periods may not be a good idea. Why some people and not others suffer from altitude sickness is still a mystery for medical science, so prior experience is still the best method of trying to predict how your body will cope up high.

● **Find other people who have done the trek** Use the internet to search for blogs, or reports on the same or similar treks. Is their experience the sort of thing you are looking for? Are they the sort of people you would expect to be trekking with?

Your choice of trek style should reflect your experience and expectations: is this your first time to Nepal? Do you want a cultural experience? Do you want to explore remote areas or climb a trekking peak? Do you have specific needs or require more flexibility than an organised tour will allow? Do you want to camp or use teahouses? And is it necessary to be an experienced camper/trekker/mountaineer before booking?

The major trekking routes in Everest, Annapurna and Langtang are well equipped with teahouse and camping grounds, but the convenience of not having

---

❏ **Crossing high passes**

A feature of many treks is a high-altitude pass, for example the Cho La and Renjo La in the Solu-Khumbu (Everest Region), the Thorong La or Mesokanto La in the Annapurna. These passes are difficult and very challenging for the majority of walkers. Steep terrain combined with the effects of altitude mean that some people fail to cross what is an unavoidable part of their itinerary.

If you plan to book a trek that incorporates one or more passes it is essential that you develop a high level of fitness and walking experience before you depart. You should also ensure that there is sufficient acclimatisation time in your itinerary to allow both you and your group to adjust to higher altitudes. It is wise to also add an extra day or two of flexibility into your itinerary to accommodate bad weather and illness that could delay your group while attempting to cross each pass.

❏ SUMMARY OF TREKKING STYLES

A summary of the three trekking styles and most common decision factors:

	INDEPENDENT TREKKING WITHOUT A GUIDE	TEAHOUSE TREKKING WITH A GUIDE	TREKKING WITH A CAMPING CREW
IDEAL DESTINATION	Everest, Annapurna, Langtang	Everest, Annapurna Kanchenjunga, Langtang, Makalu, Manaslu, Mustang, Rolwaling and Tamang Heritage Trail	Anywhere in Nepal
AVERAGE NUMBER OF DAYS ON THE TRAIL	5 to 10 days	5 to 20 days	10 to 30 days
LEVEL OF FLEXIBILITY IN YOUR ITINERARY	Good, you dictate your own pace	Generally poor, but depends on arrangements.	Generally poor, but depends on group arrangements
COST LEVEL	Low to medium	Medium to high	Medium to high
FITNESS & EXPERIENCE LEVEL	Need to be strong and fit to carry all your gear. Prior experience advisable	Training advisable but not with a heavy pack. Prior experience sometimes necessary	Training and experience advisable depending on trek
AMOUNT OF TIME TO ORGANISE THE TREK IN KATHMANDU	Short (a few hours to one day)	Medium (a couple of days)	Long (at least three days)

PLANNING YOUR TREK

to carry camping gear means that teahouses are often the preferred option. In Kanchenjunga, Manaslu, Makalu, Mustang, the Rolwaling and the Tamang Heritage Trail there are some small, basic teahouses that you might want to use but you might need to camp if they are full or closed. In the remoter regions of Humla, Dolpo, Ganesh Himal, the Far west of Nepal and the valleys that were once closed to foreigners, it is wise to assume you will have to camp all of the time. It is rare to find a bad campsite, even when exploring the remotest and least accessible areas of Nepal but sometimes finding flat ground can be tricky. Whatever your choice of destination, a good crew (guide, sherpas, cook and kitchen, and porters) will become your surrogate family and maybe lifelong friends.

Each trekking region covered in this book includes a summary of trail options and trekking styles. However, there are always exceptions and options, so for example, although the Everest region is an ideal teahouse-style area there are still some trails where camping is essential.

TREK DURATION

Trekking agents are often asked: 'What is a good length of time to go trekking?' or 'There are treks from three days to treks that last months, is any one duration better than another?' The simple answer is no, any amount of time that matches your vacation plans is a good amount of time, but there are some issues you should consider before trying to squeeze in as much as possible to your itinerary:

● **Trekking grade** Trekking grades (see below and opposite) give you a good idea of whether you should allow for a little extra time, or speed things up along the trail. For example, the Everest Base Camp trek is normally operated as a 13- to 15-day itinerary, but could be done in 10 days by pre-acclimatised or very fit people, or 20 days should you want to explore around each village along the trail.

● **Festivals** If your visit coincides with a major festival (see pp20-3) either in the Kathmandu valley or out in the hills you should try and extend your itinerary to give yourself time to enjoy the event. You may also need to leave some spare time in case of transport delays during festival periods.

● **Weather buffer** The mountains always have unpredictable weather and only in exceptional circumstances will you have perfect weather every day.

Flights to mountain airstrips are particularly susceptible to delays or cancellations, so it is wise to add an extra day or two to your trip just in case you can't make a connection.

TREKKING GRADES

There is no generally accepted trekking grade system in Nepal. The system used in this book is similar to that promoted by the Swiss Alpine Club and many countries around the world. However, due to the local demands of Himalayan trekking and the effects of altitude this grade system is slightly different.

These trekking grades are designed to give you a clear idea of whether each trail is suitable for you.

There are five grades (see opposite), and every trek is rated according to the highest rating it receives across the grades. So, for example, if one criteria of a trek is Grade 3 when the others are Grade 2, it will receive a Grade 3 overall rating.

There are no Grade 1 treks described in this book as it is designed for city and prepared trail walks of very short duration. Most of the city walks in the Kathmandu and Pokhara chapters are rated Grade 1.

See pp32-41 for details of the grade for each trek in this guide as well as some information about the trek – highlights, when to go and the accommodation available; additional specific information – such as the highest point reached – is given in the trek summary box for each trek described in the route guide.

TREKKING GRADES

	GRADE 1	GRADE 2	GRADE 3	GRADE 4	GRADE 5
SYMBOL					
DISTANCE TO COMPLETE WALK	Not more than 5km per day.	Average not more than 10km a day.	Average not more than 20km a day.	Not important to grade and may be greater than 20km a day.	Not important to grade and may be greater than 20km a day.
GRADIENT	Flat and any slight slopes are suitable for a wheelchair.	Gentle slopes and hills where gradient is no steeper than 1:10.	Short steep sections and gentle hills where gradient is occasionally more than 1:10.	Very steep with some arduous climbs and steep arduous sustained gradient exceeding 1:10.	Very steep and difficult with long sections or climbs, sustained steep gradients and may require rope hand lines.
QUALITY OF PATH	Well-formed track on hard surface.	Formed track on natural surface.	Formed track, some obstacles.	Rough track, many obstacles.	Rough unformed track.
QUALITY OF MARKINGS	Clearly signposted at beginning, end and during walk.	Clearly signposted at beginning, end and during walk.	Signposted at beginning, end, major intersections and indistinct points.	Limited signage at occasional waymarkers	No directional signage.
EXPERIENCE REQUIRED	No experience required.	No experience required. Suitable for most ages and fitness levels.	Some walking experience required. Walkers may encounter natural hazards such as steep slopes, unstable surfaces, minor water crossings.	Experienced walkers require navigation skills. Users need to be self-reliant, particularly for first-aid and possible weather hazards.	Very experienced walkers with high level of specialised skills including navigation in difficult conditions. Users need to be self-reliant – as for Grade 4.
TIME	High & low estimate of time needed to complete track (eg 1½–2hrs).	High & low estimate of time needed to complete track each day (eg 5–6½hrs).	Average time needed to complete track in hours for each day.	Average time needed to complete track in hours for each day.	Average time needed to complete track in hours for each day.
STEPS	Ramps provided if there are steps.	Occasional steps are quantified day/hours.	Steps most days and not quantified.	N/A – steps not included in grade.	N/A – steps not included in grade.

Where to trek?

From the landscaped, broad walking tracks of the classic trekking routes, to remote craggy trails occasionally used by locals, or high alpine passes that will challenge the most experienced, there is a path somewhere that is almost tailor-made for you. There is an enormous disparity in the number of visitors to various regions of Nepal. By far the most popular trekking region is the Annapurna, where tens of thousands of visitors flock to destinations such as Poon Hill, the Annapurna Sanctuary and Circuit trails. However, you only need to walk a few hours away from the main route and you'll find yourself immersed in Nepali hill culture with rarely another tourist in sight. This is even more true for the remoter trekking regions to the extreme of the Api Nampa Conservation Area in Far West Nepal which receives a trekking group every few years.

SUMMARY OF THE MAIN TREKKING AREAS

Kanchenjunga   [see pp115-24]

Kanchenjunga is the most easterly of the Nepal Himals and forms a natural border with the Indian state of Sikkim. The mountain's south-west face, south ridge and west ridge form a massive and rarely visited horseshoe-shaped valley system around Yalung and includes sections of the Singalila National Park. Village-to-village trekking routes connect Singalila with Taplejung and numerous trails towards Makalu and the Solu-Khumbu (Everest) regions.

The main Kanchenjunga Base Camp trekking route heads to the mountain's north face and stone huts at Pangpema. The isolated communities of Olangchun Gola and Yangma are adventurous side trips that can be used as bases to visit some of the most far-flung corners of Nepal. There are many ethnic groups in the region, including Limbu, Rai, Sherpa, Lhomi as well as Tibetan nomads who cross the border to trade.

Makalu   [see pp124-35]

Makalu is sandwiched between Kanchenjunga and the Solu-Khumbu (Everest Region), but that doesn't mean to say it's any half measure! This is perhaps the most stunning and challenging of Nepal's wilderness trekking areas. The standard route to the base camp of the fifth highest mountain in the world, Mt Makalu, is reached after an arduous trek over the Khongma Danda to the incomparable beauty of the Barun Nadi valley.

For those who want to immerse themselves in Nepal, the wilderness and community-based trails that criss-cross the Buffer Zone to the south of Makalu-Barun National Park are one of Nepal's best-kept secrets. Both the park and buffer zone are also home to Rai, Lhomi and Sherpa people, making this perhaps the most comprehensive trekking region in the Himalaya.

(continued on p36)

TREK SUMMARIES – EAST NEPAL

TREK, GRADE AND DURATION	HIGHLIGHTS	SEASONS	ACCOMMODATION
Kanchenjunga Base Camp (p117-21) About 20 days — GRADE 4	Lush forests to the north face of the third highest mountain in the world	Apr-May/ Oct-Nov	Basic teahouse and/or camping
Kanchenjunga BC to Olangchun Gola via Nango La (pp121-3) About 3 days — GRADE 4	Add the intriguing village of Olang for the complete east Nepal experience	Apr-May/ Oct-Nov	Camping
Olangchun Gola to Chyamtang (see pp123-4) About 4 days — GRADE 5	High route across the Lumbha Sambha that links the Kanchenjunga and Makalu Regions	Apr-May/ Oct-Nov	Camping
Makalu BC Trek (pp126-30) About 15 days — GRADE 4	The trail to the fifth highest mountain on the planet is high and wild	Apr-May/ Oct-Nov	Basic teahouse and/or camping
Makalu BC, Sherpani Col, West Col & Amphu Labsta to Chhukung (pp134-5) About 5 days — GRADE 5	Add the high passes to the Solu-Khumbu and really get among Himalayan peaks	Apr-May/ Oct-Nov	Camping
Arun-Salpa Trail (p131) About 9 days — GRADE 3	The Salpa pass is a wonderful viewpoint between Lukla & Tumlingtar	Mar-May/ Oct-Jan	Basic teahouse and/or camping
Chyamtang to Makalu BC (pp131-4) About 8 days — GRADE 5	An amazing exploratory wilderness trek beyond compare	Apr-May/ Oct-Nov	Camping
Everest Base Camp & Kala Patthar (pp138-41) About 14 days — GRADE 3	The classic must-do trek to the base of the highest point on Earth.	Mar-May/ Oct-Jan	Teahouse and/or camping
Everest BC, Kala Patthar, Cho La & Renjo La (pp138-43) About 20 days — GRADE 4	Put all the best of the best in one amazing trek	Mar-May/ Oct-Jan	Teahouse and/or camping
Rolwaling & Tashi Labsta Trek (pp146-53) About 23 days — GRADE 4	Mountains, glaciers and valleys merge into a trekking extravaganza	Apr-May/ Oct-Nov	Camping
The Last Resort to Jiri via Bigu Gompa & Laduk (p153) About 8 days — GRADE 4	A bit of wild combined with an authentic cultural trek	Oct-May	Camping

For notes about the various grades see p31.

PLANNING YOUR TREK

TREK SUMMARIES – CENTRAL NEPAL

Trek, grade and duration	Highlights	Seasons	Accommodation
Kathmandu to Gosainkund Trek (pp155-8) About 9 days	Pure Himalaya magic; great views, sacred lakes and amazing wild flowers	Mar-May/ Sep-Dec	Teahouse and/or camping
Langtang Valley Trek (pp158-61) About 10 days	Comfort, convenience and a quality Himalayan experience	Sep-May	Teahouse and/or camping
The Last Resort to Syabrubesi via Tilman's Pass (pp163-8) About 14 days	Wilderness, culture, and history... and all starting just a day from Kathmandu!	Mar-May	Camping
Tamang Heritage Trail (pp169-73) About 9 days	An easy-going trek through the most vivacious ethnic communities in Nepal	Oct-May	Basic teahouse and/or Camping
Ruby Valley Trek (pp174-7) About 8 days	A true gem of a trek in more ways than one!	Oct-May	Camping
Manaslu Circuit (pp178-83) About 16 days	One of the best experiences in the Himalaya and a fabulous trek	Mar-May/ Oct-Dec	Teahouse and/or camping
Tsum Valley (pp184-5) About 5 days	Wonderful cultures and amazing mountain scenery in a remote corner of Nepal	Mar-May/ Oct-Dec	Camping
Naar, Phu & Thorung La Trek (pp188-94) About 17 days	Traditional Tibetan villages and the extraordinary Kang La	Mar-May/ Oct-Jan	Teahouse and/or camping
Annapurna Sanctuary Trek (pp195-8) About 10 days	Fabulous mountain amphitheatre and all the comforts of some great teahouses	Mar-May/ Oct-Jan	Teahouse and/or camping
Poon Hill and Khopra Ridge Trek (pp198-202) About 7 days	There are lots of reasons why this is the most popular trek in the Himalaya!	Oct-June	Teahouse and/or camping
Teri La (pp203-4) About 12 days	A dramatic link between Annapurna and Mustang across the Great Himalaya Range	Apr-May/ Oct-Dec	Camping

For notes about the various grades see p31.

PLANNING YOUR TREK

TREK SUMMARIES – WEST NEPAL

TREK, GRADE AND DURATION	HIGHLIGHTS	SEASONS	ACCOMMODATION
Mustang Circuit (pp205-13) About 12 days — GRADE 3	Like nowhere else does today collide so obviously with the Middle Ages!	Mar-Nov	Basic teahouse and/or camping
Chhosar & Thinggar valleys (p214) 2-3 days — GRADE 3	Add the valleys and gompas along an ancient trade route to Tibet	Apr-Nov	Camping
Mustang, Luri Cave, Damodhar Himal to Phu (p215) About 20 days — GRADE 5	The remote Damodar Kund and trails to Phu via Saribung La	Apr-Nov	Camping
Upper Dolpo Circuit (pp217-25) About 20 days — GRADE 4	Mysterious, spectacular, rarely visited and authentic cultures	Apr-Nov	Camping
Dhorpatan to Jumla via Dunai (pp225-6) About 16 days — GRADE 3	An enticing blend of wilderness and lower Dolpo cultures	Apr-May/ Oct-Dec	Camping
Lower Dolpo Circuit (p226) About 12 days — GRADE 4	Amazing variety in the Trans-Himalayan biodiversity area	Apr-Nov	Camping
Kagbeni to Chharka Bhot (pp226-8) About 14 days — GRADE 4	Wonderful remote wilderness and ancient communities in a trans-Himalayan odyssey	Apr-Nov	Camping
Kagbeni to Gamgadhi – high route via Chharka Bhot & Pho (pp231-4) About 20 days — GRADE 5	Nine 5000m+ passes and authentic cultures make this beyond compare	Apr-Nov	Camping
Rara Lake Circuit (pp240-5) About 13 days — GRADE 3	Sublime beauty, old-growth forests and ancient history all in one trek	Apr-May/ Oct-Dec	Basic teahouse and/or camping
Khaptad National Park (pp245-9) About 9 days — GRADE 3	Where the Gods choose to honeymoon away from the crowds...	Mar-May/ Oct-Dec	Camping
Karnali Corridor: Rara to Simikot (pp249-53) About 12 days — GRADE 4	A trans-Himalayan delight and a wonderful insight	Apr-May/ Oct-Dec far west Nepal	Camping
Limi Valley Trek via Hilsa (Yulsa) (pp253-9) About 17 days — GRADE 3	Fascinating local history and cultures, dramatic trans-Himalayan scenery	Apr-May/ Sep-Nov	Camping
Far west discovery: Darchula to Rara Lake (pp259-67) About 20 days — GRADE 4	An amazing adventure with unbelievable hospitality and gorgeous landscapes	Mar-June/ Sep-Dec	Camping

For notes about the various grades see p31.

PLANNING YOUR TREK

Everest (Solu-Khumbu) region [see pp136-44]

The Everest Region, known locally as the Solu-Khumbu, is one of Nepal's premier trekking locations. Tens of thousands of tourists visit each year, mainly in the post-monsoon months of October and November, but come out of season and the well-maintained trails are almost empty. This is a region where you can stop at any point and absorb stunning scenery that will rival mountain grandeur anywhere, and of course, there's the 'Big E', Mt Everest, the world's highest peak at 8848m. Add the famous hospitality of the Sherpa people, comfy teahouses, plenty of culture and history and you can see why some trekkers keep coming back year after year.

Rolwaling [see pp145-53]

Rolwaling lies beyond the western boundary of the Everest region and the mighty Tashi Labsta pass (5760m). One of the least-visited areas in Nepal, the mountains and valleys of this region offer unbridled opportunities for the remote trekker and mountaineer. Bordered by the Arniko Highway (the Kathmandu to Tibet road) to the west, the Rolwaling also includes some excellent medium-altitude trails over Tinsang La and through Bigu Gompa. Tamang, Gurung and Sherpa people offer a genuine welcome to any visitor, and consider combining your itinerary with a bungy jump at The Last Resort.

Helambu and Langtang [see pp153-67]

Helambu and Langtang, to the north of Kathmandu, are perhaps the most convenient of all the trekking areas; it is even possible to begin your trek from your hotel door in Thamel! Any visitor to Nepal in April should see the rhododendron forests that cover the northern slopes of Helambu; these are only rivalled by those in the Kanchenjunga region. The Bhotia people here are just as friendly as the Sherpa elsewhere, and the intermingling with Brahmin, Chhetri and Newar people is a reminder of Nepal's harmonious ethnic diversity. It is almost unbelievable that so few trekkers continue past Kyangjin Gompa to visit Langshisa Glacier, or cross the Tilman Pass, where the mountains are simply amazing.

Ganesh and Manaslu Himals [see pp167-85]

Ganesh Himal and Manaslu lie in the geographical centre of Nepal and are one of the country's best-kept trekking secrets. Many would argue that the Manaslu Circuit is the perfect combination of nature, culture and history, and for those wanting to immerse themselves in some wild, but not high-altitude trekking, Ganesh Himal is the place. Gurung, Tamang, Magar, Larke and Siar people blend to create perhaps the most ethnically interesting series of valleys throughout the Himalaya. Add some majestic peaks, including Mt Manaslu, the 8th highest mountain on earth, and these regions should be high on anyone's list.

Annapurna, Naar & Phu region [see pp186-204]

For many years Annapurna has been the most popular trekking region of the entire Himalaya. Despite recent road construction, trekkers and tourists continue to flock to Pokhara and the trails around the majestic Annapurna massif.

The new roads are increasing accessability to what is still one of the most beautiful, comfortable and convenient areas of Nepal to explore. When you add the variety of landscapes that you'll find in Naar, Phu and Tilicho it is easy to see that the region still has lots to offer.

Mustang and Dolpo regions [see pp205-35]

Mustang and Dolpo both lie in the 'rain-shadow' of the Annapurna and Dhaulagiri massifs and are unique when compared to the rest of Nepal. Both regions are repositories of largely unchanged Tibetan culture, dating back at least 1200 years. Lush lower valleys lead up to an arid alpine desert and some of the highest permanent settlements on earth. Nomads herd yaks over windswept passes, and tales of sorcery and magicians are woven into everyday life.

The Far West region [see pp236-68]

The least developed of the trekking regions of Nepal is the Far West of the country and includes Humla, Rara, Khaptad National Park and the Api and Saipal Himals. The local Khas and Chhetri people have rarely, if ever, seen trekkers, so be prepared for a touching and heartfelt welcome wherever you go. Logistics are a challenge throughout the region but the extra effort of organising a trek here is the price you pay for an authentic experience you will never forget!

GREAT HIMALAYA TRAIL – NEPAL ROUTE SUMMARY

Many tens of thousands of trekkers visit Nepal every year and they often want to return to explore new areas of this magnificent country. The traditional trekking routes all offer wonderful trail experiences but there is more to Nepal than the Annapurna, Solu-Khumbu and Langtang regions. It was while exploring the 'off-the-beaten-track' places that the concept of the Great Himalaya Trail (GHT) really took shape. The goal of the GHT is to share the benefits of tourism with as many remote communities as possible by focusing on a trail network and the 'how' you trek. However, for this to work in practice it requires you, your guide and trekking company to act responsibly at all times. Please follow the GHT Code of Conduct (see box p12) and share the trail wisely.

The Great Himalaya Range stretches 2400km, forming a natural barrier between India and China, with Nepal covering the central third (865km) of the highest peaks. The eastern third of the Nepali GHT connects Kanchenjunga with Makalu and Solu-Khumbu (Everest) regions, and then on into Rolwaling. A central section joins Rolwaling to the Langtang valley, then on through the Ganesh Himal before ending in Manaslu. The western section links the Annapurnas to Mustang, Dolpo, Mugu and ends on the banks of the Mahakali Nadi or in the north-west region of Humla.

Trekking the GHT

The Nepal section of the Great Himalaya Trail takes between 90 and 160 days to walk, depending on the route. So for most folks, the whole trek will entail multiple visits (tourist visas are limited to 150 days each calendar year), even if you can get the leave approved!

The Great Himalaya Trail is a 'way of exploring the Himalaya' rather than a specific trail. It is a trail network; a collection of options that you can use to develop your own personal GHT. An increasingly popular approach is to combine the main tourist regions with lesser-known areas to provide a more authentic Nepal experience. There are extreme routes that cross high passes through to lower village trails suitable for the novice trekker or for those who want to immerse themselves in Nepali culture. The remote sections of the GHT require full camping equipment, but for many of the trails in the main trekking areas or lower routes it

❏ Giving something back

Many people who visit Nepal fall in love with both the country and her people. However, the level of poverty and tragic circumstances that some of the locals are suffering from often results in a desire to help. There are many 'pro-poor' or poverty alleviation programmes throughout the country as well as community development schemes from providing and distributing emergency stretchers to installing toilets and water pipes.

The GHT is designed to help local communities by encouraging trekkers to visit areas 'off the beaten track' in the belief that any help is better than no help. Nearly all the programmes and initiatives currently operating in Nepal rely on donations and volunteer assistance, so if you want to get involved and make a positive difference there is always a cause to suit.

If you are providing support to someone attempting a long section of the GHT you might, in your spare time, want to offer your services to a local organisation. The notice board at Kathmandu Guest House in Thamel is a good place to begin searching for an organisation that matches your interest. There are also some websites (💻 www.ngofederation.org, 💻 www.ain.org.np and 💻 www.nepalngo.org) that list registered organisations.

A couple of popular organisations for volunteer work in the Kathmandu valley are Just One (💻 www.just-one.org) that works with marginalised children and impoverished mothers, and Maiti Nepal (💻 www.maitinepal.org) who help victims of human and sexual trafficking. You could also check with your embassy or consulate to see if they are sponsoring any projects you can help with.

On a final note, you might like to check the prisons to see if there are any foreigners doing time. They always appreciate visitors, and gifts such as fresh fruit, bread, cigarettes and batteries. The food supplied in prisons is meager and not good quality, so any supplement you can give is welcome. These people are not supported by their embassy and rely on the kindness of strangers to get by.

Community

The financial benefits to a community are obvious in the main trekking regions of Everest, Annapurna and Langtang. But when you visit the remoter regions of the GHT it becomes apparent that even US$10 can make a difference to some villages. By spreading tourist dollars the GHT helps to alleviate poverty and address the enormous wealth disparity in Nepal.

For anyone wanting to make a difference for the better, the GHT offers many opportunities to support almost countless causes along the trail.

There are several International Non-Government Organisations (INGOs) that have long-term projects in Nepal. If you choose to help a local NGO you should carefully check its credentials. A few examples of ones that operate in areas of particular interest for mountain communities and projects are:

● **Eco Himal** (💻 www.ecohimal.org) is an Austrian initiative that specialises in grassroots projects to help create sustainable village living. They have created the Eco Himal lodges in Rolwaling.

is possible to rely on teahouses or local lodges for accommodation. Logistical issues, fitness and weather all combine to make trekking long sections a major challenge for even the most experienced and well-equipped trekkers.

For some remote sections, campsites and trails are very hard to locate, requiring local guides to help you find your way. For any route in Nepal, it is

- **ICIMOD** (International Centre for Integrated Mountain Development, 💻 www.icimod.org) aims to help the people of the Himalaya understand the effects of globalisation and climate change on their delicate ecosystems, and develop economically sustainable practices.
- **The Nepal Trust** (💻 www.nepaltrust.org) is based in the UK and provides integrated rural development in the Far West areas of Nepal and is probably the most active organisation in the poorest regions of Humla and Mugu.
- **Ten Friends** (💻 www.tenfriends.org) is a group of people who work in the Sankhuwasabha (between Kanchenjunga and Makalu), who first started donating emergency stretchers to remote villages. They are now involved with orphanage and school programmes, water filtration, sanitation and female empowerment projects in both East Nepal and Kathmandu.
- **Australian Himalayan Foundation** (💻 www.australianhimalayanfoundation.org.au) runs a number of projects in education, health & medical services and the environment, mainly in the lower Solu-Khumbu area. It aims to ensure, where possible, the long-term viability of schools, to provide health, education and medical services and to support environmental projects for remote communities.
- **The Hillary Himalayan Trust** (💻 himalayantrust.co.uk) founded by Sir Edmund Hillary is perhaps the most famous of the NGOs operating in Nepal. Its successes in the Sherpa region of the Solu-Khumbu have been outstanding and are considered to be a role model for best practice by many.
- **The Mountain Institute** (TMI; 💻 www.mountain.org/himalayas) empowers communities in the Himalayas (and elsewhere around the world) through education, conservation and sustainable development. Since its founding more than 38 years ago, TMI has worked closely with the people who know mountains best – those who actually live there – to help identify and implement solutions to challenges that threaten their livelihoods and the health of their local environments.
- **IPPG** (International Porter Protection Group; 💻 ippg.net) works to improve the conditions of mountain porters in the tourism industry worldwide and is active in Nepal. With representatives throughout the world, it is possible to assist this organisation both at home and overseas.

Environment
Many communities continue to hunt and log without any thought for the environment upon which they rely so heavily. By promoting sustainable tourism throughout the Himalaya it is hoped that remote communities will stop destroying pristine habitat and that the government will see the benefit in declaring more conservation and National Park areas. Eventually, this could link current reserves and create the first international trans-border animal corridor, truly a goal of Himalayan size!

The **World Wide Fund for Nature** (💻 nepal.panda.org) is active throughout the country and is always in need of support. The **National Trust for Nature Conservation in Nepal** (💻 www.ntnc.org.np) is a local organisation that has projects in various districts, all of which require support and volunteers.

PLANNING YOUR TREK

advisable to purchase large-scale topographic maps (see *Maps, GPS waypoints and Walking Guides*, pp42-3) to assist route-finding; a GPS and a satellite phone are handy too. Groups should carry the minimum possible and rely on the least number of tents (ideally not more than ten), as most places to camp are very small. Villages will probably not be able to sell you much food, so expect to be self-sufficient for most of the time.

The highest routes involve crossing many high passes, some requiring ropes and climbing equipment, so groups should have alpine climbing and rescue experience. Plans and contingencies for emergencies should be taken seriously; rescue from many areas along the trail could be very difficult. However, the experience of exploring remote regions, meeting the challenges of route-finding, crossing passes, and sharing in the life of communities who are always surprised and pleased to see you, is simply amazing. There is no 'tourist trail' that can duplicate the joy and sense of achievement of the Great Himalaya Trail.

Section 1: Eastern Nepal – Kanchenjunga to Thame

● **Higher trails** In the far north-east corner of Nepal is Jhinsang La, an extremely remote pass on the north side of Kanchenjunga. From here the trail heads down the main trekking route from Kanchenjunga Base Camp (KBC) to Ghunsa, and then westwards over Nango La to Olangchun Gola. Head north-west up and over the remote Lumbha Sambha, down through Thudam and along the Arun Nadi to Hongon. Climb back to the Tibetan border towards Popti La and then head west before the pass to the Saldim Khola and over to the Barun Nadi. Pass through Makalu Base Camp and over the Sherpani Col, West Col and Amphu Labsta to the Solu-Khumbu (Everest region), where you cross Cho La and Renjo La to Thame.

● **Lower trails** From the Singalilla National Park viewpoint of Phalut, head cross-country to Taplejung and then over the Milke Danda following an ancient trade route to Khadbari. Then choose from some fantastic community and wilderness trails that cross the Makalu Barun Buffer Zone towards the upper and lower Solu-Khumbu.

Section 2: Central Nepal – Thame to Kagbeni

● **Higher trails** Cross the Tashi Labsta and descend through the Rolwaling. Take the most northerly exit route towards Kodari, cross the Bhote Kosi and trek up to Bhairav Kund. Then cross the Balephi Khola and climb to Panch Pokhari before crossing Tilman Pass to the Langtang valley. Descend to Syabrubesi, continue to Gatlang and then cross the Ganesh Himal foothills to the Manaslu Circuit. Continue around to Dharapani and then around the Annapurna Circuit to Kagbeni.

● **Lower trails** There are dozens of intriguing cultural trails throughout the lower Solu Khumbu that will either lead you to Jiri or directly to Kathmandu. From Jiri, head north and visit the lower Rolwaling, especially Bigu Gompa, before heading across to the sites of Helambu. Panch Pokhari and/or Gosainkund are worth including as part of a cultural route to the Ganesh Himal, and then to the ancient capital of Gorkha and the comforts of Pokhara.

Section 3: Western Nepal – Kagbeni to Hilsa (Yulsa) or Darchula

● **Higher trails** From Kagbeni head north-west into Upper Dolpo via Chharka Bhot and then pick one of two routes: westwards to Dho Tarap and Ringmo and then north to Pho; or, head north-west from Chharka Bhot to Shimen and then head west to Pho. From Pho there are two routes to the Mugu Karnali Nadi valley; both descend to Gamgadhi. After visiting Rara Lake, a trans-Himalayan route along the Karnali corridor takes you to Simikot and the last section of trail up to the border post at Hilsa (Yulsa).

● **Lower trails** From Pokhara, cross the Dhorpatan Hunting Reserve to Dunai and follow an ancient trade route through Lower Dolpo to Jumla and Rara Lake. An extensive network of trails heads west connecting some of the least-visited regions of the entire Himalaya; all are worth the effort to explore! Eventually you arrive at Darchula on the banks of the Mahakali Nadi and the border with India.

Before departure

Life in Nepal is more 'fluid' than what you might be used to, which makes working with the locals' concept of time and efficiency a potential source of frustration for many tourists. If you are planning and organising an independent trip make sure you pack some patience and a smile – anger achieves only negative results. If you are on a packaged trip let your tour leader do the worrying and just go with the flow. Whatever your plans, once you have decided to visit Nepal the first thing to do is book your flight as most airlines run at full capacity in peak season.

VISAS AND PERMITS

Barely a year goes by without a change to the **entry visa regulations** to Nepal. You can check arrangements with one of the Nepali embassies or consular offices, but the most reliable source of information is currently the Nepal Department of Immigration website (⌨ www.immi.gov.np).

Many tourists organise a visa prior to arrival in Nepal by applying through the Department of Immigration website (see ⌨ www.online.nepalimmigration .gov.np/tourist-visa), but it is also straightforward to apply for a visa on arrival in Kathmandu at Tribhuvan International Airport (currently US$100 for 90 days, US$40 for 30 days, US$25 for 15 days, payable in a range of major currencies or Visa or MasterCard).

The visa available on arrival tends to be cheaper than applying for one from an embassy or consular office. To save time, complete the current visa application form (which can be downloaded from the website above) prior to arrival, and remember to bring some passport photos. Other entry points are Kodari (on the Tibet border and normally only open for groups), and nine overland borders with India, for current details see the website above.

Similarly, the **trekking permit system** undergoes almost constant change. Currently most trekking itineraries require: (1) a National Park or a Conservation Area Permit, and (2) TIMS (Trekkers Information Management System) permit. You may also require a Controlled Area Permit and/or a special trekking permit depending on the region. It is essential that you organise Controlled Area Permits through a registered trekking company, and if this is all you do the company will charge you a processing fee. You should always carry a photocopy of your passport when trekking, and be prepared to register at police check posts whenever requested to do so.

A final formality is to register online, or in Kathmandu, with your embassy or consulate or register at the Himalayan Rescue Association (see box p87). If there is no consulate, find out which, if any, country represents your country in Nepal. This can be determined from your Foreign Affairs Department, or corresponding office, in your country.

The essential information required by your embassy is your name, an emergency contact number, passport number and itinerary. It is also a good idea to provide the contact details of your hotel and trekking agency in Nepal should you need to be contacted. One major benefit of this process is to facilitate your rescue and repatriation should it be necessary.

INSURANCE

Most travel insurance policies will cover you while you are trekking and will include emergency medical evacuation costs. However, you should read the policy carefully and check for any exclusions. For example, using a rope (even as a handline) or itineraries that go higher than a stipulated maximum altitude during your trek could void your policy.

It is also vital that you establish some contacts in Kathmandu that could help you should an accident occur, see *Rescue and Emergency* pp69-70 for more details.

MAPS, GPS WAYPOINTS AND WALKING GUIDES

During the 1990s, INGO Finaid sponsored a new topographic survey of Nepal, which resulted in a broadsheet 1:25,000 (covering the terai and pahar) and 1:50,000 (covering the high mountains) series of maps of the entire country. These are the most accurate maps in Nepal and are sold from a small shop on Bhaktapur Road in Kathmandu called Maps of Nepal (near Everest Hotel, New Baneshwor) for the modest amount of NRs150 each. However, the geographic grid system they use does not mesh with the more recent WGS 84 (used by Google Earth, GPS devices and most mapping companies) so if you are using a GPS with the Finaid maps for navigation make sure you can change your settings.

Himalayan Map House publish a range of Great Himalaya Trail maps designed to work in combination with this guidebook. They are accurate to scales between 1:100,000 and 1:150,000 depending on the region, waterproof and updated every two years. For more information, free downloads or to buy the maps online see 🖳 www.greathimalayatrail.com/ghtProducts.php.

There is also a broad range of less expensive and less accurate maps in Nepal. The best of these are produced by *Kartographische Anstalt Freytag-Berndt und Artaria*, Vienna, Austria (normally referred to as the *Schneider* maps after the original cartographer) but the place names on these maps often do not reflect local pronunciation, some of the routes have now changed and they only cover the main trekking regions.

For those wanting to plan treks on Google Earth or create waypoint files for a GPS, there are **free download GPX files** for almost every trekking route in Nepal online, see 🖳 www.greathimalayatrail.com/gpsFiles.php.

The best of the specialist pocket trekking guides currently available are from Trailblazer: *Trekking in the Everest Region* by Jamie McGuinness and *Trekking in the Annapurna Region* (currently being updated) by Bryn Thomas. There are many older publications (from the mid-1990s) that review the major trekking routes, or the Annapurnas, Manaslu and Kanchenjunga in detail, but they are now quite out of date. Himalayan Map House also publish some specific field guides to the Manaslu and Dolpo regions, both of which are up to date and available through their website see 🖳 www.himalayan-maphouse.com.

WEATHER REPORTS

It is a good idea for those walking long sections of the GHT to receive regular weather reports. This is most commonly done via mobile phone along the main trails and satellite phone systems in remoter regions. Reliable and comprehensive weather reporting websites are hard to find and it always makes sense to check for second or third opinions.

For those trekking in remoter regions it is recommended you familiarise yourself with all the following websites and choose the most applicable.

● 🖳 www.monsoondata.org/wx/ezindia.n.html;
● 🖳 www.imd.gov.in/section/satmet/dynamic/iso.htm;
● 🖳 squall.sfsu.edu/scripts/nhemjetstream_model.html
● 🖳 www.wunderground.com/global/Region/A2/2xJetStream.html
● 🖳 www.stormsurfing.com/cgi/display_alt.cgi?a=nindi_250

● 🖳 weather.cnn.com/weather/forecast.jsp?locCode=NPXX0002&zipCode=93664825748
● 🖳 www.bbc.co.uk/weather/1283240
● 🖳 www.weather.com/weather/today/Kathmandu+Nepal+NPXX0002
● 🖳 www.meteoexploration.com/index.php
● 🖳 www.expeditionweather.info/index.php?page=200

EQUIPMENT

Kathmandu has several outdoor shops that sell a broad range of equipment for anything from light day walks to high-altitude expeditions. Prices and quality vary enormously and it is wise to know what to look for in a product as shop staff will promise the world. In general, it is wise to equip yourself at home as you then have the opportunity to wear-in and become familiar with your kit.

This may be something as simple as getting used to carrying things in certain pockets, to breaking-in your boots, to developing an exercise programme around an increasing pack weight.

Footwear

You are about to embark on a walking holiday so choosing footwear is normally the first equipment decision. Be prepared to take a considerable amount of time to shop around reputable outdoor-gear shops and find the **boots that fit you perfectly**; make sure that there is no discomfort when you wear them! Your feet will swell and become more sensitive at altitude, your sense of balance may change and the terrain may provide unknown challenges, so a full boot that immobilises the ankle joint and has excellent grip is advisable. It is relatively simple to adjust lacing for varying thicknesses of sock, so pack a few different types to suit terrain and climate. Thin, skin-hugging liner **socks** are always a good idea for

> ❑ **Top tip**
> To let your boots breathe out moisture overnight open them up by pulling the tongue forward. This is a good habit when in freezing temperatures as it will make them much easier to put on in the morning!

longer treks as they reduce the need to launder thick socks (which are hard to dry), and help to keep the skin surface dry (thus reducing the chance of blistering). You also need a pair of **light shoes or sandals** to wear when you finish trekking for the day. These will allow your feet to dry out and relax. Sandals can also be used for river crossings, and when showering.

Packs

The range and methods of using packs is almost limitless, whether you are carrying all your own equipment, or just a small daypack. The majority of trekkers use a 40-litre (2200 cu in, or thereabouts) pack for all the items they are likely to need throughout the day and a kit bag (carried by a porter or pack animal) to stow the remainder of their equipment. Packs should have a number of generic features, like at least one lid pocket for bits and pieces, external stash pockets and compression straps, and a method of keeping wet and dry gear separate. However, the most important feature of a pack is that it should fit properly and that you learn how to re-adjust it (see opposite).

The back panel length of a pack should match your own back length, try on different models and check in a mirror to see if the lengths match. You should understand the principle and placement of balance straps and how to adjust a harness to fit. It is inevitable that your pack will need readjusting at some point on the trail and knowing how to do this is as important as knowing how to lace your boots. The kit bags a trekking company might give you to stow spare equipment are not waterproof so to protect valuables, your sleeping bag and spare clothing against water damage use roll-top, durable, waterproof stuff sacks.

Trekking poles

If you want to be walking in your dotage use trekking poles now! The prolonged impact of steep downhill on ankles, hips and especially knees will have a

ADJUSTING YOUR RUCKSACK

Begin by adjusting the harness system with no weight in the pack, then once you think the pack is as comfortable as possible put roughly your average carry weight inside the pack and try it on again. Try to distribute the weight inside the pack as you would for a trip – the ideal is to make the load distribution as realistic as possible. Walk around for 10-20 minutes to feel how the harness performs as you move – this is the only accurate way of appraising a harness system. To adjust the harness:

• Loosen the pack's shoulder straps, top stabiliser straps and hip belt.

• Lift the pack using the haul loop (never lift or move the pack with the pack harness – and slide your arms through the shoulder straps.

• Bend over so that the pack sits on your spine allowing you to adjust the straps without the pack sliding down your back.

• First do up the hip belt making sure that it straddles your pelvis (iliac crest) and then tighten the straps. Note that the two ends of the hip belt should not be touching, nor pushing into your stomach.

• Cinch the shoulder straps so that they fit snugly (no gaps should be visible) over your collar bone – check that the top stabilisers connect with the pack about 3cm above your shoulder. The shoulder straps should not compress your spine, nor restrict your arm movement – they are there to take about 20% of the load, the hip belt takes the rest.

• Adjust the shoulder and hip stabiliser straps for comfort. The pack should not swing or bound as you walk, it should remain stable over your natural gravity. Make sure that the shoulder straps do not extend beneath your armpits; they will chafe if they do. Use the sternum strap to prevent the shoulder straps from slipping sideways and make sure that you do not hit your head on the pack when you look up.

• Now check for comfort by moving around. Walk up and down stairs, crouch down, hop from spot to spot and move your arms about – make sure that the harness is not causing any irritation or overly restricting movement.

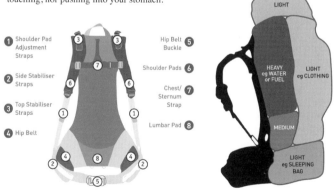

1 Shoulder Pad Adjustment Straps
2 Side Stabiliser Straps
3 Top Stabiliser Straps
4 Hip Belt
5 Hip Belt Buckle
6 Shoulder Pads
7 Chest/ Sternum Strap
8 Lumbar Pad

LIGHT
HEAVY eg WATER or FUEL
LIGHT eg CLOTHING
MEDIUM
LIGHT eg SLEEPING BAG

PLANNING YOUR TREK

noticeable effect on everyone in your group. The best and most reliable method for reducing shock on joints is to use trekking poles – that's a pair of collapsible poles, not a single stick. It is wise to purchase them well before your trek so that you have time for their use to become second nature.

Clothing

There are days that barely an hour goes by without having to make some adjustment to your clothing so most trekkers and mountaineers rely on a series of clothing layers while on the trail. When you think about layers there are three distinct types of fabric:

● **Next-to-skin fabrics** are soft, easy to launder (that is, they dry quickly) and may be thermally insulating. Three, or even four, different fabrics are ideal: (1) **for warm to hot conditions** – a very light synthetic that can dry in minutes, is UV resistant, and has an antibacterial treatment; (2) **for cool to warm conditions** – a light long-sleeved top with a pocket, that can be worn as sun protection or as a lightweight insulator on a cool evening; (3) **for cold to cool conditions** – a thermal fabric that can be worn all day or as a night shirt; (4) **for very cold conditions** – a very warm thermal shirt for high altitudes or very cold nights. It is also handy to have a loose-fitting, well-ventilated synthetic shirt for warmer or more humid days. Cotton is NOT advisable next to your skin in the mountains as it can increase the chances of hypothermia.

● **Mid-layer fabrics** include synthetic fleece garments for warmth, especially when you stop walking and need to protect against a sudden cooling, and soft-shells for warmth in wind and/or light rain. Soft-shell garments come in an enormous range of combinations; the most popular are lighter-weight fabrics that can be worn while walking in a cold wind so that you don't have to put on your weatherproof shell. However, it is important to make sure that the garment provides some insulation, and is made from a fairly tough fabric, as you will be wearing it under your pack harness at some point.

● **Shell fabrics** are 100% waterproof and windproof, preferably breathable, and/or well ventilated. Whenever you venture into the Himalaya it is essential that you always carry a waterproof jacket and pants. Pit-zips (under-arm zips) or similar ventilation is a good way to prevent condensation from building up, especially in less-breathable garments.

You should also pack a sun hat, warm hat, warm and weatherproof gloves, a light pair of liner style gloves, and a light scarf to wrap around your face on dusty sections of trail, especially when a train of yaks goes past!

Lightweight walking trousers/pants with detachable legs have become popular with some trekkers. For cultural reasons this might not be a good idea in some areas, see pp61-2.

Sleeping gear

You are going to spend roughly one-third of your holiday in your **sleeping bag** so it is worth making sure you're comfy inside it! The European Union has introduced a sleeping bag insulation rating system, which is a good method of comparing and choosing a bag. Most treks in Nepal require a bag that can keep you warm at -10°C but

> ❏ **Top tip**
> Check the size of any trekking equipment you are given by the trekking company before you begin your trek and make sure it is the right size, especially the sleeping bag! If you are not a standard size it might be better to purchase your own things.

that you can also sleep in when it's 15°
or 20°C at night.

A full side zip, and preferably a
foot zip, adds a little weight but it
makes your bag more versatile across
a broad range of temperatures. It is
also a good idea to use a **sleeping bag
liner** to prevent body oil or sweat from
making your sleeping bag smelly. Silk
liners are a popular choice as they are
lighter, easier to launder and slightly
warmer than those made from cotton.

❏ **Top tips**
● Don't overdress in your sleeping
bag. Try to minimise redundant air
space inside the bag – let the sleeping
bag insulation do its job! If you are
still cold, add layers to the outside of
the bag rather than putting too many
layers on your body.
● Barking dogs are common across
the Himalaya, so take some ear-plugs
if you are a light sleeper.

A good-quality **insulation mat** is also recommended for teahouse and
camping trekkers alike. In most teahouses you are provided with a foam mattress, which can have a well-worn pit in the middle, which an insulating mat
will negate. Camping treks sometimes provide sleeping mats but it is normally
a good idea to take your own mat as well, unless you are certain that you will
be comfortable and well insulated from the ground.

Shelter
Nearly all camping treks will provide **tents** for the trip. However, if you want
to take your own for an independent trek it is worthwhile to choose one that: (1)
can withstand extreme winds – such tents are normally rated as 'alpine', '4 season' or 'extreme'; (2) has enough room for people and gear as sometimes it is
unsafe to leave your kit in a vestibule; (3) is well ventilated – most treks start in
the hot and humid lower valleys before climbing in to alpine regions.

Bring a footprint or light tarp for use on wet ground, and carry an extensive
field repair kit, as even glue can be hard to find in the hills.

Cooking gear
If you are planning to do a teahouse trek to high altitudes and/or out of season
(when the chance of snowfall is higher) a **small gas stove** is a good safety measure. Some people find it very difficult to sustain body heat at altitude and the
ability to quickly prepare a hot drink can prevent frost nip or frost bite. **Gas fuel**
is widely available in Kathmandu.

Camping groups tend to prefer locally made heavy **kerosene stoves**, as they
are robust and easy to maintain. For expedition-style treks the MSR Whisperlite
International® and MSR XGK Ex® models both burn low-grade kerosene
(good-quality fuel is rare in Nepal) and are fairly easy to field maintain; it is
essential that you carry a **field repair and maintenance kit** for your stove as it
will clog and require cleaning on a regular, almost daily, basis.

Miscellaneous
A **first-aid kit** is essential – see p48, p49 and p66.

Perhaps the most useful item you will need is a **head torch**: for reading in
bed, finding gear in the bottom of bags and to be hands free in the toilet. An
essential piece of equipment is a **water bottle or bladder**, which should ideally

❏ FIRST-AID KIT – MEDICATIONS

Name	Uses	Dosage	Remarks
Betadine liquid iodine	Water sterilisation, throat gargle	8 drops/litre leave for 30 mins, or 2 drops/20ml for gargle	For external use when cleaning cuts & grazes, water treatment and throat gargle
Antiseptic cream/ Savlon™	Burns, grazes	Apply directly on affected area	External use only
Aspirin	Aches, pains, flu, headache, fever	1-2 tablets up to 4 times a day	May cause indigestion, stomach bleeding
Paracetamol	Aches, pains, flu, headache	1-2 tablets up to 4 times a day	Best painkiller at high altitude
Ibuprofen	Pain with inflammation	400mg 3 times a day with food	May cause indigestion, stomach bleeding
Norfloxacillin (Norflex™)	Chest, skin, urinary infections	500mg every 12 hours for 5-10 days	Avoid for quinolone-sensitive patients
Ciprofloxacillin (Cipro™)	Diarrhoea (except giardia, amoebic dysentery)	500mg every 12 hours for 2-3 days	First choice for non-specific diarrhoea. Give on empty stomach. Avoid alcohol
Erythromycin (Erythrocin™)	Alternative for penicillin-/sulpha-allergic patients	250mg every 6 hours for 5-10 days	Avoid alcohol
Tinidazole (Tinibar™), Metronidazole (Flagyl™)	Specific for giardia and amoebic dysentery	2g in single dose daily for 3 days	May give metallic taste. Avoid alcohol
Maxolon, Stemetil™	Nausea/vomiting	Maximum one every 8 hours	Avoid at altitude. Avoid alcohol
Immodium, Lomotil™	To slow bad diarrhoea	One tablet 3 times a day	Do not use if blood present. Will not cure you.
Acetozolamide (Diamox™)	Altitude sickness	Half tab morning and night	May produce tingling in extremities. Use with caution – better to descend. Avoid in sulfa-sensitive patients
Antihistamine	Allergies, bites	Usually one a day; check packet	Avoid at altitude. Avoid alcohol
Tyotocin eardrops	Earache, ear infection	3-4 drops, 3-4 times a day	Antiseptic, anti-inflammatory, pain-killing eardrops

PLANNING YOUR TREK

❏ Dressings and miscellaneous

alcohol swabs	ear plugs to help keep wind out	Steri-strips
antacids		surgical gloves (disposable)
anti-itch cream	elastic bandages	
antibacterial hand gel	eye drops/saline solution	sweets or gum to keep mouth and throat lubricated
Bandaids	eye infection drops	
blister pads	gauze squares	
butterfly closures	Lemsip (generally not available in Kathmandu)	thermometer
cotton buds (Kathmandu ones not very good)	moisturiser	thin panty liners – to keep pressure on wounds
cough medicine (very good herbal one in Kathmandu; avoid preparations containing alcohol)	rehydration salts	Tiger Balm/Vicks
	roll of cotton wool	triangular bandages
	roll of sticking plaster	tweezers
	safety pins	Vaseline (use inside nostrils to stop drying out)
crêpe bandages	scissors	
Dettol (small bottle)	SPF 30 lip balm	waterproof storage bags
	SPF 30 sun lotion or zinc cream	Wet wipes (Wet Ones)

have the capacity to carry a minimum of two litres. You also need to pack **biodegradable soap**, a **travel towel**, and **general toiletries** in a waterproof bag.

Instead of cotton hankies, which can become quite unpleasant, it is a good idea to use **lightweight kitchen cloths** (for example Chux®, Super Wipes®, J-Cloths®), these are very easy to clean, dry incredibly fast and weigh very little. Use different colours for hankies and washing yourself as it's a good idea to know which is which!

Technology in the shape of a **GPS or wrist-computer** can be invaluable when used as a backup to a map and compass (declination in most of Nepal is a marginal 2 or 3°) but make sure you carry enough **batteries** that will continue to work in cold conditions.

Waterproof stuff sacks of different colours make identifying items very easy. Clothing items are quickly found in heavy-duty transparent **compression bags**, Eagle Creek® make some good ones. A spare bag for a clean set of

❏ Top tips
● Use stick deodorants as pump action and liquid roll-ons tend to leak at altitude and aerosols are very cold.
● Take a few tampons for (1) packing or dressing deep cuts, (2) a fast way to help light a fire, and (3) just in case any women in your group should need some. It's also a good idea to pack some condoms, as they are useful for making hand and foot dressings waterproof.
● Use iodine gargle when you first feel a tickle in your throat as it is a great way to prevent infections.
● Always take spare lip-protector and sun cream.
● Honey or eucalyptus throat lozenges are great for high altitude and/or very dry environment trekking.
● Put hot water in your bottle or water bladder at night when in cold temperatures and use as it as a hot water bottle. Similarly, put cold water in your bottle in the morning when in hot temperatures.

PLANNING YOUR TREK

clothing to be left in Kathmandu should be lockable, and take another lock for your on-trail kit bag. **Small zip lock bags** (sandwich size) are handy for toilet rolls, bottles of liquid, and to protect your money and documents.

> ❏ **Top tip**
> Bring some family photos and/or a magazine from your home country to show locals – it's a great icebreaker and the local children will love to see where you come from.

Think about what might break down on the trail and how you might carry out repairs. A **sewing kit** is handy, as well as a **strong glue** for boots, a polyurethane glue or sticky patches for when repairs need to be flexible, a **repair kit for your sleeping mat**, enough spare batteries (those available in Kathmandu

---

TYPICAL GEAR LIST FOR SOMEONE WITH A TREKKING GROUP

Clothing
- Waterproof jacket and trousers both ventilated (pit zips, side zips, etc)
- Down jacket and maybe pants for high-altitude treks
- Windproof soft-shell jacket and trousers for windy/cold days.
- Fleece top and trousers
- 2 thermal tops
- 1-2 thermal long johns depending on how much you feel the cold
- 4 pairs of liner socks
- 2 pairs of warm weather walking socks
- 2 pairs of cool weather walking socks
- Pair of cold weather walking socks that can also be used as bed socks
- 2 sets of underwear for cool/cold weather
- 2 sets of underwear for warm/hot weather
- 2 pairs of walking trousers
- 2 loose-fit trekking shirts with pockets
- 2 lightweight synthetic T-shirts
- Pair of waterproof walking boots that can take crampons
- Pair of sandals to let feet breathe in the evenings and for washing
- Broad-brimmed sun hat
- Warm hat and gloves
- Polarising sunglasses with 100% UV protection
- Buff or trekking scarf

General Gear
- Sleeping bag rated to -15°C/ 3°F

General Gear (cont'd)
- Sleeping sheet and pillow (you will be given a pillow if you prefer)
- Inflating sleeping mat (you will be given a mat if you prefer)
- 40-ish litre pack for trekking
- Pair of trekking poles
- Head torch and spare batteries
- Sun block
- Lip balm with sun block
- Mosquito / fly repellent
- Toiletry bag with essentials (no hairdryers!!)
- Towel
- Neck pillow for plane/bus trips if required
- Camera with back-up batteries if needed
- 2-3 litres of water bottles or bladder system depending on consumption
- Some waterproof compression bags for storage in tote bag (different colours)
- Reading material/diary/spare pens
- General repair kit
- Tent for appropriate conditions
- Tote bag for spare gear you do not carry
- Pillow or stuff sack for clothing
- Medical kit

Optional
- Chair kit for sleeping mat
- Shorts/costume for bathing/swimming in rivers
- Closed cell foam mat
- Sarong for sunbathing, around camp on hot days.

are frequently adulterated), a **pen knife or multi-tool** of some description, and a length of 3 or 4mm **cord** as a washing line, spare laces, etc. If you write a diary it is worth carrying some spare **pens**, and a few **photos of your family and friends** will help to build new friendships wherever your path takes you.

The lists opposite and below are designed for camping groups who want to explore remote regions; if you are teahouse trekking you can omit many items!

Power and re-charging on the trail

Re-charging electrical devices while in the hills can be problematic. Many villages have at least one building with a solar panel connected to a 12V battery to provide low-wattage lighting. These set-ups often look very rudimentary with bare wire connections, but they can be a useful source of power in an emergency. It is now commonplace to pay a per hour rate for charging from a local battery (roughly US$4 per hour). Alternatively, purchase one of the many compact and lightweight solar panel and in-built battery chargers.

Many satellite phones require higher ampage outputs than regular mobile phones and they may require additional connectors. This is also true of different

---

TYPICAL GEAR LISTS FOR CLIMBERS AND CAMPERS

Hardwear (for group of eight including clients). Note that this is a general indication of the sort of equipment you might need and not a definitive list – you MUST consult with trained and experienced experts before embarking on any technical trek or climb.

- Crampons for each group member
- Harness for each group member
- Helmet for treks with rock fall hazard
- Ice axe for each group member (or trekking pole if non-technical)
- 2 large slings >2m
- 2 medium slings 1.5-2m
- Medium to large ice screw
- 60m static rope 8-9mm
- 2 screwgate karabiners for each group member
- 2 single prussiks for each group member
- Snowstake/medium to large deadman
- 4 spare screwgate karabiners

Kitchen (minimum for group of eight including clients)
- 2 medium-sized bowls for food preparation and washing
- 2 medium-sized saucepans for cooking vegetables

Kitchen *(cont'd)*
- Pressure cooker
- Frying pan
- Kettle
- 4-8 plates depending on weight considerations
- 4-8 soup bowls depending on weight considerations
- 4-8 cutlery sets depending on weight considerations
- 8 cups
- Roti cooking plate
- 2 plastic jugs
- Peeler
- Small chopping knife
- Large knife or cleaver
- Ladle
- Egg lift
- Water jerry approx 20Lt
- Kerosene jerry approx 20Lt
- 3 small towels
- 2 tea strainers
- Chopping board for meat
- Chopping board for vegetables
- 3 MSR stoves (EX model is best)
- 3m x 5m tarp
- Kitchen tent or similar

generation iPods and other MP3 players for which you may need to purchase special adaptors.

Solar-charging times are often more than eight hours so you might need to consider two chargers for longer trips or during cloudy months (eg before and during monsoon). Thorough testing of your charger with your device is highly recommended prior to embarking on your trek.

❏ **Ultralight and unguided on the Great Himalaya Trail (GHT)**
The traditional way of hiking in Nepal involves guides, porters, and teahouses. This is the system most people use and what people envision when they plan a trekking trip in Nepal. Despite the overwhelming majority who participate in this fashion, it is not obligatory.

People can take the ultralight style of hiking and use it on the GHT. There are no predetermined weight classifications, but generally the ultralight paradigm encompasses carrying all the belongings you will need to be self supported in a kit that weighs less than 7 or 8 kilos, not including food, which will vary depending on the location and conditions. In some summer-time locations, packs can weigh as little as 2 or 3 kilos, without food.

Ultralight means paring down your kit to just the necessary items – those items that you use every day or almost every day. Then look at how you can save weight on those items. For example, use a down sleeping bag instead of a synthetic bag, or a 100g wind jacket instead of a bulky fleece. Look for items that will serve multiple purposes. You can use your trekking poles to help set up a tarp shelter. Ultralighters bring minimal full-changes of clothes, instead preferring a versatile layering system and thereby reducing the amount of clothes you have to pack.

Planning is also very important. If you have a good idea of the conditions that you may encounter then you can carry the proper equipment for those situations. If the temperatures will only hit the freezing mark at night you don't need a -20 degree sleeping bag. If you carry a bag tailored for the conditions you will save the excess weight and space. Furthermore, you will be able to efficiently plan your food and water, without packing too much or too little. Food can weigh about 1kg per day per person and water is much heavier. If you are crossing streams every kilometre (like you do most of the time in the Himalaya), why carry 5 kilos of water?

People are hesitant to take an ultralight mentality into the Himalaya, for fear that it will let them down in the biggest mountain range in the world. However, if you have experience and are comfortable with your equipment a standard ultralight system is fully functional, despite the lofty elevation. Using an ultralight system increases self-sufficiency and comfort levels. You can cover longer distances and hike for more hours, while exerting less energy. Furthermore, you can carry more food weight to meet the demand of the long stretches on the GHT without resupply.

Overall the weather conditions that we faced on the GHT were not much different than many other thru-hikes that we have done. The nights were chilly when we were at high elevations and sometimes there were snow and whiteout conditions. Other days at lower elevations were warm and humid. Ultralight is not always right, but despite people's hesitance to use ultralight equipment on the GHT, in my opinion it is practical, efficient, and without a doubt the right gear for the trail.

Justin 'Trauma' Lichter
Author of *Trail Tested: A Thru-Hiker's Guide to Ultralight Hiking and Backpacking*
💻 *www.justinlichter.com*

Nepal and you

Yes, the mountains are spectacular, but it will probably be the people who draw you back to Nepal time and again. Nepali people live life 'immediately', they have been accused of wearing their hearts on their sleeve and lacking foresight, but they are disarmingly openhearted and hospitable. For them, the opportunity to make a friend today is more important than what might or might not happen tomorrow.

CHOOSING A GUIDE AND CREW

Trekking with a guide and a crew is a wonderful opportunity to develop a better understanding of Nepal. Building relationships with your crew and those around you will not only enhance your holiday, it may well change your perspective on your own life. So, if you have the opportunity to select your own guide it is worth spending a little time in making the right choice. Once you've found your ideal guide they will take responsibility for the choice of crew, but you can have input as well. If you are on a fully organised trek and the guide is already chosen for you there are issues and ideas that you should be aware of, so please take the time to read this section.

Finding a guide can be difficult in peak season, but if you arrive before the rush of groups in mid October or April you should be able to find a good candidate in a couple of days. A good start is to ask returning trekkers, or some local trekking agencies if they know any guides with knowledge of a specific area or issue and the 'grapevine' will do the rest.

Guides sometimes present their trekking or climbing history in a scrapbook or simple resumé, and it is important to ask for, and then check, references from the outset. Perhaps choose a modest local teashop as a place to meet for a snack or lunch as a 'get-to-know-you' session. Try only to ask open questions as most Nepalese will almost certainly answer 'yes' rather than lose face. It is surprising how many 'guides' will assert knowledge of places they have heard about second or third hand. So your first question could be, 'What is it like in … ?' If they have been there before, how many times, how long ago, and have they been the senior member or guide of the group each time? Perhaps your guide's home village is in or near the region you wish to trek, if so can you take the time to visit their home? Such opportunities are a great way to really get to know what life is like in rural Nepal.

Your guide's general experience is also important. A long history of leading groups to different regions proves

> ❏ **Top tip**
> When researching treks or contacting trekking companies by email remember to use open questions, itemise questions and try to use the simplest possible language.

a deep level of competence. Having taken 'a few groups teahouse trekking in the Everest region' should not inspire confidence. There are a few formal technical mountaineering and climbing courses run by the Nepal Mountaineering Association, which are world class in standard, and qualifications are evidence of genuine skill and ability. However, you should be cautious of the Trekking Agency Guide Identity Card for which very little training or few qualifications are necessary.

Rates of pay for guides vary depending on experience, level of responsibility, trek difficulties and demands. You may not get to negotiate with many guides as they will insist on using a particular agency to organise your trip. This has become common since the introduction of TIMS (Trekkers Information

❏ Trekking as a single female

There are many specialist trekking agencies in Nepal, including some who target the female-only trekking group market by providing only female staff. They have some highly skilled guides, cooks and sherpas, and can organise anything from a light trek to climbing Mt Everest!

If you plan to trek on your own with a male guide and/or porter you should choose your staff carefully. Make sure you interview them, preferably with a friend or someone from your hotel present, and get some contact details from them. Check their ID and leave details with your hotel when you go trekking. Generally speaking, an older, more experienced guide will be better in these situations than a younger one, who may just believe everything he has seen on MTV.

Always make sure you carry your money and any valuables you take in the bag you are carrying every day.

Local customs throughout Nepal deem it improper for you and your staff to share a room in a teahouse, and even innocent offers to help room allocations can be misconstrued or cause offence. It is a good idea to make it clear to your guide before you hire him that you will not tolerate any advances, and that he will be fired if he tries to become intimate.

One major problem for female trekkers is hygiene. As it is not always possible to get a shower, wet wipes are always a handy thing to have in your pack. Thin panty liners help keep your knickers fresh and may keep thrush at bay. You may not be able to wash your undies every day, and even if you do you'll need to hang them like flags off the back of your daypack to get them dry. Although a local would never display their underwear like this it is accepted as 'one of those things tourists do'.

Another problem that really irritates many female tourists who come to Nepal is their 'invisibility'. The shopkeepers see you, the beggars see you, but nobody seems to hear you! Traditionally in Nepal, women (especially Hindu and Muslim women) do not usually travel alone, nor do they speak out in public. You may have a conversation with your guide about where you will walk to, or where you would like to stay, only to find that you have been completely ignored. It's all part of the Nepali culture. It's not unusual for your guide to believe that he has a much better idea of where to stay or walk than you do, and he is just trying to make sure you have a good day. The more experienced your guide is at dealing with Westerners, especially women, the less likely this will happen. Standing by the side of the trail and shouting at him won't make any difference, it's best just to sit down with him and tell him that you are disappointed that he overruled you and next time if he disagrees with your choice he should say so. That way nobody loses face and you can all still be friends **Judy Smith**

Management System) and porter insurance. KEEP (Kathmandu Environmental Education Project), IPPG (International Porter Protection group) and the Nepali government all have recommended minimum wages and conditions for guides and crew. By trekking with a crew you are undertaking to look after the welfare of your staff, so also ask your trekking company, IPPG and KEEP about your responsibilities towards your crew. You should also develop a clear idea of which jobs and responsibilities belong to you, and those your guide will handle.

Some guides can speak multiple languages and dialects from Nepal (there are more than eighteen ethnic groups each with a distinct language), which can make bargaining and trail finding much easier. You should also test the first-aid knowledge of your guide; many have only a very basic idea. After you have asked all your questions and developed a good idea of how well you get along together, you can discuss plans for the trek.

Perhaps the most common problem trekkers suffer from is the Nepali propensity to answer questions with a 'yes'. As well as using open questions, also make sure the person is qualified to answer your questions. It's amazing how often you hear trekkers asking how long it takes to walk somewhere and being answered by a local who doesn't own a watch and has a completely different concept of time!

Before you and/or your agency start buying food, booking tickets and employing staff you need to get the rules of the trek agreed with your guide and/or trekking agency. Some common issues you should be completely clear about:

> ❏ **Top tip**
> Trekking in Nepal is about trekking responsibly so, whether you are doing only one trek or the whole GHT, please check out our GHT Alliance trekking operators listed on pp277-8 when researching and getting a quote for your trip.

● How do you organise a rescue? Is the trekking agency going to organise a helicopter if needed? You might need to obtain details of a rescue organisation before you depart. Leave a copy of everyone's insurance details with the agency.

● Who decides on rest days? Is your itinerary rigid or could you take an extra day here or there to rest and explore a place?

● If there is an injury, who treats the patient? The crew are considered your responsibility as well as that of the guide and agency.

● Does anyone in the group have any special dietary needs?

● Is anyone in the group on medication? Are there any other pre-existing medical conditions that the guide or agency should know about?

● If equipment is damaged or lost who pays for the repair or replacement?

● Will you be happy if the crew drink alcohol or smoke in camp? If you have a little party or celebration, who is paying for the drinks?

Once you have a clear understanding about the roles of the agency, guide and your own responsibilities it is time to select a cook, sherpa assistants if necessary, kitchen crew and porters. Normally your agency and guide handle all the recruiting and planning, but you can be involved should you have particular needs.

Cooks vary greatly in skill: from almost as bad as the extremely comical Pong described in WE Bowman's *The Ascent of Rumdoodle*, to five-star hotel-trained cooks who produce seven- to eight-course gourmet meals. Your guide should be able to find a cook who can cater for your tastes; if you have special dietary requirements don't be afraid to ask for a sample meal to check their skills. Your cook will normally select the kitchen crew, who tend to be staff they have

PLANNING YOUR TREK

❏ BRAHMINS, CHHETRI AND NEWARS

Brahmins These are the highest 'rank' in the Hindu caste system, and with the Chhetris (who formed the ruling Rana class) still form the majority of wealthy and influential society in Kathmandu. They speak Nepali and are spread throughout the country, especially in the pahar and terai.

Of the **Chhetri** castes, the Thakuris have the highest social, political and ritual status, so many of the influential Khas, Gurung, Bhotia and Magar people who have converted to Hinduism have aspired to become Thakuris.

In most parts of Nepal Brahmin and Chhetri homes are painted with red ochre, or whitewashed and traditionally repainted during the *dasain* festival (see p23). The inside is usually whitewashed and the mud and cow dung floors are swept daily. Around the outside of their homes is a line formed from where rainwater falls from the roof. This is the external boundary for low-caste people approaching a home, the next boundary is the veranda and reception room (in larger houses) where you, and people of a similar caste, may be invited to rest and have a cup of tea. Same-caste marriages organised by the family still predominate, although love and inter-caste marriages do occasionally occur.

Brahmins (who originally came to Nepal from India) form the priestly caste and, as such, are often conservative in their outlook. Brahmin and Chhetri boys are given a 'sacred thread' when young, and every year this is replaced. This thread is worn diagonally across the body under clothing, and never removed.

Almost everyone you meet in Nepal who is in any position of responsibility will be Brahmin or Chhetri. This has made many of the lower castes feel marginalised, and in some way led to the Maoists success with the promise of social change.

Newar people Newars are the indigenous inhabitants of the Kathmandu Valley and claim an ancestry dating back to the 6th century BC. They are a cultural entity rather than an ethnic group, and have Mongoloid and Mediterranean features. They speak Nepali and Newari. Newars traditionally travelled for trade or business and many now live west of Kathmandu in Pokhara, Butwal and Silgadhi. Newar houses are usually several storeys high, with a veranda, and large framed doors and windows. Many of the beautiful old buildings in Kathmandu highlight the complexity and beauty of their woodcarving. Newars may be either Hindu or Buddhist, and sometimes both, so they celebrate most festivals and feast days. There are 1600 sub-castes in Newar culture, as every profession forms its own caste.

Newars, particularly the Hindus, still prefer arranged marriages. Every family is a member of a *guthi* or club, which come together for religious services (such as weddings and cremations), social events (picnics and the like) and public services (maintaining temples, rest houses and bridges). This means that Newar communities are close knit and can be difficult to understand. Newar woodcarvings and stone masonry are famed throughout the Himalaya, including India and Tibet, and have influenced many of the most popular works of Asian art.

worked with in the past. The kitchen crew may also lend a hand when pitching tents or dismantling camp if necessary. Porters carry the heaviest loads, normally 25-30kg, but sometimes they might elect to carry a double load up to 60kg for short periods. You should not encourage double loads. Regional Maoist groups often check porter loads and you will have trouble continuing your trek if the loads are considerably over 30kg and/or your staff are too young. As the majority of staff on any trek or expedition are porters, it is important to take a little time in their selection.

The Sherpa people of the Solu-Khumbu (the Everest Region) have developed a reputation for enormous energy and skill at assisting climbers to Himalayan summits. In recognition of this senior role within a group, 'sherpa' has come to mean someone who helps clients along the trail, scouts ahead to find the safest route, and prepares and dismantles camp on a daily basis. Many groups employ at least one or two sherpas on teahouse treks to go ahead and book rooms for the night, be a helping hand on tricky sections of trail, and they may serve your meals to help out the teahouse owners.

Although the Nepalese are very socially and religiously tolerant, different castes may chose to prepare and eat meals separately, so ideally, you shouldn't have just one or two porters from a different caste as this may make meal times hard work for them. There are several theories about the selection of Hindu versus Buddhist staff but none is reliable. The bottom line is, you can always get a bad apple in a group but the chances are small.

Encouraging your crew to have a small party after a day on the trail is an excellent idea for a number of reasons: sharing a communal bowl of *chang* (a locally made beer throughout Nepal) is the best way to break the ice and get to know your crew. By making the effort to share a little social time you will find your crew willing to share stories and relax. Nepalese love a party and it will help to bond the crew together, and you will notice that the whole crew will start to work as a team. Some low-impact dancing will help to flush lactic acid from tired muscles, thus make the walking easier tomorrow.

SHOPPING, BARGAINING AND TIPPING

Trekkers in a camping group are less likely to buy soft or alcoholic drinks and snacks along the trail, whereas teahouse trekkers have such luxuries within temptation's grasp reach everyday. Prices vary dramatically; in the first days of a trek a bottle of soft drink may cost US$1-2, but in the highest teahouses it may be US$5-6. Beer, chocolate and luxury snacks are more expensive.

Money issues like bargaining, tipping and the payment process are perhaps the most common complaints tourists have when visiting Nepal. This need not be so when you understand a few simple principles. Firstly,

> ❏ **Top tip**
> When you are out in the hills you should always confirm prices before accepting a service or product. Some teahouses may even charge you for sitting in a dining room, especially if you do not order something from their menu. Check if there is a room surcharge if you choose to eat elsewhere.

PLANNING YOUR TREK

you are the visitor and are therefore perceived to be wealthier than the vast majority of Nepalese you will meet. Traditionally, a wealthy person travels in Nepal with an entourage of family, servants and assistants, so the expectation exists that you will do the same. This expectation is reinforced when you see all the support that comes with a trekking group. The simple fact that you are travelling in Nepal, and it is very difficult for a Nepali to travel in your country, probably exacerbates the perceived wealth divide.

It is perhaps no surprise, therefore, that the government charges a higher price for entry to places of interest for tourists than for locals (the average annual income in Nepal is only around US$1500 per capita, 2012 est). You will also begin most negotiations with a seemingly outrageous amount being quoted by the vendor, which is just a 'water-test' and all part of the process.

Bargaining

Bargaining can be a harrowing or fun experience depending on your expectations. The entire process is as much about the vendor and purchaser getting to know each other as it is about actually buying something.

A major complicating factor in making a purchase is ethnicity. Some ethnic groups do not negotiate at all; they just offer a fixed price, whereas others expect to haggle. The best way to find out what to do is to be relaxed, start haggling, and if the vendor won't move on the price, make up your mind if you are happy to pay that price or move on.

A few ideas to make 'haggling' more enjoyable:

● Start haggling over something you do not want to buy to help build your confidence and rapport with the vendor. Then progress on to your desired object but do not show much enthusiasm, as this will push the price up. It is best to only start haggling if you genuinely have an interest to purchase something from the vendor.

● Your first counter offer should be less than half the first price quoted by the vendor. The vendor will undoubtedly act offended, but this is all part of the process. If the vendor insists that you make the first offer, say half of what you are prepared to pay and then work up to what you think is a fair price.

● Have the actual amount of money you are prepared to pay ready in your pocket. If the negotiation has hit stalemate showing that you have the money ready can sometimes swing the deal. Also, when it comes to paying most transactions happen very quickly with the transfer of goods ending the conversation.

● Always keep smiling, keep the conversation friendly and not too serious, and never, ever get angry.

Tipping

For many tourists the tipping process either in Kathmandu or at the end of a trek leaves them confused and sometimes feeling offended. However, tipping is a traditional part of Nepali life and a vital component of a local's income. Tipping is therefore expected and you could seriously offend if you do not tip. The big question is: *how much*?

Tipping in restaurants is normally 10%, but this is now optional in tourist restaurants, which, as per union demands, add an automatic service charge. Your bill must specify if the service charge has been included. Nearly all local restaurants, that is, those out of the main tourist areas, will not add this surcharge, so pay a tip as you see fit.

Tipping your staff at the end of a trek is more complicated; a general rule is US$1 per day for a porter or kitchen crew, US$1.25 for sherpa helpers, US$1.50 for your cook and US$2 for your guide. However, these amounts depend on the duration and difficulty of your trek, how well the crew as a whole has performed and individual performance. It is reasonable to increase or slightly reduce tips for each crew member, and to tell them why, when you give them out on the last night of your trek. You should put tips in individually named envelopes. Your crew won't open the envelope immediately as it is considered rude to do so; they'll just put the envelope in their pocket and say 'thank you'.

It is therefore important that you have sufficient cash for your general expenses and tips before you start the trek. You'll need to take a mix of rupee note denominations (make sure the notes are in good condition) with you for the trek. It is almost impossible to get additional cash in the mountains!

SECURITY

Since the Maoist 'People's War' there has been a breakdown in law and order in some areas of Nepal; combined with an increase in the availability of weapons, this has led to a general increase in crime across the country. However, serious crimes very rarely involve tourists, who are much more likely to suffer from opportunistic theft. It is also more likely that the thief will be a fellow tourist rather than a local.

Most Nepalese are still very respectful of other people's possessions and are often protective of your belongings. Some ethnic groups, most notably nomadic Tibetans, have been known to take items which they think have been discarded. So when you leave a solar charger or some laundry in a sunny spot make sure it is watched. Any bags left unattended, including those on bus roofs and checked onto domestic flights, should be locked. Keep spare money on your person in a money belt or buried deep inside your pack, your kit bag is not as safe as the bag you always carry with you.

> ❏ **Top tip**
> Never carry something around town or on the trail that you can't afford to lose.

The role of women in Nepali society is changing in good and bad ways; strip bars and pornography accompany greater emancipation. The Nepali government is trying to cope with an underground sex industry that now flourishes throughout the country. It is unfortunate but perhaps no surprise therefore that women sometimes suffer from sexual harassment from young males, especially in urban centres or if a woman's attire seems suggestive, for more information see p62.

PLANNING YOUR TREK

COMMUNICATION

Nepal's **phone system** has expanded rapidly, and the cheap cost of calls is hugely enabling for local and visitor alike. The downside is almost perpetually overloaded circuits. It can take multiple tries to get through between different service providers and line interference is common. International calls are still comparatively expensive and it may take many re-dials to finally make a connection. The unreliability of the landline system means **mobile phones** are now very popular throughout the country. Inexpensive and good-quality internet phone services are also cropping up and a subsidised satellite network is spreading throughout mountain areas. If you want to set your phone to roaming it is wise to first check call charges, and that your provider offers roaming in Nepal. You may find it easier to buy a SIM card in Nepal (available at the airport on arrival through Ncell or Nepal Telecom); you will require photo ID and they generally cost about US$12 (with US$8 worth of calls).

> ❏ **Top tip**
> The best time to call is in the early morning when the mobile network is less congested.

Recharge scratch cards are widely available and come in many denominations, the largest being NRs1000 for which there is a NRs10 charge. You will find that calls home are pretty reasonable, and calling local numbers and even other mobiles in Nepal is inexpensive, but the service can sometimes be erratic. There is no voicemail in Nepal. Texting is popular as is 'give me a missed call' when arranging to meet people. When you try to call and can't get through you will receive one of a variety of messages – they range from the phone is unavailable the caller is busy to the number called doesn't exist. Persist, as the other person may just be on the phone. Expect to be cut off at some point in most calls.

Thuraya **satellite phones** can receive SMS directly from the Thuraya website (🖳 sms.thuraya.com) for no charge and there is a local operator who sells phones and accessories, see 🖳 www.constellation.com.np. There is also a new phone on the market in Nepal from Isat PhonePro; it is available for US$700. More information is at: 🖳 www.isatphoneproreview.com.au.

When a Nepali answers a call they do not say their name, which can cause a great deal of confusion. Likewise, they do not normally say 'goodbye', they just hang up. Years of bad phone connections mean that most locals talk very loudly or even shout down the line and expect the line to cut out at the most inopportune moment.

Internet access is readily available in nearly all urban centres, and during the climbing season there is even a satellite internet café at Everest Base Camp! **Wi-fi** is available at many hotels and guesthouses in Kathmandu and Pokhara.

Snail mail operates from the GPO (Sun-Fri 10am-4pm), a 25-minute walk south of Thamel on the corner of Kanti Path and Prithvi Path. When sending a letter or small package don't put it in a post-box but ask them to frank it or the stamps may be removed and resold. Sending mail is easier done through the various bookshops in Thamel, which are usually more reliable than the hotels.

For **parcels**, in addition to the GPO you have the choice of international couriers with reliability at a price, and cargo agents who specialise in bigger consignments. The cargo companies will often accept much smaller airfreight shipments for the same price per kilo, usually around US$5, for common North American and European destinations.

HOW NOT TO CAUSE OFFENCE

Almost anyone who visits Nepal returns with a story of another tourist's inappropriate behaviour or dress. To commit the occasional faux pas is inevitable when exploring foreign shores and Nepali people will often make light of your indiscretion. However, taking advantage of traditional hospitality without understanding the implications, overt ostentation, disrespecting ceremonies or customs, and dressing inappropriately are all considerable insults and should be avoided at all costs. If you are unsure how to behave follow the lead of a Nepali, and if necessary ask questions. Everyone will understand that you are trying to do the right thing and you'll be given all the support to participate in local lives to the fullest. This list of advice is by no means exhaustive, so please apply liberal amounts of common sense to your day.

Respect cultures and traditions
● **Consideration** Be a considerate guest at all times. Nepali culture is rich and diverse and can sometimes confuse a visitor but if you are friendly, approachable and consider those around you before yourself, you will always earn the respect of locals.
● **Photos** Ask before taking a photo, as many people prefer not to be photographed for personal, cultural or superstitious reasons. You should also be careful of taking photos in and around places of worship.
● **Gift giving** The complex patina of Nepali society sometimes calls for gift giving or making a donation; this may be to a monastery or shrine, at a wedding, or at a cultural programme. Whenever you are faced with needing to give a gift you should seek the advice of a Nepali to work out what is appropriate. The method of, or the formality associated with, giving a gift is often as important as the gift itself so make sure you are aware of any protocols.
● **Affection** Do not show affection in public.
● **Bathing** Showing your genitalia when bathing is offensive. Use a sarong, modesty screen or shower tent and when visiting a hot spring try to behave modestly.

Benefit local communities, commercially and socially
● **Share skills and experience** Teach when you can, offer a fair rate of pay for services, participate in activities whenever invited.
● **Do not publicly argue, drink excessively, or fight** Demonstrations of anger are considered an embarrassing loss of face on your behalf.
● **Begging** Of all the negative impacts tourists have had in Nepal, the encouragement of begging along the trail is probably the most problematic. Handing

out candy (referred to as sweets, *mitai* or bonbons) to children who never clean their teeth is thoughtless and irresponsible. Giving money to small children in return for picked flowers is destructive and illegal in all National Parks.

If your conscience struggles with the wealth divide provide skills through training and education, or donate to one of the major charities in Kathmandu or Pokhara. But do not just give away items along the trail and so perpetuate a habit that ultimately only reduces self-esteem and can cause long-term problems. If you aren't convinced of the negative effects of pandering to cute children then trek away from the main trails and experience the genuine, openhearted joy that children show tourists without the expectation of a 'reward'.

Adopt new customs

● **Clothing** Do not wear tight or revealing clothing, especially if you are a woman. There is a firm dress code followed by Nepalese and it is only not observed by the very poor or for special reasons.

It is considered offensive to expose your knees, shoulders and chest at all times and especially in any place of worship. This means that detachable leg trousers/pants are not very useful in Nepal, and cropped tops of any description should be avoided. Men can wear long shorts but should avoid exposing their chests. It is also considered offensive to highlight genitalia, so avoid wearing stretch or very tight clothing around the chest or groin area.

● **Entering homes** It is critical that you wait to be invited into a home. The caste system prescribes a rigid hierarchy of which rooms you may or may not be allowed to enter so respect the wishes of the homeowner. The cooking-fire area is often sacred so always check if you can dispose of burnable rubbish before consigning it to the flames.

● **Greetings** Nepalese greet each other with the traditional, 'Namaste!' Sometimes they will shake hands, especially if they are involved in the tourism sector or have retired from the Royal Gurkha Rifles, but in general you should avoid touching people, especially of the opposite gender. A namaste, or thanks, or taking a little time to play or practise English is always preferable to a short or quick reply. It will both build respect and relieve any stress you may feel from curious locals.

● **Eating** Do not use your left hand to eat or pass objects. Traditionally Nepalese eat only with the right hand, the left being considered unclean. Therefore pass foodstuffs to another person with your right hand and use your left as little as possible. You should also avoid touching the lip of a vessel to your mouth; just pour the drink into your mouth.

● **Offering payment and/or gifts** It is respectful to use both hands, or offer with your right hand while touching your left hand to your right elbow.

● **Language** Learn some basic Nepali phrases and use them as often as possible.

Environment

● **Tread softly** Stick to trails and recognised camping areas. Avoid creating new tracks, or damaging the environment in any way. Follow the adage: take only photos, leave only footprints.

● **Pack it in, pack it out** Avoid taking tins, glass, or plastic containers and bags unless you plan to carry them back to Kathmandu or Pokhara.

● **Conserve water quality** Wash away from water sources and always use local toilet facilities when available. Bury all organic waste at least 30cm below the ground and 50m away from water sources.

● **Conserve natural resources** What few resources there are belong by right to the locals. Always ask permission before using anything along the trail. It is illegal to disturb wildlife, remove animals or plants, or buy wildlife products.

❏ How long does it take to decompose?	
Cotton rags	1-5 months
Paper	2-5 months
Orange peels	6 months
Wool socks	1-5 years
Plastic bags	10-20 years
Leather shoes	25- 40 years
Nylon fabric	30-40 years
Aluminium cans	80-100 years
Plastic bottles	Forever

© WorldWise, Inc (🖥 www.world wise.com)

Safety

● **Beware of altitude sickness** Use the buddy system to watch for symptoms of altitude sickness. Make sure everyone remains fully hydrated by drinking water throughout the day, every day. Stay together along the trail and communicate frequently with everyone.

● **Be safe** Carry an extensive first-aid kit and know how to use it. Have multiple plans for emergency evacuation and designated decision makers. Leave your itinerary details with someone responsible at home.

● **Be self-reliant** Don't assume you will receive help or assistance. Ensure your group has extensive field-craft and navigation skills. Research thoroughly: is your route appropriate for your party? Do you have the necessary skills, experience, resources and equipment?

● **Remain hydrated** Drinking between two and four litres of water per day will help prevent altitude sickness and improve your body's recovery time.

● **Don't rush** There are no prizes for coming first on the trail and rushing will probably over-stress your body and may increase your chances of suffering from altitude sickness. Frequent stops to drink water and rest often become photo opportunities and a chance to chat with locals.

● **Trekking poles** That more people aren't impaled by absent-minded trekkers swinging their poles is amazing. Be aware of the pole tips, especially when crossing bridges or negotiating narrow or steep trails.

● **Beware of yaks** Many porterage animals you meet along the trail are yaks or hybrids of yaks and cattle, and all of them can be dangerous. Every season at least one tourist will die because they got too close to the large horns or were knocked from a bridge. If you see any pack animals (even donkeys cause accidents) coming along the trail you should scramble up the hillside of the trail and wait until they pass.

● **iPod use** Rather than listening to the noise of life along the trail some people prefer to plug in to an iPod. Doing so puts you at greater risk from animals and rockfall.

● **Common courtesy** The trail is often busy, especially at steep or difficult sections. A common courtesy is to give way to people walking uphill, or to those who are obviously struggling or carrying a very large load.

TEMPLE AND SHRINE ETIQUETTE

Many temples are closed for periods throughout the year and you should check if the 'key-holder' is nearby otherwise you might have a pointless walk. Personal contact is frowned upon, so you should avoid touching monks or nuns at all times. You should ask if it is necessary to remove your footwear when entering any religious building. Both men and women should have their chests and shoulders covered at all times, whereas your head should be uncovered.

Remain quiet and avoid speaking loudly. Also turn off your phone. Many Buddhists make prostrations when they enter a temple. If you do not wish to do the same, either bow your head slightly with the palms of your hands together at the chest or simply stand quietly until others have finished.

If you enter a monastery or shrine you may be led to the main statue where you can pay respect to the Buddha or deity by laying down a *khadag* (aka *khata*; ceremonial scarf) in front of the Buddha in the same way, as you would present it to a lama – folded correctly and with your palms facing towards the sky. Lighting a candle is another way of paying respect; this should be done facing towards the central Buddha or deity statue. Do not touch the Buddha statues, or any of the ritual objects around the temple.

When teachers, monks and nuns enter and leave the main shrine room, visitors should stand to show respect. Otherwise, it is good manners to bow down low when walking directly in front of people, in particular monks, who may be sitting against the walls of the temple.

Sit with your feet folded cross-legged or folded under yourself. If you feel the need to stretch your legs while in a temple, do so in such a way so as not to point your feet directly at the teacher or altar.

If you wish to take pictures, verify beforehand that it is acceptable to do so, and find out when a good time would be so as not to disturb any ceremonies.

Always ask before you enter Hindu temples, as many do not allow non-Hindus inside. Please respect their wishes and do not go in if the people outside ask you not to. You will need to remove your shoes and any leather objects you are carrying (wallets, belts etc). If you are allowed inside, do not touch any of the objects and always ask before taking photos.

Greetings and blessings

Religious practitioners of all faiths are normally happy to show you around their temple/shrine and answer questions, but there is a strict etiquette to follow when in their company. They will greet you with a 'namaste' by placing both hands together in front of their chests and a light bow of their head. You should respond in the same way. Shaking hands is not required unless the other party extends a hand. If you do shake hands, your sleeves should always be unrolled to show respect.

If you are a guest, you should begin by handing over a khadag. Use two hands with the palms towards the sky and take the khadag between your thumb and the palm of your hand. This is a traditional greeting in order to pay respect to your host, who may, as a sign of respect, hand back the khadag, hanging it over your head onto your shoulders. Receiving a khadag from a *lama* is considered a form of blessing. Your khadag should be folded three times widthwise and presented with the opening towards the receiver; to not do so will be considered offensive.

When receiving a blessing from the lama or presenting a khadag, monks and nuns are generally asked to go first, in order of seniority. In Buddhist cultures, monks go before nuns. You approach the lama holding out a khadag; he may then touch your head with his hands as a blessing, and then either he or his assistant may give you a red blessing cord with a small knot on it. The cord should be treated with respect and not dropped. Buddhists tie the cords around their necks or place them in their shrines. You should knot the thread around your right wrist or your throat, depending on the size. You may also receive a blessed parcel or small picture amulet, which can be suspended from the thread, like a pendant. You should not remove this (unless for washing) as you will also remove the blessings it bestows. It is always polite to offer money to the temple when you receive a blessing – NRs100 or more is reasonable.

If a Hindu holy man, or *sadhu* approaches you on the street with a little tray of coloured powder or flowers and you accept a blessing, it is appropriate to give NRs5-10 – this is his way of living. However, if you take a blessing from a sadhu, especially in tourist areas and places of interest, expect to pay a few hundred rupees at least.

Health and well-being

Trekking is good for you! The daily exercise, consumption of significant volumes of water and controlled exposure to sunlight all combine to make many feel healthier than they ever have before. However, there are occasions when this is not the case, and being aware of your and your group's health is critical to safe trekking.

This chapter is not an exhaustive review of health, first-aid and rescue issues; it is merely a guide to help you understand what information and experience you need to have to trek safely. It is essential that somebody in your party has up-to-date first-aid knowledge, that everyone has a clear idea of general health problems and their prevention, and that your party and guide understand what to do in an emergency situation.

An excellent resource for anyone trekking into mountainous regions is *Pocket First Aid and Wilderness Medicine* Drs Jim Duff and Peter Gormly (Cicerone Press). Every group should carry at least one copy.

GENERAL HEALTH ISSUES

All trekking companies and medical staff recommend a regular **exercise** programme of increasing difficulty some months prior to embarking on your trek. If you arrive in Nepal in an unfit state you will find trekking tough on both your body and mind.

Regular aerobic exercise for a couple of hours at a time is the least you should be able to achieve. It is also wise to take at least one long walk a week, for up to five or six hours (of walking time), so that your body is not unfamiliar with sustained exercise. The fitter you are before you arrive the faster your body will adapt to the rigours of walking all day on sometimes rough and difficult trails. It is often hard for people to imagine that you can spend *days* walking up just one hill and that a climb of 100m or 200m is considered *flat* by most Nepalese. Aerobic fitness will also make acclimatisation easier for you as your body will begin to adapt to, rather than just coping with, reduced levels of oxygen.

You must visit your doctor at home and **check your immunisations** and any general health requirements or issues. It is also a good idea to get some recommendations about specific **medications** for your trip and research potential health issues. Whenever you prepare a field first-aid kit there is one major consideration: only pack what you know how to use. Any items or medications that you are not familiar with will at best be a waste of time, at worst, they could cause a serious problem. You should also include enough supplies to cover your crew as well as group members.

When you are trekking you will come across **health posts** in some villages, if you have additional medical supplies these could be a good place to leave them. You should avoid giving out medications to locals unless absolutely necessary and you know exactly what you are doing. It is far better for everyone that you encourage them to visit their health centre as quickly as possible. Sometimes, you may be asked to give medicines to people along the trail or in villages; this is because many Nepalese believe foreign medicines are stronger and more effective than those available locally. If this should happen, ask your guide to explain that your medicines are the same as those prescribed by their local health practitioner. Local people frequently use traditional remedies to cure general ailments, but as you may react to them, it is wise to avoid them.

Although malaria is rare in Nepal, **mosquitoes** and numerous other **insects** and nasties that bite, including bed bugs, fleas, small spiders, leeches (in the wetter months), horse flies and ticks are common. Packing both an insect repellent (with DEET) and a bite-balm is a good idea, especially for remoter trips.

If you wear **contact lenses** you will probably find the chance of an eye infection higher than at home, especially on dusty trails. Pack sufficient amounts of sterilising/disinfecting solutions and do not exceed recommended wearing times. Use boiled water that has cooled for cleansing, and remove con-

tacts at the first sign of irritation. The
disposable extended-wear lenses tend
to perform better than those you
change or clean daily.

The supply of plastic bottles of
water in the mountains is causing a
major environmental problem, and
boiling water frequently puts a strain
on meagre fuel supplies. Taking a
water filtration or purification treatment means that you can be sure your

> ❏ **Top tips**
> ● Use wrap-around, UV A and B
> lens-protection sunglasses.
> ● To avoid having to get out of their
> sleeping bag and tent on a cold night,
> men can use a pee bottle, but should
> make sure the lid is water-tight. Wash
> out with used face-washing water in
> the mornings.

water is good to drink. Ultra-violet light (for example Steri-pen®) and chemi-
cal treatments tend to be easier to use and lighter to carry than pump systems.

FOOD AND DIARRHOEA

It's rare that some form of stomach malady doesn't affect the trekker at some
point, and you should be prepared with a range of medications, see *Pocket First
Aid and Wilderness Medicine*.

Many travellers to Nepal pick up a stomach bug in Kathmandu and continue to suffer while trekking. It is important that you eat and drink correctly prepared food from the moment you arrive in Nepal and maintain high levels of
personal hygiene throughout your trip. However, there are a few general precautions that will make the chances of sudden dashes to the toilet less likely.

● Only eat food that has been freshly prepared, which is normally *dhal bhat*.
Many teahouses are guilty of preparing food hours, or days, in advance, which
will certainly cause a stomach upset at least. If you doubt the level of hygiene
visit the kitchen and check for yourself before ordering.
● Avoid excessively oily food.
● Keep to regular eating times.
● Increase the amount of vegetables in your diet, even to the extent of avoiding
meat altogether when in the mountains.
● Drink plenty of treated water.
● Only consume raw vegetables and fruit if properly treated.
● Be very careful of all roadside restaurants, even if they are busy serving fresh
food, as hygiene in these places is frequently very poor.

ALTITUDE SICKNESS

The effects of altitude are many and various, and still largely a mystery to modern medicine. One year someone may suffer from altitude sickness, but not the
next, even if they are doing exactly the same trek at the same time of year. For
this reason the effects of altitude have become the most common dinner conversation in teahouses and dining tents alike.

For a comprehensive review of HAPE, HACE, AMS and related issues see
Pocket First Aid and Wilderness Medicine. If someone is beginning to feel

PLANNING YOUR TREK

unwell then first assumption is always altitude sickness until proven otherwise. A healthy level of observation should exist between all group members and each trekker should have a 'health buddy', normally a tent or roommate, with whom you will form a 'watch me, watch you' relationship. Sometimes the effects of altitude are subtle, eg a slight slurring of speech, or loss of coordination, that only regular examination will notice.

It is essential that all group members take altitude seriously and maintain a vigilant approach and openly discuss how they feel; self-medication without telling anyone is extremely dangerous. When ascending, most people suffer from some symptoms of altitude sickness, but cautious acclimatisation and continuous vigilance will help to limit the effects you will feel.

LOOKING AFTER FEET AND JOINTS

Carry a **blister-treatment** kit and examine your feet regularly for any signs of irritation or nail problems. When you have finished trekking for the day it is a good idea to remove your boots and socks and let your feet 'breathe'. Some people like a footbath but these are best saved for times when your feet can completely dry out. Trim your toenails regularly and clean out any dead skin from around the nails. If you develop any aches or pains in your feet you should first check that your boots are laced correctly, your sock or boot lining hasn't creased or folded differently, or that your laces are not too tight. If pains persist it is wise to rest and seek medical attention.

Legs and joints can frequently feel painful with deep **muscle aches** lasting for days. Pack a little massage oil and softly apply it to affected areas, if pain persists seek medical attention. If a joint is twisted or sprained first apply something cool: along the main trails this is frequently a chilled bottle of soft drink. Then compress and elevate the joint, make sure the patient is comfortable and relaxed and then give pain and/or anti-inflammatory medication.

See *Pocket First Aid and Wilderness Medicine* for more information on blister treatment and also easing pain in your legs/joints.

HYPOTHERMIA AND HEATSTROKE

Two very common conditions suffered along the trail are hypothermia (aka exposure) and heatstroke, and even mild forms (including dehydration) can significantly reduce your walking performance. See *Pocket First Aid and Wilderness Medicine* for a comprehensive review of symptoms, diagnosis and treatments.

Hypothermia occurs when your body loses heat faster than it can create it, and is most common in cool to cold conditions during or after periods of high exertion. Typical combinations of factors that cause hypothermia are physical exhaustion, wet or insufficient clothing, cold and/or wet weather conditions, failure to eat enough food, dehydration and high altitude. Ultimately it can result in death. The patient needs to be warmed immediately, ideally with a hot drink, high-energy food, and hot water bottle next to the skin. They should also be insulated from the weather using a sleeping bag, and/or a blanket/mat wrapped around them.

Heat exhaustion, and the more severe **heatstroke**, is common at lower altitudes, especially at the beginning of the trek. It occurs when your body's ability to regulate temperature fails, normally in hot and/or humid conditions, especially when you have arrived from a very different climate. Symptoms include dizziness, vagueness, rapid heart rate, and possibly nausea, vomiting and headache. It is best avoided through the regular intake of substantial quantities (up to eight litres a day) of water, salt, resting at the hottest periods of the day and the application of moist scarfs to the head and neck. Rest and avoiding vigorous exercise for a few days is the best method of recuperation.

FIRST AID

A comprehensive first-aid kit suitable to cater for the needs of your party is essential. It should be kept available throughout the day and not packed away in a porter's load that will not be seen again until camp. There are two components to most first-aid kits: medications and dressings.

A simple list and explanation for your reference is given on p48 & p49 but see *Pocket First Aid and Wilderness Medicine* for a comprehensive guide, and remember to keep your first-aid skills updated through regular training. It is also a good idea to have a small subsidiary first-aid kit with the person responsible for your crew during the day.

RESCUE AND EMERGENCY

None of the rural health posts in Nepal can provide the sort of emergency care that tourists take for granted back home. If an emergency occurs you must evacuate the patient by either land, or at times of a life-threatening emergency, by rescue helicopter, see p70 and p94 for more information. Some tourists are wealthy enough to pay for non-medical evacuations and if you choose this option you must explain that it is a not life-threatening situation.

Telecommunication options (see *Communications* pp60-1) in Nepal are expanding year by year and it is rare that you will be more than a few days away from a telephone, better still, carry your own satellite phone system to contact the emergency services. However, phone numbers frequently change in Nepal and it is essential that you confirm emergency contact details before you start your trek. It is wise to have a clear idea of the costs of a rescue before you start your trek, you may also need to organise a method of payment in Kathmandu and obtain permission from the relevant insurance company prior to rescue.

When you make an emergency call you must relay the following to your trekking company and the pilot of the helicopter:

● Degree of urgency: **Most Immediate** means death within 24 hours; **As Soon As Possible** is used in all other cases.

● The patient's present location or, if the patient is going to be moved, where to and how quickly. You should provide a latitude, longitude and altitude if possible, alternatively a map reference with publisher's name and title, and give as many local details as possible.

● Name, age, sex, nationality, passport number, visa and permit details, trekking agency name and contact details, and any other relevant contact details (family, embassy, etc).

● Medical information, including sickness or injury details, and any special requirements for the rescue, eg is supplementary oxygen or neck brace required?

● Is a doctor present or does one need to come in the helicopter to administer treatment prior to and during the flight?

● The names, ages, nationalities and sex of all the people who need to be evacuated.

● The name and organisation of the person who is going to pay, and the method of payment. Most helicopter charter companies will only fly once a payment guarantee has been provided in writing or paid in cash in Kathmandu.

A rescue may take a number of days to organise, especially if the weather is bad. Wait until 10 or 11am each day before moving the patient to give the helicopter a chance of arriving when the weather is normally clearest. In each cleared landing location mark your location with a large emergency orange 'X' – you may need to light a large smoky fire if it's hard to spot your location from above. Try to make a windsock and a signal mirror, which should be used with great care. If you are signalling to a helicopter stand at the end of the landing site with your back to the wind and wear brightly coloured clothing. As the helicopter prepares to land remove the 'X' marker.

Do not signal a helicopter if you cannot direct it to the victim or you are not directly involved in a rescue. Do not approach the helicopter until indicated to do so, and only approach from the front.

If the worst should happen and a porter or trekker dies you will probably have to charter a helicopter to transport the body; domestic airlines will refuse transport. It is best to organise a cremation and have it witnessed by at least one senior local, perhaps a village chairman, policeman or teacher; they should not be associated with anyone in your group. Record all personal possessions and details if known and have at least one witness sign to the effects. There are many logistical issues facing the transport of bodies to Kathmandu and then out of Nepal; if you need to do this, contact your embassy.

KATHMANDU

The Kathmandu Valley is enigmatic and unique. For almost two millennia people from across the Himalaya, and now the world, have been drawn to this broad and fertile valley and its three cities of Kathmandu, Patan and Bhaktapur.

The colour, chaos and complexity of life in Nepal's capital will fill your days with wonder and amazement. It's said that if you belong nowhere else on earth, this is your home.

HISTORY

Origins

According to legend, the Kathmandu Valley was once a lake upon which a beautiful lotus grew surrounded by light. The Buddhist deity Manjushri (Buddha of Transcendent Wisdom) drained the lake by cutting a gorge at Chobar so he could examine this lotus. The flower settled on a hill now called Swayambhunath and the retreating waters left rich soil in the Valley that was ideal for grazing cattle and buffalo. The founder of the first dynasty here was a sage known as Ne and in ancient chronicles the area became known as Ne-pāla, literally 'the land protected by Ne'.

By the second half of the first millennium BC the invading Kiratas, who are distantly related to the Limbu (p115) and Rai (p127) people, had occupied a number of sites in the region. They were succeeded by the Lichhavi in the 9th century AD. The settlements were centred around religious sites known as piths or power places, usually on the tops of hills. The Lichhavis worshipped the sun and the moon, which are two symbols that appear on Nepal's uniquely shaped flag, and they are responsible for many of the oldest religious sites in the Valley, although none of their architecture remains.

A transitional period, also called the 'dark period' of the Valley's history, began with the disintegration of the Lichhavi empire towards the end of the 9th century. A series of shadowy kings ruled a Valley that was rarely at peace, but the period is notable for the founding of Kathmandu city at some point between AD980 and 998. The towns of Patan and Bhaktapur were already established by then. The name Kathmandu is believed to be a corruption of Kasthamandap ('square house of wood'), the 1000-year-old *dharamsala* (rest-house) that still stands in Durbar Square.

Everything changed in 1200AD when Ari Malla founded a dynasty that was to last until 1769. However, the early years of a peaceful unified Malla empire soon ended with the creation of the three separate city-kingdoms of Kathmandu, Patan and Bhaktapur. The cities had their own courts, which frequently engaged in intrigue, quarrelled and went to war against one another. Competition between the Valley's kings helped to create some of the region's most notable buildings and art. Throughout this period the Valley grew wealthy on trade with Tibet and India, which led to ever-grander and more flamboyant festivals and events. The success of the three cities meant that the Valley became synonymous with Nepal as a whole, and this largely excluded the surrounding kingdoms to the east and west.

Times present

While the Malla kings squabbled, the nearby kingdom of Gorkha grew stronger to become the dominant power in central Nepal. In 1769, Pritvi Narayan Shah conquered the Valley and so began a dynasty that unified dozens of regional principalities into what has become modern Nepal. However, the rule of the Shahs was often challenged. One night in 1846 almost the entire court was massacred thus making Jung Bahadur Rana de facto ruler of Nepal. For almost 100 years the Rana family kept Nepal isolated from the rest of the world, yet they travelled widely. They introduced garish Western-influenced building styles incorporated into enormous palaces throughout Kathmandu. The tight control held by the Ranas didn't extend much further than the edge of the Valley beyond which the concept of a unified Nepal meant little. Ethnic groups throughout the country identified themselves with clan, caste and district far more than a national identity.

In 1951, the Shahs returned to power with the support of India, who also encouraged the new King Tribhuvan and his son, Mahendra, to adopt democracy. A system of local government through village committees known as Panchyat was established across the country in 1959. Although this system continues to work well in India the rampant corruption and self-interest in Nepal undermined its effectiveness. A series of riots and civil unrest throughout the country led to democracy in 1991, where the Nepali Congress (symbol: the tree, a neo-conservative, pro-business party akin to the UK Conservatives or US Republicans) won, putting the United Marxist Leninists (UML; symbol: the sun, a strongly socialist party akin to the UK Labour or US Democrats) and the royalist RPP into opposition. However, corruption continued unabated as governments regularly fell and what seemed like a procession of the same old faces moved in and out of power.

When in 1994 the UML split sending the charismatic Baburam Bhattarai and his Communist Party of Nepal 'underground' no-one predicted the extent of suffering Nepal was going to endure. The subsequent 'People's War' between the Maoists and the Nepal army and police services killed 15,000 people and many more died or suffered indirectly through the conflict. Accusations of war crimes will continue for many years to come.

Two of the most tangible changes in Nepal during what is euphemistically called, 'the troubles', were a gradual creation of national identity so that impoverished and marginalised groups realised they had a voice and a right to be heard, and perhaps more importantly, the monarchy was removed as head of state making Nepal a Federal Democratic Republic. At the same time many Nepalese left their country to work overseas, a practice that continues today. The funds sent home keep the economy afloat and it's hoped that exposure to stable governments elsewhere is, in some way, positively influencing expectations and practices back in Nepal.

As the country lurches forward in fits and starts and attempts to write a new constitution it is hard to see other short-term gains from what seems to be an extension of a traumatic, feudal history. The peace seems to be holding, tourism growing again and everyone hopes that law and order will prevail and that corruption and self-interest are replaced by good governance, altruism and a system of government that benefits every Nepali.

Modern Kathmandu

Kathmandu today is plagued with the problems that beset all rapidly expanding cities in the developing world: overcrowding, severe pollution and traffic congestion to name but a few. Many parts of Kathmandu have degenerated into an urban sprawl of unsightly concrete block buildings. The district of Thamel, that today looks no different from tourist ghettos in the other Asian capitals on the backpackers' route, was largely fields 40 years ago. The population of the Kathmandu Valley stands at around 1.8 million, with a very high growth rate of almost 5%.

ARRIVAL AND DEPARTURE

By air

● **Arrival** Tribhuvan International Airport (🖥 www.tiairport.com.np) is a 20-minute drive from the centre of Kathmandu. The domestic terminal is next door.

After completing **visa formalities** (see p41) head down to the baggage claim and then pass through **customs** where you may be required to put all your luggage through an X-ray machine.

Reaching the main hall, pick up a free city map at the **tourist office** here. There's also a **post office**, **communications agency** (for telephone calls), **bank** and **hotel reservations counter**.

Outside, screens and barricades attempt to keep an enthusiastic mob of hotel touts and taxi drivers at bay. If you stop to negotiate a fare expect to be quickly surrounded. Anyone other than your driver who pushes your trolley, even a few metres, will expect a tip. However, some hotels (and even some of the budget places) offer free transport from the airport. Taxis to the city centre and Thamel should cost Rs600 if you get your own, or Rs750 with the pre-paid taxi desk just outside to the left of the arrivals exit. If you're really counting the pennies you can reach the bus stop for the crowded local bus by walking to the end of the airport drive and turning left.

● **Departure** At the bank in the international terminal you can convert into hard currency (usually US$) only up to 15% of the rupees for which you have encashment certificates. Alternatively you can dispose of surplus rupees at the shop in the corner of the departure hall, that sells gift packs of tea and Coronation Khukri rum in exotic khukri knife-shaped bottles.

By road

Some of the tourist buses will take you all the way to Thamel. Most go no further than the new bus station about 3km north of the city. Buses from the Everest region still use the old bus station by the clock tower in the town centre. Frequent shuttle buses link the two, passing by the northern end of Thamel. Sajha buses usually stop at the GPO, which is closer to Thamel.

ORIENTATION

Greater Kathmandu, which includes Patan as well as Kathmandu itself, lies at about 1400m/4593ft. The Bagmati River runs between these two cities. The airport is 6km to the east, near the Hindu temple complex of Pashupatinath, with the Buddhist stupa at Baudha 2km north of Pashupatinath. The other major Buddhist shrine, Swayambhunath, is visible on a hill in west Kathmandu. The third city in the Valley, Bhaktapur, is 14km to the east.

Within Kathmandu, most hotels and guesthouses are to be found in Thamel, north of Durbar Square, the historic centre of the city. Freak Street, the hippie centre in the '60s and '70s, which still offers some cheap accommodation, is just off Durbar Square. Some of the top hotels and the international airline offices are along Durbar Marg, which runs south from the modern royal palace.

WHERE TO STAY

Guesthouses and hotels in Kathmandu, even in the cheap bracket, now often have rooms with an attached bathroom and hot water, a TV and wi-fi as well perhaps as an air-conditioner and heater.

Cheap accommodation should also provide clean sheets, blankets and a desk while the better places will also supply towels and toilet paper and perhaps be carpeted. They may also have their own restaurant and a good number now accept credit cards.

Wherever you are check that the hot water works and try to get a room that faces away from the roads – Kathmandu is plagued by noisy dogs and honking taxis. Other features to check are: is there a vent or window in the bathroom?; a clothes line?; and a rooftop garden? You may also want a place which offers a lift from the airport; this may only be offered for the cheap rooms if you stay for more than one night.

Note that many places offer accommodation in a range of prices so do look in all the categories. All the hotels included in this guide have their own website and many offer online booking.

For additional accommodation options it is worth looking at 💻 www.hotel nepal.com.

Hotel areas

● **Thamel** Most travellers find Thamel the most convenient area to stay in, although it's largely a tourist ghetto. Everything you could want is available here, with over 100 guest houses and hotels, many good restaurants, souvenir shops, book shops, communication centres. *(continued on p78)*

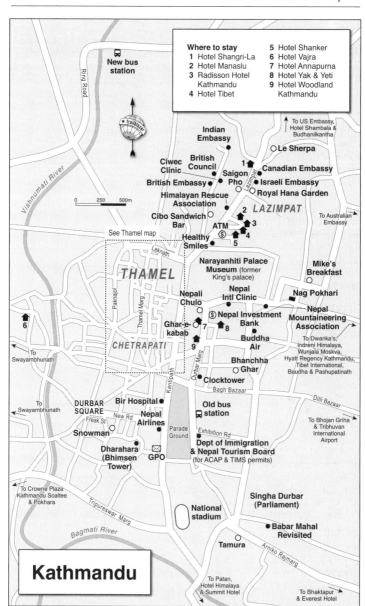

New bus station

Ring Road

Where to stay
1 Hotel Shangri-La
2 Hotel Manaslu
3 Radisson Hotel Kathmandu
4 Hotel Tibet
5 Hotel Shanker
6 Hotel Vajra
7 Hotel Annapurna
8 Hotel Yak & Yeti
9 Hotel Woodland Kathmandu

trailblazer

Vishnumati River

0   250   500m

To US Embassy, Hotel Shambala & Budhanilkantha

Indian Embassy

○ Le Sherpa

Ciwec Clinic

British Council

1

Canadian Embassy

Saigon Pho

Lazimpat

British Embassy ●

● **Israeli Embassy**

○ **Royal Hana Garden**

Himalayan Rescue Association

LAZIMPAT

To Australian Embassy

Cibo Sandwich Bar ○

2

See Thamel map

ATM ⓈⒶ

3

4

Healthy Smiles ●

5

Leknath

Narayanhiti Palace Museum (former King's palace)

Mike's Breakfast ○

THAMEL

Paknajol

Thamel Marg

Nepali Chulo

Nepal Intl Clinic

Nag Pokhari

Ⓢ **Nepal Investment Bank**

Nepal Mountaineering Association

6

Ghar-e-kabab ○

7

8

Buddha Air

To Dwarika's, Indreni Himalaya, Wunjala Moskva, Hyatt Regency Kathmandu, Tibet International, Baudha & Pashupatinath

CHETRAPATI

9

Kantipath

Durbar Marg

Bhanchha Ghar ○

To Swayambhunath

Clocktower

Bagh Bazaar

Dilli Bazaar

DURBAR SQUARE

Bir Hospital ●

To Swayambhunath

Freak St

New Rd

Nepal Airlines

Old bus station

To Bhojan Griha & Tribhuvan International Airport

Snowman ○

Parade Ground

Exhibition Rd

Dharahara (Bhimsen Tower)

✉ **GPO**

Dept of Immigration & Nepal Tourism Board (for ACAP & TIMS permits)

To Crowne Plaza Kathmandu Soaltee & Pokhara

Tripureswar Marg

Singha Durbar (Parliament)

National stadium

● **Babar Mahal Revisited**

Bagmati River

Tamura ○

Arniko Rajmarg

Kathmandu

To Patan, Hotel Himalaya & Summit Hotel

To Bhaktapur & Everest Hotel

KATHMANDU

Hotels in Thamel – keyed to map opposite

Where to stay

1   Family Peace GH
2   Tibet Peace GH
3   Kathmandu Peace GH
4   Hotel Manang
5   Hotel Alpine
6   Pilgrim's Guest House
7   Hotel Encounter Nepal
8   Dolphin Guest House
9   Gaju Suite Hotel
10 Annapurna GH
11 Hotel Norbu Linka
12 Hotel Shakti
13 Souvenir Guest House
14 Hotel Malla
15 Hotel Impala Garden
16 Hotel Tenki
17 Hotel Marshyangdi
18 Hotel Cosmic
19 Hotel Courtyard
20 Hotel Florid Nepal
21 Pilgrim's Hotel
22 Hotel Visit Nepal
23 Hotel Lily
24 Kathmandu Eco Hotel
25 Hotel Buddha
28 Shree Tibet Family
      GH
30 Hotel Vaishali
31 Karma Travellers
      Home
32 Hotel Thamel
33 Samsara Resort
34 Holyland Guest House
38 Hotel Hana
41 Hotel Red Planet
42 Acme Guest House
43 Tasi Dhargey Inn
44 Yeti Guest Home
47 Hotel Mandap
52 Holy Lodge
53 International GH
54 Hotel Metropolitan
      Kantipur
55 Kathmandu GH
59 Hotel Nana
63 Dalai-la Boutique
      Hotel
66 Ambassador Garden
      Home

Where to stay (cont'd)

69 King's Land Hotel
73 Hotel Potala
77 Hotel Blue Horizon
78 Hotel Magnificent
      View
80 Red Planet GH
83 Hotel Excelsior
92 Hotel Horizon
93 Happy Home
95 Thorong Peak GH
96 Siesta House
97 Thamel Eco Resort
99 Hotel Silver Home
100 Hotel Discovery Inn
101 Hotel The Great Wall
102 Hotel Harati
104 Mandala Boutique
      Hotel
105 Tibet Guest House
106 Nirvana Garden Hotel
108 Hotel Tayoma
109 Potala Guest House
112 Om Tara Guest House
116 Namtso Rest House
119 Mustang Holiday Inn
120 Hotel Holy Himalaya
121 Fuji Hotel
122 Hotel Norling
123 Hotel Osho Home
124 Hotel Utse
125 Hotel Friend's Home
126 Hotel Mum's Home
127 Kantipur Temple
      House

Where to eat

7   Kathmandu Grill
14 Hotel Malla
26 Bamboo Club
27 Rum Doodle
29 BK's
35 Thamel House
      Restaurant
36 Café des Arts
37 Yangling Tibetan
39 Gillingche
40 Mo:Mo Star
45 Sam's
46 Krua Thai

Where to eat (cont'd)

47 Mandap
48 Celtic Manang
49 Zibro Resto & Bar
50 Nirmala
51 Places Bar &
      Restaurant
56 Northfield Café
57 Crazy Burger
58 Full Moon
60 Tom & Jerry's
61 Nargila's
62 New Orleans
64 Brezel Bakery
65 La Dolce Vita
67 Pub Maya
68 K-too
70 Tashi Deleg
71 KC's
72 OR2K
74 Maya Cocktail Bar
75 Pumpernickel
76 Kaiser Café
79 Dechenling
81 Himalayan Java
82 Fire & Ice
84 Ying Yang
85 Third Eye
86 New China Town
87 Tibet's Kitchen
88 Roadhouse Café
89 Weizen
90 Helena's
91 Koto
94 Typical Nepali
98 Hot Sandwich
103 Everest Steak House
106 Samsara
107 Nepalese Kitchen
110 Pilgrim's Feed 'n'
      Read Restaurant &
      Bar
111 Rosemary Kitchen &
      Coffee Shop
113 Café Mitra
114 Cha Cha Café
115 Omei Chinese
117 Kilroy's
118 Gaia Coffee Shop
124 Utse

To new
bus station

Leknath

Thamel Marg

Paknajol

Zee St

Cinema

Satghumti

HMB
Ultimate
Descents

ATM $

Pilgrim's
Bookshop

THAMEL

Shrine

Temple

Shrine

Amrit Marg

Pharmacy

Thamel
Chowk

Best
Shopping
Centre

Tri Devi

Taxis

ATM $

ATM $ $

ATM $ $
Himalayan 82
Bank

Kaiser Library
(Ministry of
Education
& Culture)

KEEP

Global $
Bank

Kanti Path

JP School Rd

Paknajol

Trekking
shops

Thamel Marg

To
Swayambhunath

CHETRAPATI

Many small
mountaineering
shops

$ Nabil
Bank

KATHMANDU

Motorbikes
for hire

Thahity
Chowk

Jyatha

Mandala
Book Point

0   50   100   150m

Thamel
& Chetrapati

To Durbar Square,
Freak St & New Rd

● **Freak Street** In the halcyon days of the '60s and '70s when Kathmandu was a major stopover on the hippie trail, Freak St, just off Durbar Square, was the place to hang out. Although the hash dens are now all closed it still retains a quaint charm. Its hotels are generally in the rock-bottom to cheap bracket.

● **Other areas** Away from the intense tourist scene are many other hotels scattered throughout Kathmandu. In **Patan** there are some good budget and upmarket hotels both in and off Durbar Square; see p83.

Baudha and **Swayambhunath** have some simple hotels favoured by Buddhists but also by travellers.

Budget accommodation (US$10/£6.50) In Thamel, particularly in the north of Thamel, there are some places where you can still get a bed in a dorm, or a very basic room, for $10 or less; in some you'll even get an attached bathroom.

Places in this area to consider include: *Pilgrim's GH* [6; see p80]; *Souvenir GH* [13; see opposite]; *Holyland GH* ([34; see opposite]; and *Shree Tibet Family Guest House* [28; see p80].

Hotel Silver Home [99; see opposite] is the most centrally located of the places listed here and comes highly recommended. Also worth considering is *Om Tara GH* [112; see opposite].

These budget options are all **keyed to the map on p77**.

Cheap hotels/guesthouses in Thamel (US$10-20/£3-12) The wonderful *Hotel Potala* [73] (☎ 470 0159, 🖳 www.potalahotel.com; sgl $8-12, dbl

---

❏ **Rates**
Many hotel owners quote their rates in **US dollars ($)**; you pay in rupees, though. Given the changing rate of inflation in the country, this is a sensible idea so US dollars are also used here. The dollar/pound exchange rate hovers around US$1.55=£1.

Intense competition means you can find bargain accommodation in all price brackets. Although it is still possible to get a bed for as little as US$3.50, cheap accommodation with a communal bathroom is more usually around the US$5-10 a night mark for a double room. Most accommodation, though, now comes with an attached bathroom. However, don't expect much if you are only paying US$10; for a nicer room expect to pay around US$20, and up to US$60 to get more services and facilities. Four-/five-star hotels start at about $100 but many cost much more.

Accommodation tariffs can vary enormously between low season and peak season. In the low season many hotels cut their prices or offer significant discounts – sometimes 50% or more for stays of more than one night. Since there is plenty of choice it is worth looking around. Discounts are often available on many hotel websites for advance bookings so also it is worth booking as soon as you can.

Rates quoted are for single (**sgl**) and double (**dbl**) rooms (often the beds in double rooms can be separated to make a twin room); where available the rates for triple (**tpl**) rooms are also quoted. However, most places also offer to put an **extra bed** in a room.

Note that most hotels add a 13% **government tax** to the bill as well as a 10% service charge; however, some places include these in the rate.

$13-18, tpl $17-22) is run by a Tibetan family, and comes with a satellite TV lounge and a roof terrace, but is near night clubs so can be noisy.

Kathmandu Guest House [55; see p81] is actually a three-star hotel but it also has rooms in this price bracket (simplicity room sgl/dbl $8/12, basic room $12/16).

Recommended places include: *Holyland GH* [34] (☎ 443 3161, 🖥 www .lodgenepal.com; dorm $3.50, sgl $5-10, dbl $12-15, tpl $18); *Holy Lodge* [52] (☎ 470 1763, 🖥 www.holylodge.com; sgl $8-40, dbl $12-50, extra bed $5-10); *Karma Travellers Home* [31](☎ 441 7897, 🖥 www.karmatravellershome.com; sgl $14-20, dbl $18-25, extra bed $5; *Acme GH* [42] (☎ 470 0236, 🖥 www .acmeguesthouse.com; sgl $8-35, dbl $10-40, tpl $30-45; *King's Land Hotel* [69] (☎ 442 1060, 🖥 www.kinglandhotel.com; rooms $10-12); and *Hotel Silver Home* [99] (☎ 426 2986, 🖥 hotelsilverhome.com; dorm bed $3.50, sgl $8-12, dbl $10-15, tpl $16-18). Both Holyland GH and Hotel Silver Home have dorm beds.

For a bit of peace and quiet away from Thamel, check out some of the guest houses just to the north. Worth considering are: *Tibet Peace Guest House* [2], (☎ 438 1026, 🖥 www.tibetpeace.com) sgl $12-16, dbl $16-25, tpl $22-28) which has its own garden area; *Hotel Cosmic* [18] (☎ 470 0415, 🖥 www.hotel cosmic.com) sgl $15-22, dbl $18-30, budget tpl $20); *Hotel Visit Nepal* [22] (☎ 470 1384, 🖥 www.hotelvisitnepal.com) sgl $8-10, dbl $12-15, tpl $13-16); and *Hotel Lily* [23] (☎ 470 1264, 🖥 hotelthamellily.com) sgl $10, dbl $15-25, tpl $20, de luxe $25.

The following cheap hotels/guesthouses are also **keyed to the map on p77**:

1 Family Peace GH (☎ 438 1138, 🖥 www.familypeacehouse.com) sgl $12, dbl $14, tpl $16

3 Kathmandu Peace Guest House (☎ 426 2597, 🖥 www.peaceguesthouse.com) sgl $8-20, dbl $12-26, tpl $15-32

10 Annapurna GH (☎ 441 7461, 🖥 www.annapurnaguesthouse.com) sgl $7-15, dbl $9-20, tpl $11-25

13 Souvenir GH (☎ 441 8225, ☎ 441 0277, 🖥 www.souvenirguesthouse.com) rooms $5-25

20 Hotel Florid Nepal (☎ 470 1055, 🖥 www.hotelflorid.com.np) sgl $10-25, dbl $15-35, tpl $45

38 Hotel Hana (☎ 442 4683, 🖥 www .hotelhana.com.np) sgl $10-20, dbl $14-26

41 Hotel Red Planet (☎ 470 0879, 🖥 ho telredplanet.com) sgl $10-13, dbl $14-20, tpl $34

59 Hotel Nana (☎ 470 0251, 🖥 www .hotelnana.com.np) sgl $9-12.50, dbl $13-18, tpl $15

80 Red Planet GH (☎ 441 3881, 🖥 red planetguesthouse.com) sgl $13-17, dbl $17-20, extra bed $5

99 Hotel Silver Home (see above)

100 Hotel Discovery Inn (☎ 422 9889) rooms $15-25

112 Om Tara GH (☎ 425 9634, 🖥 om taraguesthouse.wordpress.com) sgl $6-12, dbl $8-14, tpl $18

116 Namtso Rest House (☎ 425 1238, 🖥 www.hotelinthamel.com) sgl $15-22, dbl 10-28, tpl $25-32

KATHMANDU

The **Kathmandu phone code** is 01 and the **country code** is +977.
If phoning from outside Nepal dial ☎ +977-1.

Moderately priced hotels ($20-60/£12-38) There are numerous reasonable hotels in this price range, most of them with a restaurant.

Pilgrim's Guest House [6] (☎ 444 0565, 🖳 www.pilgrimsguesthouse.com; budget room $10 no breakfast; B&B sgl $16-25, dbl $26-30, suite $40-45) is set in its own peaceful and sunny grounds at the northern end of Thamel.

Both *Nirvana Garden Hotel* [106] (☎ 425 6200, 🖳 www.nirvanagarden .com/new; sgl $40-80, dbl $50-75) and *Hotel Courtyard* [19] (☎ 470 0476, 🖳 www.hotelcourtyard.com; sgl $40-60, dbl $45-95, extra bed $25) have large tranquil gardens; see also box p87.

Other recommended places are: *Shree Tibet Family Guest House* [28] (☎ 470 0902, 🖳 www.hotelshreetibet.com; dorm bed $4, sgl $16-19, dbl $20-26); *Hotel Encounter Nepal* [7] (☎ 444 0534, 🖳 www.encounternepal.com; sgl $30-60, dbl $35-75); *Hotel The Great Wall* [101] (🖳 www.hotelgreatwallnepal .com; sgl $20-35, dbl $25-40, tpl $30); *Happy Home* [93] (☎ 421 6807, 🖳 www.hotelhappyhomenepal.com; rooms $30-75); and *Hotel Utse* [124] (☎ 422 8952, 🖳 www.utsehotel.com; sgl $25-40, dbl $35-45, extra bed $9).

Hotel Vajra [see map on p75] (☎ 427 1545, 🖳 www.hotelvajra.com; sgl $33-85, dbl $38-90) was conceived and paid for by a Texas billionaire, and built by Newar craftsmen, with wall-paintings by Tibetan and Tamang artists. There are also cheaper rooms (sgl $14, dbl $16) with wash-basins and shared bathrooms. It is located near **Swayambhunath**.

The following moderately priced hotels are also **keyed to the map on p77**:

5 Hotel Alpine (☎ 470 1435, 🖳 alpine hotelnepal.com) sgl $35-55, dbl $45-65, apartment sleeping two $80

8 Dolphin GH (☎ 442 9280, ☎ 442 5422, 🖳 www.dolphinguesthouse.com) sgl $15-25, dbl $30-40

12 Hotel Shakti (☎ 444 1593, ☎ 441 0121, 🖳 www.hotelshakti.com.np) sgl $26-40, dbl $39-60, extra bed $12-20

15 Hotel Impala Garden (☎ 470 1549, 🖳 www.hotelimpala.com.np) sgl $20-30, dbl $30-45, tpl $60, de luxe $60, extra bed $12

16 Hotel Tenki (☎ 470 0694, 🖳 www.ho teltenkinepal.com) sgl $30-40, dbl $40-50, extra bed $10

17 Hotel Marshyangdi (☎ 470 0105, 🖳 www.hotelmarshyangdi.com) sgl $40-80, dbl $50-90, extra beds $20-30, suites $200

21 Pilgrim's Hotel (☎ 470 0600, 🖳 www.hotelpilgrimsnepal.com) sgl $40-70, dbl $45-75

25 Hotel Buddha (☎ 470 0366, 🖳 www .hotelbuddhanepal.com) sgl $10-40, dbl $35-45

32 Hotel Thamel (☎ 442 3968, 🖳 www .hotelthamel.com) sgl $40-55, dbl $50-65, extra bed $10

43 Tasi Dhargey Inn (☎ 470 0030, 🖳 ho teltashidhargey.com) sgl $15-20, dbl $20-25, extra bed $8

44 Yeti Guest Home (☎ 470 1789, 🖳 www.yetiguesthome.com.np) sgl $12-26, dbl $20-35, extra bed $7-10

47 Hotel Mandap (☎ 470 0321, 🖳 www.hotelmandap.com) sgl $35-40, dbl $45-50, suites $65-70

53 International GH (☎ 425 2299, 🖳 www.intguesthouse.com) dorm bed $8, sgl $24-60, dbl $28-60, tpl £58

54 Hotel Metropolitan Kantipur (☎ 426 6518, 🖳 www.kantipurhotel.com) sgl $15-40, dbl 25-50, extra bed $10

77 Hotel Blue Horizon (☎ 442 1971, 🖳 www.hotelbluehorizon.com) sgl $20-40, dbl $25-45, extra bed $10

78 Hotel Magnificent View (☎ 443 7455, 🖳 www.hotelmagnificent.com) sgl $15-40, dbl $20-50, extra bed $8

83 Hotel Excelsior (☎ 425 7748, 🖳 www .excelsiornepal.com) sgl $25-58, dbl $30-65

92 Hotel Horizon (☎ 422 0904, 🖳 www .hotelhorizon.com) sgl $20-25, dbl $25-30, tpl $30-40

95 Thorong Peak GH (☎ 426 2980, ☎ 425 3458, 🖳 www.thorongpeak.com) sgl $20-28, dbl $28-50, extra bed $8
96 Siesta House (☎ 421 2818, 🖳 www .siestaguesthouse.com) sgl $15-18, dbl $20-40, tpl $50
97 Thamel Eco Resort (☎ 426 3810, 🖳 www.thamelecoresort.com) sgl $45-150, dbl $50-180, extra bed $20
105 Tibet GH (☎ 426 0383, 🖳 www.tibet guesthouse.com) sgl $16-90, dbl $20-100, extra bed $8-10
108 Hotel Tayoma (☎ 422 9885, ☎ 425 5977, 🖳 www.hoteltayoma.com) sgl $22-70, dbl $30-75, extra bed $10
109 Potala GH (☎ 422 0467, 🖳 www.po talaguesthouse.com) sgl $21-24, dbl $33-58, tpl $46, extra bed $10
119 Mustang Holiday Inn (☎ 424 9041, 🖳 www.mustangholiday.com) sgl $20-50, dbl $30-70
120 Hotel Holy Himalaya (☎ 426 3172, 🖳 www.holyhimalaya.com) sgl $28-60, dbl $36-70, tpl $52-80
121 Fuji Hotel (☎ 425 0435, 🖳 www.fuji hotel.com.np) sgl $22-50, dbl $32-80, extra bed $13
122 Hotel Norling (☎ 424 0734, 🖳 www .hotelnorling.com) sgl $17-23, dbl $22-39, tpl $41, extra bed $6
123 Hotel Osho Home (☎ 415 2083, 🖳 www.hoteloshohome.com) rooms $40-50
125 Hotel Friend's Home (☎ 415 2065, 🖳 www.hotelfriendshome.com) sgl $35, dbl $55, tpl $60-65
126 Hotel Mum's Home (☎ 415 2026, 🖳 hotelmumshomes.com) sgl £45, dbl $55, tpl $60-65, extra bed $20

Three-star standard hotels ($60-100/£38-65) The best known of the hotels in Kathmandu must be the long-running **Kathmandu Guest House** [55] (KGH ☎ 470 0632, 🖳 www.ktmgh.com/kathmandu-guest-house.html), a Thamel landmark. Popular with groups, it's bursting in the high season. It offers many options ranging from cheap accommodation (see p79) up to very comfortable options (standard sgl/dbl $60/80, garden-facing $80/100, superior $120/140, de luxe $160/180, suite $180/200, extra bed $20-40 depending on room).

Nearby and often recommended is **Ambassador Garden Home** [66] (☎ 470 0724, 🖳 www.aghhotel.com; sgl $51-87, dbl $63-105, extra bed $24).

In north Thamel **Hotel Manang** [4] (☎ 470 0993, 🖳 www.hotelmanang .com; sgl $80-95, dbl $95-110, extra bed $22, suites $150) is popular with trekking groups. Nearby, with a large garden area is the modern and completely non-smoking **Samsara Resort** [33] (☎ 441 6466, 🖳 www.samsararesort .com; sgl $70-80, dbl $80-95, extra bed $20-22). Also good is **Hotel Harati** [102] (☎ 425 7907, 🖳 www.hotelharati.com.np; sgl $50-60, dbl $60-80, extra beds $10-15, suites $100).

Other hotels in this price bracket include:

● Keyed to Thamel map, p77
9 Gaju Suite Hotel (☎ 443 2281, 🖳 gajusuite.com) sgl $80, dbl $90, extra bed $20; apartments sgl $110, dbl $150 extra bed $30; suite $170
11 Hotel Norbu Linka (☎ 441 0630, 🖳 www.hotelnorbulinka.com) rooms $60-250
24 Kathmandu Eco Hotel (☎ 444 0195, 🖳 www.kathmanduecohotel.com) sgl $50-90, dbl $60-100
63 Dalai-la Boutique Hotel (☎ 470 1436, 🖳 dalailaboutiquehotel.com) rooms $80-120, suites $200-500
104 Mandala Boutique Hotel (☎ 425 4511, 🖳 mandalaboutiquehotel.com.np) rooms from $60

● Keyed to Kathmandu map, p75
4 Hotel Tibet (☎ 442 9085, 🖳 www .hotel-tibet.com.np) sgl $65-86, dbl $75-93
2 Hotel Manaslu (☎ 441 0071, 🖳 www.hotelmanaslu.com) sgl $60-75, dbl $60-80, extra bed $25

● **Three-star hotels marked off Kathmandu map, p75**

Indreni Himalaya (☎ 411 3711, 🖥 www   **Hotel Shambala** (☎ 465 0251, 🖥 www
.hotelindrenihimalaya.com) rooms $85-150   .shambalahotel.com) rooms $95-200

Four- and five-star hotels (from $100/£65) Most of the city's top hotels are much like expensive hotels anywhere in the world.

The oldest of Kathmandu's hotels is the overpriced and under-serviced *Hotel Yak & Yeti* [8; map p75] (☎ 424 8999, 🖥 www.yakandyeti.com; rooms from $240 to $750). Centrally located, it has everything you'd expect from a five-star hotel, although the modern wings don't exactly blend with the old Rana palace which forms part of it. The Yak & Yeti Bar, with its excellent Chimney Restaurant, was moved here from the Royal Hotel (Nepal's first hotel) when it closed.

However, there are some good hotel options for those wanting genuine four- or five-star service. Probably the best hotel in Kathmandu is *Dwarika's Hotel* (☎ 447 9488, 🖥 www.dwarikas.com). If Kathmandu is a living museum, this is the ultimate place to experience it. The red-brick buildings are decorated, inside and out, with ornate panels lovingly restored from old Kathmandu houses. Every room (sgl $220-275, dbl $240-95, suites $350-1800) is an individual work of art, and the restaurants' offerings are similarly deliciously exotic. Rich Nepalis, however, consider *Crowne Plaza Kathmandu-Soaltee* (☎ 427 3999, 🖥 www .ichotelsgroup.com) as the best of the big hotels, although it's not so well located, being to the west of the city, in Kalimati. Rooms range from $129 to $935.

Two popular options are *Hotel Shanker* [5; map p75] (☎ 441 0151, 🖥 www.shankerhotel.com.np; rooms $70-140) and *Hotel Himalaya* (☎ 552 3900, 🖥 www.hotelhimalaya.com.np; rooms $160-250 but good online deals), both of which have a pleasant outdoor pools.

Hotel Malla [14] (☎ 441 8385, 🖥 www.hotelmalla.com; sgl $130-150, dbl $156-182, suites $204-268, extra bed $42), just north of Thamel, is pleasant and has a fitness centre and swimming pool though some of the rooms are rather tired. The best value in this group is *Hotel Shangri-La* [1; map p75] (☎ 441 2999, 🖥 www.hotelshangrila.com), in Lazimpat, with rooms from $140 and a peaceful garden.

On Durbar Marg is *Hotel Annapurna* [7; map p75] (☎ 422 1711, 🖥 www .annapurna-hotel.com) with rooms for $160-550 and a large pool and excellent cake shop!

Both *Radisson Hotel Kathmandu* [3; map p75] (☎ 441 1818, 🖥 www.radisson.com) and *Hyatt Regency Kathmandu* (☎ 449 1234, 🖥 www.kathmandu .regency.hyatt.com), which is near **Baudha**, have rooms from around $160 per night, though considerable discounts are available at both throughout the year especially if booked in advance.

The Indian-owned *Hotel Vaishali* [20] (☎ 441 3968, 🖥 www.hotelvaishali .com), with pool, was Kathmandu's first four-star hotel. Rooms are around $90 (sgl) and $110 (dbl) but you should be able to negotiate substantial discounts.

Other hotels in this price range worth considering are: ***Hotel Woodland Kathmandu*** [9; map p75] (☎ 422 0540, 🖳 www.hotelwoodlandktm.com; sgl $125, dbl $150, tpl $200, extra bed $30); ***Kantipur Temple House*** [127] (☎ 425 0131, 🖳 www.kantipurtemplehouse.com; sgl $90-250, dbl $115-250, extra bed $40); and ***Tibet International*** (☎ 448 8188, 🖳 www.hoteltibetintl.com.np; rooms $200-450, extra bed $50).

Where to stay in Patan
There has been an explosion of good-quality boutique hotels in the Kathmandu Valley, especially in Patan. Service quality is generally very good and accommodation is much nicer than the concrete buildings that dominate Thamel.

The traditionally decorated ***Summit Hotel*** (🖳 www.summit-nepal.com; sgl $120-140, dbl $130-155) is popular with expeditions wanting a peacefully located hotel. They also have a budget annex where twin rooms with shared bathroom are $44 ($37 single occupancy). Both have a pleasant atmosphere, attractive gardens, restaurants and the usual amenities.

The Inn (☎ 985 1052 006, 🖳 theinnpatan.com; sgl $70-85, dbl $80-95 extra bed $35-40) is a heritage hotel, originally a Newari house, in Patan's Durbar Square. Another Newari house, but north of the Square, is ***Newa Chen*** (☎ 553 3532, 🖳 www.newachen.com; sgl $17-35, dbl $45-50, extra bed $10).

Other places worth considering are: ***Goodwill Hotel*** (☎ 554 4520, 🖳 hotelgoodwill.com; sgl $40-65, dbl $50-65); and ***Hira Guest House*** (☎ 553 3273, 🖳 www.stayinnepal.com; sgl $50, dbl $60).

WHERE TO EAT

Kathmandu's restaurants have long been renowned amongst travellers throughout South Asia for their ability to serve passable approximations of Western dishes. Until recently, however, you'd probably have been more appreciative of Kathmandu's apple-pie and enchilada cuisine after a trek rather than on arrival direct from the West. It's surprising how quickly you forget how things are really supposed to taste! Standards have risen quite considerably over the last few years with restaurants competing for more authentic dishes, some even importing chefs from abroad. The better restaurants charge 13% VAT; sometimes this is included in the menu price but in upmarket restaurants it is usually added to the bill. Some restaurants also add a 10% service charge to the menu prices.

Be especially careful about what you eat before you set out on your trek; you're more likely to pick up a stomach bug in a Kathmandu restaurant than in the hills. A test on the quality of the tap water in Thamel showed it to contain more than 10 times the WHO-recommended safe maximum level of faecal matter. The better restaurants are serious about hygiene but don't believe all restaurants that tell you their salads are washed in iodine. Similarly, filtered water is not reliably clean; stick to bottled or hot drinks.

There are too many restaurants to mention every one but some current favourites are reviewed overleaf; unless specified these are **keyed to the Thamel map on p77**. More are marked on that map and on the Kathmandu map (p75).

Breakfast

Most hotels and guesthouses offer breakfast and snacks either as room service or in their own snack bars. Most of the Thamel restaurants have set breakfasts that can be good value and there are numerous bakeries that do a roaring trade in cinnamon rolls, bagels and other pastries and cakes. For a leisurely breakfast it's worth searching out places with sun terraces or gardens.

The original is *Mike's Breakfast* (see map p75) where you breakfast on authentic American (hash browns, pancakes and syrup, fresh coffee with free refills etc) and Mexican fare in a garden. Mike is no longer around but he was an ex-Peace-Corps volunteer who loved Nepal so much he just couldn't leave.

Other good breakfast places include *Rosemary Kitchen & Coffee Shop* [111; see also below], *Northfield Café* [56; see also opposite], *New Orleans* [62] and *Helena's* [90] (⌨ www.helenasrestaurant.com); it may be several flights of stairs to Helena's rooftop, but the view is well worth it.

Lunch and dinner

Tibetan restaurants are amongst the cheapest places to eat in Thamel. The best-known Tibetan place here is *Utse* [124], at the hotel of the same name (see p80). The pingtsey soup (meat soup with wontons) is excellent, as are their momos (vegetable, mutton, buffalo or pork). Given a couple of hours' notice, they will prepare a complete Tibetan banquet. *Yangling Tibetan* [37] is also recommended, particularly for its momos which come with a range of fillings; the chilli momos are very good.

Many restaurants serve pizza and pasta but one place stands way above the rest: *Fire & Ice Pizzeria & Ice Cream Parlour* [82] (⌨ www.fireandicepiz zeria.com) has to be experienced to be believed. Run by an Italian woman who imported her own computer-controlled Moretti Forni pizza oven, some of the best pizzas on the subcontinent are now turned out here – to the sound of Pavarotti. Queues can be long, though.

For authentic pasta try *La Dolce Vita* [65], which has great food (especially salads, pesto and desserts).

In the southern part of Thamel, *Rosemary Kitchen & Coffee Shop* [111] is very popular. The menu includes chicken satay, sizzling garlic prawns and a good range of vegetarian dishes. There's an attractive open courtyard section to the restaurant and you can get wine as well as beer here.

❏ Babar Mahal Revisited

This place (see map p75; ⌨ www.babermahal-revisited.com) has to be seen to be believed! The crumbling stables of a Rana palace near the parliament building have been converted into a chic shopping centre. There are some distinctly exclusive boutiques and some excellent restaurants.

Chez Caroline is one of Kathmandu's best, with authentic French cuisine, wine and good patisserie. There's also *Baithak* (☎ 426 7346), where, in the grand long gallery, past Ranas stare down from their portraits as you feast on 'delicacies from the Rana court'.

❏ **Stylish traditional dining**
There are now some very upmarket traditional restaurants in Kathmandu. *Bhanchha Ghar* (see map p75; 🖥 www.nepalibhanchha.com) was one of the first restaurants here to serve a 9- to 13-course banquet with lots of complimentary *raksi*, floor seating, and traditional singing and dancing. Located in an old Rana building in Bagh Bazaar, Bhanchha Ghar (meaning Kitchen House) offers wild boar or dried deer meat to accompany drinks, and the dinner menu is similarly exotic.

Others include *Bhojan Griha* in Kamaladi and *Nepali Chulo* (see map p75) on Lazimpat behind Hotel Gangjong, which occupies an extensive Rana palace that's worth exploring especially if you want a private dining room.

Similar in spirit, though classier – and without live entertainment – are *Baithak* in Babar Mahal Revisited (see box opposite) and the spectacular *Krishnarpan* at Dwarika's Hotel (see p82), where the service and décor are entertainment enough.

At the slightly bizarre end of the scale is *Wunjala Moskva* (🖥 www.nepalicuisine.com) in Naxal. At this Russian-Newari eatery, you sit in a garden courtyard eating blinis and momos, watching Nepali dancing and knocking back vodka!

Thamel House, in Thamel, is in a well-maintained 100-year-old Newari building. As at the other places, you can order á la carte or go for the set meal.

Kaiser Café [76], run by Dwarika's Hotel (see p82), occupies a very peaceful location in the wonderfully named **Garden of Dreams** (🖥 www.gardenofdreams.org.np; Rs200 entry charge), a short walk but seemingly a million miles away from hectic, polluted Thamel. The cuisine is Austrian-themed.

Café des Arts [36] is French-run with a (short) menu featuring excellent French and Asian dishes. The garden setting perfectly complements the food. Wine and beer are available. For a fancy dinner with gleaming silver, china, linen, and good service visit *Café Mitra* [113] (🖥 www.cafemitra.com). The tossed salad, Zen mackerel and cheese soufflés are excellent, as is the pannacotta. This two-floor resto-bar has lounge seating, a private dining room, art on the walls, and the best toilet in Thamel.

Saigon Pho is the only Vietnamese restaurant in Kathmandu but given the success of this place no doubt others will open soon. They serve excellent *pho* (noodle soup) and delicious papaya salad. It's in Lazimpat (see map p75). Further north in Lazimpat is *Le Sherpa* (🖥 www.lesherpa.com.np), which has an attractive outdoor dining area. The pasta here is recommended and there's an imaginative menu including roast quail and rabbit ravioli.

Pilgrim's Feed n' Read [110] serves Indian and Nepalese cuisine and is the only decent place in Thamel that serves southern Indian Masala dosas – which make a great lunch. Their momos are original too. *Northfield Café* [56] was the first place in Thamel to have an open clay oven. *Third Eye* [85] (🖥 www.thirdeye.com.np) is another place known for its Indian cooking.

However, the top Indian restaurant is *Ghar-e-kabab* in Hotel Annapurna [7 map p75; see also p82]. It specialises in the rich cuisine of North India, and there's live music in the evenings. You may need to book.

For a quiet multi-cuisine restaurant with a garden setting consider *Samsara Restaurant* [106] in Nirvana Garden Hotel.

KATHMANDU

Many places have steak on the menu; usually (but not always) this is buffalo steak. It's often served as a 'sizzler' and arrives in front of you on a heated cast-iron plate doing just that. The enduring ***Everest Steak House's*** [103] speciality is a wide range of real beef fillet steaks. ***Kathmandu Grill*** [7], in Hotel Encounter Nepal (see p80), is another good place to go for a steak; they also do a range of other dishes at this popular open-air restaurant.

All restaurants have some dishes for vegetarians who are sick of daal bhat. The top veggie and vegan restaurant is probably ***OR2K*** [72] (🖳 www.or2k.net); it is clean and comfortable, specialises in Israeli and Middle eastern dishes, and there's relaxed seating on floor cushions with low tables as well as a nice rooftop terrace. ***Places Restaurant & Bar*** [51] (🖳 www.facebook.com/Places Kathmandu) is another busy veggie and vegan place that's often recommended and there's sometimes live music here.

The Rum Doodle Restaurant & 40,000½ft Bar [27] (🖳 www.therumdoodle.com) is a Kathmandu institution, with yeti prints on its walls inscribed by the members of many mountaineering expeditions. As well as a wide range of drinks (eg hot buttered rum), the food here is good although a little expensive. Try the chicken with almond sauce and mashed potatoes, or a steak. In winter enjoy a real fire without guilt: the logs are made from crushed rice husks.

Zibro Resto & Bar [49] (🖳 www.facebook.com/zibro.restaurant) is also more of a bar with food, a place to chill out, than somewhere to go for dinner. There's often live entertainment here and great views from the rooftop.

SERVICES

Banks
Larger hotels can change money at reception and around every corner in Thamel are authorised money-changers. You can withdraw unlimited amounts in person from banks, either in rupees or travellers' cheques but not in foreign currency.

There are numerous **ATMs** in central Kathmandu. In Thamel the most convenient machines are in the courtyard of Kathmandu Guest House next to its main gate, and adjacent to Roadhouse Café. There is also one next to La Dolce

---

❏ **Embassies and consulates**
- **Australian Embassy** (☎ 437 1678, 🖳 www.nepal.embassy.gov.au), Bansbari
- **British Embassy** (☎ 441 0583, 🖳 www.gov.uk/government/world/organisations/british-embassy-kathmandu), Lainchaur
- **Canadian consulate** (☎ 444 1976, 🖳 www.canadainternational.gc.ca)
- **French Embassy** (☎ 441 2332, 🖳 www.ambafrance-np.org), Lazimpat
- **German Embassy** (☎ 421 7200, 🖳 www.kathmandu.diplo.de), Gyaneshwar
- **Indian Embassy** (☎ 441 0900, 🖳 www.indianembassy.org.np), Lainchaur
- **Israeli Embassy** (☎ 441 1811, 🖳 embassies.gov.il), Lazimpat
- **New Zealand** (Honorary Consul ☎ 442 6427, 🖳 nzconsulate@tigermountain.co.np), Ramalaya
- **US Embassy** (☎ 423 4000, 🖳 nepal.usembassy.gov), Maharajgunj

❏ **KEEP and HRA**
Kathmandu Environmental Education Project (KEEP) raises environmental awareness among trekkers and the trekking industry. They have an information centre (☎ 441 0952, ☎ 441 0935, 🖳 www.facebook.com/keepnepal, 🖳 www.keepnepal .org, Sun-Fri 10am-5pm) which is well worth visiting. It offers unbiased trekking information, trekker logs, a coffee shop and library, plus a free embassy registration service; unless you're trekking with an organised group, you're advised to do this since your embassy's assistance is necessary if a helicopter rescue is required for you. They also sell iodine, potable aqua and steri pens for water purification. The notice board here is a good place to look for trekking companions.
  Himalayan Rescue Association (HRA; ☎ 444 0292, ☎ 444 0293, 🖳 www.hima layanrescue.org) was founded in 1973 with the primary aim of saving lives in the mountains by alerting trekkers to the dangers of altitude sickness. It's largely due to their unfailing efforts (passed into guidebooks) that the death toll from altitude sickness is now very low. They have an information centre in Kathmandu upstairs near Best Supermarket where they have an altitude-awareness talk at 3pm each day during the main trekking seasons. They also have forms here so you can register with your embassy (see above).
  In addition to the Kathmandu information centre the HRA has medical posts at Manang, Thorong Phedi, Pheriche and Everest Base Camp. They operate only during the peak trekking seasons: from early October to early December, and March to April.

Vita and another on the right-hand side on the road down from Fire & Ice. These last two are tiny brightly lit cubicles.
  There have been no reports of theft or muggings around ATMs but you should use your judgment at night. There is a withdrawal limit of Rs10,000 per transaction set by the machines but some will allow up to five withdrawals a day if your card limit permits.
  The most convenient bank foreign exchange counter is **Himalayan Bank** in the same building as Fire & Ice. **Global Bank** and **Nabil Bank** on Kantipath are convenient too. **Nepal Investment Bank** on Durbar Marg works 365 days a year, though only from 9am to noon at weekends and on public holidays.

Bookshops and libraries
Kathmandu has some of the best bookshops on the subcontinent, including many small second-hand shops where you can trade in your novel for another. Most international news, computer and fashion magazines are regularly available.
  The original **Pilgrim's Book House** (🖳 www.pilgrimsbooks.com)

❏ **Trekking talks**
Chris Beall (🖳 www.chrisbeallphoto .com) is a professional photographer and expedition leader who for many years has also done slide presentations covering the main trekking regions of the country. These are held regularly during the trekking seasons in the Movie Hall at Hotel Courtyard (see p80); he offers good unbiased advice for trekkers about to head into the hills and the presentations (including a dinner) are well worth the ticket price. See Chris Beall's website (click on Slide presentations) for further details.

KATHMANDU

was destroyed by fire in 2013 but the business reopened soon after near Ying Yang restaurant and still sells a wide range of books. **Mandala Book Point** (🖳 www.mandalabookpoint.com) is geared more to academic books.

Kaiser Library (🖳 klib.gov.np), Kaiser Sumshere Rana's private collection, is worth visiting as much for the building as for the 30,000 plus musty volumes. This Rana palace just west of the modern royal palace is now the Ministry of Education & Culture. There's also an old garden with six pavilions in the same compound. This is now being renovated and turned into an upmarket shopping, café and bar area to be called the Garden of Dreams.

The **British Council Learning Centre** by the British Embassy is open to all and has the main UK newspapers and plenty of magazines.

Left luggage
All hotels and guest houses are happy to store excess luggage for you free of charge while you go off on your trek, although they expect you to stay with them on your return.

Medical clinics
CIWEC Travel Medicine Center (☎ 442 4111, 🖳 www.ciwec-clinic.com, Mon-Fri 9am-5pm for consultations, 24hrs for emergencies) is an exceptionally competent clinic. It's in a building opposite both the British Embassy and the British Council. Credit cards are accepted.

Nepal International Clinic (☎ 443 5357, 🖳 www.nepalinternationalclinic .com; open Sun-Fri 9am-5pm, appointments only on Sat) is also excellent. It's opposite the Royal Palace, slightly east of Durbar Marg.

For dental problems the best option is **Healthy Smiles** (☎ 442 0800, 🖳 heal thysmiles.com.np) in Lazimpat. The dentists are competent and experienced, and have been trained overseas.

WHAT TO SEE

You could easily spend a month in the Kathmandu Valley, such is the rich concentration of sights here. Several companies operate bus tours (ask in the larger hotels and travel agencies) but renting a bicycle and wandering round independently is rather more rewarding. Getting lost is all part of the fun.

The first seven places mentioned here have been declared World Heritage Sites, making the Kathmandu Valley one of the most significant cultural heritage sites in Asia.

Durbar Square
First stop on the Kathmandu sightseeing trail is Durbar Square (see map p75), also known as Hanuman Dhoka, named after the Hindu monkey god and patron saint of the Mallas.

This complex of ornately carved temples and monuments includes the **old royal palace** (closed Tuesday; entry is Rs100), the **Kumari Bahal** (the home of the Kumari, the 'living goddess', a young girl chosen as the incarnation of the Hindu goddess, Durga), the **Kastha Mandap** (the wooden pavilion from which the city's name is said to have been derived), the tall **Taleju temple**, built in the 16th century and Kathmandu's protective god, the **Black Bhairab**, whose statue is of unknown origin and antiquity. The best time to be here is early in the morning when people are going about their daily pujas.

The authorities charge foreigners an entrance fee of Rs750 to get into the square. While this has raised a number of complaints from travellers, nobody should begrudge paying it – the entire square has, after all, been declared a World Heritage Site by UNESCO and a vast amount of funds are required to restore and maintain the square's many buildings. It's a good idea, having paid the fee, to go straight to the offices lining the southern end of Durbar Square (to the west of the entrance to Freak Street, behind the souvenir market) to convert your entry ticket into a Visitor Pass. You will need one passport photo and your passport. The authorities will then provide you with a pass that will be valid for the duration of your stay in Nepal, and which will allow you to visit Durbar Square as many times as you like for up to a week without further payment.

Baudha (Bodhnath)
This Buddhist stupa is one of the largest in the world. Seven kilometres from the city centre (about Rs400 in a taxi from Thamel), it's a major place of pilgrimage, especially for Tibetans. There's a large Tibetan community here and several monasteries. There's now an entrance fee of Rs250 for foreigners.

From dawn to dusk the faithful make their circumambulations (always in a clockwise direction) under the fluttering prayer-flags and the all-seeing eyes of the giant white stupa. It's a fascinating place to visit, especially at the time of a new or a full moon when there are special festivities. Legend tells of a woman who wanted to build a stupa and asked the king for as much land as the hide of a buffalo could cover. The king agreed and she cut the hide into tiny strips, laying them in a giant square. The king gave her the land, but at the time there was a bad drought. The woman laid sheets of cloth on the ground to collect morning dew to make cement, so Baudha is known as the stupa of a million dewdrops.

Swayambhunath
Offering the best view of Kathmandu and the first place of pilgrimage in the Valley is the Buddhist stupa at Swayambhu. A popular 40-minute walk west from Thamel, this is the best place to watch the sun set on a clear evening. There's now an entrance fee of Rs250 for foreigners.

Mythical creatures guard the entrance steps, while the all-seeing eyes of supreme Buddhahood gaze out over the valley and up to the snowy peaks along the border with Tibet. Statues from the 7th and 8th centuries have been found around the stupa but it is thought to date from a much earlier period. It's also known as the '**Monkey Temple**' on account of the troupes of macaques here. Don't feed them as they can get vicious when your supplies of biscuits run out.

Pashupatinath
Hindu pilgrims come from all over the subcontinent to this Nepalese Varanasi. It's a very extensive complex of temples beside the Bagmati River, 6km from the city centre. You can walk here from Baudha; leaving Baudha, turn left and

cross to the small dirt track squeezed between the buildings on the opposite side of the road (look for the sign saying 'Peace snooker'). It's a 20-minute walk from there (take a right at the fork in the path halfway along). There is an entrance fee of Rs1000.

Pashupatinath is the oldest Hindu site in the Kathmandu valley and derives its fame from the metre-long linga, carved with four faces of Shiva which is kept in the main temple (closed to non-Hindus). The first rites at Pashupati are lost in the haze of time, but it was well established by the time the Lichhavis arrived in the 1st century. The whole complex is dedicated to Shiva and is a focus for sadhus, wandering ascetics, some of whom may have walked here from as far away as south India. As at Varanasi, people perform their early morning ablutions from the ghats here. It's also the most auspicious spot to be cremated in the country. The funeral pyres by the river have become something of a tourist sight, attracting coachloads of scantily-clad foreigners who behave with astounding insensitivity, lenses zooming in on the burning bodies.

Patan

Also known as Lalitpur (meaning City of Beauty), Patan is the oldest of the three main city-states in the Kathmandu Valley but now just a suburb of the capital (Rs500 by taxi from Thamel).

Patan's Durbar Square (Rs750 entrance fee), probably the best collection of late Malla architecture in the country, is rather less touristy than Kathmandu's Durbar Square.

If there's only one museum you visit in Nepal it should be **Patan Museum**, (🖳 www.patanmuseum.gov.np) in the palace compound of Keshav Narayan

---

❏ By road around Kathmandu

If you want to **cycle** and brave the traffic and pollution problems, which get worse each year, there are lots of rental stands around Thamel. No deposit is required; you sign the book and pay the first day's rental. Be sure you check the tyres, brakes, lock and bell before you cycle off. Lock the bike whenever you leave it as you'll be held responsible for its replacement if it gets stolen. If you're renting for more than one day (a good idea as you can keep the bike overnight at your guest house) you can usually negotiate lower daily rates.

A number of places in Thamel, particularly around Thahity Chowk, rent out **motorbikes**, mostly 100-250cc Japanese bikes made under licence in India. A cash deposit is sometimes required, usually they simply want to know where you're staying. You're supposed to have either an international driving licence or a Nepali one.

There are lots of **taxis** but it's difficult to get drivers to use their meters, especially if you pick one up in a tourist district such as Thamel or Durbar Marg. There are also **auto-rickshaws**, metered and costing about a third less than taxis.

Kathmandu's **cycle-rickshaw** wallahs understand just how your delicate Western conscience ticks, so hard bargaining is required if you're going to pay anything like local prices.

There are extensive **bus** routes around the city and out to the airport but this is a very slow and crowded transportation option.

Chowk on Durbar Square. The museum gives an idiot's guide to the Hindu and Buddhist faiths using statues, icons and sculptures from the tenth century onwards. Marvellous stuff. It's open daily except Tuesday; entry is Rs250 for foreigners.

It's also worth visiting **Kumbeshwar Square**. Water in the pond here is said to flow directly from the holy lake of Gosainkund in Langtang. At the north-east corner of the square is **Kumbeshwar Technical School**. Visitors are welcome at this school and orphanage set up to help the lowest castes in the area. Tibetan rugs and sweaters of considerably higher quality than those on sale in Thamel can be purchased here.

Bhaktapur

The third city, Bhaktapur, is a mediaeval gem, visited only fleetingly (if at all) by tourists. Fourteen kilometres east of Kathmandu, it's an almost entirely Newar city that is strongly independent of Kathmandu. Some of the people who live here can't even speak Nepali. Much more than in Kathmandu or Patan, an atmosphere of timelessness pervades this place.

Bhaktapur's main attraction is its **Durbar Square**, with its Palace of Fifty-Five Windows, but here, as in the rest of the city, many buildings have been damaged by earthquakes. Much of the reconstruction work has been done by the Bhaktapur Development Project, a German-sponsored urban renewal programme. To help support further restoration programmes there is a Rs1500 entrance fee, which is expensive but you can really see the benefit throughout Bhaktapur.

It's an hour-long cycle-ride to Bhaktapur from Kathmandu or you can take the electric trolley-bus from Tripureshwar which will drop you across the river, a 15-minute walk from Bhaktapur's Durbar Square. A taxi costs around Rs1200.

Narayanhiti Palace Museum – The Royal Palace

The former palace of King Birendra and the other members of the royal family murdered here in 2001 is now open to the public as Narayanhiti Palace Museum. You're shown round the modern building, finished in 1970, on a guided tour which takes about 1½ hours and includes innumerable stuffed animal trophies, the opulent dining and sitting areas, overgrown gardens and the site of the massacre. Entry costs Rs500.

Nagarkot

The most popular mountain-viewing spot near Kathmandu is Nagarkot, 32km from the city on the road that passes Bhaktapur. Since the view, which includes Everest and four of the other ten highest peaks in the world, is best in the early morning, most people spend the night here. There are, however, tours that leave Kathmandu before dawn to catch the sunrise. You can also get here by taxi (Rs2500), bus from Bhaktapur (2hrs), on foot or by mountain-bike.

KATHMANDU

❏ STAYING ON IN KATHMANDU – LONG STAY TIPS AND IDEAS

If your partner or friend is walking the GHT, they may need someone in Kathmandu to look after logistics such as: crew changeovers, weather reports, trekking permits, food resupply, government departments, plane tickets, and just to be a voice at the end of the phone. You won't be doing all the touristy things, but you won't really be an expat either.

Getting organised
First, make sure that your hotel has **enough space** in your room to store all the stuff you will need to 'keep handy' – spare tents, stoves, clothes – all sorts of things have littered my room over the years. I find a blue plastic barrel handy as I can lock things in it, and use it as a side table as well. If you are buying food to restock, this is the place to keep it. If you can get a room with a balcony, you will be able to air things like down jackets, sleeping bags, boots and tents. Next best option is the rooftop garden of your hotel. Always try to make sure that you stay in a hotel with an outside place inside! Never leave your belongings out overnight.

Negotiate a **'long-term' room rate** with your hotel. Most places are happy to offer discounts to long-termers, and you will find that they are usually willing to do extra little things for you. If you go away for just a few days on a resupply visit, keep your room – it's worth the few dollars you pay while not in it to have everything in the same place when you get back. Just like home – well, it is home for now.

Thamel is the main tourist area and everything is in walking distance, which is a handy feature in a transport strike, but many people prefer the quieter areas like Lazimpat. You should always make sure the room has **good ventilation**, decent **locks** on the doors, and **bars and mosquito mesh** on the windows. Try to avoid ground-floor rooms (monsoon floods or little squeaky visitors are no fun) and if the hotel has a generator try to stay as far away from it as possible. An airy sunny room is your best option, and if you are staying a while you may be able to negotiate a rearrangement or replacement of furniture to suit your needs. Make sure you have **wi-fi and/or cable TV** (even cheap hotels have it these days) and check to see if it is backed up by inverters or battery power when the power cuts begin after the monsoon (ask your hotel for the current schedule). Some of the wi-fi can be fairly unstable, especially if you are trying to video Skype someone. If you are taking the laptop for an outing, remember to take the power lead and adapter/powerboard as many places have outlets at every table. And a word of warning, most Nepali computer owners don't use anti-virus protection. Don't let them use their USB stick in your computer, tell them to email whatever it is to you. Make sure your anti-virus etc is up to date before you leave home.

Many hotels have solar-heated hot water, which is fine until there is no sun for a day or two. During the colder months it's a good idea to purchase an **electric kettle** and a thermos, and borrow a bucket from the hotel. Have the kettle filled and ready to go so that when the power comes on (often at 3am) the water boils and then store it in the thermos till you need it later that morning.

Buy yourself a local **4-point powerboard** so that you can recharge everything at once. Most local boards have universal holes so that any sort of power plug will fit. That way your computer, phone, camera, iPod and whatever else will always be charged. Just get into the habit of plugging everything in every time you're in the room.

If you would prefer an **apartment**, there are many places available, it is just a matter of finding them. Check the local English newspapers, or the magazine *ECS* (though places listed there can be rather expensive), and ask the staff whenever you are somewhere for food or drinks. Almost everyone knows someone that has a room or apartment to rent. You should expect to pay around Rs20,000-35,000 a month for a small unfurnished place; Rs30,000+ furnished. On top of this there will be utilities such as water, electricity, gas bottles for cooking, and the 'didi' (house help) who will come to clean and cook for you. Then you have the cost of buying food to cook (this will keep you busy for quite some time as you generally can't store food for long due to the lack of electricity for the fridge).

If you want to buy anything like a new mattress, sheets etc go to Bag Bazaar and haggle. It may be worth taking a local with you. Beware of the sprung coir mattresses as they get hard and lumpy quite quickly. The best linen is by Bombay Dyeing, and the Korean acrylic blankets with ghastly floral patterns (unless you get the one with the horse on it) are surprisingly warm.

Once you're settled in

Many 'long-termers' hang out in Sam's Bar, Celtic Manang, New Orleans or Tom and Jerry's (all in Thamel) or Upstairs Jazz Bar (Lazimpat) in the evenings and they are a wealth of useful information as well as good company. If you tell people what you are doing and what help you think you need, they are usually happy to offer whatever advice they can. Never leave your room without a small **notebook and pen** as you won't remember everything. Always make sure you have a head torch in your bag or pocket, too. Get yourself some **business cards** – they don't need to be flash but you should make sure they have your local phone number on them.

You will want to be in close discussions with the **trekking agent** who has organised your friend's trip, to make sure that all arrangements are going fine, and that they don't need new permits (the government often introduces new permits part way through a season), tickets, tents or whatever. Depending on the level of service you have requested and paid for, you may need to take a greater role in the forward planning. You will definitely need to have access to US dollars cash for the unexpected things that pop up – extra staff and charter flights are the big dollar items that you need to have money set aside for.

Make sure you know when any major **festivals** are coming – Dashain is the main one, usually in October, when the country effectively shuts down for about 10 days. This is a Hindu festival, so you should still be able to get some Sherpa staff, but don't try to set out anywhere in the days just before the festival as all the buses and planes are booked solid. There are plenty of one-day festivals that you can see in Kathmandu – just check the festival calendar and the local papers, or ask around.

If you stay in Thamel or nearby, most of what you will need to access is within walking distance. Taxis are plentiful but the prices can vary wildly. Always agree on a fare before you jump in. Ask the hotel what a fair price is before you head off. Try not to use the taxis that just cruise around Thamel clogging up the roads. There are a few taxi ranks close by – TriDevi Marg outside the Mountain Hardwear shop – and you get a choice then if you don't like the first quoted price.

At some point you will need to go to the **Immigration Office**, which is inconveniently located in Maitighar – it is a taxi ride from just about anywhere in Kathmandu where you might be staying. Get the driver to wait while you extend your visa and pay the staff the 'express fee' to get your visa in 10 minutes – it is actually cheaper than two taxi rides there and frees you up from having to return later that day.

Judy Smith

KATHMANDU

MOVING ON

By air

Flying in Nepal is the fastest and most convenient method of getting around the country. There are several domestic carriers, all with expert pilots who cope with tricky navigation, rough runways, and the vagaries of mountain weather every day of the week. However, do not expect flying in Nepal to be like a city hop back home; the entire process from booking in, to reclaiming your luggage will appear chaotic and at times quite thrilling!

Since the deregulation of domestic airlines some years ago many operators have started and almost as many have gone out of business. Two which haven't are **Yeti Airlines** (☎ 421 3012, 🖥 www.yetiairlines.com) and **Buddha Air** (☎ 554 2494, 🖥 www.buddhaair.com); both fly daily to Pokhara as well as to a number of other destinations in Nepal.

Other airlines include: **Simrik Airlines** (☎ 410 6691, 🖥 www.simrikair lines.com) which flies at least once daily to Pokhara, Jomsom, Lukla and Bhairahawa; and **Tara Air** (☎ 421 3012, 🖥 www.taraair.com) which, in conjunction with Yeti Airlines, claims to fly to more destinations in Nepal than any other airline; Tara has seven STOL (Short Take-off and Landing) planes and operates both scheduled and charter flights. **Goma Air** (☎ 400 7612, 🖥 www .gomaair.com) operates flights in western Nepal and the airline has a brand new plane for their Lukla flights.

Saurya Airlines (☎ 449 1598, 🖥 www.sauryaairlines.com) started operating in November 2014 and is the first Nepalese airline to use jet aircraft. However, at present they only fly to Biratnagar and Bhairahawa.

The oldest airline is the notoriously unreliable **Nepal Airlines** (☎ 422 0757, 🖥 www.nepalairlines.com.np), though it flies to a number of destinations.

If you are going to need many flights, or you're helping with the logistics of a long trek get to know a good travel agent – one that takes your calls at all sorts of hours and can arrange charter flights (plane or helicopters) at short notice. If there is an accident where someone needs air evacuation, you or your trekking agency will need to be able to deposit about US$7000 as a surety before the helicopter will leave. The going rate for helicopters is around US$2800 an hour but it depends on the size of the helicopter. There are a few helicopter charter businesses now offering custom services throughout the country, and rescue pick-ups for when your luck runs out; see *Rescue and Emergency*, pp69-70.

Fares do not vary a great deal from one airline to another, however, reliability does. Departure tax is included in the fare for all flights. There is a strict luggage allowance on most domestic flights; the maximum for checked-in luggage is generally 10kg and 5kg for hand luggage. It is worth being aware that security luggage checks can occasionally result in opportunistic theft.

Flights are frequently cancelled, delayed, and rescheduled due to bad weather, which can be frustrating. But remember that every year air accidents result in the tragic death of Nepalese and foreigners; it always pays to be patient when flying in Nepal.

Bus services

● **To Pokhara** The easiest way to get to Pokhara is on one of the **tourist buses** that run from Thamel, leaving in the early morning. Tickets can be bought at most travel agents for Rs400 upwards.

Top of the range are the air-con buses operated by Greenline Tours (☎ 425 7544, 🖳 www.greenline.com.np), on the corner of Kantipath and the main road into Thamel. They have daily buses at 07.30 to Pokhara (US$23; 7hrs) and Chitwan (US$20; 5hrs); lunch is included.

More interesting since they're also used by Nepalis, though not necessarily recommended, are the **local buses** which run from the Central Bus Station. Expect to pay about Rs500.

Minibuses to Pokhara (from Rs700) leave every half an hour, beginning at 08.00, with the last at 14.00.

Note that as at March 2014, a national highway development programme has created roadworks on the Pokhara–Kathmandu Highway that can cause long delays, with trips taking 17 hours or more.

● **Other destinations in Nepal and India** From the new bus station there are buses to most towns in Nepal, many departing early in the morning. Avoid the night buses, not only because they don't exactly make for a restful night but also because you'll miss some spectacular views. For Jiri and the Everest region, buses use the old bus station in the centre of town.

If you're going on to India watch out for 'through' tickets. Since everyone has to change into an Indian bus at the border, there's actually no such thing. Travel agents give you a bus ticket to the border and a voucher to exchange with an Indian bus company with whom they've got an arrangement. Since things don't always run as smoothly as they might it's safer, cheaper and just as easy to buy the tickets as you go along. It also gives you a choice of buses and the option to stop off where you want.

The best crossing point into India is via **Sunauli** for Gorakhpur, Varanasi or Delhi. From the main bus station for Sunauli ordinary buses (9-12hrs; about Rs900) leave between 06.00 and 09.00 and there are also night buses (tickets available from the second counter from the right at the new bus station). From Sunauli to Varanasi bus services (9hrs; about Rs600) operate fairly regularly.

For Patna and Kolkatta it's better to go via **Birgunj/Raxaul** (11hrs). Buses leave from the main bus station.

For Darjeeling you'll first have to make the gruelling trip to **Karkabhitta** (12-14hrs; around Rs160) on overnight buses leaving between 15.00 and 16.30.

POKHARA

*In all my travels in the Himalaya I saw no scenery so enchanting as that which
enraptured me at Pokhara.* **Ekai Kawaguchi** *Three Years in Tibet*

Pokhara's superb mountain scenery has been enrapturing foreign visitors since Ekai Kawaguchi, the town's first foreign visitor, came this
way in 1899. Modern travellers are no less impressed; there can be
few other towns that are so close to such high mountains. Pokhara
(pronounced 'POKE-rah') lies at 850m/2789ft yet peaks of over
8000m/26,267ft rise above it in a breathtaking panorama.

Two hundred kilometres (125 miles) west of Kathmandu,
Pokhara is the starting and ending point for most of the treks in the
Annapurna region, except the Annapurna Circuit (usually started
from Besisahar). It's also the perfect place to rest weary limbs after
a trek and the town's relaxed atmosphere causes many travellers to
stay rather longer than they'd originally planned. Along the eastern
shore of Phewa Tal (Lake) a waterside version of Thamel offers
accommodation to suit every budget.

The joy of Pokhara is that there really is very little to do here
except laze around by the lake and over-indulge in those culinary
delights you may have been pining for while away on your trek.

HISTORY

Origins
Probably at the same time that the Kathmandu Valley was a lake
(about 200,000 years ago) the Pokhara Valley was also under water.
Now just a few lakes (tals) remain: Phewa Tal in Pokhara, and
Begnas Tal and Rupa Tal 10km to the east are the largest.

Very little is known about the early history of this area but
Pokhara's location between the mountain passes and the plains has
made it a focal point for peoples from both sides of the Himalaya for
centuries. The area was controlled by numerous small kingdoms,
usually situated on hilltops around the valley, populated by people
who had migrated from Tibet. They were the ancestors of the Gurung
who now live in Pokhara and the surrounding hills.

In the 14th century, Moghul persecution of Hindus in India
forced refugee communities north into Nepal and some settled in the
Pokhara area. Rajput princes from Rajasthan brought their entire
courts and armies with them to carve out their own principalities.
These Indo-Aryans developed the agriculture of the Pokhara Valley

and whilst the high caste Brahmins and Chhetries remained in their mountain strongholds, the lower castes were sent to work the land below.

Shah Rulers of Kaskikot

In the 17th century, Pokhara was being ruled as part of Kaskikot, one of the most powerful of the Chaubise kingdoms in Central Nepal. These Chaubise kings were cousins of the Shah kings of Gorkha (Nepal's last royal family). Kulmandan Shah is the best known of Kaskikot's kings and also the first of the Shahs to rule a Nepalese Kingdom. He is credited with establishing a winter capital in Pokhara and he encouraged trade along the Kali Gandaki Valley through Mustang to Tibet. Mule trains brought salt and wool down from Tibet to exchange for grain from Pokhara.

By the late 18th century the Chaubise kingdoms were no longer closely united. Prithvi Narayan Shah, the king of Gorkha who had conquered the Kathmandu Valley, turned his attention west to these kingdoms, sweeping through with his powerful army to conquer Kaskikot in 1785. In the period of peace and stability that followed Pokhara quickly grew to become the major trading town in the region.

The Ranas

Although the Rana prime ministers who ruled Nepal from 1846 to 1950 could claim ancestral connections to the Kaskikot area, only Jung Bahadur, the first of the Ranas, showed any particular interest in the region, declaring himself Maharaja of Kaski and Lamjung. None of the Ranas ever visited the Pokhara area.

Under the Ranas, Pokhara became the capital of Kaski and Lamjung districts. That there are few old buildings to see in Pokhara today is the result of a devastating earthquake in 1934, and in 1948 of a fire offering being made by a priest in the Bindyabasini temple that got out of control and reduced much of the town to ashes.

Pokhara since 1950

Until the middle of the 20th century, the only way to reach Pokhara from Kathmandu was on foot, a six- or seven-day journey. In 1951 the airfield was built but it was not until 1973 that the road linking Pokhara with the capital was finished. By the turn of the century another major communications project, the Pokhara–Baglung–Beni highway, was complete, and by 2008 a dirt road had been constructed from Beni all the way to Jomsom. While some argue that the road has improved communications to the valley's remote communities there is no doubt that it has had a very damaging effect on the Kali Gandaki valley as a trekking destination, as is evident from the sudden drop in trekker numbers and the boarded up lodges and teahouses.

Improved communications brought people from the surrounding villages to swell the town's population from just 5400 in 1961 to over 200,000 in 2008. The Chinese invasion of Tibet in 1951 brought 15,000 exiles to Nepal, many to Pokhara. Dervla Murphy spent some time working with Tibetan refugees in the 1960s and *The Waiting Land: A Spell in Nepal* provides an interesting description both of her experiences and of a Pokhara before apple pie and chocolate cake were being served on the shores of Phewa Tal. Numerous international aid agencies now have their regional headquarters in Pokhara.

Pokhara is the main recruiting area in Nepal for troops for the Gurkha regiments in the British and Indian armies. Together with tourism, army wages and pensions form the mainstay of the local economy. In recent times, the Gurkha contingent in the British army has decreased, however, tourism growth has more than compensated despite the negative impact of the Maoist insurgency.

Since the end of the Maoist struggles in 2007 and the slow road to political stability, Pokhara's fortunes have improved. Investment in tourism facilities is increasing and construction sites are popping up all over the expanding city. This once sleepy backwater is rapidly developing as the vibrant multi-adventure hub of Nepal.

ORIENTATION

The lake is the main focus for travellers. It's on the western edge of town and there are two main accommodation areas here, Lakeside (Baidam) and Damside (Pardi). Lakeside is one long strip of hotels, guest houses, restaurants and shops with more places to stay up the paths among the trees. Damside is the smaller district beside Pardi Dam, to the south of the lake.

The airport and bus station are also in the southern half of the town, a long walk or a short taxi ride from the lake.

In the centre of Pokhara is the modern town; the old bazaar is to the north. Pokhara is a surprisingly spread-out town, sprawling for several kilometres down an incline that is unnoticeable until you try to ride your gearless Indian Hero from the lake to the bazaar.

WHERE TO STAY

There is no shortage of accommodation options in Pokhara so you shouldn't have any difficulty finding a place to stay. A lot are simple guest houses with just a few rooms, many run by ex-Gurkhas, but there are also upmarket options. As in Kathmandu many places have rooms for a range of budgets so do look in all the categories.

It is often possible to have an extra bed put in the room but be aware this may not always be a real bed so if this is important to you check when you are booking. Also many places can book treks and adventure activities.

Although there is some accommodation near the bus station and in the centre of Pokhara, everyone heads for the lake. Not surprisingly therefore **Lakeside** has the greatest choice of places to stay and almost all the restaurants and shops. Many of the cheaper places lie at the northern and southern ends of Lakeside, and there are a few which stand on the western side of the road overlooking the lake. *(continued on p102)*

POKHARA

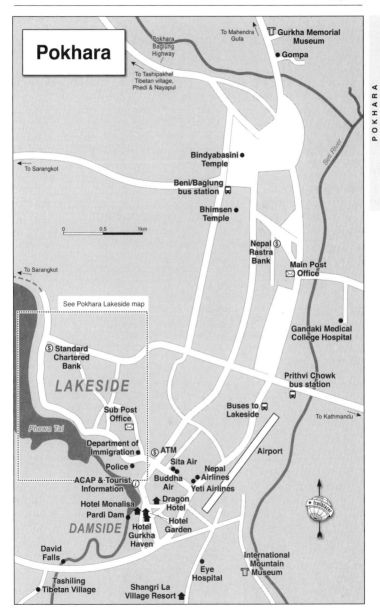

Pokhara

To Mahendra Gufa

Pokhara Baglung Highway

To Tashipakhel Tibetan village, Phedi & Nayapul

Gurkha Memorial Museum
● Gompa

Seti River

To Sarangkot

Bindyabasini Temple ●

Beni/Baglung bus station

Bhimsen Temple ●

0   0.5   1km

To Sarangkot

See Pokhara Lakeside map

Nepal Rastra Bank ⑤

Main Post Office ✉

Gandaki Medical College Hospital ●

⑤ Standard Chartered Bank

LAKESIDE

Prithvi Chowk bus station

Phewa Tal

Sub Post Office ✉

Department of Immigration ●

⑤ ATM

Police ●

Sita Air ●

ACAP & Tourist Information ⓘ

Buddha Air ●

Nepal Airlines ●

Yeti Airlines ●

Buses to Lakeside

Airport

To Kathmandu

Hotel Monalisa
Pardi Dam ●

Dragon Hotel ●

Hotel Gurkha Haven ●

Hotel Garden ●

DAMSIDE

David Falls ●

Tashiling
● Tibetan Village

Eye Hospital ●

Shangri La Village Resort ●

International Mountain Museum

★ trailblazer

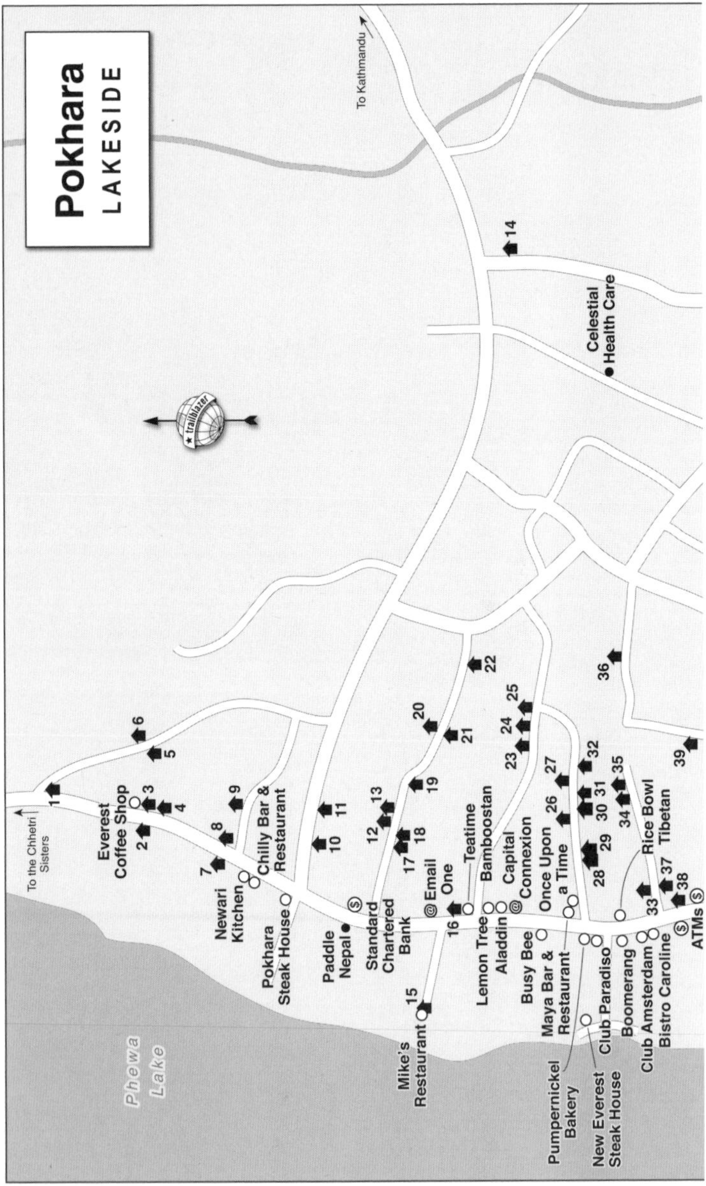

POKHARA

Pokhara
LAKESIDE

To Kathmandu

To the Chhetri Sisters

Phewa Lake

Celestial Health Care

Everest Coffee Shop

Newari Kitchen

Pokhara Steak House

Chilly Bar & Restaurant

Paddle Nepal

Standard Chartered Bank

Teatime

Bamboostan

Email One

Aladdin

Capital Connexion

Once Upon a Time

Rice Bowl

Tibetan

Lemon Tree

Busy Bee

Maya Bar & Restaurant

Club Paradiso

Boomerang

Club Amsterdam

Bistro Caroline

Mike's Restaurant

Pumpernickel Bakery

New Everest Steak House

ATMs

1 2 3 4 5 6 7 8 9 10 11 12 13 14 15 16 17 18 19 20 21 22 23 24 25 26 27 28 29 30 31 32 33 34 35 36 37 38 39

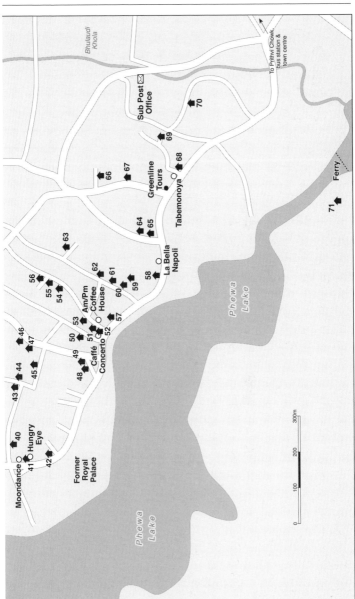

POKHARA

Bhulaudi Khola

To Prithvi Chowk, bus station & town centre

Sub Post Office

70

69

66 67

Greenline Tours 68

Tabemonoya

64 65

63

62 61

56 58

55 54 59

Am/Pm 60

53 Coffee House

46 50 51 57

47 52 Concerto

44 49 La Bella Napoli

43 45 48 Caffé

40

Hungry Eye

41 42

Moondance

Former Royal Palace

Phewa Lake

Ferry

71

Phewa Lake

0 100 200 300m

(continued from p98) **Damside** is quieter and it has better views of the mountains; many of the guest houses here also have dining rooms so you don't have to go to Lakeside to eat.

Wherever you are it is worth paying a little bit extra to have a room with a view over the lake and the mountains; if your budget doesn't stretch to this look for places with a rooftop garden.

Rates

Hotels and guesthouses here generally quote their rates in US dollars ($) though you are likely to pay in rupees; a number of places now accept payment using one of the major credit cards.

The rates quoted in this book are for single (**sgl**), double (**dbl**), and triple (**tpl**) rooms and are given as a guide only – many factors affect what you will actually pay: intense competition means you can find bargain accommodation in all price brackets. For the cheaper places you may get 20-40% off but for mid-range hotels you might be able to get a larger discount, depending on how many people are chasing rooms at the time.

A 13% government tax and 10% service charge is payable on most accommodation but make sure you ascertain whether this is included in the agreed price.

Cheap accommodation (up to US$20/£12)

Several of the hotels which used to offer rooms for just a few dollars a night spruced them up and increased their prices; thus it is harder to get budget accommodation. The lower rates are generally for rooms with common bathrooms.

Peace Eye GH [54] (☎ 461699, 🖳 www.peaceeye-guesthouse.com; Rs600-1200) has friendly, helpful staff, clean rooms, a quiet location, and serves good food in its restaurant.

For a very central location as well as friendly, helpful staff try *Pushpa GH* [26] (☎ 984-646 5974, 🖳 pushpapokhara@hotmail.com; sgl $12, dbl $15).

Also with an excellent location and highly recommended is *Sacred Valley Inn* [42] (☎ 461792, 🖳 www.sacredvalleyinn.com; $6-30). It is an efficiently run place with a variety of lovely clean rooms, some with mountain views.

For clean rooms and a quiet location consider *The Mountain House* [22] (☎ 465015, 🖳 pokhara-guesthouse.com; rooms $15-25). The popular *Hotel Noble Inn* [34] (☎ 464926, 🖳 www.nobleinn.com; sgl $12-17, dbl $14-24, tpl $22-32, extra bed $7-10) has large and well-kept grounds.

Nanohana Lodge [67] (☎ 464478, 🖳 www.nanohanalodge.com; rooms $12-35) lacks large grounds, but has some lovely views from the balconies for the rooms on the upper floors.

The manager of the aptly named *New Solitary Lodge* [14] (☎ 461804, 🖳 www.newsolitarylodge.com; sgl $8-30, dbl $12-40, tpl $15-50), a hotel right on the eastern edge of Lakeside, is justifiably proud of the rooms and the tranquillity of his hotel, though some may find it a little too far from the lake to be ideal.

POKHARA

ACCOMMODATION IN POKHARA – Keyed to map on pp100-1

1	Hotel Tropicana
2	Phil's Inn
3	Pokhara Village Resort
4	Hotel Crown
5	Hotel Yokohama
6	Hotel Tibet Home
7	Hotel Peace Plaza
8	Hotel Blue Heaven
9	Hotel Mandala
10	Little Tibetan GH
11	Fairmount Hotel
12	Hotel Celesty Inn
13	Tranquility Lodge
14	New Solitary Lodge
15	Hotel Fewa
16	Hotel Monal
17	Hotel Khukuri
18	Butterfly Lodge
19	Temple Villa
20	The Silver Oaks Inn
21	The North Face Inn
22	The Mountain House
23	Hotel Stupa
24	Hotel Lake Palace
25	Hotel River Park
26	Pushpa GH
27	Nepali Cottage GH
28	Hotel Lake Diamond
29	Vardan Resort
30	Hotel Travel Inn
31	Hotel Serenity
32	Unique Mountain GH
33	Hotel Tulsi Pokhara
34	Hotel Noble Inn
35	Hotel Fishtail Villa
36	Harvest Moon GH
37	Hotel ABC
38	Hotel Snowland
39	Hotel Family Home
40	Hotel Barahi
41	Hotel Landmark
42	Sacred Valley Inn
43	Green Tara Hotel
44	Hotel Panorama
45	Blue Planet Lodge
46	Hotel Himalayan Star
47	Placid Valley Lodge
48	Karma GH
49	Hotel Nirvana
50	Hotel View Point
51	Broadway Inn
52	Hotel Glacier
53	Gauri Shankar
54	Peace Eye GH
55	Rustika GH)
56	Shanti GH
57	Trek-O-Tel
58	Mount Kailash Resort
59	Moonlight Resort
60	Lake View Resort
61	Temple Tree Resort & Spa
62	Hotel Grand Holiday
63	Blue Heaven GH
64	Hotel Yeti
65	Hotel Bedrock
66	Mum's Garden Resort
67	Nanohana Lodge
68	Baba Lodge
69	New Pokhara Lodge
70	New Annapurna GH
71	Fish Tail Lodge

Damside (see map p99)
- Hotel Monalisa
- Hotel Gurkha Haven
- Hotel Garden
- Dragon Hotel

If you're a woman travelling on your own, ***Chhetri Sisters' Guest House*** (🖳 www.3sistersadventuretrek.com) is particularly recommended. Run by Lucky, Dicky and Nicky, the guesthouse is in the north of Lakeside, along the road that runs parallel to the lake. Double rooms with breakfast cost $12-25 (shared bathroom) and $15-30 en suite ($8-15 & $10-20 for single occupancy). They also run a trekking agency for women (see p110).

The following places also have rooms in this price bracket and are **keyed to the map on pp100-1**.

1 Hotel Tropicana (☎ 462118, 🖳 www .hoteltropicana.com.np) rooms $15-25

2 Phil's Inn (☎ 462009, 🖳 www.phil .rinnet.de) sgl $15-20, dbl $20-25

4 Hotel Crown (☎ 464821, 🖳 hotel crownpokhara.com) rooms $15-20

10 Little Tibetan GH (☎ 531898) sgl $8-10, dbl $10-15

12 Hotel Celesty Inn (☎ 984 602 0486) sgl $12, dbl $20

13 Tranquility Lodge (☎ 463030, 🖳 bai dam.com/tranquility.htm) sgl $10, dbl $15

POKHARA

19   Temple Villa (☎ 521203) rooms $10-25
17   Hotel Khukuri (☎ 462110, 🖳 hotel khukuripokhara.com) rooms $10-15
27   Nepali Cottage GH (☎ 461637) sgl $10-15, dbl $15-20
28   Hotel Lake Diamond (☎ 462064) sgl $12, dbl $20
30   Hotel Travel Inn (☎ 462631, 🖳 www .hoteltravelin.com) rooms from $15
31   Hotel Serenity (☎ 463098, 🖳 www .hotelserenitypokhara.com) rooms $10-17
32   Unique Mountain GH (☎ 532720) rooms $12-25

49   Hotel Nirvana (☎ 463332) sgl $15, dbl $20
48   Karma GH (☎ 984 604 9867) sgl $12, dbl $15
51   Broadway Inn (☎ 465796, 🖳 www .hotelbroadwayinn.com.np) sgl $10-15, dbl $15-20
53   Gauri Shankar (☎ 462422, 🖳 www .gaurishankar.com) dorm Rs200, sgl Rs600-1200, dbl Rs750-1500, tpl Rs1800
55   Rustika GH (☎ 465138) rooms $10-25
56   Shanti GH (☎ 463645) dorm $6; sgl $8-12, dbl $12-20

Lower mid-range (US$20-50/£12-32)

A way to avoid the crowds is to go for a hotel with a big garden, of which there are plenty to choose from. *Hotel ABC* [37] (☎ 461934, 🖳 www.hotelabc.com .np; sgl $22, dbl $28) is run by an affable man whose pride and joy is his lovely, well-kept garden.

The popular *Hotel Yokohama* [5] (☎ 466651, 🖳 www.yokohamapokhara .com; sgl $18, dbl $25-40, tpl $30-36) is in a great location and provides good breakfasts. The friendly *Hotel Tibet Home* [6] (☎ 463101, 🖳 www.hotel tibethome.com; sgl $20-35, dbl $26-45, tpl $34-41), also at the northern end of Lakeside, is one of many places owned by a former soldier in the British Army Gurkhas. The hotel boasts rooms with bath tub, TV, phone and mountain views.

Also in a good location and almost opposite each other are: *The Silver Oaks Inn* [20] (☎ 462147, 🖳 hotelpokhara.com; sgl $25-40, dbl $30-50, tpl $35-508), where you can expect a good breakfast and comfortable rooms; and *The North Face Inn* [21] (☎ 464987, 🖳 www.northfaceinn.com; dbl $25-55, tpl $30), where in addition to the rooms in the main building there are two cottages each sleeping up to three people. The grounds here are lovely and the service is good.

Vardan Resort [29] (☎ 985-602 0241 or ☎ 465830, 🖳 www.vardanresort .com; cottages sgl $24-35, dbl $29-42, tpl $35-49, apartments $60-99) also has cottages but more unusually its rooms are self-catering apartments; the accommodation is clean and the service friendly. Vardan gives 10% of its profits to support kids at a school in Lalitpur.

Hotel Family Home [39] (☎ 463024, 463005, 🖳 www.familyhomepokhara .com; rooms $40-55) has clean rooms and helpful staff.

New Annapurna Guest House [70] (☎ 465011, 🖳 newannapurna.com; sgl €14-25, dbl €18-44, extra bed €4-8) is in a pleasant, intimate little spot set back from the lake at the far southern end of the lake; there are great views from here.

New Pokhara Lodge [69] (☎ 462493, 🖳 www.pokharalodge.com; sgl $20-45, dbl $27-60) is also recommended; the rooms on the top floor have a mountain view, but there is also a rooftop terrace and breakfast can be eaten in the garden.

The following places also have rooms in this price bracket and are **keyed to the map on pp100-1**.

8 Hotel Blue Heaven (☎ 461450, 🖳 www.hotelblueheaven.com.np) sgl $15-25, dbl $20-30, tpl $30-35

9 Hotel Mandala (☎ 464690, 🖳 www.hotelmandala.com.np) sgl $15, dbl $20, tpl $30

11 Fairmount Hotel (☎ 463252, 🖳 www.hotelfairmount.com) sgl $20-30, dbl $25-40

16 Hotel Monal (☎ 461459, 🖳 www.monal-zorba.com) rooms $30-40

23 Hotel Stupa (☎ 462608, 🖳 www.hotelstupa.com) sgl $47, dbl $72, tpl $90

24 Hotel Lake Palace (☎ 462027) sgl $46, dbl $50, suite $60

25 Hotel River Park (☎ 462756, 🖳 www.hotelriverpark.com.np) sgl $30-70, dbl $40-70

35 Hotel Fishtail Villa (☎ 462451) sgl $17, dbl $24, tpl $30

36 Harvest Moon GH (☎ 462647) sgl $16, dbl $26

38 Hotel Snowland (☎ 462384, 🖳 www.hotelsnowlandpokhara.com) sgl $45-70, dbl $55-80

43 Green Tara Hotel (☎ 462698, 🖳 www.greentarahotel.com) rooms from $20

44 Hotel Panorama (☎ 463763, 🖳 www.hotelpanorama.com.np) sgl $20-30, dbl $30-40

45 Blue Planet Lodge (☎ 465706, 🖳 www.blueplanetlodge.com) rooms €20-40, apartment for €45; singles 10% discount

46 Hotel Himalayan Star (☎ 463846, www.hotelhimalayanstar.com) sgl $25-40, dbl $35-50, tpl $45-60

47 Placid Valley Lodge (☎ 465193, 🖳 placidvalleylodge.com.np) sgl $30-35, dbl $40-45, tpl $40-45

50 Hotel View Point (☎ 464648, 🖳 www.hviewpoint.com) sgl $30-40, dbl $40-50, tpl $50-60

63 Blue Heaven GH (☎ 461450, 🖳 www.hotelblueheaven.com.np) sgl $15-25, dbl $20-30, tpl $30-35

64 Hotel Yeti (☎ 462768, 🖳 www.hotelyeti.com.np) sgl $15-23, dbl $21-32

65 Hotel Bedrock (☎ 465524, 🖳 www.hotelbedrock.com) sgl $18-40, dbl $25-48

68 Baba Lodge (☎ 462997, 🖳 baba-lodge.com) rooms from $20

Damside (see map p99)
● Hotel Monalisa (☎ 463863, 🖳 www.hotelmonalisa.com.np) sgl $20-40, dbl $30-50
● Hotel Gurkha Haven (☎ 464527, 🖳 gurkhahaven.com) sgl $30-40, dbl $35-45
● Hotel Garden (☎ 463681, 🖳 www.hotel-garden-nepal.co.uk) rooms $25-70
● Dragon Hotel (☎ 460391, 🖳 dragonhotelgrp.com) rooms $35-80

Higher mid-range (US$50-80/£32-52)
Several recommended places in this category are at the southern end of Lakeside. *Trek-O-tel* [57] (☎ 464996, 🖳 www.acehotelsnepal.com/trekotel; sgl/dbl $50/70, extra bed $20) has a neatly manicured front lawn. All the rooms have a bathtub.

Hotel Grand Holiday [62] (☎ 984-505 0480, ☎ 462967, 🖳 hotelgrandholiday.com; sgl $40-53, dbl $53-67, tpl $67, quad $80) has a rooftop balcony which is great for views. The rooms are a good size and the service here is friendly and welcoming.

Lake View Resort [60] (☎ 461477, 🖳 www.pokharahotels.com; sgl $45, dbl $50) has a range of rooms including huts which sleep up to three people; this is the place to come if you would like to learn more about the Nepalese performing arts as there is a show every night.

Mum's Garden Resort [66] (☎ 463468, 🖳 www.mumsgardenresort.com; rooms sgl $55, dbl $65), one of the more charming places in Lakeside, is tucked away in secluded splendour. Constructed out of hand-cut stone, all the rooms have a terrace with mountain views, and twin beds.

The following places also have rooms in this price bracket and are **keyed to the map on pp100-1**.

3 Pokhara Village Resort (☎ 462427, 🖳 www.pokharavillage.com) sgl $38-65, dbl $48-85

7 Hotel Peace Plaza (☎ 461505, 🖳 www.hotelpeaceplaza.com) rooms from $55

15 Hotel Fewa (☎ 463151) sgl $62, dbl $72-84)

18 Butterfly Lodge (☎ 461892, 🖳 www.butterfly-lodge.org) sgl $50-70, dbl $60-80

52 Hotel Glacier (☎ 463722, 🖳 www.glaciernepal.com) sgl $38-46, dbl $48-56, quad $70

59 Moonlight Resort (☎ 465704, 🖳 www.pokharamoonlight.com) sgl $50, dbl $70

Expensive (US$80/£52 plus)

The centrally located *Hotel Landmark* [41] (☎ 462908, 🖳 www.landmarkpokhara.com; sgl $106-143, dbl $118-155) is a pleasant place to stay; there can be attractive discounts on the rooms so check online. There's also good food in its Hungry Eye restaurant.

Hotel Barahi [40] (☎ 460617, 🖳 www.barahi.com; sgl $115, dbl $145, extra bed $55) is surrounded by large grounds and has its own swimming pool.

The old favourite, and another place with a pool, is *Fish Tail Lodge* [71] (☎ 465071, 🖳 www.fishtail-lodge.com; sgl $170, dbl $180, tpl $215); its main attraction is its superb location on the southern side of the lake; it's worth visiting just for the wonderful view of the mountain panorama reflected in the water. It's also set in well-kept gardens and is reached by raft across a narrow stretch of the lake.

Temple Tree Resort & Spa [61] (☎ 465819, 🖳 www.templetreenepal.com; sgl $160, dbl $180, suite $200, extra bed $40) is arguably the best in the class in Pokhara.

Shangri La Village Resort [see map p99] (☎ 462222, 🖳 www.hotelshangrila.com) has great mountain views from the swimming pool but is set away from the lake.

Other places to consider are: *Hotel Tulsi Pokhara* [33] (☎ 462895, 🖳 www.hoteltulsipokhara.com; sgl $67-77, dbl $94-114) and *Mount Kailash Resort* [58] (☎ 465703, 🖳 www.mountkailashresort.com; sgl $128, dbl $136) which is centrally located and by the lake. It is also a modern hotel with good-sized rooms.

A 10-minute drive from Lakeside and on the northern shore at **Pame** is *Waterfront Resort Hotel* (☎ 466303, 🖳 www.waterfronthotelnepal.com; sgl $120-200, dbl $145-200). The hotel is part of the Kathmandu Guesthouse Group and is very comfortable and situated right on the lake. They provide a free shuttle service back to Lakeside.

WHERE TO EAT

Calorie after delicious calorie lines the main street of Lakeside, from the cake shops laden with waist-expanding chocolate croissants, to the larger establishments offering ever more scrumptious ways of putting the wobble back in your walk after weeks on the trail. It's difficult to give specific recommendations for restaurants: things change so fast. Some of the old favourites are listed below.

Breakfast

Many guest houses have a limited breakfast menu including porridge, muesli, toast and eggs. There's also great competition amongst the restaurants along Lakeside to provide all-inclusive breakfast specials. These range from Rs100 for a (more than adequate) set meal of eggs, toast, hash browns, tomatoes, and coffee, up to Rs120 or more for an 'American' or 'Trekkers Special' – a huge feast that usually includes steak. Some of the best bowls of muesli and curd with fruit is served by the numerous small fresh fruits stalls.

One place that's often recommended for its breakfasts, and also for its location, is *Mike's Restaurant*. If you want something simple like a roll and coffee there are several bakeries along the main road in Lakeside. They are not quite up to the standards of Thamel bakeries, yet, though there is a branch of Kathmandu's *Pumpernickel Bakery* in Pokhara.

The tiny *AM/PM Coffee House* is also good and they do half-decent coffee. For organic coffee head to *Moondance* (🖥 moondancepokhara.com); Moondance sources a lot of its ingredients from its own farm.

For a post-trek celebratory breakfast binge try one of the top hotels since they often have all-you-can-eat breakfasts; you should phone first to check, though.

Lunch and supper

● **Western/Have-a-go-at-anything** 'Tourist-friendly' restaurants now proliferate on Lakeside's main street. Characterised by thatched roofs and Western music, a new addition to one restaurant's menu is quickly emulated by the other restaurants here, thus most menus now look decidedly similar. That said, the food is usually of a fairly high standard, the attempts at copying different national cuisines continue to achieve higher levels of authenticity – and the beer's always cold. Most places have video screenings to entice customers in.

One restaurant that is consistently recommended is *Once Upon A Time*, particularly favoured by Westerners living here.

A number of other places on this main central drag, such as *Moondance* (see above) and *Lemon Tree*, have similar fare; the latter also does the most exquisite banana smoothies in Pokhara.

Further north, the long-established *Teatime Bamboostan* is still going strong and the food isn't bad at all. *Maya Pub & Restaurant* has an extensive menu and the food is generally good; it is worth going up to the second floor for the views.

Many restaurants have gardens stretching down to the lake. Very pleasant in the early evening as the egrets swoop by, it is also possible to get some decent nosh, provided the mosquitoes don't devour you completely first. *Boomerang* (🖳 www.boomerangrestaurantpokhara.com) is good, as is *Bistro Caroline*, a French restaurant with a lovely little back garden. *Mike's Restaurant* (see p107) may be known for its breakfasts but serves good food throughout the day.

The popular *New Everest Steak House* (400g for Rs700, 600g for Rs1000) is a branch of the Kathmandu restaurant. There is a cheaper steak house, *Pokhara Steak House*, further up the road where the food is very good and the staff friendly.

Chilly Bar & Restaurant (🖳 www.chillybar.com.np) has lovely exclusive balconies that look out to the lake. The menu covers a range of world cuisines and the food is good.

As you might expect, the top hotels have good restaurants.

● **Italian** The best Italian food is served at *Caffè Concerto*, in south Lakeside. There are pizzas, fresh pasta, gnocchi and even tiramisu. *La Bella Napoli* offers similar fare but also has Nepali dishes.

● **Nepali/Tibetan** Opposite Boomerang is *Rice Bowl Tibetan* with reasonable food and live music. *Newari Kitchen* (🖳 newarikitchen.com.np) offers typical Newari dishes.

● **Chinese** *Lan Hua*, in the south of Lakeside, is an authentic place with a wide choice on the menu. A large selection of Chinese food can actually be found at many of the places here. Usually these are just variations on fried rice, but are nevertheless tasty and filling.

● **Japanese** *Tabemonoya* (🖳 www.tabemonoya-nepal.com), at the south-eastern end of Lakeside, offers standard Japanese fare.

● **Indian** Most of the restaurants make fair attempts at Mughal and Tandoori dishes. *The Hungry Eye* in Hotel Landmark (see p106), in central Lakeside, is worth trying.

● **Vegetarian** All restaurants have some vegetarian dishes.

NIGHTLIFE

Try *Club Amsterdam* in Lakeside; there's live music most nights and it's open late. They do cocktails, serve bar snacks, such as fried chicken, and there's a pool table. Another place with live music and a pool table is *Busy Bee Bar & Restaurant*; locals may also come here. *Maya Pub & Restaurant* (see p107) is a smaller and quieter affair, though the beer's just as cold and there is still some live music. These places are open during the day, too.

There are **cultural shows** at several hotels. Tickets are sold at the hotels or in some travel agents and bookshops.

SERVICES

Banks
Standard Chartered Bank has a branch on Lakeside with an ATM; they will also do cash advances on Visa or MasterCard. There is a branch of **Nepal Rastra Bank** near the main post office.

There are **exchange counters** dotted all the way along the main drag; they all seem to offer exactly the same rates, too, though in the early morning there are some differences between them, depending on whether they have managed to hear the new rates yet. As a result, this may be the best time to change money with them. None of the moneychangers charges commission. Doublecheck your money here as shortchanging always seems to work in their favour.

Bookshops
As in Kathmandu, there's no difficulty in finding something to read here with numerous bookshops and kiosks in the Lakeside area. They stock new and second-hand titles and most operate book exchanges.

Communications
● **Wi-fi/internet access** Most hotels and many restaurants offer wi-fi and/or internet access; the service is generally reliable and either free or cheap. However, if you have problems or are travelling without a laptop or phone there are some internet centres along Lakeside, which charge a fixed rate. If you are staying on Lakeside, Capital Connexion is the friendliest of the internet cafés, and offers a **photocopying** service, too.
● **Post** The main post office (GPO; Sun-Thur summer 10am-5pm, winter 10am-4pm, Fri to 3pm) is a long bike ride into the centre of town. The sub post office in Lakeside has the same opening hours.
● **Phone and fax** In Lakeside and Damside it's easiest to use the phones in guesthouses, shops and kiosks for international calls; some of the internet cafés also offer internet phone calls, though they charge more than Kathmandu and the service is generally even less efficient. There are many **fax** facilities in Pokhara and most hotels will be willing to send faxes for a fee.

Left luggage
As in Kathmandu, most hotels and guest houses will store excess baggage free of charge, as long as you promise to spend at least one night more there on your return. Keep all valuables with you, though.

Medical clinics
Gandaki Medical College Hospital (☎ 538595, ▭ www.gmc.edu.np) is a teaching hospital and is based near the main post office. If you're hospitalised in Pokhara you may need a friend to bring you food and help look after you as nursing is minimal. Unless, that is, you are staying at **Celestial Health Care** (see map p110; ▭ celestialhealthcare.com). Situated on the edge of Lakeside, this is a plush clinic with beds for 40 people, with each room furnished with TV and bathtub. A one-off $30 consultation fee covers all medicines and any further consultations. Call outs with medication cost $60, while overnight stays should be covered by your travel insurer.

CIWEC (☎ 463082, ▭ ciwec-clinic.com/ciwec-pokhara) has opened a clinic in Pokhara behind Hotel Meera. It is open 24 hours a day, 365 days a year. Payment is expected on the day of treatment and can be made by cash, credit

card or through your insurance policy as long as the insurance company has
guaranteed the payment.

Himalaya Eye Hospital (🖥 www.heh.org.np) treats foreigners needing
specialist eye treatment for a nominal fee. Staffed by one Dutch and two Nepali
opthalmologists it's to the south of the airport.

Shopping

Pokhara is the perfect place to browse and there are rows of kiosks and small
shops in which to do it. However, all the goods on sale here are also available
in Kathmandu and it may be more convenient to do your shopping there.

Few travellers, though, escape the pushy charms of the Tibetan curio-sellers
who work the streets in pairs with considerable success.

You can watch carpets being woven at Tashiling and Tashi Palkhiel Tibetan
villages. Prices here can also be better than in the tourist shops in Lakeside.

Also worth visiting is the group of thangka shops just north of Lakeside,
near Pokhara Village Resort. Another place to check out is the excellent
Dhukuti, which sells local crafts – knitwear, brassware, crockery and cutlery –
at reasonable prices.

For supplies the grocery shops in Lakeside (Safeway, 7to7, 7Eleven, etc)
stock everything a trekker could wish for. Alternatively there is a branch of
Bhatbhateni supermarket and department store on New Rd.

Some of the bakeries sell delicious wholegrain trekking bread too. It's
worth pointing out, however, that for most treks you really don't need to stock
up on anything.

Trekking agencies

There are several agencies (and hotels) here who will happily organise a complete trek, should you want their services.

To hire a porter, it's usually cheaper to cut out the middleman and arrange
things yourself. See pp53-7 for more information.

If you're a woman looking for a female crew, or a female-only trek, contact
Chhetri Sisters' Guest House (see p103). They are also happy to arrange a range
of adventure activities; see their website for details.

Trekking equipment rental

As in Kathmandu, it's possible to rent most things from down jackets to sleeping-
bags but don't expect any fancy climbing gear.

Annapurna entry permits

The **ACAP desk** (daily 10am-5pm) is in the **tourist information office** in
Damside. Permits for entry into the Annapurna Conservation Area cost Rs2000,
which is half the price of the same permit bought at one of the offices on the
trails (which may or may not still be selling them by the time you read this).

Next to the ACAP desk is the TIMS (trekkers information management system) desk. You need to get a **TIMS** card from here, which is free, before you
set off on your trek. For both the ACAP entry permit and the TIMS card you
will need to show your passport and bring along two passport photos for each.

It's possible to turn up in Pokhara, get your ACAP permit and TIMS card and get at least as far as Birethanti in the same day. It's not yet possible to get visas for the north Mustang area here; you need to get this from the immigration office.

Visa extensions
Since April 2014 all visa extensions are meant to be done online (⌨ www .online.nepalimmigration.gov.np/tourist-visa). However, it seems this doesn't always work so you may well need to go to the Immigration Office (☎ 465167; Sun-Fri 10.30am-3pm) which is now more conveniently located in Lakeside. In general it seems it is much easier to extend visas here than in Kathmandu. Do bring your passport, a spare photo and some money though.

Transport
Taxi Some taxis have meters but most are meterless and you pay as much as the driver thinks you will stand.

Between the airport or bus station and Lakeside you probably won't get away with paying less than Rs250; however if you have booked accommodation you may get a free pick-up.

Bus Local buses are based at Prithvi Chowk Bus Station (Bus Park) in the centre of town. Buses run from here to Lakeside, to the airport, and to Besi Bus Park (for buses to Nayapul for Birethanti etc).

Bicycle and motorbike The best way to get around Pokhara is by **bicycle**. There are lots of places to rent them from and prices are around Rs100-300 a day; if you want to explore further afield expect to pay considerably more for a Western mountain bike.

In Lakeside you can rent **motorbikes**; an Indian Escort RX100 (licence-built Yamaha) costs around Rs600 per day. You will need a driving licence and your passport will be kept as surety.

WHAT TO SEE AND DO
Resting on or beside Phewa Tal is possibly the number one activity in Pokhara for locals and tourists alike. There are not many major sights to visit but there are plenty of things to do if you want to explore.

Mountain viewing
The Pokhara panorama is undeniably impressive and dawn is the best time to view it. Fish Tail Lodge is the best place to view it from. Machhapuchhre is the most easily recognisable peak; from Pokhara it has a classic pointed shape; it looks like a fish tail only from the north.

From left to right the major peaks you can see from Pokhara are Dhaulagiri (8167m/26,795ft), Annapurna I (8091m/26,545ft), Machhapuchhre (6993m/22,942ft), Annapurna III (7555m/24,767ft) – shaped like an elephant, Annapurna IV (7525m/24,688ft) and Annapurna II (7937m/26,041ft).

P O K H A R A

Museums and exhibitions

To the south of the airport the huge **International Mountain Museum** (⌨ www.internationalmountainmuseum.org; daily 9am-5pm, Rs400), housed inside what appears to be an enormous hangar, is a project managed by the Nepal Mountaineering Association; exhibits include actual gear used in ascents (particularly for the mountains in Nepal that are over 8000m) as well as photos and information about the peoples and flora and fauna. There is also a section about the impact of climate change.

Gurkha Memorial Museum (⌨ gurkhamuseum.org.np; Rs200, daily 8am-4.30pm) is at the northern end of Pokhara near the Seti Gorge (see Pokhara map p99). It has pictures of various renowned Gurkhas, their uniforms, and the medals they have won serving the Indian and British armies; there are also some films (about 25 mins) about Gurkha history which can be seen for free. It's more for those with a serious interest in the subject, and those that don't will probably find it a little dull.

Temples

The most important Hindu temple here is **Bindyabasini Temple**, just above the old bazaar. It's dedicated to Durga, the goddess of death and manifestation of Parvati, Shiva's consort. She is appeased by the sacrificing of goats, cocks and buffaloes and, especially during festivals such as Dasain, the streets flow red around this temple. South of Bindyabasini is the smaller **Bhimsen Temple**.

You can visit **Barahi Temple**, on an island in Phewa Tal, by boat.

There are modern Buddhist temples at the two Tibetan villages (see below) and a gompa a kilometre east of the telecommunications centre. For the energetic, climb to **Pokhara Shanti Stupa** on a ridge to the south of Lakeside. It's visible from Lakeside, and the views of Pokhara and the mountains from there are awesome.

Bicycle excursions

Pokhara's other sights make pleasant bicycle excursions; see p111 for details about renting a bicycle.

In the south there's **David Falls/Devi's Fall** (Rs50). The origins for its name get more confused with each guidebook that's published. A tourist named David, Davy, Devi or Miss Davis is said to have been swimming here when the sluice-gates on Pardi Dam, a couple of kilometres upstream, were opened. He (or she) was drowned. The falls are quite impressive after the monsoon; much less so in the winter and spring.

Nearby you can visit the **Tashiling Tibetan Village**, where there's a carpet factory. Tibetan trinket sellers will soon home in on you here and you'll also meet them in Lakeside.

To the north you could visit **Tashipakhel Tibetan Village**, which has a restaurant, guest house, gompa and carpet factory. Follow the Pokhara–Beni Highway for 3km to reach it.

Also in the north but past the British Gurkha camp is **Mahendra Gufa**, a large dark natural cave full of bats that's not really worth the long ride up here.

However, if you do decide to go take a torch as even though there is lighting it isn't always reliable.

Seti Gorge is very impressive and so deep and narrow you may not be aware of its existence. You get a good view of it from the bridge near the Gurkha Memorial Museum.

POKHARA

Boating and swimming
Hiring a boat to paddle yourself around the lake or out to the small temple on the island gives you a chance to admire the views from a different perspective and relax. There are lots of boat-hire places in Lakeside; some places list their prices in English but you may still have to bargain. You will be required to hire a life jacket whether you self-paddle or take a boatman. Rates depend on the size of boat and whether it comes with a boatman. Prices start at Rs500 per day, Rs200 per hour, or Rs250 'with boatman'.

You can swim in the lake (best from a boat in the middle – but wear a swimsuit) and the water can be surprisingly warm.

If there's enough wind (there usually isn't) you can rent a small sailing dinghy from Hotel Fewa or Hotel Monal for Rs300 per hour.

Golf
The 18-hole Himalayan Golf Course (www.himalayangolfcourse.com; US$50 for green fees, clubs and caddy hire; balls extra), 7km from Pokhara, is deemed one of the most unique courses in the world; expect to come across cattle and buffalo roaming freely.

Ultra-lights, paragliding ... and falconry
There are four companies in Pokhara offering the chance to get airborne in a number of terrifying ways. Avia Club of Nepal (www.aviaclubnepal.com; ultralight flights $95 for 15 mins up to $390 for 90 mins; paragliding $90 approx 25 mins, $130 approx 50 mins) operate ultra-lights and paragliding over the lake and foothills surrounding Pokhara.

Frontiers Paragliding (www.nepal-paragliding.com; Rs7500 for 5-10 mins up to Rs18,000 for 90-120 mins) offers a variety of packages.

Blue Sky Paragliding (www.paragliding-nepal.com) offer a similar deal. The company also offers the chance to go parahawking (www.parahawking.com), that is paragliding with a trained bird of prey that will find the best thermals, and to learn how to handle falcons and other birds of prey.

Rafting and kayaking
Pokhara is a good place to organise a rafting trip. Paddle Nepal (464754, www.paddlenepal.com), based in the Center Point complex in Lakeside, offer white-water kayaking, white-water rafting and canyoning as well as adventure packages combining activites.

MOVING ON
By air Get to the airport early as flight departure times are approximate. It's not unknown for a flight to leave early but you're more likely to be kept waiting.

With several new airlines now offering services on these routes timings are likely to change. Fares do not vary much between the airlines.

Note that both the Pokhara–Jomsom and the Pokhara–Manang routes are subject to delays or cancellations if the weather is not perfect. The Manang route is not operated during the monsoon season.

Buddha Air (☎ 465997, 🖥 www.buddhaair.com) has up to six flights a day to and from Kathmandu.

Yeti Airlines (☎ 464888, 🖥 www.yetiairlines.com) has 11 flights a day to and from Kathmandu and, in conjunction with **Tara Air** (☎ 464888, 🖥 www .taraair.com), provides services to most airports in Nepal.

Nepal Airlines (☎ 465021, 🖥 www.nepalairlines.com.np) has two daily flights to Kathmandu. There are flights to Jomsom daily (2-4/day) but departure times vary depending on the day; flights to Manang (2/day) operate on Friday only.

Simrik Airlines (☎ 465887, 🖥 www.simrikairlines.com) flies from Pokhara to Kathmandu and Jomsom.

By bus For services **to Kathmandu** it is simplest is to get a ticket from one of the agencies that operate tourist buses from Lakeside and Damside. Tickets can be bought at most travel agents for Rs400-500. The journey takes 7-9 hours and they will pick you up from your hotel.

Top of the range are the air-con buses operated by Greenline Tours (☎ 464472, 🖥 www.greenline.com.np), near the south-eastern end of Lakeside. They have daily buses at 08.00 to Kathmandu (US$23, seven hours) and Sauraha (US$20, five hours) for Chitwan.

Of the public buses, Sajha day buses are the cheapest. They leave from outside the GPO, in the centre of Pokhara, 4km from the lake. From the ticket office here you can make reservations up to three days in advance for Kathmandu (Rs125 for early morning) or Sunauli. Buses to Kathmandu leave at 06.00, 07.30 and 19.00.

From the bus station there are lots of buses for Kathmandu (Rs310 daytime) between 05.30 and 11.00 for the day buses, and 19.30 and 20.45 for the night buses (when running).

From the main bus station there are three buses direct to **Gorkha** (four hours) at 07.00, 10.50 and 12.20 (Rs180), but most other buses will get you to the turn-off to Gorkha from where you can pick up a connection. For **Dumre** (two hours), you have a wide choice of buses: most pass through this town. For **Tansen** (six hours), the direct bus leaves at 07.00. To **Begnas Tal** (Rs25, 60 mins), there are buses starting at 07.00 and continuing every 30 minutes or so throughout the day.

Direct buses to **Tadi Bazaar** (Rs270, six hours) for **Chitwan**, leave at 07.30, then every hour until 10.30; Greenline also operate a daily bus at 08.00 direct to Sautara for Chitwan.

To reach **the border with India**, the best route is through Sunauli (Rs445, nine hours). There are numerous buses between 05.30 and 22.00.

Kanchenjunga region

Lush rhododendron forests, dramatic mountain vistas, communities that abound in folklore and the third highest peak in the world, Mt Kanchenjunga, all combine to make this a paradise for trekking off the beaten path. Located in far-eastern Nepal, on the border with Sikkim, Kanchenjunga Conservation Area (KCA) was one of the first areas of the Himalaya to be explored in the 19th century, and yet it remains largely unvisited by tourists outside of October.

The Nepal side of the Kanchenjunga massif is split into three distinctive trekking regions:
● The north face to Kanchenjunga Base Camp – described in detail on p117.
● The remote valleys that lie beneath the horseshoe-shaped south-west face and ridges, around Yalung (summary only; see p122).
● The *pahar* trails that lead north–south and east–west through the regional hub of Taplejung.

Along the higher trails, communities are isolated from the lower valleys by a maze of ridges and peaks. So, treks to this region are a little longer than those to the most popular areas, but spending a little extra time here will prove more than worthwhile as you get to explore one of the wilder corners of the Himalaya.

❏ **Limbu people**
Limbuwan (the Limbu homeland) extends east from the Arun Nadi to the Indian border at Sikkim, and includes Taplejung and Ilam. Most of their villages are between 750 and 1200 metres in altitude. Like the Rai, their houses are in the middle of their fields and are generally single-storey stone buildings with thatched roofs. Richer folk use slate for their roof, and the house will be larger than average with a wooden balcony running around the first floor. They cultivate maize, rice, wheat and millet, which they use for food and for *rakshi* and *tongba* (locally made alcohol). Limbus have arranged marriages, but more often prefer capture/abduction or elopement. Abduction marriages are where a girl is 'taken' from a public place and kept in the boy's home for three days. If the girl agrees, the wedding will be arranged; if not she is free to return to her parents. This is certainly a less expensive alternative to big arranged marriages. Limbu marriage customs and religions are similar to Rai (see pp127), who can be described as ethnic cousins.

Most trekkers arrive at Taplejung (by road via Ilam or the Suketar airstrip), which attracts a lively combination of Sherpa, Limbu, Rai and Gurung people, especially for the Saturday market. However, if you are trekking to Phalut, on the border with India, your trek will begin from the jeep road-head at Chyangthapu (Phunlading). Note that you will need a special permit from the police station here to trek to the border and stay at or near Phalut.

The KCA is the first region in Nepal to be managed by local communities and this has so far proved very successful along the main trail, but is yet to be fully effective in remoter valleys. Trekking is still in its infancy in much of the KCA so tread lightly and encourage sustainable practices wherever you can.

As at March 2014, the trekking permit fee for the Taplejung District/ Kanchenjanga Region (includes Olangchung Gola, Lelep, Papung and Yamphudin) is US$10 per person (pp) per week. Plus the Kanchenjunga National Park entry fee of Rs2000pp.

ROUTE GUIDE

Kanchenjunga region

KANCHENJUNGA BASE CAMP TREK

See the 3rd highest mountain in the world up close, trek on glaciers, challenge yourself on high mountain passes, enjoy spectacular forests of rhododendron and the openhearted hospitality of the Sherpa, Limbu, Rai and Lhomi communities.

GRADE 4

- **Duration & distance**: About 20 days total; daily distance is not important to grade
- **Gradient**: Some steep and arduous sections
- **Quality of path**: Formed & rough tracks, some obstacles
- **Quality of markings**: Limited signage
- **Experience required**: Some walking experience required
- **Walking times**: Less than 6½ hours per day
- **Steps**: Steps not included in grade
- **Highest point**: 5143m
- **Best season**: Apr-May/Oct-Nov
- **Accommodation**: Camping or basic teahouses
- **Recommended map**: NP101 GHT Series Kanchenjunga Region, Himalayan Map House, 2013

KANCHENJUNGA BASE CAMP TREK

The return trek to Kanchenjunga Base Camp takes about 20 days and can be combined with a number of trails to explore some magnificent wilderness areas. If you want to visit the southern valleys of Kanchenjunga, combine trails to Yalung via Ghunsa and Yamphudin. Another great option is over Nango La from Ghunsa to the intriguing communities of Olangchun Gola and Yangma, from where you can explore some really remote mountains.

There are two main seasons (April-May and October-November) for visiting Kanchenjunga; both offer very different trekking experiences. Being isolated

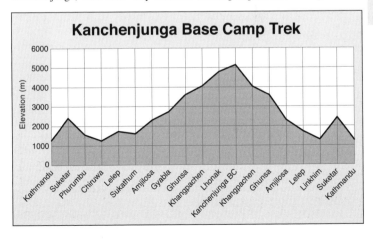

Kanchenjunga Base Camp Trek

from the other main ranges in Far East Nepal, Kanchenjunga is renowned for making its own weather and suffering from heavy monsoonal rains. After the monsoon has finished the mountains are free of lingering cloud and the views in late October and November are probably at their best. By mid-December snow closes the higher trails, which will not open again until mid to late February at the earliest. The pre-monsoon period is famous for the stunning forests of rhododendron that begin at Suketar and continue throughout the trek, and are perhaps the most extensive throughout the Nepal Himalaya.

Getting to and from the Kanchenjunga region can be time consuming. In the main trekking seasons a scheduled flight operates between Biratnagar and Suketar a few times a week. For the remainder of the year, you either have to drive to Taplejung or Phidim, or charter a helicopter to Suketar.

ROUTE GUIDE

DAY 1: KATHMANDU–TAPLEJUNG/ SUKETAR   2HRS
The only scheduled flights to Suketar (2420m) from Kathmandu are on Sunday and Wednesday (Tara Air), for the rest of the week you either have to fly via Biratnagar (causing an overnight delay), or charter your own flight, or use a combination of flight and bus to the large Limbu settlement of Taplejung (1820m). Flights can be delayed due to bad weather so it is wise to organise a second option, just in case. If you arrive late in the day at Suketar there are some simple teahouses next to the airport, alternatively it is an easy downhill walk for two hours to Taplejung.

DAY 2: SUKETAR/TAPLEJUNG– PHURUMBU   4HRS
Suketar sits within a web of trails that can easily confuse, so make sure you walk with your guide or ask locals for directions at trail junctions. From the airstrip follow a grass-covered trail northwards for 20-30 minutes which brings you to a major trail junction where you turn right; ask for Bhotegaon if you are confused. The trail slowly descends providing views of the Tamor Khola valley below to your left. This is a very fertile region with three crops being produced per year; depending on the season and altitude it might be rice, millet, corn, potatoes, cauliflowers or green vegetables that surround you. Slowly curving northwards the trail moves on to a spur that suddenly steepens at Gadidanda (1890m, 2½hrs).

The 350m descent is on a hard-earth trail that is slippery when wet, so take care. There is a good camping site in the school at Phurumbu (1542m, 1hr) to the left of the trail just before the steep section is finished.

DAY 3: PHURUMBU–CHIRUWA 6HRS
The trail dips and climbs slightly as you pass a stream, and then again after Baishakhe (sometimes also called Moyam; 1520m, 1hr). Now the descent towards the Tamor Khola continues, first to Linkhim (1300m), then Tawa (1120m, 1hr) before finally reaching the valley floor before Nagadin (1050m, 4hrs). The villages you pass through are part of a historically important region in Nepal; this is where the Kirati warriors came from who first tried to unite the many kingdoms of the Himalaya into a single sovereign state.

The trail climbs slightly as you approach Chiruwa (1270m, 40 mins), a compact settlement of teahouses, shops and school, all squeezed between the river and steep hillside. The school sportsground, which doubles as a campsite, is 10 minutes further on and off the main trail to your left.

DAY 4: CHIRUWA–SUKATHUM   5½HRS
After the heat of the previous afternoon it's a relief to start walking in the cool morning air from Chiruwa. The main trail remains on the river's south bank and if you get an early start you won't need to walk in the sun until just before the National Park

checkpost at Taplechok (1380m, 1¾hrs). It is necessary to stop and complete formalities with the National Park staff, perhaps over a cup of tea, and confirm if there are any landslides ahead, which might mean taking an alternative trail.

From Taplechok, the main trail crosses a long suspension bridge to the west bank (true right) trail. You first wind through cardamom fields and then into dense forest before gradually climbing away from the Tamor Khola to Lelep (1750m, 3hrs) which has a small teahouse. A trail descends rapidly from Lelep to a suspension bridge across the Tamor Khola to Sukathum (1576m, 40 mins) and a large campsite.

The old route, only used if the main trail is broken, takes the east bank (true left) trail and follows the river before climbing a little after Tamewa (1420m, 2hrs), then down to Simbuwa Khola at Hellok (1550m, 1hr) where there is a small teahouse. A trail winds around to the Ghunsa Khola valley and across a suspension bridge to Sukathum (1576m, 30 mins) and the campsite.

DAY 5: SUKATHUM–AMJILOSA
6HRS

This is the toughest and most dramatic day of the trek so far. Cross the suspension bridge at the Sukathum campsite to the true left bank of the Ghunsa Khola, and follow a trail through dense forest until the valley narrows into a deep gorge (2hrs). Waterfalls cascade down both sides of the valley; the sound of the river will make conversation difficult. It is essential you concentrate on the trail. Locals have built a stone walkway beneath a cliff-face along the river's waterline, which makes for some great pictures but care is needed at all times. After negotiating this section, there is another hour of dense forest trail before you cross a bridge at the base of a steep climb. Switchbacks ascend 350m (2hrs) before the gradient eases, about one hour before Amjilosa (2308m).

DAY 6: AMJILOSA–GYABLA
(KYAPRA)   5HRS

The trail leaving Amjilosa wastes no time in climbing a minor ridge to a sharp turn to

the north (30 mins). The forest is dense and dark as you again descend towards the Ghunsa Khola at Thyanyani (2405m, 1hr) and the first of a few slippery log bridges across streams. There are a few small stone shelters here which are normally only used by herders in monsoon.

For the first time in a number of days the trail doesn't seem to continually climb up and down, as the valley widens slightly and feels less claustrophobic. After the third bridge (2hrs) the trail climbs another steep track for roughly 300m (2hrs), the last section beside a stream can be slippery so care is needed. You crest the climb and find yourself on the outskirts of the picturesque village of Gyabla (Kyapra, 2730m). For those with time and energy there is a pleasant walk up behind the village with views of the Birdhungga Danda.

DAY 7: GYABLA (KYAPRA)–GHUNSA
4½HRS

After the previous week this day marks a noticeable change in the flora and fauna along the trail. At first, the trail seems much like that of the previous afternoon; a broader valley bottom permits views of the river and hillsides, which continue for 1½ hours. Then the trail climbs for 200m (1hr) and suddenly you notice rhododendron, camellias and azaleas rather than bamboo and cardamom beside the trail. The village of Phale (Phere, 3140m) is spread over a large area. The first houses are the winter village for Ghunsa, before the village proper (30 mins). This is a Tibetan refugee settlement where it's possible to buy handicrafts and homemade rugs from some of the locals, ask around when you arrive and potential sellers will soon find you! From Phale a pretty trail winds through dwarf conifer and pine forest before crossing a suspension bridge (to the true left bank) and arriving at Ghunsa (3595m, 1½hrs) in a broad section of valley. Waterfalls fall from the steep cliffs above this Sherpa village that feels like the edge of nowhere on a cloudy day.

DAY 8: GHUNSA   ALL DAY

As you have now passed the 3000m mark, it is wise to take an acclimatisation rest day

ROUTE GUIDE

at Ghunsa. You can relax and explore the village. Sherpa hospitality is legendary and the local school is proud to show off its computer (you can charge iPods here for a donation).

Alternatively, explore the Yamtari Khola which boasts a fantastic view of Jannu (7711m) from the south – first follow the water pipe for the village hydro-generator and climb on the true right side of the river until you reach some herders' huts, then cross boulders to reach the viewpoint. This valley is also the route to the disused and dangerous Lapsang La (5161m), as well as Sele La (4290m) and Sinion La (4440m) both of which offer interesting route variations to/from Yalung if you have camping gear (see *Other Trails in the Kanchenjunga Region*, opposite).

DAY 9: GHUNSA–KHANGPACHEN (KHAMBACHEN) 5½HRS

Deodar pine and rhododendron forest, grassy glades dotted with wild flowers, and increasingly spectacular mountain scenery combine into what is perhaps the most impressive section of trail along the entire trek. It will take about 1½ hours to reach a bridge that crosses to the true right bank of the Ghunsa Khola and Rampuk Kharka (3720m). Note that the bridge is often blocked with sticks to prevent yaks from

---

❏ The Kanchenjunga School Project

The Kanchenjunga School Project (KSP) funded the building of the Ghunsa and Phale schools and medical clinics in 1990 and 1992. Since then the KSP has maintained these facilities, provided salaries and training for the health-care worker, a midwife and pre-school teachers. The Nepal government provides primary-school-level teachers and some support for the health posts. KSP always need additional support and donations, which can be made locally through businesses in the villages or through 🖳 www.kanchenjunga.org.

---

wandering. The trail now climbs almost 400m past, and then through, a large landslide (beware of rockfall) beside the terminal moraine of the Kanchenjunga Glacier to 4100m (2½hrs). A brief traverse of the hillside offers a good view of Jannu before descending to the yak farming settlement of Khangpachen (Khambachen, 4050m, 1½hrs).

DAY 10: KHANGPACHEN (KHAMBACHEN) ALL DAY

A day to acclimatise is normally taken at Khangpachen (Khambachen), where there are two great day walks to help you adjust to the 700m altitude gain tomorrow. One route is to explore the valley directly behind Khangpachen and walk up to the base of Tha Nagphu (5980m), a massive snow and rock dome that you can see from the village. Alternatively, for those feeling fit, cross the river and climb the true right (left-hand) side of the Kumbhakarna Glacier lateral moraine to the popular pilgrimage site beneath the massive vertical north face of Jannu – there is a large boulder and plenty of prayer flags to mark a viewpoint.

DAY 11: KHANGPACHEN (KHAMBACHEN)–LHONAK 5HRS

The trail away from Khangpachen is surprisingly easy as you gradually climb scrubby lateral moraine for one hour. Then comes perhaps the hardest and most dangerous section of the entire trek, a climb up a long section of landslide, mostly across large boulders, which takes about 2½ hours. It is wise to keep moving, however slowly, across this section and complete the climb as early as possible as the risk of rockfall increases throughout the day. Once across the stream from the waterfall section the trail climbs steeply (beware of rockfall) for a short section to the top of an ancient lateral moraine at 4670m (a popular lunch stop), where the gradient eases as you cross some scrubby and grass-covered moraine. On the far side is the Lhonak Khola, which you follow to a seasonal bridge and a few stone shelters at Lhonak (4780m, 2hrs).

DAY 12: LHONAK   ALL DAY

The large sandy bed of the Lhonak Khola offers an inviting walk for an acclimatisation trip. It is important that you are prepared for and understand the hazards of river crossings if you want to fully explore this valley. It is possible to explore a rough track along the western edge of the Lhonak glacier to the confluence of the Chabuk and Chijima glaciers at 5080m, 5 hours' return. Alternatively, you can enjoy the views of Gimmigela, Wedge Peak, Nepal Peak and Tent Peak (Tharpu Chuli) that line and head the valley to the east. Try to spot the rock pinnacle on the far side of the glacier, just at the point it turns south-west.

DAY 13: LHONAK–KANCHENJUNGA
BASE CAMP   4HRS

The trail from Lhonak climbs gently along the massive lateral moraine of the Kanchenjunga glacier for the first 2 hours. It's hard not to stop and admire the views of the peaks and the glacier below. A short steep section of loose rock and landslide formed by a side river will take 40-60 minutes to cross. The trail then climbs more gently for another hour before you reach the few stone huts of Pangpema and Kanchenjunga Base Camp (5143m). Expedition groups will probably not have a permanent camp here as an advanced base camp across the glacier has become a preferred spot.

DAYS 14-21

Return to Suketar along same route, then fly to Kathmandu.

ROUTES FROM KANCHENJUNGA BASE CAMP

[See maps opposite inside back cover] If you have experienced crew, or can employ a local guide, it is worth the effort to continue along a small, dangerous trail that climbs around the massive curve in the glacier to the north. This route is very rarely trekked and after three hours will require you to traverse and then walk across a glacier; beyond here you will need ropes and associated climbing equipment. After two days you reach Jhinsang La and the border with Sikkim and Tibet. Expect to take another two days to return. Be paranoid about the weather, this is not a place to get caught out.

The small river that creates the landslide and loose rock about an hour below Kanchenjunga Base Camp flows from a glacier complex on Mera Peak. On either side of the river are two minor rocky summits of close to 6000m, which do not require permits to climb and are fantastic viewpoints.

OTHER TRAILS IN THE KANCHENJUNGA REGION

[See maps opposite inside back cover] From **Ghunsa**, there is a trail to Olangchun Gola via **Nango La**, which takes a total of three days to complete, see *Kanchenjunga Base Camp to Chyamtang* on p122 for details. The trail from Olangchun Gola back to Lelep/Sekatum takes two days; there is a convenient riverside camp at Magawa, after 3½ hours of walking on the first day.

It is possible to trek to a remote 5700m Tibetan border pass via **Yangma** without any additional permits. Camping is the only option, but if you have the time this is one of the most remote corners of the entire Himalaya. Allow three to four days from Ghunsa to Yangma, then four days minimum (without an acclimatisation stop) to reach the border and return to Yangma, and a further two tough days to Olangchun Gola, where it would be wise to rest for a day or two.

ROUTE GUIDE

❑ **Olangchun people**

One of the most important trade routes from Nepal to Tibet passes along the upper Tamur Valley, with its centre at Olangchun Gola (known locally as Holung). A local legend tells of a wolf that showed a passing trader the trail to Tibet, thus the village name Olang (wolf), chun' (trader) and Gola (place or village). The people here are closely related to the Thudam and Topke Gola communities. Exports to Tibet include cloth, cotton thread, grain, *gur* (brown sugar), matches, cigarettes and other items from India. These are exchanged for Tibetan salt, wool and carpets. Holung people travel extensively for trade, as far as Lhasa, Delhi and even Mumbai, and they are therefore relatively well informed about the outside world compared to many of the mountain neighbours. Their houses are built of stone to the floor level and then completed with wood. The ground floor is for storage and the living quarters are above. The village houses are built in a row along a paved street. They practise Buddhism and have a beautiful, old gompa in the village, which desperately needs some repairs.

An alternative route from Suketar to Ghunsa goes via Yamphudin, Cheram (Tseram) and **Yalung Base Camp** and is a great trail to create a circular trek. It requires camping gear and takes 10-14 days depending on your route and time spent at Yalung. Note that a major landslide has made access to Yalung dangerous and it is not advisable to take laden porters.

The border with India and the spectacular **Singalila National Park** are restricted areas that require a special permit issued from the police station in Chyangthapu (Phunlading) or a valid Indian tourist visa. From Phalut, trails head almost due west to Taplejung in about six days via Sablakhu and Kande Bhanjyang. En route you pass near to **Phathibhara Temple**, a very popular pilgrimage site and a worthy side trip to any itinerary. Trails further westwards to the Makalu region from Taplejung either head through Dobhan or Topkegola.

Kanchenjunga Base Camp to Chyamtang

GHT through-hikers tend to either begin or end their journey in the Kanchenjunga Base Camp area or on the Singalila ridge near Phalut. The remotest starting point for the Great Himalaya Trail in east Nepal is Jhinsang La, a 2- to 3-day walk from Kanchenjunga BC. The approach to the pass is along the true right (left-hand) side of Jhinsang Glacier and although locals don't visit the area often, it might be possible to employ a local guide from Ghunsa. Crossing the pass into Sikkim is not permitted. From the pass, follow the main trail to Ghunsa (see *Kanchenjunga Base Camp Trek*, days 9-13 in reverse, pp120-1) and then to Olangchun Gola. Note that a major landslide has damaged sections of this trail such that it might be closed. Consult local communities before attempting the route between Ghunsa and Olangchun Gola described below.

Ghunsa to Olangchun Gola (Holung)
From Ghunsa, descend the main trail beside the Ghunsa Khola for 1½ hours to a trail junction, just before the Yangma Samba Khola (before Phale) that descends from the Nango La valley to your right. Ascend a small trail, first through scrubby pine forest and then grassy hillside for 3¼ hours to a series of *kharka* (summer grazing pasture), which offer some rough tent platforms.

The following morning get an early start for Nango La (4776m, 1¼hrs), as cloud often obscures the view. Once over the pass descend to a bowl-shaped valley to a *dharamsala* (emergency shelter) in 30 minutes. Livestock have made the ground around the dharamsala very muddy so only stay here if you have no other choice. Descend to the west on the true right (northern) bank of a stream, which rapidly grows in size and often involves some route finding through scrubby rhododendron.

There is an excellent grassy campsite at Lanjong Kharak (3734m, 3hrs from the dharamsala) towards the end of the valley before you descend through dense woodland to the Yangma Khola valley. Once beside the river, the trail swings north, upstream, for about one hour before descending to the Yangma Khola bridge (3430m, 2hrs), which you cross. There are many minor up and downs as you walk downstream on the true right (western) bank of the Yangma Khola and then turn west (right) into the Tamor Khola valley (2800m, 3½hrs). Do not cross the bridge over the Tamor Khola: you must stay on the true left (northern) bank following a broad trail to Olangchun Gola (3191m, 1½hrs).

Olangchun Gola (Holung) to Chyamtang/Hongon

From Olangchun Gola head north-west for 3½ hours along the Tamor Khola, which brings you to a river confluence and bridge, which you cross to head up the Dingsamba Khola. There is a campsite at the confluence of the two rivers (3712m). A small trail through dense rhododendron forest climbs the true left side of the valley to a large, flat area used by herders (1½hrs).

At the end of the valley a trail climbs up and over a black rock band into another, smaller valley (4453m, 2½hrs), where you should camp. A stream cascades down a rocky slope on your left; climb the broken trail on the true left (north-west) side of the stream. You then reach a plateau (1½hrs) with a lake and views of the Lumbha Sambha. Climb the ridge on your right (northern side of the small plateau), heading for the northernmost of three obvious saddles. There is a small trail to follow but snow often obscures your route. You should crest the saddle (5136m, 1hr; Finaid: Topkegola, sheet: 2787 07, ref: 658 697) after another hour. Do not descend into the Palun Khola valley below! There is a small trail that traverses beneath a peak marked 5422m on the map to another saddle and the Lumbha Sambha La proper (5159m, 30 mins; Finaid: Topkegola, sheet: 2787 07, ref: 642 688), with views of Kanchenjunga and

---

❏ **Thudam people**

West of Olangchun Gola is a series of valleys where the people of Thudam, which is a place name rather than an ethnic group, live. These people have no land of their own, so they rent a little farming land east of the Arun Nadi from the Lhomi people.

Individual families own pulping mills where they make juniper wood incense, which is very popular in Tibet. The mills are very basic: a wooden shaft a metre or so long is turned by a waterwheel. The rough block of sandstone, which is attached to the ground, is scraped with the small juniper log – the resulting pulp is dried in the sun and then sold. They also keep yaks, which are mainly used as pack animals and traded with Tibet.

Jannu to the east and Makalu to the west. An easy-to-follow trail descends to the north-west into a large valley and the source of the Lapsi Khola (1hr). This valley has many campsites and the following day you should reach the strongly Tibetan-influenced community of Thudam (3556m, 4hrs).

The trail gradually becomes overgrown and harder to follow as you descend the Medokchheje Khola. Just before a large wood-cutting camp the trail climbs (3020m, 1½hrs; Finaid: Tiptala Bhanjyan, sheet: 2787 03, ref: 512 707) and splits again after 30 minutes of climbing, take the west (left) fork. A sometimes scrambly trail winds around ridges and climbs to a minor pass (3369m, 2hrs) before descending into dense forest beyond where you can camp in a small sloping kharka (1½hrs). The trail continues in much the same vein to another kharka (2hrs) dominated by a large rock. The trail goes to the right of the rock and climbs steeply to another minor pass (2820m, 1hr) before a long descent to a bridge over the Arun Nadi below (1850m, 2hrs). You are bound to receive a warm welcome from the Lhomi people (see box below) in Chyamtang (2187m, 1hr), where you can now enjoy the luxury of a main trail!

It is an easy day to Hongon (2323m, 5½hrs) where you will need to stock up on food and fuel before embarking on the next section to the Makalu region.

Makalu region

The Makalu region is known for being wild and high, and has some of the most dramatic mountain scenery in the Himalaya. Sometimes described as the Yosemite of Nepal, but with glaciers on top of the mountains, this region offers unbridled wilderness to explore. Sandwiched between Kanchenjunga and the Solu-Khumbu (Everest) regions, the massive Makalu-Barun National Park and Buffer Zone rarely sees more than a few hundred trekkers each season.

Dozens of peaks surround the Honku Khola and Honku Basin in the west of the National Park, including the popular Mera Peak (6461m) and the infamous

---

❏ **Lhomi people**
Lhomi live in the upper Arun Nadi valley in eastern Nepal in Sankhuwasabha district, one of the most remote regions along the northern border of Nepal. Their 'main' villages are Hatiya, Hongon (Hangaun) and Gomba (which has one of only two gompas for the region), which cling to the steep slopes above the Arun Nadi gorge. They are often isolated from each other and they mainly trade to the south as far as the terai.

Lhomi marriages are always by choice. They grow enough maize, millet, barley wheat and potatoes for their own needs, and the villagers keep cattle and *dzum* (yak crossbreeds) for ploughing, and sheep for wool and meat. They have only recently learned how to milk their cows. The dzum are often sold to Olangchun Gola people. Their houses are erected on piles, with bamboo walls and wild straw thatch. Although not well off economically, they are friendly, hospitable and cheerful. They are not ardent Buddhists, as they will kill animals for meat and follow Shamanism.

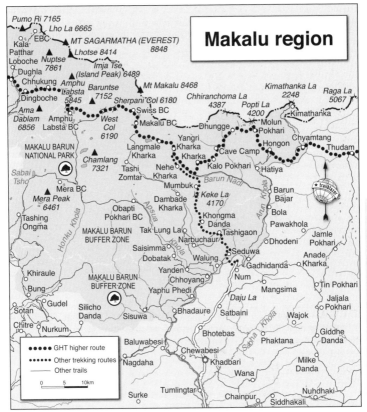

Amphu Labsta pass. To the north, Mt Makalu (8468m) straddles the border with Tibet and is reached via the Barun Nadi, which flows east to join the Arun Nadi in Lhomi country. An outgoing mix of Sherpa and Rai communities populate the valleys in the southern Buffer Zone; the centre of the Park is home to many endangered species including snow leopard and red panda but is not inhabited by people.

Most trekkers begin their adventure from Tumlingtar, a sprawling Rai settlement, and then drive along a ridge-top dirt road to Num (via Khadbari), before crossing the Arun Nadi. The next few days are tough as you climb up and over the Khongma Danda, but the views and cloud forest adorned with orchids are ample reward. You then descend to join the sparsely populated Barun Nadi valley to Makalu Base Camp (route described in full on pp126-30).

Intrepid trekkers will enjoy the route between Makalu Base Camp and Chyamtang, along some wild and remote trails parallel with the Tibetan border (described on pp131-4). Also in this chapter is a description of one of the highest and most challenging trekking routes in the world, from above Makalu Base Camp and across some technical alpine passes: the Sherpani Col (6180m), the West Col (6190m) and Amphu Labsta (5845m) to the Solu-Khumbu (Everest region).

For those who prefer to avoid the rigours of high-altitude passes, there are multiple trails from Tumlingtar and Khadbari that connect to Chyamtang, Lukla and Taplejung. Passing through the Makalu-Barun Buffer Zone, both cultural-based village-to-village homestays and more remote wilderness routes are options, and almost certainly without meeting another trekker!

A recent burst of teahouse-building activity means the trail to Makalu Base Camp has a ready-made stop for each day/night of the trek. Facilities and food are basic, and a little on the expensive side for Nepal, but it does mean you can avoid carrying tents and cooking equipment during the main trekking seasons.

Makalu-Barun is the second largest of Nepal's National Park and Buffer Zones. Local herders are permitted to graze animals and are encouraged to take an active role in conservation projects.

As at March 2014, the trekking permit fees for the Sankhuwasabha District/Makalu Region areas (including Kimathanka, Chepuwa, Hatiya and Pawakhola) are: for the first 4 weeks US$10 per person (pp) per week; and after 4 weeks US$20pp per week. Plus the Makalu Barun National Park and Buffer Zone entry fee of Rs3000pp.

MAKALU BASE CAMP TREK

The return trek to Makalu Base Camp takes about 15 days if you take a jeep to Num from Tumlingtar and return via the same route. However, you could create a longer mountaineering route across the high passes to the Solu-Khumbu

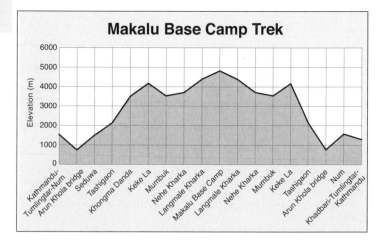

MAKALU BASE CAMP TREK

A genuine Himalayan wilderness experience, with towering cliffs and hanging glaciers. Stand at the foot of the massive bulk of Makalu, while old growth rhododendron and pine forests surround picturesque and welcoming Rai and Sherpa villages.

GRADE 4

● **Duration & distance**: About 15 days total; daily distance is not important to grade
● **Gradient**: Some steep and arduous sections
● **Quality of path**: Formed & rough tracks, some obstacles
● **Quality of markings**: Limited signage
● **Experience required**: Some walking experience required

● **Walking times**: Less than 7½ hours per day
● **Steps**: Steps not included in grade
● **Highest point**: 4825m
● **Best season:** Apr-May/Oct-Nov
● **Accommodation**: Camping or basic teahouses
● **Recommended map**: NP102 GHT Series Makalu Region, Himalayan Map House, 2013

(Everest region), either via Amphu Labsta or by descending the Honku Khola. Both of these routes can eventually take you to Lukla where you can either fly to Kathmandu or take the trail to Jiri (see *Other trips in the Solu-Khumbu*, pp144). If you are returning to Tumlingtar from Makalu Base Camp, consider taking the slightly rougher, but pretty riverside trail along the Arun Nadi instead of retracing your steps via Num.

Like many mountain regions in Nepal, the best time to visit is during the main trekking seasons of April-May or October-November. Throughout winter (December to March) and the monsoon (June to mid-October) the Arun Nadi

ROUTE GUIDE

❏ Rai people
Rai settlements are along the Dudh Kosi and Arun Nadi, usually between 1000 and 2000 metres in altitude. They live in single-storey stone houses with thatched or slate roofs. Their villages are generally spread out, like Sherpas', with each house in the family field. Some Rai houses are built up on wooden piles, with a notched ladder to get you up to the first floor. Animals live under the veranda, and the walls and roof are made from bamboo. They use wet and dry fields to grow rice, maize, wheat, millet and vegetables and fruit such as beans, potatoes, bananas and guava.

Men and women often smoke cigarettes of locally grown tobacco. Rais have arranged marriages, but more commonly capture/abduct or elope. Their religion is quite complex having been influenced by Tibetan Buddhism and Hinduism, and incorporates many local mountain deities. Within the home, the cooking fire is sacred and visitors should never throw anything into the flames. They frequently build stone *chautara* (resting platforms) and wooden benches shaded by a pipal tree, which provide shade and rest for travellers (yes, even trekkers!) as a memorial for their dead. Along with the Limbu (their ethnic cousins, see p115), they often join one of the Gurkha regiments.

and Barun Nadi valley systems funnel wet weather towards Mt Makalu, dumping large amounts of snow on the both the Khongma Danda and Shipton's Pass (aka Tutu La), closing them. During the pre-monsoon spring season the extensive rhododendron and orchid forests that cover the Khongma Danda bloom in a multitude of colours and provide a welcome distraction from the tough climb. The clear air of the post-monsoon period makes for some excellent mountain photography and is probably the best time of year to cross the high passes to the Solu-Khumbu.

There are several scheduled flights a day between Tumlingtar and Kathmandu, and Tumlingtar and Biratnagar, as well as bus services. If you cross to the Everest region make sure you have purchased your flight tickets out of Lukla, as there can be long waiting lists in October.

DAY 1: KATHMANDU–TUMLINGTAR –NUM   ALL DAY

It is a good idea to get the earliest possible flight to Tumlingtar's grass airstrip (410m) and take the first available jeep to Num, but should you need to camp there is a good grassy site near the airport as well as some simple teahouses. The return jeep journey from Num to Tumlingtar will mean you'll have to overnight near the airstrip, so it is prudent to book your teahouse accommodation or camping space in advance when you first arrive.

For those wanting to walk to Num, either because they have the time or the road is closed, the trek takes 3 days. From Tumlingtar ascend a long ridge running north from the edge of the sprawling town around the airstrip to the Newari and Rai village of Khadbari (1040m, 3hrs walking from the airport), it's an exposed trail so take plenty of water and sun cream. Khadbari is the administrative centre for the enormous Makalu-Barun National Park and Conservation Area and you will need to register at the park office. Try and coincide your visit with a market day on Wednesdays and Saturdays. There is a campsite next to the large school in the middle of the town.

The following day continue along the ridge through picturesque villages to Mane Bhanjyang (1100m, 1hr), where you can see the trail climbing a small hillside basin to a minor pass at Bhotebas (1740m, 3½hrs). On a clear day there are good views of Makalu from a point about 10 minutes

beyond the pass and from spots along the trail for the next few hours. The next village, Gogane (1720m, 20 mins) offers an excellent campsite if you are running a little late. Follow the road through moss-covered forest along the ridge to Chichira (1980m, 1hr) and a large camping area; there are also some simple teahouses here.

It's a good idea to get an early start on the final day to Num to get clear views of Mt Makalu before the jeeps drive by and kick up dust. The village of Kuwapani (2010m, 1hr) sits hunched on a narrow section of ridge at a major trail junction. Take the right-hand trail that traverses beneath a triangular hill and passes through Satbaini (Sakurate, 1920m, 20 mins). After another hour you come to a minor pass, Daju La (Dhara Deurali, 2100m) before descending, gradually at first, and then through a steep section of forest with many trails. It is important to stick together through this forested section, as some trails lead down to the Arun Nadi valley and it is easy to take the wrong path. From the pass it is 2½ hours to the large village of Num (1560m), which has a grassy campsite and some teahouses.

DAY 2: NUM–SEDUWA   4½HRS

If you look across the valley to the northwest, you will see the day's destination, the village of Seduwa. The main trail from Num continues along the ridge before curving back on itself to lose height. However, there is also a direct route down some rough steps, which is hard to locate and begins near the village centre (ask around for directions). In 1½ hours you should reach the Arun Nadi (760m) and cross the suspension bridge. The dense, moist forest of the east bank contrasts to the open deciduous forest on the west bank before giving way to cultivation.

It will take about 3 hours to climb to Seduwa (1500m), a large trading village with views of countless mid-hills receding in to the distance. You will need to register again with the National Park office.

DAY 3: SEDUWA–TASHIGAON 4HRS

Today is the last day of walking through villages as you draw closer to the Khongma Danda, the large and imposing forested ridge at the end of the valley. An easy trail to Murmidanda (1560m, 1hr) brings you to a school where the children will almost certainly break class to ask you questions. The climb to Narbugaon (2000m, 1½hrs) eases to become a straightforward trail that traverses hillside through cultivated fields. As Tashigaon (2100m, 1hr) is the last village on the trail, your guide will spend some time re-stocking food and fuel supplies.

It is important that you also research trail conditions for the coming days, check if there is any snow or hazards on the trail, and that locals are using the route. You will be told that there are no supplies up the Barun Nadi valley; this is not true during the main trekking seasons, as all basic supplies are available, although expensive, all the way to Makalu Base Camp.

DAY 4: TASHIGAON–KHONGMA DANDA   7HRS

The trail climbs, often steeply, through some of the most impressive cloud-forest in Nepal. It is important that you climb slowly, rest frequently, and perhaps take some time to admire the clusters of orchids hanging above. Make sure you have enough water and snacks to last the day, as there is no convenient lunch spot with running water. Unshisa (3110m, 5hrs) is the first potential campsite and there is a small teashop open in the main trekking season. You now climb on to the Khongma Danda

and your campsite (3500m, 2hrs) will offer morning views of Makalu, with Peak 6 and Peak 7 in the foreground. When you reach camp you should check the entire group, including your porters, for symptoms of altitude sickness.

DAY 5: KHONGMA DANDA   ALL DAY

Acclimatisation day. It is important that you begin the day by checking again for any signs of altitude sickness. Some of your group may have had a restless night, make sure they remain hydrated and rest. There is not much to do other than explore the surrounding forest and enjoy the views, so relax and unwind, soak your feet and consume as much water as possible.

DAY 6: KHONGMA DANDA–MUMBUK   7½HRS

Today is the toughest day on the trek so far and you must be on the lookout for altitude-sickness symptoms in the party. The day begins by continuing along the ridge past the prayer-flag-covered Kauma La (3603m, 1½hrs) with views of Makalu, Chamlang, Baruntse, and if the weather to the east is clear, Kanchenjunga and Jannu.

The trail now climbs to the left of the main ridge up to Shipton's Pass (aka Tutu La, 4125m, 2½hrs) before descending for 200m to a large lake called Kalo Pokhari, which can offer sublime reflections of Peaks 6 and 7 and Chamlang in calm, clear conditions.

A short climb up to Keke La (4170m, 1hr) gives views of the Chamlang range and Tibet to the north, the Barun Nadi flows almost 1000m below. The 2½-hour descent is steep and rocky all the way to the stone huts and campsite of Mumbuk (3540m).

DAY 7: MUMBUK–NEHE KHARKA   4½HRS

The trail descends to the Barun Nadi before turning upstream on the true right bank and traversing steep hillside, which is often affected by landslides.

Note: In 2013, locals were discussing building a bridge to the far bank of the Barun Nadi to avoid rockfall sections. Seek local advice for developments.

ROUTE GUIDE

You should take care when crossing any loose ground, as well as watching for rockfall from above. Then about 4½ hours of alternate loose landslide and stable trails brings you to Nehe Kharka (3700m) and a good campsite in a meadow surrounded by pine trees. During the monsoon, normally for the August full moon, there is a fertility festival here as a tradition tells that a famous Buddhist sage, Guru Rimpoche, stayed in a cave high above.

DAY 8: NEHE KHARKA–LANGMALE KHARKA   5HRS

More loose sections of trail, with an occasional well-formed path, continue beside the Barun Nadi before crossing on a log bridge to a wide grassy field called Yangri Kharka (Yangla Kharka, 3557m, 2hrs). There are a number of teahouses here, along with basic supplies and a large campsite. The next section of trail is one of the most spectacular in the entire Himalaya as you wind through rhododendron, fir and pine forest. Yosemite-like cliffs form an enormous U-shaped valley crested with glaciers and a series of snowy peaks including Pyramid Peak, Peak 4, Peak 6, Chamlang and Peak 5 all show themselves. In one monstrous rock-face a massive cave contains a waterfall in freefall. *Lumdar* (strings of prayer flags) are suspended from poles to mark a pilgrimage site popular during the July/August full moon, when it is said that the waters here can cure many illnesses. For 3 hours you'll keep stopping and absorbing the evolving panorama,

before arriving in Langmale Kharka (4410m), which has a couple of teahouses and campsites spaced well apart.

DAY 9: LANGMALE KHARKA– MAKALU BASE CAMP   4HRS

The avenue of mountains that line your route become ever more spectacular as Peak 3 and the snout of the West Barun Glacier appear. From Langmale Kharka the trail enters an ancient lateral moraine through which the infant Barun Nadi flows. A large glacial lake fills the valley to your left and an easy to follow trail leads to Shersong (4630m, 2½hrs), a large grassy area used by yak herders in the monsoon months. Turn right and follow an obvious trail that climbs more moraine, and, once on top, maintain your height; do not descend into the valley to your left. A number of small trails (formed by yak herds) stay about 100m above the valley floor before finally descending to a small bridge and the stone huts of Makalu Base Camp (4870m, 2hrs). Expeditions have left all sorts of supplies here over the years and it is possible to buy anything from wine to kerosene to apple jam and dehydrated meals. To the north, the massive bulk of Makalu rises about 3598m (11,824ft) to a pyramid summit; this is truly one of the most spectacular mountain viewpoints in Nepal!

DAYS 10-15

Return to Tumlingtar along same route, then fly to Kathmandu.

MAKALU ADVANCED BASE CAMP

Makalu Base Camp has become a staging post for expeditions rather than a full-blown base camp. Most expeditions now climb to a valley on the north-east side of Makalu to an advanced base at 5780m.

To get there, follow the trail up and past Hillary Base Camp before descending to and crossing the Barun Glacier on a loose trail (3hrs). A few small tracks run through the lateral moraine on the far north side of the glacier, beware of rockfall in this area.

You eventually reach a small waterfall and the trail turns in to the Makalu La valley (2hrs). Some small stone shelters have been built by porters at 5500m, advanced base camp lies further up this valley on the left-hand side (2hrs).

OTHER TRAILS IN THE MAKALU REGION

[See maps opposite inside back cover] GHT through-hikers have a simple choice in the Makalu region, to go over the high passes (see *Sherpani Col, West Col & Amphu Labsta*, pp134-5), or take a southerly route along the Arun-Salpa Trail (summary below), which could also include heading up the Arun Nadi to Thudam or continuing directly to Taplejung.

One of the least-visited regions in the Himalaya is the **Milke Danda**, a long ridge that runs south from the Lumbha Sambha and is covered in rhododendron forests, alpine lakes and craggy peaks. The ridge almost bisects eastern Nepal and in the heart of the region is Topkegola, a community renowned for trade with Tibet and India. From Taplejung, it is only a two-day hike from the road-head at Papung to reach Topkegola and another two days to Thudam. Trails across the Milke Danda link Dobhan with Khadbari via Chainpur (5-6 days, village-to-village route) and Jaljala Pokhari (6-8 days, wilderness route).

Kimathanka lies beside the upper Arun Nadi on the border with Tibet. From Tumlingtar, it takes 10-12 days to reach and return from the most isolated district centre in Nepal.

A comprehensive 8- to 10-day village-to-village route (Grade 3) between the Arun Nadi and Kharikhola/Lukla via Salpa Bhanjyang (known as the **Arun-Salpa Trail**) is one of the new trekking gems of the lower Solu region. The trail follows an old trade route used by Sherpas visiting Sikkim and offers some wonderful views and immersion in a range of hill cultures. Typical itineraries include: Lukla–Kharikhola–Panggom, Sibuje, Khiraule, Bung/Cheskam, Gudel, Salpa Pokhari, Silicho Danda, Dobhane and Baluwabesi to Tumlingtar.

For those who want a wilderness challenge, the as-yet-undocumented routes along the **Apsua Khola** and **Isuwa Khola** lead into the heart of Makalu-Barun National Park. The Isuwa Khola route crosses to Shershong, just below Makalu Base Camp, whereas the Apsua Khola system leads to the Honku Khola and routes to and around Mera Peak.

Chyamtang to Makalu Base Camp

The 'highest' route through the Makalu region is probably the most difficult navigational section of the Great Himalaya Trail network as it follows some *shikari bato* (hunters' trails) rarely used by locals when they search for medicinal plants, has many river crossings (especially post-monsoon), and three of the highest and most technical passes in the Himalaya. Only small (maximum 12 trekkers with crew), experienced groups who have climbing skills and equipment should attempt this route.

This section of the GHT begins with some particularly remote and small trails with occasionally confusing junctions, so you would be foolish not to employ a local guide from Chyamtang or Hongon at least until the Barun Nadi valley. This trail can be very hard to follow in the Dhunge Khola and Saldim Khola valleys, even with Finaid maps and GPS. You should take a 30m rope for river crossings.

If you want to climb the high passes you should have a guide or climbing sherpa who knows the route very well. Identifying the route can be very difficult especially if snow covers the trail and alpine-climbing skills are required for glacial travel.

Note: there is a direct route to the Popti La plateau and thence Molun Pokhari from Chyamtang, which avoids Hongon. This route takes the same amount of time as going via Hongon but has better views. Ask in Chyamtang for a local guide.

From Hongon, climb a well-used trail that goes straight up to a ridge behind the village. There are some tall prayer flags beneath the ridge that mark a burial site. Avoid going there or taking photos of the site as it will only offend the locals and your crew will believe that any disrespect will bring bad luck. There are many small trails towards the top of the ridge, most of which are created by grazing animals, so it might take a little time to find the *chorten* that marks a minor pass (2710m, 1½hrs Finaid: Kimathanka, sheet: 2787 02, ref: 354 726).

Just after the pass the trail forks: you must go right; do not descend to your left. The trail traverses a hillside, crosses a stream and then climbs a small ridge before meeting the Tojo Khola. You need to stay on the true left (east) bank of this river and follow a trail made by woodcutters through rhododendron forest covered in moss. Eventually the trail crosses the Tojo Khola to the true right bank and Bakim Kharka (3020m, 2hrs; Finaid: Kimathanka, sheet: 2787 02, ref: 338 749) is a good campsite. After another hour there is a smaller campsite at Khazakhani Kharka (3480m). The trail becomes steep and rocky but offers great views south of the Arun Nadi valley. Climb for nearly 500m (2½hrs), as you near the top of the plateau (3950m) there are some scrambling sections. A series of chortens mark the end of the climb and the edge of Molun Pokhari, a picturesque lake.

Wind around the north side of the lake to a large campsite in a valley to the west (3954m, 40 mins; Finaid: Kimathanka, sheet: 2787 02, ref: 328 774). The trail to the Tibetan border, Popti La (4200m, 3hrs) can be seen heading north out of the valley. A small trail climbs a ridge to the south of the campsite, before heading south-east, then east to a rocky ascent that climbs a minor pass (4201m, 1hr; Finaid: Kimathanka, sheet: 2787 02, ref: 316 767). Be careful not to take a small trail that heads south just before the pass. Just after the pass is a great view of Tin Pokhari and the eastern edge of the Makalu-Barun National Park. An easy to follow trail descends a ridge to your left; there will probably be some yaks around the lake. At a small lake on your left is another trail junction (30 mins), head to your right and continue descending next to a small stream to the valley bottom. Cross the Dhunge Khola (the plank bridge is often washed away) to a large kharka on the far bank and continue down the valley on the true right bank to a drier campsite, which normally has a bamboo structure over a kharka (3590m, 1hr; Finaid: Kimathanka, sheet: 2787 02, ref: 290 772).

A small trail through dense forest continues to follow the true right (west) bank of the Dhunge Khola. After 1½ hours, and rounding a ridge that draws you away from the main river valley, the trail forks beneath cliffs in the middle of a small clearing. Either descend a steep stream bed to your left (which doesn't look like a trail at all), or continue on a small trail that bears right and into the tributary valley of the Kholakharka Khola.

The streambed trail will take you to a large hollow tree used by locals as shelter before descending a couple of metres to the watercourse. A large tree has been felled creating a bridge across the river, but you will require a couple of safety lines as the log can be slippery (45 mins, note you only need to use the log if the stream is in spate). Cross the Kholakharka Khola, about 80m upstream of the confluence with the Dhunge Khola – after heavy rain this is a very difficult river crossing.

The right-hand trail goes to a point where the river crossing over the Kholakharka Khola is safer but will add up to 1½ hours to your day.

Either route will mean you cross to the true bank (west) bank of the Dhunge Khola and then follow a small, overgrown trail to the Saldim Khola (2hrs; Finaid: Kimathanka, sheet: 2787 02, ref: 267 736).

A-hard to-find trail in dense rhododendron forest then climbs briefly, heading parallel to the Saldim Khola. The trail gets lost in the gouged out river-bed (almost certainly caused by a GLOF, Glacial Lake Outburst Flood) and you will need to find your own way across a boulder-strewn and shifting route (for about an hour) until you can see a large slightly overhanging rock-face on your left. Scout around and you should find a small trail that leads to the base of the rock-face, which makes an acceptable campsite (3115m; Finaid: Kimathanka, sheet: 2787 02, ref: 259 738). Apparently there is an alternative trail up the real Saldim Khola to another possible camping spot, but we didn't see the trail junction.

Climb the watercourse a little further before exiting on the true right (left) on a small trail that ascends just to the left of a much steeper watercourse, which looks more like a cascade. Ascend steeply (for 350m) between two streams on a small trail (1½hrs) before the gradient begins to ease; you can then cross the stream to the true right (left) and head up a shrub-covered slope. Pass a small lake and continue to climb to a waterless kharka and on to the ridge top (3855m, 1hr), which you will follow before descending slightly to an east-facing kharka and possible campsite. You then climb a craggy trail around a ridge to a minor pass (4207m, 1hr; Finaid: Kimathanka, sheet: 2787 02, ref: 252 711), before dipping through a shallow valley and climbing another ridge (4253m, 1hr) to arrive at a black water lake (4192m, 30 mins), where there is enough room to camp. Climb the next ridge to a pass (4624m, 1½hrs) before a steep, rocky descent, which is treacherous if snow-covered. From the valley bottom the trail climbs another ridge to a minor pass (4457m, 1½hrs), where you can see a large valley and campsite below, it will take another 1½ hours to descend through dense rhododendron shrubs and walk a little way up the valley to a kharka (4097m; Finaid: Bala, sheet: 2787 05, ref: 206 696).

The slight downhill to the lip of the valley gives you a moment to identify the blue-roofed Mumbuk teahouses on the far side of the valley before you enter a beautiful forest of fir, pine and large rhododendron, and the trail steepens. Before you reach the Barun Nadi the trail heads upstream (true left bank, north-west), past another rock overhang cave (3366m, 1½hrs), and then after crossing several streams, finally into the open valley bottom. You now follow the Barun Nadi along an easy trail broken by occasional landslides to Yangla (Yangri) Kharka (3557m, 2½hrs).

You are now on the main Makalu Base Camp trail, which you should follow
and then cross the Sherpani Col, West Col and Amphu Labsta before arriving in
Chukhung in the Everest region. Good luck!

Sherpani Col, West Col and Amphu Labsta

Those with mountaineering experience and equipment may choose to cross
three passes of roughly 6000 metres (Sherpani Col, West Col and Amphu
Labsta) into the Solu-Khumbu (Everest Region). If you want to attempt the high
passes you should have a guide or climbing sherpa who knows the route well.
Identifying the route and avoiding crevasses can be very difficult, especially if
snow covers the trail.

From Makalu Base Camp follow the well-defined trail to Hillary Base Camp
and then continue along a smaller trail on the south side of the Barun Glacier valley. Do not descend to the *ablation valley* (created by snow and/or ice melt from
a glacier) beside the glacier until forced to do so, and camp at a small area known
as the Swiss Base Camp (3hrs; Finaid: Mount Makalu, sheet: 2787 01, ref: 049
825). Just beyond the campsite the trail becomes hard to follow as it climbs
towards a steep boulder-filled gully formed by a cascading stream (Finaid:
Mount Makalu, sheet: 2787 01, ref: 043 829) that flows from a valley approxi-
mately opposite the one that leads to Makalu Advanced Base Camp. Identifying
this valley can be difficult, especially in cloudy weather. Climb to boulders to the
north (true left) of the watercourse for about 300m. The gradient then eases and
ahead you will see a small trail ascending the northern side of a rocky valley.
There is a small flat area (1½hrs) before the trail climbs further. After another
hour you reach the Sherpani Col Base Camp (5688m), at the snout of a glacier.
There are two routes that climb either side of the glacier snout, so you will need
to do some reconnaissance to decide on the appropriate route.

The first is to the south (true right) of the snout and climbs mixed rock and
ice, before veering onto the glacier. Beware of rockfall and crevasses on this
route. The second option is to climb the rocky slope and gully to the north (true
left) of the glacier snout. Once the gradient levels, step across onto the glacier.
On the glacier, head towards the base of a rock-face on the southern (true right-
hand) side of the glacier, where it begins to rise towards the Col. Do not get too
close to the rock-face as there is constant danger from rockfall. Traverse across
the base of the rock-face to a point beneath some prayer flags, which are easily
spotted on the rocky ridge above. Climb towards the prayer flags from rocks
beside the glacier; this will require a handline (20m) for the first, loose scrambling section, and possibly another fixed rope for an easy 20m rockclimb to the
top of the Sherpani Col (6180m, 3-4hrs from Base Camp; Finaid: Mount
Makalu, sheet: 2787 01, ref: 007 819).

You will need to abseil (35m) down to the West Barun Glacier, which you
reach after crossing a snow-bridge over a *bergschrund* (a deep crevasse between
a glacier and mountainside). Beware of rockfall while descending to the glacier!
Cross the glacier (2-3 hours – beware of crevasses!) to Baruntse Advanced Base
Camp and the only spot on the glacier with some shelter from constant wind.
Most groups elect to camp here and prepare the abseil over the West Col for

early the following morning. There are two routes over the West Col and they vary according to snow conditions each year. One route is over the snow bulge at the northern end of the West Col ridge, but this will involve crossing more crevasses at the bottom of the descent. Alternatively, take a route over the southern end of the West Col ridge (6190m; Finaid: Sagarmatha, sheet: 2786 04, ref: 993 805). To reach the ridge cross another bergschrund and climb a loose rocky route at the far southern end of the distinct rockwall that forms the pass. From the summit there is a 200m abseil into the Honku Basin and some potential campsites (3hrs) if you are going to head to the Amphu Labsta, or Baruntse Base Camp (4hrs) if you are exiting via the Honku Khola route. The full traverse normally takes about 11 hours, as time is lost preparing the abseils and fixing a rope up and down the Sherpani and West cols. If you have a large group it is advisable to run two ropes, one for clients/porters and the other for equipment.

The route to, and over, Amphu Labsta (5845m; Finaid: Sagarmatha, sheet: 2786 04, ref: 929 832) to Chukhung is now popular with groups who have climbed Mera Peak. However, this is still probably the most dangerous pass in Nepal and care needs to be taken on both the ascent and descent. Most groups that attempt the pass camp beside one of the Panch Pokhari lakes and get an early start. A collection of cairns are reached after about an hour, which mark the point where you have to choose one of two routes to the pass: the more popular is up a series of ice cliffs, while the other climbs an exposed, steep rocky and snow-covered section direct to the pass. Full climbing equipment is required for either route and it is wise to fix any ropes in the afternoon prior to crossing. The descent is a bottleneck as there is a short abseil (30m) to a ledge, which then leads down steep rocky ground to the Amphu Labsta Glacier and the trail to Chukung (4730m, 11-15hrs from West Col base depending on group size).

❑ **Sherpa people**
The famous Sherpa people live in the Solu-Khumbu (Everest) region and are similar to the Bhotia of Helambu (north of Kathmandu) and other ethnic groups dotted through the eastern districts of Nepal. Their mountain settlements are always higher than anyone else's, no matter where they are living. During the cold winter only the elderly stay in the village to look after livestock; the younger of them go down to the plains and valleys to look for manual work.

Many Sherpas own or work for trekking and mountaineering companies, while others run lodges and shops in Kathmandu or along popular trails. Most families make a part of their income from tourism. Sherpa people keep yaks, dzum and dzo (a cross between cattle and yak) to work the fields, carry loads and provide meat, milk and wool.

The traditional Sherpa house has two stories made of stone with a sloping shingle roof. On the ground floor potatoes and firewood are stored, and this is where their livestock will be sheltered during bad weather. The family lives upstairs, normally in one large room, which functions as bedroom, sitting room and kitchen. Sherpas follow Tibetan Buddhism and generally pick their own marriage partner. They grow millet, maize and barley, and make their own alcohol, called chang, which is a fermented beer.

Solu-Khumbu (Everest) region

Mt Everest, known as Sagarmatha to most Nepalese and Chomolungma to the
local Sherpas, has become one of Nepal's premier trekking destinations. The
proliferation of comfortable teahouses (many with en suite rooms) and well-
maintained trails accommodates tens of thousands of tourists each season. The
region is popular for good reason; some of the most spectacular and beautiful
mountain scenery in the world combines with the famous friendliness and hospitality of the Sherpa people to make a visit a must for any walker.

The Everest Region, known locally as the Solu-Khumbu, fans out into a
series of impressive glacier-filled valleys above the main trading centre of
Namche. The eastern side of the fan includes the main trail route to Everest

❏ **The Hillary Himalayan Trust**
Schools and programmes operated by the Hillary Himalayan Trust, started by Sir Edmund Hillary, are famous for kick-starting the economy of the Solu-Khumbu region. The key to the success of its projects is the involvement of locals. Sir Edmund believed locals could help themselves if given sufficient opportunity and resources. The Trust mostly provides funds and the villagers provide land, materials and labour. This approach means that the villagers 'adopt' the projects and take pride in maintaining and further developing schools, hospitals and bridges all over the Solu-Khumbu. For more information see, 🖳 www.himalayantrust.co.nz.

Base Camp (EBC) and the viewpoint of Kala Patthar, along with the Chukhung valley that leads to Amphu Labsta (see *Sherpani Col, West Col & Amphu Labsta*, pp134-5) and the popular trekking peak of Imja Tse (Island Peak). The centre of the fan is the Gokyo valley, which contains a series of turquoise glacial lakes beneath the impressive bulk of Cho Oyu (8201m). To the west is the less frequently visited Bhote Kosi valley system that leads first to Thame and then west to Tashi Labsta (see *Rolwaling & Tashi Labsta*, pp146-53) or north to Nangpa La, a pass used by Tibetan traders and refugees. The trek described on pp138-43 links the main valleys of the Solu-Khumbu by following a route to Everest Base Camp and then over Cho La to Gokyo and Renjo La to Thame before returning to Lukla.

The vast majority of visitors to the Solu-Khumbu now fly in and out of Lukla rather than do the 4- to 5-day trek from Jiri. Beyond Lukla, Namche offers a convenient and comfy acclimatisation stop and the opportunity to get to know the local Sherpa people a little better. Khumjung and Khunde are above Namche, and this is where Sir Edmund Hillary began his pioneering work with local development projects (see box above). The famous Tibetan Buddhist gompa at Tengboche is only a day further, and then the highest settlements of Pheriche and Loboche lead you to Gorak Shep, a staging-post for both Everest Base Camp (where there isn't a view of Mt Everest's summit) and the viewpoint of Kala Patthar (where there is). A popular side trip is to Chukhung, or over Cho La to Gokyo, which for many is a worthy destination in itself. Renjo La offers perhaps the best viewpoint of the entire region and leads to the Thame valley, which can feel eerily remote compared to the main trails.

The 'Khumbu' in Solu-Khumbu refers to the higher-altitude areas of the Solu region, which actually extends far to the south. The 'lower' Solu is rich in Sherpa culture, sacred sites, fantastic viewpoints and not another tourist in sight! Dozens of trails are open for most, and sometimes all, of the year, and all are worth an unhurried exploration.

Sagarmatha National Park was declared a World Heritage Site in 1979 and has a comprehensive management structure. Use of firewood is prohibited and locals rigorously monitor environmental protocols.

As at March 2014, the trekking permit fees for Solu-Khumbu District are $10 per person (pp) per week for the first 4 weeks and after that $20pp per week. Plus the Sagarmatha National Park entry fee of Rs3000pp.

ROUTE GUIDE

EVEREST BASE CAMP, KALA PATTHAR, CHO LA & RENJO LA

Many trekking groups who only visit Everest Base Camp do the return trek (Grade 3) to Lukla in about 14 days, but if there is any chance of staying longer the effort will pay dividends. Crossing Cho La and adding the viewpoints of the Ngozumba Glacier and Gokyo Ri increases your trek duration by a mere 4 days!

Another great add-on is Renjo La and a trip to Thame, which takes just one more day than returning down the main Gokyo valley. In short, this is the most convenient place to experience the immensity of the Himalaya in Nepal and in less than three weeks!

There is almost no bad time of year to visit the Solu-Khumbu as there is always something going on. A major re-forestation programme in the 1980s and 1990s has once again given a bloom of colour to the lower slopes in the pre-monsoon. The most popular season is October to December, when the air is clear and offers the best shots of the highest mountain in the world. The popular passes of Cho La and Renjo La are open for most of the year except for a brief period from mid-February to March. All the main routes in the valleys are open year-round.

The region used to have a reputation for tough trekking but a significant increase in teahouses and trail maintenance has made it an option for novices and experienced trekkers alike. Access is very easy with multiple daily flights to Lukla year-round; just remember to reconfirm the day before you fly as waiting lists can be long in peak season.

For comprehensive trail, accommodation and local information see Jamie McGuinness's, *Trekking in the Everest Region*, Trailblazer.

ROUTE GUIDE

EVEREST BASE CAMP, KALA PATTHAR, CHO LA & RENJO LA

Everyone should see Mt Everest at least once in their life! Trek to the famed Kala Patthar viewpoint, cross Cho La and Renjo La, enjoy the natural open-hearted friendliness of the Sherpa people – if you only visit Nepal once, this is the trek to do.

Grade 4

● **Duration & distance**: About 20 days total; daily distance is not important to grade
● **Gradient**: Very steep sections with some arduous climbs
● **Quality of path**: Formed & rough tracks, some obstacles
● **Quality of markings**: Clear signs at beginning, end and during trek
● **Experience required**: Some walking experience required

● **Walking times**: Less than 6½ hours per day
● **Steps**: Steps not included in grade
● **Highest point**: 5550m
● **Best season**: Mar-May/Oct-Jan
● **Accommodation**: Camping or a range of teahouse qualities
● **Recommended map**: NP103 GHT Series Solu-Khumbu (Everest) Region, Himalayan Map House, 2013

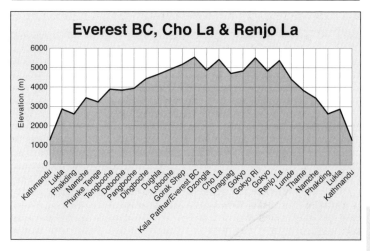

Everest BC, Cho La & Renjo La

**DAY 1: KATHMANDU–LUKLA–
PHAKDING/BENKAR   ALL DAY**
The 200km flight to Lukla (2840m) has
great views of the eastern Himalaya; sit on
the left-hand side of the plane for the best
views. Many guides like to meet your crew
and purchase supplies in Lukla, so do not
be surprised if you are delayed before heading out of town. From the airport head north
along the main paved trail crowded with
shops to a *kani*, where you then head downhill. After 45 minutes you should reach
Chheplung (2660m), the first of many col-
lections of teahouses and the carved *mani*
stones, prayer wheels and chortens built by
all Buddhist communities throughout the
Himalaya.
  The trail now undulates through
Nurning and Ghat, punctuated by short sections of scrubby pine forest and painted
mani stones, until you reach Phakding
(2610m, 2hrs). Many trekking groups stay
in this extensive village so you might want
to continue for another 20 minutes to Zam
Fute (2730m), or about an hour to Benkar
(see Day 2).

**DAY 2: PHAKDING/BENKAR–
NAMCHE   5HRS**
From Phakding the trail crosses a long sus-
pension bridge to the true right bank before

again following an undulating route, which
many Nepalese would call 'flat'. A pretty
waterfall attracts photographs just before
Benkar (2630m, 1½hrs), after which you
re-cross the Dudh Kosi to the true left bank
and climb a little to the village of Monjo
(2835m, 40 mins). Ahead, you can see the
trail climbing to a cleft between by a huge
finger of rock and the hillside, which is the
site for the Sagarmatha National Park entry
post where you register.
  Stone steps descend to another suspension bridge, which you cross to Jorsale
(2740m, 45 mins) on the true right bank.
Continue on a broad trail to another bridge,
which you cross to the true left bank and
follow an easy riverside track before a
slight climb to Larja bridge (40 mins) festooned with prayer flags. Cross the bridge
and begin a long climb during which you
can look forward to finally sitting down and
resting in Namche (3440m, 2½hrs). Early
on the first section of switchbacks the trail
turns a sharp left on the edge of the ridge
and you can catch your first glimpse of Mt
Everest. The trail climbs switchbacks,
which gradually ease as the trail follows a
route that winds north-west through pine
forest. There is a police checkpost 15 minutes before entering Namche where you
must register.

ROUTE GUIDE

DAY 3: NAMCHE   ALL DAY

As you have now passed the 3000m mark, it is a good idea to take an acclimatisation day and rest from the previous day's climb. Namche is an extensive market town, where there is always something to see and places to explore. If you are here on a market day (Saturday) make sure you get up early to see Tibetan and Sherpa traders bargaining before the tourists arrive.

If you have the time it is worth completing a looped day walk to Sagarmatha National Park Museum (on the ridge above the town), and the combined villages of Khunde (3840m) and Khumjung (3780m), which is the site of the first Himalayan Trust school, as well as many chorten and mani walls.

DAY 4: NAMCHE–DEBOCHE 5½HRS

It is a good idea to get an early start today, as the trail up to Tengboche can be hot and dusty in the afternoon. First climb to the ridge above Namche and Sagarmatha National Park Museum and then continue along a slightly rising trail to Khyangjuma (3550m, 45 mins), where there are a couple of teahouses and a wonderful view of Ama Dablam on the far side of the valley. A stone paved trail descends to Phunke Tenga (3250m, 1½hrs), before climbing switchbacks through pine forest and traversing across Tengboche hill to a final switchback only 5 minutes from the gompa (see Day 5), campsite and some teahouses (3860m, 2¼hrs). Accommodation has been problematic in Tengboche for many years as the local teahouse owners sometimes take a very 'commercial approach' to trekking groups. A way to avoid this is to visit the gompa and then continue to Deboche (3820m, 20 mins) or Milingga (3750m, 40 mins) through a delightful pine, rhododendron and birch forest.

DAY 5: DEBOCHE–DINGBOCHE
                                    3½HRS

Wake up early and head back up to Tengboche for the morning *puja* (prayers), which you should try to get to by 7-7:30am. Please enter the gompa as quietly as possible and remember to make a donation

before you leave. Bring a *khadag* (silk blessing scarf) to offer as thanks if you want to receive a blessing from the abbot or senior monk. This Nyingmapa-sect gompa is a World Heritage site, originally built in 1916 but destroyed by an earthquake in 1934. The rebuilt gompa was again destroyed in 1989 by fire, but the grand new buildings are true to the original designs and form an idyllic setting for the thirty or so young monks who live here.

Once you have finished exploring the gompa it is worth the effort to climb the ridge that rises from Tengboche. Views of the surrounding peaks including Mt Everest and Ama Dablam improve with height once you reach a chorten after climbing for 30 minutes.

Leaving Deboche you first descend an easy trail before crossing a bridge and climbing to Pangboche (3930m, 1hr), which boasts the oldest gompa in the region.

Note: Many people stay at lower Pangboche as part of a slower acclimatisation programme.

The trail from Pangboche follows the Imja Khola and leads to a major trail junction (4175m, 1½hrs) and the site of a teashop. The left fork leads to Pheriche (site of the Trekker's Aid Post), but take the right trail and descend to and then cross a bridge. The trail continues up above the Imja Khola on a broad trail to Dingboche (4410m, 1hr).

DAY 6: DINGBOCHE   ALL DAY

The ascent to Dingboche (or Pheriche) frequently produces mild altitude sickness symptoms so an acclimatisation day is an excellent idea. There are three options for a day walk from Dingboche of varying difficulty. Perhaps the most impressive, and exerting, is a trail that crosses the Imja Khola by a small wooden bridge at the southern end of the village. From there, climb about 400m (2hrs) to a valley with a series of small lakes at the base of the north face of Ama Dablam. Continue up a slight ridge on your left, where you can see the pyramid summit of Makalu in the distance.

For a walk of a similar duration but on easier trails it is a good idea to follow the main trail to Chukhung (4730m, 3hrs) but stop short and return. As you climb through the Chukhung valley the popular Island Peak becomes increasingly dominant ahead and the massive Lhotse wall dwarfs everything. There are good views of Tabuche, Cholatse and Ama Dablam.

The easiest and shortest walk climbs the ridge to the north of Dingboche to a series of chortens and good views of all the surrounding peaks.

DAY 7: DINGBOCHE–LOBOCHE
3½HRS
Take any one of a number of trails that lead to a white chorten on the top of the ridge behind Dingboche. The ridge is the edge of an ancient lateral moraine and the trail takes an obvious route along the top, providing views of Ama Dablam (behind), Pheriche (below) and Loboche Peak (ahead) among other peaks on either side.

The trail will eventually descend to cross a small river that emits from the end of the Khumbu Glacier, on the far side is the small settlement of Dughla (4620m, 1½hrs). Climb the lateral moraine on the north side of the glacier snout on a well-defined trail to a series of stone memorials for climbers killed on the surrounding peaks. Cross a bridge over a stream flowing from Loboche Peak and continue to the often crowded teahouses of Loboche (4910m, 1½hrs).

DAY 8: LOBOCHE   ALL DAY
Some trekkers decide to take an acclimatisation day at Loboche despite the cramped conditions. However, you may choose to continue to Gorak Shep if you are not suffering from the gain in altitude, and explore around Loboche on your return trip. Directly behind the teahouses is a ridge that climbs to form the east flank of Loboche East Peak.

There is a small trail that climbs to about 5400m (2½hrs) and really good views of the surrounding peaks including Everest. Alternatively, cross the Khumbu Glacier on a good trail and climb a scrambly, rocky track to Khongma La (5528m, 3½hrs), where it is possible to continue on

to the summit of Pokalde (5806m, another 1½hrs), but remember it is a long descent to Loboche (or the Chukung/Dingboche valley) so exercise caution if you decide to continue.

DAY 9: LOBOCHE–KALA PATTHAR–
GORAK SHEP   5HRS
The trail continues on the same side of the glacier past the trail junction to the Italian Research Centre pyramid and over the Changri Shar glacier snout. Kala Patthar (meaning black rock) is clearly seen ahead and Gorak Shep is the cluster of teahouses beside the small lake. Your crew will want to go to straight to Gorak Shep (5140m, 3hrs) to deposit their loads, and you should take a rest to check everyone for symptoms of altitude sickness before attempting to climb Kala Patthar.

It is important to take your time and monitor your group for symptoms of altitude sickness throughout the climb and when resting on the summit. From the teahouse, climb north by north-east to a prayer-flag-covered rocky summit (5550m, 1½hrs) for one of the best views of the highest point on earth, Mt Everest, and the surrounding peaks of Nuptse, Lhotse, and Pumo Ri. Your descent will take 45 minutes, or longer if you wait until sundown (when it gets very cold very quickly).

DAY 10: GORAK SHEP–EVEREST
BASE CAMP (EBC)–LOBOCHE
4HRS
From Gorak Shep the trail curls around the base of Kala Patthar, continuing along the side of the Khumbu glacier. After an hour you will move on to the glacier itself and care needs to be taken not to walk off the track. As you approach EBC (5350m, 30 mins) views of the notorious Khumbu Icefall appear on your right, it looks far more intimidating from here than from other viewpoints. Most expeditions do not appreciate you walking around their camps for security reasons, so respect their wishes and avoid intruding. The return trip to Gorak Shep along the same trail takes about 45 minutes and a further 2 hours down to Loboche.

ROUTE GUIDE

DAY 11: LOBOCHE–DZONGLA 5HRS

Descend from Loboche for about 20 minutes towards Dughla and turn right before crossing a stream (4835m); after crossing a flat area, follow an obvious trail that climbs up and around a grassy hillside, with views all the way to Pheriche and beyond. The trail continues to climb an easy gradient up natural contours in the hillside, the turquoise Chola Tsho (lake) lies below the rugged summits of Cholatse and Arakam Tse. The teahouses of Dzongla (4830m) are across another stream and up a small rise, and should be reached in 2 hours from the Loboche–Dughla turnoff. If you are camping continue for another 40 minutes to a large meadow surrounded by a horseshoe of impressive peaks.

DAY 12: DZONGLA–CHO LA–DRAGNAG (THANGNAK)   5HRS

An obvious trail loops over a grassy hill behind Dzongla and then gradually climbs a large meadow to a rocky bluff near the end of the valley. The trail switchbacks up to a rock-face and then climbs to the right, up a worn boulder-strewn trail to an area of smooth rock slabs covered in cairns, next to a glacier. Stick to the true right (south) side, rather than climbing onto the glacier immediately, on a track that is frequently covered in snow, before crossing the glacier just before Cho La (5420m, 2½hrs). There aren't any views of the highest peaks but there are many lesser peaks that fill the western horizon. Beneath is a steep rocky trail that will be covered in parts with snow and ice. Take care on the descent but keep moving as the lower section is prone to rockfall from a craggy peak to your left. In less than an hour you should reach an easier gradient; cross a minor boulder-covered ridge, which leads to a good campsite in a trough. Climb the grassy hill on the far side of the campsite to a large obvious boulder and then a long steep descent brings you to the teahouses and campsites at Dragnag (Thangnak, 4700m, 1½hrs).

DAY 13: DRAGNAG (THANGNAK)–GOKYO RI–GOKYO   5½HRS

Of all the glaciers in the Everest region the most impressive is the Ngozumba, which you must cross on a trail to the west of Dragnag. Ask locals which route is currently recommended and take your time while crossing the glacier to catch mountain reflections in the turquoise lakes. Once on the far side of the glacier turn north (right) and join the main Gokyo trail just before a large lake (1hr from Dragnag). The trail to Gokyo (4790m), located on the east bank of another large lake, takes a further hour. After depositing unnecessary gear in your teahouse or camp, head out of the village on a trail that crosses a broad shallow watercourse crossed by stepping stones and rock platform. The track up Gokyo Ri is badly eroded in the lower section but it soon becomes a substantial ridge trail all the way to the summit (5483m, 2½hrs). This rocky, prayer flag covered peak offers one of the best views of Mt Everest and surrounding peaks in the entire region. It will take an hour to descend back to Gokyo.

❏ **The life of a teahouse owner**
Running a teahouse is a tiring and often difficult occupation, but few can have had more challenges than Pasang Bhotie Sherpa, Namaste Lodge, Gokyo.

The eldest of four sisters, Pasang was sent to tend her family's yak herd in the Gokyo valley at the age of 12. While her sisters went to school, Pasang sold firewood and tea to trekkers from her cold and lonely stone huts, which she inhabited up and down the valley depending on the weather. After 6 years she had learnt basic English and was sending significant funds home to the family. She decided to run a small teashop at Gokyo's third lake and started saving every rupee. At 25 she met and fell in love with a Nepali trek leader with whom she has run a slowly expanding teahouse business for the last 19 years. She hopes that one day one of her sons, both of whom have a good college education, will return and continue her legacy.

DAY 14: GOKYO   ALL DAY

A great day out is to explore the higher lakes and Cho Oyu Base Camp; without crossing the watercourse, head north on a good trail from Gokyo in the ablation valley caused by Ngozumba Glacier. You will soon come to the fourth of Gokyo's lakes (1hr) surrounded by craggy peaks. Continue on the same trail to the picturesque fifth lake (4990m, 1½hrs). Here you have three options, climb one of the higher lumps of glacial moraine for views of Mt Everest reflecting in glacial lakes, or climb a ridge that comes down to the north-eastern corner of the lake to an excellent viewpoint at roughly 5500m (at least 1½hrs), or continue on a smaller trail which turns left to the foot of Cho Oyu, which reflects in the sixth lake (1½hrs). For groups with camping equipment it is worth spending a night in the sixth lake area and enjoying all of these options as well as potential sunset views of Mt Everest.

DAY 15: GOKYO–RENJO LA–LUMDE   6½HRS

From Gokyo head to the base of the Gokyo Ri climb, but instead of heading up the hill take the left-hand trail that heads around the lake. There are two trails, do not take the one by the lakeshore; instead, take the other which climbs slightly. In an hour you should reach the bottom of a steep switchback trail where the ground is loose and climbs an unrelenting gradient for another hour. At the top of the climb the gradient eases a little and heads across a rocky section, which can be icy from December to March. You now enter a broad valley, which can make an ideal high camp for those with tents. The trail heads due west across the valley and then climbs again around a rocky spur before heading up to Renjo La (5360m, 1½hrs) via a stone staircase. The trail is much easier to follow now that the people from Thame have completed a major reconstruction project. This is especially true on the western side of the pass, which is now a stone staircase in good repair. The view from the pass is one of the best in the entire Solu-Khumbu, and a terrific lunch spot. The trail down the western side of the pass rapidly brings you to the

edge of a glacial lake, where the stone steps finish. Beyond is another lake, Relama Tsho (4905m, 2hrs), which is a popular camping spot for those approaching the pass from the Thame side. A broad trail now winds around the eastern side of a hill above the lake before descending to a large sandy kharka. At the very end of the kharka the trail descends rapidly into the Bhote Kosi valley and in one hour you should reach the few teahouses at Lumde (4368m).

DAY 16: LUMDE–THAME   3HRS

An easy trail descends from Lumde to a bridge at the village of Marulung (4210m, 1hr), where there are some more teahouses. You now cross the Bhote Khosi and descend the true right (western) bank along a broad and easy-to-follow trail to Thame (3820m, 1½hrs), where there are many teahouses beyond a large moraine with some stupas on top. If you have the time, it is worth climbing this moraine and following a trail through juniper and fir forest to Thame's major gompa (at the entrance to small valley heading west from the main village); it is the site of a Mani Rimdu festival in May.

DAY 17: THAME–NAMCHE   3½HRS

The trail from Thame descends to the Bhote Kosi and crosses a steel-box bridge at the end of a canyon section carved by the river. The locals believe this is an auspicious place and have painted the rock-face above the bridge with Buddhas and prayers. The trail now climbs a little before settling into an easy downhill gradient to Thamo (3480m, 1hr). Cross the Thesbu Khola and continue on a broad trail through pine forest all the way to Namche (3440m, 1½hrs), where you will arrive next to the new helipad and many painted mani stones on the hill above the western side of the town.

DAYS 18-20: NAMCHE–LUKLA–KATHMANDU

From Namche to Phakding takes about a day to walk; the next day is a half-day walk to Lukla where many people spend the afternoon drinking beer to celebrate the end of their trek, before flying to Kathmandu on the following day.

ROUTE GUIDE

OTHER TRAILS IN THE SOLU-KHUMBU

[See maps opposite inside back cover] GHT through-hikers tend to favour two routes in the Solu, the first is for those coming from Makalu Base Camp over the passes and then continue across Cho and Renjo La to Tashi Labsta (see *Rolwaling and Tashi Labsta*, pp146-53). The other follows the Arun-Salpa Trail between Arun Nadi and Kharikhola (see the *Arun-Salpa Trail*, p131) and then on to Jiri.

Before commercial flights to Lukla became the most popular method of accessing the Solu-Khumbu, trekkers would start from the road-head town of **Jiri** (the road has now been extended to Bhandar and there are plans to go all the way to Salleri in the next few years). The number of trekkers taking this 4- to 5-day route is now so small that those who do often find it a major highlight of their trek. The contrast to the crowds and rush of the higher trails means you can enjoy the natural hospitality and friendliness of the Sherpa, Gurung and Rai communities you encounter.

In 2007, the Nepali government removed trekking restrictions for **Nangpa La** (5716m) at the head of the Thame valley. Camping equipment is necessary as well as experience in glacier travel. This is a rough and wild route, and absolutely do not cross into Tibet from here!

Perhaps the most popular trekking peaks in Nepal are **Island Peak** above Chukhung and **Mera Peak** above the Honku Khola. Access to both peaks follow established trekking routes, for Island Peak it is a simple day trip from Dingboche (5½hrs return), whereas the Honku Khola and routes over Mera La and Amphu Labsta are much more committing and normally take about 30 days to and from Lukla. For more information about both routes, see Jamie McGuinness's, *Trekking in the Everest Region*, Trailblazer.

In the lower Solu there are a number of **community-based routes** that have a combination of teahouses and homestays. These are excellent winter treks for those wanting to immerse themselves in hill cultures and enjoy the clear-air views of the Himalaya. In addition to the Arun-Salpa Trail, the most popular routes link **Salpa Pokhari** to **Parma Ri** and then to either **Salleri** or **Halesi Maratika**, where there are some of the most important Buddhist pilgrimage caves in Nepal. Each January many thousands of pilgrims visit the caves to perform a series of 'tests' passing through holes and crawling through narrow gaps as acts of devotion.

One of the best Himalaya-panorama viewpoints is from **Pikey Peak** (4068m), near Salleri. There are teahouses and community lodges for a number of circuit-trek options of 7-10 days from Jiri, although some trekkers use a flight and bus combination with **Phaplu** to reduce the trek to 5-6 days.

Rolwaling region

Often overlooked by tour companies, there is a culturally diverse and very enjoyable trekking region just a day's drive to the north-east of Kathmandu, known as Rolwaling. Whether you want high passes, mountains and glaciers, or charming villages amid old-growth forests, this region will both surprise and delight any trekker.

Although the name, Rolwaling, specifically applies to a river that is fed from the glaciers around Tsho Rolpa lake, it now includes all the valleys, hills and ridges as far west as the Arniko Highway (the road to Lhasa from Kathmandu). To the east of the region is the Solu-Khumbu (see *Solu-Khumbu/the Everest Region*, pp136-44), to which it is linked by the formidable

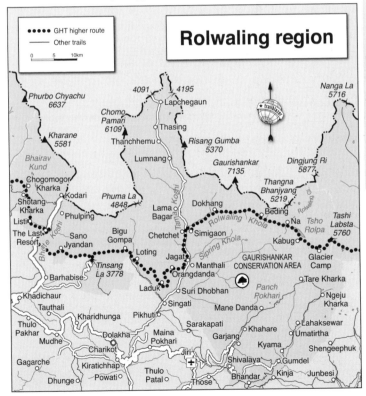

ROUTE GUIDE

Tashi Labsta pass (full route from the Arniko Highway to the Solu-Khumbu over Tashi Labsta is described below). The Great Himalayan Range in Nepal comes to an abrupt stop at the Gaurishankar Himal as the Tama Kosi cuts through the mountains. Beyond, to the west, are Tamang, Gurung and Sherpa communities, as well as some rarely explored rhododendron forests that are home to red panda and black bear.

A road is being built up the Tama Kosi valley to Tibet, which is now increasing access to Rolwaling as a whole. Another road from Barhabise to Bigu Gompa is open but often blocked by landslides. A good place to start exploring the eastern Rolwaling is The Last Resort on the Arniko Highway, where you can follow a series of ridges up to Tinsang La. From here you traverse around the Chilingkha Danda through Sherpa, Tamang and Gurung villages to Laduk. It is possible to travel by bus from Kathmandu to Singati, and reach Laduk in one day. The most popular trail in Rolwaling is a high alpine route over Tashi Labsta that heads from Laduk to Na via Simigaon and takes six days (note that you can take a jeep from Singati to Chetchet to save two days). For the truly adventurous, there is a more serious mountaineering route over Yalung La before climbing the Trakarding and Drolambu glaciers to Tashi Labsta. Lower trails head from Laduk to Jiri via Yarsa and Sarakapti.

Most of the Rolwaling region is protected as part of the Gaurishankar Conservation Area, which adjoins Sagarmatha National Park at Tashi Labsta pass.

As at March 2014, the trekking permit fees for the Dolakha District/ Gaurishankar & Lamabagar areas are US$10pp per week. Plus the Gaurishankar Conservation Area entry fee of Rs2000pp. Also see *Solu Khumbu (Everest Region)* for Sagamartha and Everest region permit details, p137.

ROLWALING & TASHI LABSTA TREK

If you have limited time you could begin your trek from Singati or Chetchet (aka Chhechet) or head over Yalung La to Na and then cross the Tashi Labsta (a 16-day trek). Some groups like to combine this trek with a trekking peak such as Ramdung (5930m), Yalung Peak (5630m) or Pachermo (6273m). Remember to include an additional acclimatisation day in the Thame valley if you are going to attempt Tashi Labsta from the Solu-Khumbu.

The best times of year to visit Rolwaling are the two main trekking seasons of March to May, and October to December. However, for those wanting to cross Tashi Labsta, the compacted snow in October offers much better conditions than in the spring months.

The approach and crossing of Tashi Labsta can cause problems as even light snow can make route finding very difficult and the trail treacherous on both the ascent and descent. The glaciers on the eastern side of the pass are hazardous and crevassed. You should also ensure that you have rock and ice climbing equipment with you, to help negotiate steep snow and/or blue ice.

Despite being a fertile area, food is often scarce in Rolwaling so ensure that you are as fully supplied as possible before leaving Kathmandu. Crossing Tashi

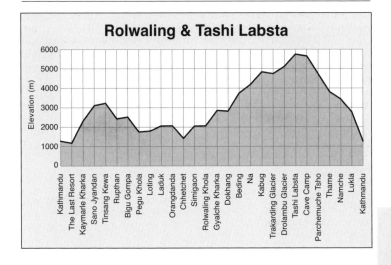

Rolwaling & Tashi Labsta

Elevation (m): 6000, 5000, 4000, 3000, 2000, 1000, 0

Kathmandu, The Last Resort, Kaymarle Kharka, Sano Jyandan, Tinsang Kewa, Rupthan, Bigu Gompa, Pegu Khola, Loting, Laduk, Orangdanda, Chhetchet, Simigaon, Rolwaling Khola, Gyalche Kharka, Dokhang, Beding, Na, Kabug, Trakarding Glacier, Drolambu Glacier, Tashi Labsta, Cave Camp, Parchemuche Tsho, Thame, Namche, Lukla, Kathmandu

Labsta requires that you have sufficient food and fuel for at least eight days prior to arriving at Na.

An Austrian development project, Eco-Himal, have built a series of tea-house-style lodges and campsites from near Barhabise on the Arniko Highway to Orangdanda, which provide an ideal route for a cultural trek via Bigu Gompa. It is worth employing a local guide to show you how to avoid the new road up and over Tinsang La from Barhabise.

ROLWALING & TASHI LABSTA TREK

Diverse cultures, picturesque villages and one of the most challenging passes in the Himalaya. A trek through the Rowaling region will delight, surprise and provide a genuine physical test for even the most experienced trekker.

Grade 4

● **Duration & distance**: About 23 days total; daily distance is not important to grade
● **Gradient**: Short steep sections
● **Quality of path**: Both formed & rough tracks, some obstacles
● **Quality of markings**: Limited signage
● **Experience required**: Some walking experience required

● **Walking times**: Less than 6½ hours per day
● **Steps**: Steps not included in grade
● **Highest point**: 5760m
● **Best season**: Apr-May/Oct-Nov
● **Accommodation**: Camping
● **Recommended maps**: NP104 GHT Series The Rolwaling & NP103 Series Solu-Khumbu (Everest) Region, Himalayan Map House, 2013

DAY 1: KATHMANDU–THE LAST RESORT   4HRS

The drive from Kathmandu up the Arniko Highway is best done early in the morning before the traffic becomes too heavy. If you reach Barhabise within 3 hours you have had a fast trip: the public bus can take much longer. If you are going to stay in the Eco-Himal lodges you will need to alight at Barhabise and trek to Karthali where Mr Sunil Rokka runs a teahouse and can organise a local guide for you.

However, if you are planning to follow the route described, continue to The Last Resort (1170m, famous for the highest bungee jump in Asia), about an hour from Barhabise.

DAY 2: THE LAST RESORT– KAYMARLE KHARKA   5½HRS

There are many confusing forest trails from the Marmin Danda to Tinsang La, so you should organise a local guide at The Last Resort. From The Last Resort, cross the bridge and climb stone steps to Tyanthali village (1390m, 30 mins). At an old service road, turn right and continue past the village school. About 400m beyond the school take a trail that turns up hill (left) and slowly climbs as it traverses to Sakhuwa village (1480m, 40mins).

After passing through some scrubby forest the trail swings around a corner to some broad terraced fields belonging to Kati village (1520m, 20 mins). Stay close to the base of the steep hillside above, which will involve stepping up from terrace to terrace. Do not enter the village. Continue on a trail that heads across a small stream on the northern side of the village and then climbs into scrubby forest that covers the hillside above. You will now climb a well-worn switchback trail to Mandre (2180m, 2½hrs).

From above Mandre village, take a major trail that turns south-east (right) where you will find the gradient eases as it traverses the south-facing slope of a prominent hill. In another 1½ hours you will reach a natural saddle between the Khagdal Khola and Gulche valleys. Camp on the terraces or saddle (2285m; Finaid: Barhabise,

sheet: 2785 04, ref: 925 811), there is a permanent water source on the north side (Gulche village side) where there are a couple of houses.

DAY 3: KAYMARLE KHARKA–SANO JYANDAN   5½HRS

Today you leave the villages behind and head up to a large forested ridge, which ultimately leads to Tinsang La. Take your time and enjoy the views; if you begin early each day there is a good chance of seeing red panda. Follow a trail to the east that heads up from the kharka along an obvious ridge. As you climb, the forest becomes thicker and after about 400m of ascent (1¾hrs) the trail veers away from the ridge and onto the northern slopes of the Nambarjun Danda.

After 40 minutes you reach a dry watercourse which you should climb to another saddle and potential campsite at Sindurche Kharka (2780m, 1hr). The trail from the kharka continues east, back up onto the forested ridge. The trail sometimes butts up against the precipitous edge of the ridge, with views down to the Khagdal Khola 700m below. As you continue along the ridge the trail rises and falls for short sections and there are small seasonal shelters used by locals when they take their cattle to the high pastures during the monsoon months. Do not take any cross trails, stick to the obvious track as close to the top of the ridge as possible.

After about 2 hours you will arrive at a kharka with two stone shelters in a large saddle, Sano Jyandan (3127m), where there is permanent water in the rhododendron-forested gully to the north of the campsite.

DAY 4: SANO JYANDAN–TINSANG KEWA   4HRS

Head due east on a trail that traverses beneath a forested hill to a very large kharka with many stone shelters called Palati Jyandan (3210m, 30 mins). **Note: camping is not advisable here as water is scarce during the trekking seasons.**

Continue to the far side of the kharka and re-enter the forest. You soon come to the head of a dry watercourse (25 mins) which you should follow as it winds down between two hills and away from the ridge. A further 30 minutes from the kharka, the trail swings east (right) and away from the watercourse and into an old-growth rhododendron forest. Continue on a good trail, which in 20 minutes from the watercourse brings you to Marmin Jyandan (3250m), where there are a few stone shelters but not permanent water. From this kharka the trail heads out across a steep rocky hillside. You should check the weather before beginning, as rain will make sections more difficult.

Climb back onto the ridge for 30 minutes before the trail slowly climbs and traverses a steep rock- and grass-covered hillside. In 45 minutes you will connect with a long north–south ridge, which leads to Tinsang La. You should be able to see the motor road leading up to the pass about 2km away.

Once you join the main ridge you are back in rhododendron forest, but do not descend all the way to the pass. Instead follow a large trail that swings east, away from the ridge, and in 20 minutes you drop down to a series of plateaus that lead to a campsite at Tinsang Kewa (3266m, 15 mins).

DAY 5: TINSANG KEWA–BIGU GOMPA 4½HRS

You will frequently cross the road as you descend via multiple short cuts through the forest. In 2¾ hours you will reach the hamlet of Rupthan (2400m) where you cross a small bridge. From here the trail begins to climb back into the forest on an easy gradient. A local guide is useful to pick the right combination of short-cut trails up to the broad plateau of Bigu Gompa (2516m, 1¾hrs), and the Eco-Himal teahouse and campsite.

Bigu Gompa is a nunnery dedicated to the thousand-armed Buddha, Avalokiteshwara (Compassion of all Buddhas), who is the all-seeing, all-knowing remover of obstacles. The nuns are happy for visitors to attend morning prayers; a donation is appropriate for even brief visits.

DAY 6: BIGU GOMPA–LOTING 4HRS

From the Sherpa village of Bigu, there are two routes to Loting, the main trail descends to the Pegu (Amatol) Khola (1700m, 2½hrs), which it crosses and then climbs a little before descending to a bridge over the Sangu Khola and then climbing to the Gurung village of Loting (1768m, 80 mins) where there is an Eco-Himal teahouse and campsite.

Alternatively, head east and gradually descend to the village of Alampu, which covers the south-east-facing hillside above the Kotheli Khola. A steep trail descends through the village to a bridge (1732m, 2hrs), which you should cross to a small hamlet. Follow the river downstream for about 30 minutes to just before the confluence with the Sangu Khola and veer left to climb about 200m through scrubby forest. In an hour you round the hillside and enter Loting (see above).

DAY 7: LOTING–LADUK 6HRS

A trail leads around the edge of some terraced fields before descending slightly to the Dorun Khola to the south-east of Loting. Climb the far bank past a large chautara and continue ascending a gradual gradient around a hillside, which is steeper on its southern flanks.

There are many trails around the hill and you should try to stick to the highest obvious track. Descend to and then cross a seasonal watercourse before climbing easy trails to Chilingkha (1839m, 2hrs), where there is an Eco-Himal campsite but no teahouse facility.

Climb through the village to another scrub-covered hillside, which has recovered from a large bushfire at the beginning of 2009. The trail traverses around the hillside to the small village of Chyasarpa (2020m, 80 mins), where you descend to another watercourse. From here the trail becomes broader as it passes through a small forest and then climbs an easy gradient all the way to the Eco-Himal teahouse and campsite at Laduk (2050m, 2½hrs).

Note: from Laduk it is possible to descend to the road at Singati and return to Kathmandu within 7-8 hours.

DAY 8: LADUK–ORANGDANDA
4HRS

A broad trail climbs an easy gradient from Laduk through pine forest that covers most of the hillside above. In 80 minutes you will reach a ridge above Bulung where you might be lucky and catch your first views of the Gaurishankar Himal. Descend to the village (1890m, 15 mins), where there is a community-owned campsite.

A trail winds around the top of the village to a chautara with two chorten where you join another trail from the valley below. Take the left fork, which heads north and descends to a stream before climbing an easy gradient across a grassy hillside to the small village of Yarsa (2020m, 45 mins). The trail descends to a small dry watercourse on the northern side of the village, which you have to climb for about 40 metres to a track that swings right and climbs to terraced fields.

In about 50 minutes you enter the ridge-top village of Orangdanda (2029m) where there is another Eco-Himal teahouse and campsite. There are great morning views of the Gaurishankar Himal from this teahouse, which is the last one along the Rolwaling trail. From here you can descend to the road in the valley below (about 700m down, 3hrs) where you can return to Kathmandu.

Note: To continue towards the Rolwaling Khola from this point requires camping equipment.

DAY 9: ORANGDANDA–RIVER CAMP
4¾HRS

Looking north from the Eco-Himal teahouse you will notice that the homes have changed from the previous days as you are now entering Tamang communities. From the entrance to the lodge, the trail contours around a broad, terraced hillside to a large landslide. There is a good trail across the very top of the landslide, do not cross lower down. Once on the far side, descend terraces to a stream, and then climb a little to the village of Deulang (1900m, 1¼hrs). You soon reach the top of the large village of Thare where you should follow the main trail that descends through the centre of the village. As you reach a cluster of homes towards the bottom of the village (1820m, 45 mins) the trail swings north and descends an easier gradient to a small Sherpa village above Gongar (1430m, 1¾hrs), which is in the valley below. Stone steps lead down to the road, which you will need to follow for about an hour to a bridge at Chetchet (1377m). Cross the Tama Kosi to a campsite on the far bank. If you are feeling strong and have enough time, you could combine today with tomorrow's trek.

DAY 10: RIVER CAMP–SIMIGAON
3½HRS

From the campsite a stone staircase climbs up and around a rocky spur that juts into the river valley. Climb steps which switchback for about 400m to the lower homes of Simigaon village (2hrs). Once you reach the first terraces the gradient eases as the trail winds between homes. It will take another 1½ hours to reach the few teahouses and campsite (2036m) on the ridge above the village, where a new gompa is being built.

DAY 11: SIMIGAON–DOKHANG
6HRS

From the gompa you can see the trail winding around the hillside to the north-east to a minor ridge (30 mins) where the trail descends through forest to a small kharka about 30m above the Rolwaling Khola (2060m, 40 mins).

Note: if you are doing this route in reverse there is a trail junction about 10 minutes into the forest from the kharka – you must take the left fork and climb from here, do not descend to the river.

From the kharka the trail begins a long and sometimes steep climb through forest. After 2 hours you should reach a large waterfall, which has a cool pool of water to soak your feet in if it's a hot day. Continue to climb for another 2 hours to Gyalche Kharka (2832m) where there is a small shop and campsite. It is now an easy descent through forest and then beside a small stream to the spacious campsite at Dokhang (2791m, 40 mins).

DAY 12: DOKHANG–BEDING
5¼HRS

After the steep climbs of yesterday, the trail gradient is now much easier as it winds a course along the south bank of the Rolwaling Khola. Rhododendron, pine and juniper shade wildflowers in mossy glades, and the river cascades beside the trail. There are a few small landslides to cross, which make ideal places to spot birds catching insects above the river.

In 2 hours you should reach a bridge to the true right (north) bank of the river, and in another 15 minutes you will reach a bridge over the Themlung Khola, which is surrounded by cairns. If you stand in the middle of the bridge and look up the steep ravine to the north you will see Gaurishankar looming overhead.

From the bridge the trail climbs a few hundred metres away from the V-shaped river valley and towards the U-shaped glacial valleys above. As you reach the top of the climb you will notice that juniper and fir trees become more common, and the snow and ice-covered bulk of Tsoboje peak fills the end of the valley ahead.

The gradient eases once again and you should reach the village of Nyamare (3550m) in another 2 hours. Beding (3740m), where there are teahouses and a campsite, is now less than an hour away.

DAY 13: BEDING–NA
4¾HRS

Today is a relatively short and easy trekking day, so take a little time to visit the gompa in the village. It is said that a Buddhist monk came and lived in a cave behind the gompa before the village was established. To mark the site, a chorten was built and to offer a khadag to the chorten is considered to bestow good luck on the giver for as long as the scarf remains attached. Please offer a donation to the gompa if you want to admire the wood-panel frescoes inside.

The trail climbs an easy gradient away from Beding through miniature fir trees along a sometimes rocky trail. After 2½ hours you should notice that the valley is becoming broader and flatter and some large boulders dot the landscape. One of the

boulders has been carved with the Buddhist prayer, *Om Mani Padmi Hum*, and must be the largest single mani stone anywhere. Just beyond is another boulder with a large painting of Padmasambhava (aka Guru Rinpoche, the Lotus Born, who first took Buddhism to Tibet in the 8th century) and a small shrine.

Na (4180m, 2¼hrs) is a scattered village on a broad alluvial fan where there are many camping options and teahouses.

DAY 14: NA
ALL DAY

It is a good idea to take a day to acclimatise in Na, and there are a couple of good day trip options.

The most popular day trip is to head up valley to a small kharka and then turn right on a small trail to Yalung Peak base camp (5hrs' return trip). Alternatively, climb to the end of Tsho Rolpa lake for views of Kang Nachago above Na (4hrs' return trip).

DAY 15: NA–KABUG
5HRS

The trail above Na climbs a slight gradient to a bridge over the Tsho Rolpa outflow. From here you have two options: the main trail ascends an ablation valley to the south, alternatively, climb the terminal moraine wall that acts as a dam for the lake. Once at the lake, the trail winds around and descends slightly to the ablation valley to the south.

About halfway along the side of the lake, at Chhukyima there are a couple of small teashops run by locals from Na and a good campsite (4580m, 3hrs). Continue to the end of the valley and climb a steep hillside for 250m (1½hrs) to a viewpoint of the lake and surrounding peaks. It is now a short descent to the broad sandy plateau of Kabug campsite (4820m, 30 mins).

DAY 16: KABUG–GLACIER SNOUT
6½HRS

Before you begin today it is worth having a good look at the Trakarding Glacier below and try to identify potential routes across it – groups often get separated here and finding each other can waste a lot of time. Cross the plateau to the furthest eastern corner above the glacier and then descend a loose earth trail to the southern edge of Trakarding Glacier (4735m, 40 mins). From here there are a number of routes that cross the glacier. If you have started early in the morning, the most obvious trail crosses almost immediately to a trail that then ascends the northern side of the glacier. However, this route is extremely prone to rockfall from mid-morning onwards. Alternative routes begin in about 30 minutes and again in an hour up the south side of the glacier. As with all glacier crossings care should be taken at all times, and your party should remain together throughout the crossing. Once on the north side of the glacier, follow a trail that leads to the snout of Drolambu Glacier. There is a large campsite at place called Noisy Knob Camp (4880m, 3½hrs). If you have time, continue to the far side of the glacier snout to where a rock scramble (use a hand line for porter safety) brings you to another campsite beneath ice cliffs (5085m, 2hrs 20 mins).

Note: many maps show a rocky route up the western side of the Drolambu Glacier snout, this route is rarely used due to rockfall danger.

DAY 17: GLACIER SNOUT–TASHI LABSTA CAMP   6½HRS
On the true left side of Drolambu Glacier (east) a stream has carved a rocky trail, climb this to access a glacial ablation valley (5350m, 1hr). Stay in the bottom of the ablation valley all the way to the base of the glacier flowing down from Pachermo (5435m, 2½hrs). The snout of this glacier has receded and you might need to put in a hand line for porter safety. Once onto the glacier, climb a natural ramp that leads all the way to the summit of Tashi Labsta (5760m, 3hrs) – be careful of crevasses! The pass is a rocky ridge, which is normally reached by climbing an icy slope on the lower flanks of Pachermo. From the top of the pass the high camp is beneath an overhanging rock-face about 100m down from the summit.

Note: close to the base of the overhang is safe from rockfall, whereas camping on the glacier below is dangerous.

If there is already a group camped here, head a little higher on the northern flank of Pachermo to a snowy plateau that is often used as a base camp for groups climbing Pachermo. The strong social and economic links between the Rolwaling and Thame valleys mean that you could even meet a wedding party camped up here during the summer months!

18: TASHI LABSTA CAMP–LAKE CAMP/THYANGBO KHARKA
5-6½HRS
From the high camp a trail traverses due east along the base of south-facing rock-face of Agole Peak. In less than an hour you should reach a broad notch in the cliff-face below, you will probably need to set a safety line for porters. The descent is about 70m to an obvious trail down rocky slopes to the campsite at Ngole (5130m, 2hrs 20 mins).

A steep trail leads down moraine from the camp to a shallow basin where there is a trail junction. The fastest route down to Thyangbo Kharka climbs the smaller moraine wall on the far side (true left) of the basin and descends around a black cliff-face before winding down the true left (northern) side of the valley to Thyangbo Kharka (4320m, 3hrs). Alternatively, turn right in the basin and head down to a series of three lakes where you can camp beside the largest, Parchemuche Tsho (4780m, 1½hrs).

DAY 19: LAKE CAMP/THYANGBO KHARKA–THAME   2-4HRS
The trail down to Thyangbo Kharka (4320m, 2hrs) is along the true left (northern) side of the valley and provides good views of a series of pinnacle-like peaks to the south. From the Kharka, where there is a teahouse and good campsite, it is an easy 2 hours, passing the famous gompa, down to Thame (3820m).

DAY 20: THAME–NAMCHE   2½HRS
The trail from Thame descends to the Bhote Kosi and crosses a bridge at the end of a canyon section carved by the river. The locals believe this is an auspicious place and have painted the rock-face above the

bridge with Buddhas and prayers. The trail now climbs a little before settling into an easy downhill gradient to Thamo (3480m, 1hr). Cross the Thesbu Khola and continue on a broad trail through pine forest all the way to Namche (3440m, 1½hrs) where you will arrive next to the new helipad and many painted mani stones on the hill above the western side of the town.

DAY 21: NAMCHE–PHAKDING 4HRS

The trail from Namche leaves the southern entry to the town and descends almost 800m to the Bhote Kosi below (2hrs). The trail then winds down the river valley first to Monjo (2840m, 1hr, the Sagarmatha

National Park entry post), then Benkar (45 mins) and then to Phakding (2610m, 1hr), where there are numerous teahouses.

DAYS 22-23: PHAKDING–LUKLA–KATHMANDU   4HRS

An easy undulating trail leads to Ghat (2590m, 1hr) where there are some fine painted mani boulders. It is then an easy climb to Lukla (2840m, 3hrs) where there are many teahouses and the famous airstrip with regular flights to Kathmandu. See *Everest Base Camp, Cho La and Renjo La*, pp138-43 for more information about the trail from Thame to Lukla.

OTHER TRAILS IN THE ROLWALING REGION

[See maps opposite inside back cover] GHT through-hikers either cross Tashi Labsta following the previous itinerary or avoid it by detouring from **Laduk to Jiri** via Yarsa and Sarakapati (Grade 4, 2-3 days) and then joining the Jiri to Solu trail. Note that accommodation is scarce on this route and you should take a tent or be prepared to sleep in the open for a night or two.

There are many ridge and valley treks in Rolwaling waiting to be explored. Trekking groups can be organised from The Last Resort to explore Kalinchok Bhagawati Danda (the ridge that flows south from Tinsang La) and Jimyal Danda (the ridge to the north of Tinsang La).

For those who want to challenge themselves with more adventurous trekking, the restricted area to the north of **Lama Bagar** is now accessible with the purchase of a US$90 trekking permit from Kathmandu. Alternatively, create a spectacular technical alpine trek by starting from Lukla, cross Tashi Labsta to Na, then over **Yalung La** to join with the passes to the south of Yalung and Ramdung peaks that link upper Rolwaling with trails to Jiri, Bhandar, Junbesi and routes that approach Lukla from the south.

ROUTE GUIDE

Helambu and Langtang

Just a day to the north of Kathmandu is the third most popular trekking region in Nepal, Langtang National Park, where there are mountains, glaciers, wildlife and rhododendron forests galore. The intermingling of Bhotia, Tamang, Brahmin, Newari and Chhetri people throughout the region is a wonderful example of Nepal's harmonious ethnic diversity. Add some folklore and some sublime sacred lakes, and it's fair to say that the Helambu and Langtang regions have it all!

Three glaciers converge at Langshisa Kharka to form the headwaters of the Langtang Khola, which flows east to west between two chains of snow-covered peaks: the Langtang and Kangja Himals. The ridges and river valleys that shape the south-facing flanks of the Kangja Himal are broadly called Helambu. An extensive trail network runs throughout the region providing treks from just a few days to up to a month. However, most trekkers stick to the teahouse routes from Dhunche to Kyangjin Gompa (described in detail on pp160-1) and Sundarijal to Gosainkund (described in detail on pp156-7).

Of the two main trails in the region the Dhunche or Syabrubesi to Kyangjin Gompa through Bhotia villages is by far the more popular. If you have camping

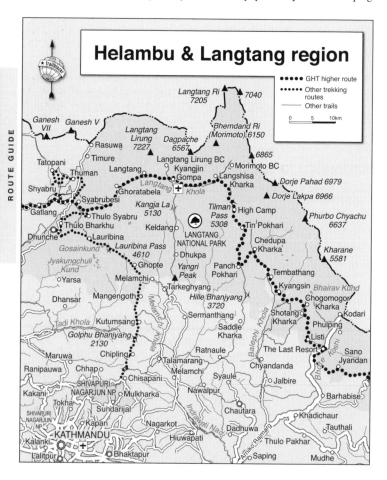

Helambu & Langtang region

* trailblazer

●●●●● GHT higher route
●●●●● Other trekking routes
——— Other trails

0   5   10km

Langtang Ri 7205
7040
Bhemdand Ri (Morimoto) 6150
6865
Ganesh VII
Ganesh V
Rasuwa
Langtang Lirung 7227
Dagpache 6567
Tatopani
Timure
Langtang Lirung BC
Morimoto BC
Thuman
Langtang
Kyangjin Gompa
Langshisa Kharka
Dorje Pahad 6979
Shyabru
Langtang Khola
Ghoratabela
Dorje Lakpa 6966
Syabrubesi
Gatlang
Kangja La 5130
Tilman Pass 5308
High Camp
Phurbo Chyachu 6637
Thulo Syabru
Keldang
Tin Pokhari
Thulo Bharkhu
LANGTANG NATIONAL PARK
Chedupa Kharka
Dhunche
Lauribina
Kharane 5581
Gosainkund
Lauribina Pass 4610
Dhukpa
Jyakungchuli Kund
Ghopte
Yangri Peak
Panch Pokhari
Tembathang
Yarsa
Melamchi
Tarkeghyang
Kyangsin Bhairav Kund
Dhansar
Mangengoth
Hille Bhanjyang 3720
Chogomogor Kharka
Tadi Khola
Kutumsang
Sermanthang
Shotang Kharka
Kodari
Golphu Bhanjyang 2130
Saddle Kharka
Phulping
Chipling
Ratnaule
The Last Resort
Listi
Maruwa
Chhapo
Talamarang
Chyandanda
Sano Jyandan
Ranipauwa
Chisapani
Melamchi
Syaule
Jalbire
Kakani
SHIVAPURI NAGARJUN NP
Mulkharka
Nawalpur
Barhabise
Tokha
SHIVAPURI NAGARJUN NP
Sundarijal
Chautara
Khadichaur
Kapan
Nagarkot
Dadhuwa
Tauthali
KATHMANDU
Hiuwapati
Thulo Pakhar
Kalanki
Lalitpur
Bhaktapur
Saping
Mudhe

ROUTE GUIDE

equipment, continue up the valley into an unspoilt mountain wilderness, which is home to snow leopard and three challenging passes: Kangja (Ganja) La, Tilman Pass and Tilman East Pass, all of which are summarised below.

There are dozens of trails through Helambu that link the sacred lakes of Gosainkund, Panch Pokhari and Bhairav Kund to villages nestled in rhododendron forests that are a blaze of colour in April. A major feature of this region is the ease of access; regular bus services from Kathmandu run to Dhunche and Syabrubesi in the west, and Melamchi, Chautara and Jalbire in the east. All these route options mean you can design your own unique Great Himalaya Trail experience in this region and it's all just a stone's throw from Kathmandu.

Established in 1976, Langtang National Park has a reputation for being well managed, where locals actively help to maintain park biodiversity and ecology. Human impact is limited but not absent as grazing is allowed in high pastures and permanent communities are permitted to exist in the heart of the Park. The Langtang National Park entry fee is Rs3000pp as at March 2014.

Note: You should not trek through the Helambu region on your own as solo trekkers have been robbed and two have disappeared in recent years; in fact the Government of Nepal is considering banning solo trekking in the whole region. Also do not leave belongings unattended at any time. Locals believe that the many foreign workers working on road construction projects are responsible.

KATHMANDU TO GOSAINKUND TREK

To trek out of the Kathmandu valley is a step back in time, to an age when all expeditions started from the valley rim. The feeling of walking away from Nepal's capital is unique and it allows you to 'grow' into the trek. Once over the rim, you head for a mountain range that fills the horizon. To the main

ROUTE GUIDE

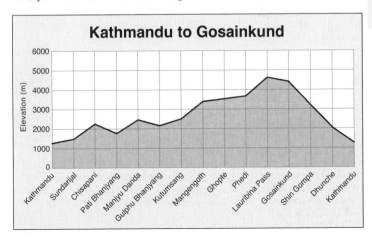

KATHMANDU TO GOSAINKUND TREK

To the north of Kathmandu is pure Himalayan magic – traditional cultures, great views, well maintained trails, plenty of wildlife, sacred lakes, rarely another trekker in sight and one of the best wildflower displays in Nepal during the spring season.

GRADE 3

● **Duration & distance**: About 9 days total; days not more than 20km per day
● **Gradient**: Short steep sections
● **Quality of path**: Formed & rough tracks, some obstacles
● **Quality of markings**: Signs at beginning, end and major intersections
● **Experience required**: Some walking experience required

● **Walking times**: Less than 6hrs a day
● **Steps**: Occasional steps on some days
● **Highest point**: 4462m
● **Best season**: Mar-May/Sep-Dec
● **Accommodation**: Camping and basic teahouses
● **Recommended map**: NP105 GHT Series Langtang & Helambu, Himalayan Map House, 2013

north–south route a series of interconnecting trails from the east and west offer an opportunity to trek to your heart's content.

Gosainkund tends to have a long trekking season from early October through to mid-February, and then re-opening in March until the monsoon begins in June. However, snowfalls are very common on Lauribina Pass throughout the year and trekkers should be careful not to become isolated on the higher trails. A major highlight is the magnificent rhododendron forests that bloom throughout April across the southern boundary of the National Park. If you want to connect with the holy lakes of Bhairav Kund and Panch Pokhari in the east of Helambu, you should be aware of sudden storms that can occur throughout the year, but they never deter the thousands of pilgrims who visit them during the monsoon months. If you have the time, consider a one-day side trip to the summit of Shivapuri and spend a night watching the twinkling of Kathmandu's city lights beneath a heaven full of stars.

Multiple daily bus services run from Kathmandu to Chisapani, Melamchi Gaon, Dhunche and Syabrubesi. An extensive new road network is under construction throughout Helambu and will include a Melamchi to Trisuli road via Kutumsang. All these roads are causing a great deal of forest damage and are unavoidable whether trekking east–west or north–south across the region.

DAY 1: KATHMANDU–SUNDARIJAL– CHISAPANI   4HRS' DRIVE
From the centre of Kathmandu, catch a bus to Chisapani via Sundarijal (1460m), where you need to register at the Shivapuri Nagarjun National Park post (1600m). There are views of Shivapuri (behind) and Himalayan peaks (ahead) from along the ridge-top road as it passes through an oak

forest to the teahouses of Chisapani (2215m, 1½hrs).

DAY 2: CHISAPANI–KUTUMSANG   6HRS
The trail is the same route as a new road project and continues down a pronounced ridge to a saddle at Pati Bhanjyang (1770m,

30 mins) and then climbs to a fork where you should take the left-hand trail to another saddle called Thankune Bhanjyang of a similar height. The trail then ascends an easy gradient before steepening to switchbacks and arriving at the village of Chipling (2170m, 2hrs). A final climb to the top of the Manjyu Danda ridge (2455m, 1hr) brings you to a large chorten, teashop and a good viewpoint of the mountains to the north. Descend for 45 minutes to the saddle village of Golphu Bhanjyang (2130m), where there are some teahouses and a camping ground next to the school if you cannot face the next climb.

The trail continues to climb a ridge to the north, take the larger track at each junction, until you reach another saddle and the Sherpa community of Kutumsang (2470m, 1½hrs). There is a Langtang National Park office here; you will need to show your Park receipt as well as register your details.

DAY 3: KUTUMSANG–MANGENGOTH 4HRS
Water can be hard to find in dry months on the next section of trail so carry a good supply. Continue up the eastern side of a ridge that climbs from Kutumsang, first through oak forest and then through an impressive forest of red-, white- and pink-flowered rhododendron. The gradient eases and from grassy meadows there are good views of the broad lower valleys and Shivapuri behind you. The trail steepens again as you climb a gully before arriving at Kyuola Bhanjyang (3220m, 3½hrs) where there are some teahouses. The trail descends a little before climbing an easy gradient to Mangengoth (3390m, 30 mins), which has a few teahouses and a large campsite surrounded by rhododendron forest.

DAY 4: MANGENGOTH–GHOPTE 4½HRS
The trail follows the undulating ridgeline north through dense rhododendron forest until it climbs to the hamlet of Therapati (3510m, 2hrs) and a major trail junction where you must go left (right descends to Melamchi village). There is frequently snow covering the trail from here to the

pass during the spring season, which could slow your group considerably. It is also important to note that you are now at a height where many people feel the effects of altitude so you may want to stop and rest for the night. If you look ahead it is possible to see the trail slowly ascending as it traverses through forest and then rocky hillside to the few teahouses and small campsite at Ghopte (3530m), which is 2½hrs away.

DAY 5: GHOPTE–PHEDI 3HRS
Most trekkers now stop at the teahouse and campsite at Phedi (3630m, 3hrs) as it makes acclimatisation easier and you have the chance of reaching Lauribina Pass (see below) while the weather is still relatively clear. Attempting the pass from Ghopte is a long and strenuous day and means making the crossing in the afternoon when clouds often obscure the view.

The climb to Phedi is along a well-established trail but the rocky terrain can be hazardous in snowy conditions. There are also a couple of waterfalls that need to be crossed and these are normally frozen in the mornings.

DAY 6: PHEDI–GOSAINKUND 5HRS
From Phedi climb a rough trail past a chorten and up into a valley dominated by Surya Peak to the north. Cross a wet or icy section of trail before ascending a series of easy slopes as you approach Lauribina Pass (4610m, 4hrs). The pass is a broad saddle between the lower slopes of Surya Peak (to the north) and Chhyarkung Chuli (to the south) and connects with a complex series of shallow valleys to the north and northeast. Each valley has at least one small lake and as many of them are sacred they each have a name.

From the pass descend into a valley past a couple of small lakes, and then over a slight rise where you can see the holiest of the lakes, Gosainkund (4380m, 1hr). There is a Shiva shrine beside the lake adorned with bells to deter demons, as well as some spacious teahouses. If you have time climb the slopes of a rocky hillside to the north for good views of Surya Peak and the lakes.

ROUTE GUIDE

> ❏ **The legend of Gosainkund**
> Thousands of pilgrims gain merit by circumambulation of and/or bathing in the lake on the full moon in July and August. There are many legends concerning Gosainkund, perhaps the most famous involves Shiva, the Hindu god of creation. It is said that the gods were once churning the ocean, hoping to obtain *amrit*, the water of immortality. However, they extracted a burning poison that Shiva, in an effort to save the gods and the world, drank. This made his neck blue and the burning sensation forced him into the mountains to find something soothing to drink. He struck his trident into the ground and three streams poured forth, creating Gosainkund. Shiva drank from the lake and quenched his thirst. There is a rock in the centre of the lake that resembles a Shiva *linga*, the sacred symbol of Hindu creation, and pilgrims often say they can see Shiva reclining on a bed of serpents in the lake's water.

DAY 7: GOSAINKUND–SHIN/SING GOMPA   4HRS
An exposed trail from Gosainkund first traverses beneath and then climbs a ridge that heads westwards. Cresting the ridge brings you to a minor pass (4165m, 1hr) and a series of chorten. You can see the ridge descending to a collection of teahouses at Lauribina (3900m, 1hr). There are good views of the Langtang range to the north-east and the Ganesh Himal to the north-west. From Lauribina continue on the southern side of the ridge on a large trail, which enters rhododendron and then pine and fir forest. The trail switches to the north side of the ridge and continues through a forest that locals believe is haunted. After 1½ hours the trail switches back to the southern side of the ridge and then descends to the village of Shin Gompa (aka Sing Gompa, 3150m, 30 mins) where there are teahouses and campsites.

DAYS 8-9: SHIN/SING GOMPA–DHUNCHE–KATHMANDU   3½HRS
The trail descends rapidly through an impressive forest all the way to the Trisuli river (2000m, 2½hrs), where there is a great spot to soak your feet in the river. Cross a bridge to the south bank and continue on a slightly undulating trail that leads to Dhunche (2030m, 1hr) where there are teahouses and transport services to Kathmandu.

LANGTANG VALLEY TREK

When you are sitting in the congested and noisy tumult of Kathmandu, it is amazing to think that in a day's bus drive you could be on the edge of pristine wilderness. Viewpoints above and beyond Kyangjin Gompa offer some stunning mountain vistas, and the opportunity to really immerse yourself in the Himalaya. Three high passes link to trails through Helambu and can be used to provide a range of loop itineraries.

The Langtang valley can be trekked year-round, and although the mountains are covered in cloud during monsoon, carpets of wildflowers compensate handsomely. The most popular seasons are early October through to mid-February, when the weather is clear and stable, and then from mid-March to the end of May when the rhododendron forests are in full bloom. Care should be taken when attempting any of the high passes; Kangja (Ganja) La, Tilman Pass and Tilman East Pass are susceptible to sudden, fierce storms and snowfall at any time of year.

LANGTANG VALLEY TREK

Stunning views of glaciers and mountains, amazingly photogenic sunsets, sacred lakes, Buddhist monasteries, Tibetan culture, and the possibility of seeing rare wildlife – Langtang is a culturally rich and beautifully diverse national park.

GRADE 3

- **Duration & distance**: About 10 days total; days not more than 20km per day
- **Gradient**: Short steep sections
- **Quality of path**: Formed & rough tracks, some obstacles
- **Quality of markings**: Signs at beginning, end and major intersections
- **Experience required**: No walking experience required

- **Walking times**: Less than 6 hours a day
- **Steps**: Occasional steps on some days
- **Highest point**: 4984m
- **Best season**: Sep-May
- **Accommodation**: Camping and teahouses
- **Recommended map**: NP105 GHT Series Langtang & Helambu, Himalayan Map House, 2013

Comfy teahouses are in every village from Dhunche and Syabrubesi to Kyangjin Gompa after which you will need camping equipment. Supplies are expensive in Kyangjin so try to carry in as much as possible. If you want to attempt the high passes you will need ropes and rock, ice and snow climbing equipment.

DAY 1: KATHMANDU–DHUNCHE
8HRS' DRIVE

The drive from Kathmandu offers good views of Manaslu, Ganesh Himal, and Langtang and brief glimpses of village life in the Himalaya. The first section is sealed road to Trisuli before a precipitous dirt road (which is slowly being upgraded) to the National Park and police checkposts on the edge of the bustling trading town of Dhunche (2030m, 8hrs). There are many

ROUTE GUIDE

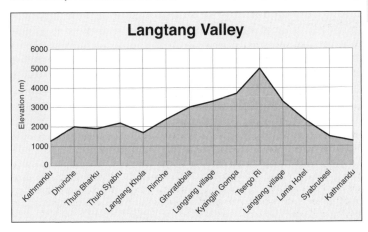

Langtang Valley

teahouses and some campsites at the far end of the main street.

DAY 2: DHUNCHE–THULO SYABRU
4½HRS

It might be possible to catch a lift with a vehicle heading towards Syabrubesi and jump off at Thulo Bharkhu (1860m, 1hr), if not, it can be a dusty walk along the road, so make sure you have a scarf to cover your face. Thulo Bharkhu is a small place and a large sign towards the end of the village indicates the start of the main trail, which quickly climbs up through oak and pine forest to Barbal (2190m, 1½hrs). If you can, take some time to visit the gompa here (and make a donation) as part of a rest break.

It is now an easy undulating trail through temperate forest with occasional glimpses of the Ganesh Himal and Langtang valley. Reach the ridgetop Tamang village of Thulo Syabru (2210m) in 2 hours, where you may have to register again at the checkpost.

DAY 3: THULO SYABRU–RIMCHE
5HRS

The trail cuts back into a gully to a bridge before rounding the hillside and dropping about 300m to the Langtang Khola below (1660m, 1½hrs). Once at the main valley trail turn upstream (east) on the true left bank and follow the Langtang Khola. In 20 minutes you will drop to the riverside and there may be a bamboo and log bridge to some hot springs on the far bank. The springs are not always accessible as landslides affect the area regularly. Just beyond the springs is a teashop and for the next 80 minutes the trail passes through some small riverside glades and minor up and downs as you approach Bamboo (1970m).

From behind the topmost of three teahouses with flower gardens the trail begins to climb more steadily. Head up into forest to avoid some landslides, although you will return to the riverside a few times before finally crossing a suspension bridge (2150m, 50 mins) to the true right bank. Cross a couple of small landslides and then begin a switchback climb to Rimche (2399m, 1hr), where there are a couple of

pleasant teahouses, a small campsite and views down valley.

DAY 4: RIMCHE–GHORATABELA
4HRS

From Rimche the trail climbs a little before dropping to the village of Lama Hotel (2487m, 40 mins).

Note: if you are camping you will probably have to stay here rather than at Rimche.

Lama Hotel doesn't have any cultivation and relies exclusively on tourists for income. You should check and confirm all fees before committing to a teahouse; some even charge you just for sitting in the dining room. From Lama Hotel you enter some beautiful oak, birch, hemlock and mountain-bamboo forests. Spanish moss hangs from trees giving the whole place a mysterious feeling. Try to make an early start from Rimche to give yourself the best chance of spotting monkey and the many birds that feed near the river. At first the trail undulates through the forest before coming to a lone teahouse at Gumnachok (2670m, 1hr) in the forest. From here the trail climbs steadily for more than 200m to Ghoratabela (3030m, 2hrs 10 mins), where there are a couple of teahouses and a campsite. If you have the time, consider visiting the small monastery, which the local headman will open for a donation.

DAY 5: GHORATABELA–KYANGJIN GOMPA
4¾HRS

Beyond Ghoratabela is an army camp where your permits will be checked. The valley now broadens and the gradient eases; Thyangsyapu (3120m, 1hr) marks the end of the dense forest and the beginning of alpine country. The small settlement of Chyamki (3110m, 15 mins) soon appears, before you then reach the gompa at Kangtangsa (3220m) in a further 45 minutes. If you are feeling the effects of altitude it might be a good idea to rest here for the night.

A short climb takes you up to views of the classic glaciated U-shaped valley and the village of Langtang (3330m), the administrative centre for the valley, in a further 30

❏ Bhotia people

Rather than being a distinct ethnic group, Bhotia people are immigrants from the Tibetan Plateau who have settled in mountain valleys along the length of the Himalaya. They can therefore be considered the 'ethnic cousins' of other Mongoloid groups like the Sherpa and Tamang, who have also migrated from the north.

Bhotia homes can be either single or double storey, and are usually made of stone for the ground floor and wood for the upper levels. Communities tend to be compact, with only small fields for growing crops and keeping livestock and a few dozen homes. Bhotia always follow Tibetan Buddhism and the particular sect they belong to is often a clue as to where they originally came from. Marriages are normally within their own community, or another Bhotia village.

The term Bhotia is considered insulting by some ethnic groups, so don't use it unless you are sure you won't cause offence; calling them 'Lama' or 'Sherpa' is likely to be safer, even if less accurate.

minutes. There are many teahouses and camping grounds to choose from, and remember to register at the checkpost.

From Langtang it is an easy climb through two Bhotia hamlets, Mundu and Sindum (3410m, 45 mins). Ahead are views of Ganchenpo (Fluted Peak) and Langshisa Ri, and Langtang Lirung rising above you to the north. The trail then climbs the terminal moraine of the Lirung Glacier and descends to the gompa and many teahouses of Kyangjin Gompa (3830m, 1½hrs). If you arrive early enough, sample the nearby cheese factory, visit the gompa, and consider trekking up the trails that run on either side of the Lirung Glacier to see ice falls and spot musk deer or blue sheep.

DAY 6: KYANGJIN GOMPA ALL DAY

The easiest viewpoint to reach is a hill to the north of Kyangjin Gompa where many prayer flags, which can be seen from the village, indicate the summit (4360m, 2hrs). For the more adventurous there are many good views on the climb of Tsergo Ri

(4984m, 3½hrs climb). There is an excellent look-out with magnificent views of Langtang Lirung and its surrounding peaks – it can be reached by climbing the slopes immediately behind Kyangjin Gompa. Further to the east of Tsergo Ri, is Yala Peak (5500m, 6hr climb), which is more spectacular, and requires a trekking peak permit, mountaineering skills and equipment.

Alternatively, a trek further up the valley towards Langshisa Kharka (4160m, 7hr return trek) provides great views of the ranges bordering Tibet and a chance for some more wildlife spotting in the early morning.

DAYS 7-10: KYANGJIN GOMPA–SYABRUBESI–KATHMANDU

Retrace your steps on the main trail. You might want to stay in different places on your descent or return to see friends. Either way a clearly marked trail follows the river to Syabrubesi (1503m) where there are many teahouses and a regular bus service to Kathmandu (10hrs).

OTHER TRAILS IN HELAMBU AND LANGTANG

[See maps opposite inside back cover] Langtang and Helambu offer GHT through-hikers a range of options from technical routes to easy trails suitable for winter hiking and mountain biking.

An enjoyable village-to-village trek that is ideal in the winter-season and for those preferring a lower-altitude route links **The Last Resort to Betrawati** via Ratnaule, Pokhari Bhanjyang, Golphu, Kharnaitar and then to Betrawati (total 6-8 days, local teahouses en route). At any point along this route you can branch north towards Langtang and cross one of the Tilman passes, Kangja (Ganja) La or Gosainkund to arrive at Syabrubesi. A road links Betrawati with Syabrubesi as well as a number of trails that head into the Ganesh Himal.

Shivapuri, the highest point on the northern Kathmandu valley rim, offers a stunning viewpoint (2732m, 6hrs) of the city below, especially on a clear night when the lights imitate the stars above. There are many trails, which often causes confusion, so take a guide who knows the way.

Panch Pokhari (translates as 'five lakes') is a very popular pilgrimage site in the monsoon and location of a Mahadev Temple. These five sacred lakes at 4010m make an excellent 9-day loop trek from the road-head town of Chautara via Sano Okhareni, Kami Kharka, Pauwa Bas, Hille Bhanjyang, Nasim Pati and then to Panch Pokhari. Instead of returning the same route, head down to Tupi Danda and then via Dhap to the road-head at Melamchi, and maybe take an extra day or two to relax en route? Chautara, where you begin the trek with a long ridge climb, is a few hours' drive from the centre of Kathmandu. The trail ascends the Kamikharka Danda above the Indrawati Khola before linking with the Hutprang Danda and then heading north to the lakes.

The villages en route are a diverse blend of Hindu, Tamang and Bhotia communities separated by extensive rhododendron, pine and fir forests, which surround the Langtang National Park. From the lakes there are great views of the Kangja Himal, Jugal Himal, Rolwaling Himal and distant views of Mt Everest, Mt Makalu and Kanchenjunga. This route can be combined with treks to/from Helambu, Gosainkund and over Kangja (Ganja) La (see below) or one of the Tilman passes (see *The Last Resort to Syabrubesi via Tilman Pass*, opposite) to the Langtang valley. Alternatively, you could combine with the other sacred lakes in the region at **Gosainkund** (see *Kathmandu to Gosainkund*, pp156-7) or **Bhairav Kund** (see *The Last Resort to Syabrubesi via Tilman Pass*, opposite) for a doubly auspicious trek!

Kangja (Ganja) La – this pass should only be attempted by experienced trekking groups with appropriate climbing and camping equipment. Kangja La offers a great circular trek back through Helambu, some fantastic views of the Langtang range and an approach to the popular trekking peak, Naya Kanga. From Kyangjin Gompa, retrace the trail towards Langtang village and after about 20 minutes take the left fork, which drops down to the river and a small wooden bridge. A small but obvious trail climbs through birch and rhododendron forest to simple teahouses and a good campsite, Ngegang Kharka (4430m, 2hrs). Continue climbing, staying on the west bank of a watercourse, across steep ground until you reach the base of moraine deposited by the glacier above, and a potential campsite (4640m, 2hrs).

The pass is a further 2-hour climb up a steep rock scramble, which is often made treacherous by snow. Mountaineering skills and a fixed rope may be necessary to reach Kangja La (5130m) and to descend. There is a steep descent on loose moraine for 3 hours, do not head towards the glacier rather, stay on the east-facing (right) slope of the valley. Continue descending past some kharka and staying high on, but not on top of, a ridge that runs almost due south above the Yangri Khola. There is a good campsite at Keldang (4420m) after another 2 hours with water from a tributary of the Yangri Khola. Continue to traverse the ridge without losing height; the next campsite is Dhukpa (4030m, 6hrs). Follow the ridge until the trail swings up to some prayer flags (1hr) and then descends steeply to Tarkeghyang and the main Helambu trails.

The main route continues to **Melamchi Bazaar** (870m, 2 days via Sermathang) or via Tharepati and Chisapani (see reverse of *Kathmandu to Gosainkund*, days 1-4, pp156-7).

The Last Resort to Syabrubesi via Tilman Pass

This route requires excellent navigation skills and/or local guides, and technical climbing experience for either the Tilman Pass or Tilman East Pass. Only fully equipped camping groups will be able to attempt the route, there are no tea-houses or major resupply opportunities between the Bhote Kosi and Kyangjin Gompa.

The route described here is from The Last Resort (1220m) on the Arniko Highway to Syabrubesi via Panch Pokhari and Tilman Pass, however, cross-country options also include linking Panch Pokhari to Kangja (Ganja) La or Gosainkund (see opposite).

Leave The Last Resort on the Arniko Highway from the main gate and pass through Panlan village immediately to the south. From here the trail climbs a steep hillside with little shade to Baldun (1890m, 1¼hrs), which the locals might refer to as Listi. However, the real Listi (2260m; Finaid: Barhabise sheet: 2785 04, ref: 893 866) is a Tamang community on a plateau further up the hill and is reached in another 70 minutes. As you approach the ridge above you will clearly see a Hindu Temple, beneath which is a community health post where you can camp.

Continue on the temple ridge to a series of chorten overlooking Listi and then swing north-east, keeping on the ridge. Do not traverse around the ridge (to your left, or more north). After 1½ hours you reach the top of the ridge above Listi and a broad grassy place (2650m) where cremations occur, so treat the area with respect. From here you can see the trail traversing a hillside to your north to a minor pass where a Sherpa village called Bagam (2705m, 45 mins) is home to some of the three hundred nuns from Bagam Gompa, situated below the ridge. There is also a school here, which would make a good campsite. To the north, you can see a steep forest-covered ridge and the trail from Bagam leading straight up to 3286m (100 mins) to a temporary dharamsala, which is just below the main ridge.

At the top of the ridge there is a trail cross-roads, turn left and continue on the ridge proper. At first the trail looks like a watercourse and you are tempted to bear right, but don't stray from the ridge and the trail soon becomes a pleasant flat walk through pine forest. Shotang Kharka (3379m; Finaid: Barhabise, sheet: 2785 04, ref: 887 920) is reached in 20 minutes; you will need to ask herders to show you where the water source is located.

From Shotang the trail continues north, climbing a ridge with good views of mountains to the north-east in Rolwaling and Tibet, and north-west in Langtang. Pilgrims who come for the August festival have made the trail broad and easy to follow to Chogomogor Kharka (3924m, 2hrs; Finaid: Barhabise, sheet: 2785 04, ref: 887 949), which is a major trail junction both north–south and east–west. If you do not wish to continue to Bhairav Kund you should camp here.

To reach the sacred lake of **Bhairav Kund**, climb a little to a chorten and then head north-east across the east-facing flanks of a rising series of craggy peaks; there is a dharamsala and campsite at the lake (4113m, 1¾hrs).

The following morning retrace your steps to Chogomogor Kharka (45 mins) and then take a trail that heads east-north-east to a kharka on the Paulan Dada (3812m, 1¼hrs; Finaid: Barhabise, sheet: 2785 04, ref: 873 956). Be careful to stay on the west-ridge trail from this kharka as many tracks lead into the forest. Descend a trail, which gradually becomes very steep as you enter dense forest. In 2 hours you reach a temporary dharamsala and series of chorten directly above Kyangsin village (2520m) to which you descend in 30 minutes. A trail then traverses a hillside to the north-east and once around the ridge descends steeply to the Nyasem Khola (1861m, 2hrs), where there is a camping place on the far side of a suspension bridge. Do not camp close to the bridge as there are quite a few ticks and lice in the area; instead pick an area about 20 or 30 metres upstream.

Climb a trail on the far side of the river for 300m to Nimatol village (2158m, 1hr) where there is a new trail that traverses the sometimes-steep hillside to Tembathang (2160m, 45 mins). You will need to employ a local guide from this village, as the trails ahead are frequently overgrown and rarely used.

There are **two options from Tembathang**:
1. A long route to Panch Pokhari via Hille Bhanjyang (3-4 days, see *Panch Pokhari*, p162) follows more substantial trails. A local guide is advisable for a confusing forested section before Hille Bhanjyang.
2. A more direct route to Panch Pokhari (2 days) heads upstream from Tembathang. Follow a flat trail north from the village to a wooden suspension bridge over a tributary but do not cross the bridge! Instead, follow a small trail that crosses the river about 10 metres downstream and then winds onto flat ground where there are some well-used kharkas. From the northern end of the kharka descend to the river. The trail now climbs the true right (eastern) side of the river course to the hamlet of Tegu where you continue to follow a trail along the bank. In 1½ hours from Tembathang you will reach the remains of Thipu village. There is a good campsite by the river before the village area.

Note: the enormous landslide area on the far bank destroyed Mahathan village and most of Thipu village but, incredibly, with no loss of life.

Do not cross the river at the village, instead continue on the true right (east) bank for one hour to a small bamboo and log bridge. Cross carefully to the true left bank and then continue north on a sometimes scrubby trail through forest to Chedupa Kharka (2513m, 1hr; Finaid: Dorle Pahad, sheet: 2885 16, ref: 774

062). From this large kharka a small trail heads north for about 50 metres before heading up the steep hillside to your left. You might need to ask a local to identify the trail. There are ticks and leeches along this track so be vigilant. Climb for about 800m to Salingling Kharka (3323m, 3hrs 40 mins; Finaid: Lantan, sheet: 2885 15, ref: 765 057), where you might be able to find water in a gully to the south. If not, continue for another 45 minutes to Nemagchukpa Kharka (3578m), where there is permanent water. Continue along the ridge through rhododendron forest to an intersecting ridge, which leads to Panch Pokhari. There is another, small kharka campsite at 4048m (2¼hrs) on the ridge. From here it is only 1½ hours to the lakes of Panch Pokhari (4074m), which you reach by crossing the main north–south ridge at 4229m (Finaid: Lantan, sheet: 2885 15, ref: 747 034).

Directly to the east of the temple at Panch Pokhari is a short climb back to the ridgeline (4245m, 40 mins), which you should cross and descend to a broad kharka (4070m, 20 mins). Follow the obvious trail north as it rises to cross a hill spur into another shallow basin. For the next 1½ hours continue north crossing similar spurs and basins between 4000m and 4200m. In the fourth basin you will see a trail junction where the left trail climbs towards a rocky outcrop and the right trail swings away to the north-east. You can take either trail, but if the north-facing slopes are covered in snow and/or ice you might find the longer, but lower, north-east trail safer. The higher route climbs to a small lake (Lingsing Kharka, 4450m, 1hr) whereas the north-east trail contours lower slopes at 4000m +/- 30m for 2 hours before climbing and rejoining the higher trail at a small basin with a well-built stone kharka (4273m; Finaid: Lantan, sheet: 2885 15, ref: 749 092). From this kharka continue north, climbing for about 100m before the trail levels and you then drop through a small valley to ascend a final ridge above Tin Pokhari (4255m, 1½hrs; Finaid: Lantan, sheet: 2885 15, ref: 754 110), although the three lakes have dried up.

From the ridge above Tin Pokhari you have a clear view of both glacier approaches to Tilman Pass and Tilman East Pass. In clear weather it is even possible to see the rocky ridge of Tilman East Pass at the base of the west ridge of Dorje Lakpa peak. Your choice of which pass to attempt will depend on time available, weather conditions and skill level. The easier route is Tilman Pass (the western of the two glaciers, described in full below), however Tilman East Pass is a spectacular option for experienced groups and is worth considering if you have time available.

Crossing Tilman Pass

From Tin Pokhari follow a trail that drops into an ablation valley to the northwest, trek through some kharka and climb for 2¼ hours until you each a campsite (4646m; Finaid: Lantan, sheet: 2885 15, ref: 731 134) at the valley's end, marked by a steep moraine wall. There are a few large boulders on top of the moraine wall, climb to the most northerly of them and descend beside a small glacial lake.

From the lake cross to the middle of the glacier and follow an indistinct trail marked by occasional cairns. In 2 hours you will reach a campsite (4867m;

ROUTE GUIDE

Finaid: Lantan, sheet: 2885 15, ref: 732 150) on the glacier just as the valley narrows, and in a further 20 minutes you will reach the base of the pass (4848m).

There appear to be two routes up the lower rocky section of the pass, but the right-hand rock-climbing option is exposed and prone to rockfall so it is better to ascend the loose scree to the right of the icefall (and to the left of the rock-climbing route). Once above the rock band, traverse around to your left and climb mixed ice and rock to the right of the icefall and beneath a steep rock-face. Once at the rock-face traverse left to the glacier and then climb directly onto the pass snowfield. Tilman Pass (5308m, 2hrs 40 mins; Finaid: Lantan, sheet: 2885 15, ref: 727 166) is through a narrow notch to the north-west of the snowfield. Beware of rockfall on both sides of your approach.

Once on the pass descend a steep snowy slope to the north-west. Beware of crevasses on your descent, it is wise to rope everyone because the descent becomes steeper as you approach a broad plateau covered in avalanche debris at 5130m (45 mins), where you could camp. Follow a snowmelt stream on the true left (western) side of the plateau to a steep drop to a glacial lake in a valley below. This section can be treacherous and care should be taken on the rock and ice-filled gullies; a handline may be needed in places. In less than 2 hours you should reach the lake, where you can camp on the northern shore (4756m; Finaid: Lantan, sheet: 2885 15, ref: 727 185). Alternatively, continue to the left (north-west) of a moraine wall to an indistinct campsite at 4720m (30 mins).

Continue to descend north-west to a small, level, sandy place (20 mins) about 200m above Langshisa Glacier. A landslide ahead along the old trail means that you must now descend to the glacier, the moraine here is very unstable, steep and prone to rockfall. Beware of patches of hard ice covered by loose moraine as you descend to the side of Langshisa Glacier (45 mins). Descend beside the true left bank of the glacier for 1½ hours when the first patches of vegetation appear. Continue descending through prickly bush as directly as you can while following some not-so-obvious stone cairns towards Langshisa Kharka (4285m, 1½hrs; Finaid: Lantan, sheet: 2885 15, ref: 703 214).

Wade the river at the shallowest point (normally near a large boulder on the true right, northern bank) and move directly away from the river to find the main trail to Kyangjin Gompa (3900m, 3hrs to your west). From Kyangjin Gompa follow the main Langtang valley trail to Syabrubesi (1503m, 9hrs, see *Langtang Valley* for trail notes in reverse, p161).

Crossing Tilman East Pass

This is a relatively new route and has only been completed a few times by groups with Sherpa staff and experienced porters. The descent from the northern side of the pass has many crevasses. Both sides of the pass are prone to rockfall. Care should be taken, as well as rock, snow and ice climbing equipment.

From Tin Pokhari follow a trail that drops towards an ablation valley to some small kharka to the north-west, the first of which has a trail that turns north (4210m, 15 mins; Finaid: Lantan, Sheet: 2885 15, ref: 745 118). Drop to the river that flows from the Tilman Pass glacier and ascend the moraine above a glacier that flows down from the north-east. The trail climbs steeply at first but as it nears an intersecting glacier from the north-west becomes more flat. There isn't a good campsite beside the glacier so continue north and camp far enough away from the hanging ice at 4675m (4¼hrs; Finaid: Lantan, sheet: 2885 15, ref: 763 152). Head out into the centre of the glacier (eastwards) and then head north, staying clear of any rockfall from crags to your left.

Ascend a slight step to a snowy basin and then climb again to Tilman East Pass (5368m, 3hrs; Finaid: Dorle Pahad, sheet: 2885 16, ref: 777 178), which is a rocky ridge about 30m high. It is then a steep descent across a crevassed snowfield to the north-north-west, to the upper reaches of Langshisa Glacier. Continue down the southern edge of the glacier to Langshisa Kharka (4550m, 12hrs from the pass).

Ganesh and Manaslu Himals

In the centre of Nepal are two trekking gems, the Ganesh and Manaslu Himals; both are the country's best-kept secrets. Many would argue that the Manaslu Circuit trail is the best general trek in the country, with colourful cultures and dramatic valleys against a backdrop of classic Himalayan peaks. The Ganesh Himal is one of the least-visited regions in Nepal, and offers a wonderfully diverse range of cultural and wilderness-exploratory treks.

Lying to the west of the Langtang valley, the Ganesh Himal is a collection of seven major peaks (one in Tibet, six in Nepal or on the border) that form a natural barrier with Tibet. Named after the Hindu elephant god, Ganesha (Ganesh IV is said to look like the head of an elephant), the range is bordered by the Budhi Gandaki river to the west and extensive forests across the southern flanks that flow to Dhading District. Beyond the Budhi Gandaki, to the west, rises a collection of peaks dominated by the 8163m summit of Manaslu. Throughout both Himals Gurung, Tamang, Magar, Ru-Pa, Larke and Siar people blend to create perhaps the most ethnically interesting series of valleys throughout the entire Himalaya.

Itinerary options abound and provide some of the most fantastic GHT routes in the Nepal Himalaya. This chapter documents all the major trails in the region, including the Tamang Heritage Trail (see map p154), which can be combined with more strenuous routes into and around the Ganesh Himal, as well as the Ruby Valley trek. Tsum, a remote Larke valley to the north of the Ganesh Himal, is accessible from the Manaslu Circuit. If you want to do the full Circuit trek and cross the impressive Larkye La, a large saddle to the north of Manaslu, you can explore the massive natural amphitheatre of mountains at Bimtang before descending to the Annapurna Circuit.

The Tamang Heritage Trail region was opened to tourists in 2002 when the Chinese and Nepali governments resolved all border claims; in contrast the

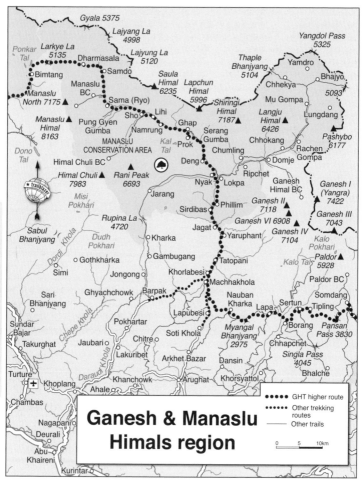

Manaslu region was opened in 1992, and yet has only become popular since 2012. The Manaslu Conservation Area Project (MCAP) provides guidance to villagers in maintaining their natural heritage and is similar to the neighbouring Annapurna Conservation Area Project (ACAP). The Tamang Heritage Trail is not protected, so logging and poaching remain unchecked. Hopefully, the Nepali Government will one day safeguard this region to link MCAP and the Langtang National Park.

As at March 2014, the trekking permit fees are:

Rasuwa District (including Thungmen and Timure) is US$10pp per week.

Gorkha District/Manaslu region is a bit more complicated: in addition to the Manaslu Conservation Area Project entry fee of Rs2000 you require:

- October to November: US$70pp for first week, after that US$10pp per day.
- December to August: US$50pp for first week, after that US$7pp per day.

For the Chhekampar & Chumchet VDC (Sirdibas–Lokpa–Chumling–Chhekampar–Nile–Chhule) areas:

- September to November: US$35pp for 8 days
- December to August: US$25pp for 8 days.

TAMANG HERITAGE TRAIL

Tamang Heritage Trail (see map p154) was created by some Nepali NGOs who worked with villagers to improve local trails, the result is an easy-going route through pristine mountain scenery. The trail was designed to showcase the local Tamang culture and is best when combined with one of the many Buddhist festivals throughout the year.

The highest point of this trek, at 3600m, also makes it ideal for those who are susceptible to altitude sickness but who still want to experience the high Himalaya. The best time for views is November to January when the air is free from haze and the mountains in Tibet can be seen clearly, but expect cold nights! The main trekking seasons (both pre- and post-monsoon) see a few small trekking groups visiting, but the region is most popular with independent trekkers who are in search of something different. The openhearted hospitality of the Tamang people makes any welcome something special, especially if you visit during festivals.

ROUTE GUIDE

TAMANG HERITAGE TRAIL

An excellent trek (see map p154) along an easy-going route through authentic villages that offer a homestay programme in traditional homes, great views of mountains in Tibet, Langtang and Ganesh Himals, set against rhododendron forests, and all just a day from Kathmandu!

GRADE 2

- **Duration & distance**: About 9 days total; days not more than 10km per day
- **Gradient**: Gentle slopes and hills
- **Quality of path**: Formed track
- **Quality of markings**: Signs at beginning, end and during trek
- **Experience required**: No walking experience required
- **Walking times**: Less than 6 hours per day

- **Steps**: Short step section on second day
- **Highest point**: 3600m
- **Best season**: Oct-May
- **Accommodation**: Camping and teahouses
- **Recommended map**: NP105 GHT Series Langtang & Helambu, Himalayan Map House, 2013

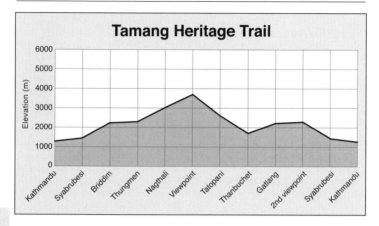

One of the highlights of the trek is the opportunity for a 'homestay' in the village of Briddim. This involves staying in a traditional Bhotia house for up to three nights.

The main trail can be extended in a number of directions, including to Dudh Kund ('Milk Lake') on the northern slopes of Langtang Lirung, Sangjung Kharka and Kalo Pokhari near Paldor Peak, Jaisuli Kund above Somdang and connecting trails to valleys to the south-west of the Ganesh Himal including the *Ruby Valley Trek* (connects at Gatlang, see p173).

Note: a new road linking the border town of Rasuwa to Trisuli is now completed and unavoidable if you want to cross the Bhote Khosi valley between Briddim and Thungmen.

DAY 1: KATHMANDU–SYABRUBESI
8HRS

The drive from Kathmandu offers good views of Manaslu, Ganesh and Langtang Himals as well as brief glimpses of village life in the Himalaya. The first section is a sealed road to Trisuli before the precipitous dirt road to Dhunche, where there is a National Park and police checkpost.

❏ **A local legend**
One of the villagers from Briddim joined our camp one evening and told an intriguing tale: 'A long time in the past, the Chinese and Nepalese had a brief war, which resulted in the Chinese army marching through Rasuwa and occupying the hills to the south of Dhunche. The defending Nepalese were caught off-guard and with few troops were not going to be able to halt the Chinese. As the invaders established their camps overlooking the valleys around the Trisuli river, the Nepali general devised a cunning plan. Each night he lit small braziers and mounted them on cattle, which the Chinese were led to believe were the countless camps of the growing defending forces. The Chinese general believed the ruse and withdrew, which saved Nepal from an embarrassing loss.'

❏ **A Briddim folktale**

Long ago the field near the gompa was a *tal* (a small lake), which the villagers some-times used for washing. One day, a great and famous high lama came to the village. He stayed in the gompa and the villagers looked after him. When he was here the vil-lagers asked him if he could do something about the tal; they already had a good river for washing and water so the tal wasn't very useful (Tibetans refuse to kill animals and therefore place little value on fish). So the lama recited some powerful *mantras* (Tibetan Buddhist prayers) and all the water and laundry that was around and in the lake spiralled up into the clouds and disappeared. The fish that had lived in the water all jumped out of the tal and into a large rock beside the field. So the tal became a field, which the lama said the villagers must protect, as it was now sacred. The vil-lagers may only sow three crops per year there, at most, and sometimes when they plough the field they find *dzee* stones (sacred stones believed by some to be fossilised caterpillars). Ask the locals to show you the fish in the rock.

Continue to Syabrubesi (1503m), where there are many teahouses and a campsite. As most of the day's drive is on dirt roads, a light scarf to protect your face against dust may be useful.

DAY 2: SYABRUBESI–BRIDDIM
4HRS

Make your way north through Syabrubesi to the checkpost located above the steps that lead to a suspension bridge across the Bhote Kosi. After leaving your details, cross the bridge and then turn upstream on the true left bank following a trail that climbs briefly before an easier gradient to the village of Wangel (1633m, 1hr). There is a water pipe in the centre of the village, take the trail, opposite the pipe, that climbs between houses. You will enter mixed pine and rhododendron forest after roughly 30 minutes. Stay on this main trail for the rest of the day, and at any trail junctions always take the noticeably larger track. It's mostly an easy gradient as you traverse hillside, but there are two steeper sections in the for-est. A deserted house is reached after 1½ hours; monkeys can often be spotted here.

For another hour the trail winds around another ridge before arriving on the edge of a basin above Briddim (2229m). You can descend and walk up through the village or traverse around to a trail above the village and then walk down. The school offers a small campsite and there is a basic tea-house, however it is far more enjoyable and

convenient to stay in one of the homestays. Many people elect to stay for two or three nights in the **homestay** to really get the feel for what life is like in a Himalayan village. There are local trails to explore up the Briddim Khola that runs beside the village and along the ridge to the south of the vil-lage. Alternatively, see how a typical household works, spin wool, and learn about traditional culture.

DAY 3: BRIDDIM–THUNGMEN
5½HRS

Take the trail that leaves Briddim past the gompa and traverse through forest above Lingling and then descend a steep trail to the Bhote Kosi (2hrs). Follow the road route for 30 minutes to a bridge that cross-es to the true right bank of the Bhote Kosi and then climb narrow switchbacks for 1½ hours to the terraces surrounding Dalphedi (2317m). The trail climbs more gradually from Dalphedi to a ridge to the south of the village. A pronounced rock outcrop marks a minor pass (visible from Dalphedi) decorat-ed with prayer flags. The trail descends some rough stone steps and then traverses a rock-face before turning west and provid-ing the first views of Thungmen (2338m, 1½hrs). An easy trail traverses around to the Palpachhe Khola before climbing slightly to the village.

There isn't a good campsite in Thungmen, but there are some simple tea-houses and a decaying wooden Nyingmapa sect gompa that is said to be 450 years old, and is definitely worth a visit. The locals don't seem to care about the state of the gompa, so please leave a donation with the key-holder who tries his best to maintain the building. If you are camping, continue up through the village to a school (15 mins) and a series of grassy fields, which can all be used as campsites.

DAY 4: THUNGMEN–NAGTHALI
4HRS

The trail is sometimes steep and there is no reliable water source so make sure you pack enough supplies. Climb a well-established trail that leads up to a series of terraces and pastures before reaching the forest (roughly 2750m, 1½hrs) above Thungmen. You are now in a fine rhododendron, juniper, pine and oak forest that attracts birds. The trail switchbacks up to a small, derelict chorten (2870m, 1hr), where the trail forks: take the left trail into a small valley. Remain on the south (left) bank of a small stream, as the trail continues to climb. Locals have cut young trees to leave stumps about 1m high as trail markers.

As you near the end of the small valley the track crosses the stream before climbing a short section to a large kharka (3010m,

1hr). There are two trails to the top of the hill, the left-hand track loops around a large thicket of dense rhododendron bushes and climbs some steps. The second heads from the herder's shelter through a narrow track that climbs a sometimes slippery slope directly to the hilltop. There are few trees on the top of Nagthali (3165m, 30 mins) and you should easily spot the small gompa and new teahouses as you approach. There are plenty of places to camp or share a room for a small fee.

DAY 5: NAGTHALI VIEWPOINT
5HRS

To the north of the gompa, nestled against the forest, is a small stone meditation hut for Buddhist hermits who visit from Tibet. You will see a track leading off to the right, which then winds around the hill through one of the most beautiful old-growth rhododendron forests in Nepal. The trail swings to the north again (3310m, 1hr) and stays on top of a narrow ridge offering views of the Ganesh Himal and Chilime valley below. During the winter months and just after dawn, red panda can be spotted in the forest along this ridge. The track then climbs again before turning right (3400m, 45 mins) and away from the forest and on

---

❏ Tamang people

Tamangs mainly live in the hills that circle Kathmandu, where you may see them on the streets, carrying their *dhoko* by a *namlo*, and always with their *khukuri* (knife) tucked into their cloth belt. No self-respecting Tamang fellow would leave the house without his knife. Tamang means horse-trader in Tibetan and they believe that they originated from Tibet and moved to Nepal countless centuries ago, where they continue to practise Buddhism. Theirs is the major Tibeto-Burman speaking community in Nepal.

They generally prefer to live in congested paved villages with terraced stone houses and wooden shingle or slate roofs. Most houses have two floors, the ground floor is where grain is stored and livestock shelters overnight, and the family live upstairs. The first floor has three wooden windows surrounded by intricate carvings and sometimes overhangs the ground floor, forming a veranda where the inhabitants will take tea, chat and work during the day. They grow their own crops of wheat, maize, millet etc and keep a few animals such as chickens, goats and buffalos.

Tamangs are skilled craftsmen and tuneful singers – so their festivals are often lively affairs which continue into the early hours for days on end! They are strong, easygoing and hardworking – many are employed as porters for trekking groups as well as local delivery work. They are the most highly sought after domestic staff because of their honesty, kindness and work ethic.

to an open hillside of dwarf azalea bushes. This track can be hard to follow when it gets overgrown, especially when it swings north (left) towards a copse of rhododendron festooned with Spanish moss. After another 45 minutes you should reach a rarely used kharka with a small stream. This eerie forest section again gives way to dwarf azalea as you continue to ascend an easy gradient to a magnificent viewpoint (3720m, 1hr) of countless peaks in Tibet, the Ganesh and Langtang Himals. Take the same route back to Nagthali (1½hrs).

DAY 6: NAGTHALI–TATOPANI
3½HRS

From Nagthali the trail heads south-west over the edge of the plateau – ask the locals in the teahouse if you are unsure. The trail drops to a small copse before turning back on itself and descending steeply, heading north-north-west. As you descend you will notice the small village of Brimdang (2848m, 1¼hrs), where there is a large chautara above a stone stairway. If you look at the houses while facing north you should see a small track that heads into the dense forest behind the buildings. If you ask the locals they might guide you along this shortcut to Tatopani ('Hot Water'). However, the main trail continues down the steps and becomes a larger track that heads north past terraces and small, forested sections. The hot springs of Tatopani (2607m, 2hrs) are ahead, marked by many prayer flags in some trees. These hot springs are probably the largest in Nepal and perhaps the most popular. Most evenings, locals and visitors congregate in the three pools and sing songs to each other. There are teahouses and a campsite near the springs.

DAY 7: TATOPANI–GATLANG
5¾HRS

Locals will probably be in the hot springs soon after dawn – feel free to join them for a dip before breakfast! From the centre of Tatopani follow a rough stone-paved trail, which descends to a single farm building before flattening out to an easy gradient. The trail steepens again before entering Gonggang (2227m, 1hr). A lone teashop

marks the end of Gonggang and a steep descent to the Chilime Khola and a suspension bridge. On the far bank take the left-hand trail that climbs to Chilime village (1762m, 45 mins), where there is an old wooden gompa. The locals here are friendly but the village is frequently dirty. Take the trail that leaves Chilime passing a small school and a series of chorten and mani walls. A long, derelict mani wall marks the entry to the Gatlang valley, and the trail again forks.

If you want to return to Syabrubesi from here, turn left and cross the suspension bridge to Thanbuchet and head straight down the valley on a trail on the north bank. At the end of the valley you will meet the Bhote Kosi, where you cross the Chilime Khola and follow the road along the true right bank (south) to Syabrubesi (2½hrs).

To visit Gatlang, turn right and cross another bridge about 200m upstream from the mani wall. The trail now climbs through oak and rhododendron forest before meeting the terraces of Gatlang (2238m, 4hrs). Along the trail are large chorten decorated with beautiful mani stones. There is a community teahouse at the bottom of the village and a private teahouse at the very top. If you are camping, you will probably be directed to the school above the village.

This is a very friendly village, although a little dirty, and the local Mother's Group is always willing to provide a show of traditional songs and dancing for a donation.

Note: for Trail connection to the Ruby Valley Trek, see p175.

DAYS 8-9: GATLANG–SYABRUBESI–KATHMANDU

From Gatlang head up to the dirt road above the village and follow it east (turn left once on the road) for 3½ hours to a small pass, Rongga Bhangyang (2187m) above Syabrubesi. If you have the time, climb to the viewpoint to the north of the pass (2320m, 15 mins). The trail continues north from the viewpoint (or directly down from the pass), descending into forest before turning back on itself and descending rapidly to Syabrubesi (1503m, 2hrs).

RUBY VALLEY TREK

Like many of Nepal's 'new' trails, this route has been around for centuries but mostly ignored by the tourism industry. Few treks offer such an authentic experience for the fit trekker plus it can be walked for most of the year. Connecting trails include the Tamang Heritage Trail and the delightful Manaslu Circuit as well as a host of potential exploratory routes in both wilderness and villages.

The Ganesh Himal's seven peaks are some of the easiest of all the Himals to get close to. The entire southern flanks drain into the Ankhu (Netrawati) Khola except for the secluded Somdang valley – the site of an abandoned ruby mine. En route you'll enjoy some fine mixed forest, sacred lakes and intriguing villages. All combine in to what a group of adventure journalists described as, 'Truly one of the best trekking experiences you can imagine!'

The trails are open throughout the year except for late January/mid-February, when snow can close the remoter areas for a few weeks. Large crowds of pilgrims visit the lakes of Jaisuli Kund during monsoon, but expect to be accompanied by a few leeches at this time. Despite the lower altitudes, this trek is ideal for fitter walkers as you have to cover some considerable distance each day. Local communities are working hard to develop more accommodation options, but for now, you will have to take a tent or expect some outdoor nights.

NOTE: Both times I have trekked this route the accompanying Finaid map for Arughat was not available, so I have quoted GPS waypoints (WGS84 grid reference) between Lapagaon and Machhakhola.

DAY 1: KATHMANDU–SYABRUBESI
                        8HRS' DRIVE
[See map p154] The drive from Kathmandu offers good views of Manaslu, Ganesh and Langtang Himals as well as brief glimpses of village life in the Himalaya.

The first section is a sealed road to Trisuli before the precipitous dirt road to Dhunche, where there is a National Park and police checkpoint. Continue to Syabrubesi (1503m), where there are many teahouses

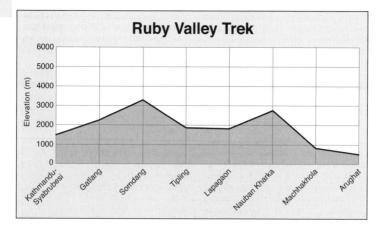

Ruby Valley Trek

Elevation (m): 6000, 5000, 4000, 3000, 2000, 1000, 0

Kathmandu-Syabrubesi · Gatlang · Somdang · Tipling · Lapagaon · Nauban Kharka · Machhakhola · Arughat

RUBY VALLEY TREK

Ruby Valley provides a true gem of a trek in more ways than one! Some terrific views combine with authentic mountain hospitality to form one of the best low-altitude treks in Nepal. Add some intriguing history about a deserted gem mine and it's time to go!

GRADE 4

- **Duration & distance**: About 8 days total; days not more than 20km per day
- **Gradient**: Short steep sections
- **Quality of path**: Formed track, some obstacles
- **Quality of markings**: Limited signage
- **Experience required**: Experienced walkers require navigation skills
- **Walking times**: Less than 7½ hours per day

- **Steps**: Steps not included in grade
- **Highest point**: 3830m
- **Best season**: Oct-May
- **Accommodation**: Camping
- **Recommended maps**: NP106 GHT Series Manaslu & Ganesh Himals and NP105 GHT Series Langtang & Helambu, Himalayan Map House, 2013

and a campsite. As most of the day's drive is on dirt roads, a light scarf to protect your face against dust may be useful.

DAY 2: SYABRUBESI–GATLANG 5¾HRS

[See map p154] There are two trails to Gatlang (2300m) from Syabrubesi: the first option follows the new valley road to the Chilime Khola valley into which you turn west (left) and follow a good trail to Thambuchet and then to Gatlang (see *Tamang Heritage Trail*, day 8, p173).

The second, faster option from Syabrubesi is to climb a trail that begins beside Buddha Guest House. This is a direct route to the Rongga Bhanjyang

(2187m, 2hrs) above Syabrubesi, and also sometimes coincides with the route of an old road to Somdang. From the pass it is an easy 2 hours and 20 minutes along the road to Gatlang (2238m).

DAY 3: GATLANG–SOMDANG 6HRS

[See maps p154 & p168] From Gatlang the road is rarely used by motor traffic as landslides and fallen trees often block it. Follow a large track from Gatlang school up to Parvati Kund (45 mins). From the lake the trail intermittently cuts across the road as it winds through pine and rhododendron forest. At 3100m (1¾hrs) you come to a large kharka where you can camp. Not far above you re-join the road

❏ **Ruby Valley**

Locals in Somdang love to tell the story of why the road exists. They say that the Nepal Army built the road to supply a security post at Somdang. The post was established to protect a nearby mine, which many believe mined precious gem stones including rubies. Others say it was a lead mine and the ensuing debate is always fun to watch!

However, there is some truth to the story. A seam of zinc and lead ore that runs through the Ganesh Himal (between 4000 and 5000m) was identified in 1981. A disused research mining facility sits beneath Paldor Peak at the head of the Somdang valley. The ore has traces of silver and some garnets and there are many stories of locals finding good-quality rubies in secret locations throughout the region. It is said that some of the jewels worn by the kings of Nepal came from here.

and follow it as it traverses a steep rocky hillside to another, smaller, kharka where the road does a U-turn. Here you take a small trail that climbs up and right, away from the road, into a gully filled with rhododendron to the Khurpu Dada Pass (3710m, 2hrs; Finaid: Somdan, sheet: 2885 13, ref: 194 171). For location reference, note a line of old powerlines (now only poles) that crosses the Khurpu Dada, small chautara and trail junction. To the north, along the ridge, is a small trail, which leads to Jaisuli Kund (Jageshwar Kund on the Finaid map, 3hrs), from where you could head to Paldor Peak Base Camp. Instead, head west and descend quickly, cutting across the road a few times, before following it again as it gradually descends to Somdang (3258m, 1½hrs), where there are some campsites and teashops.

DAY 4: SOMDANG–TIPLING 6¾HRS
From Somdang, the trail climbs up through forest and occasionally crosses an old road that was never finished. In 2¾ hours you should reach a small pass at 3780m, where the trail begins traversing steep, rocky hillside. If there has been recent snowfall care should be taken to avoid small avalanches along this section of track. The trail traverses above a large kharka before arriving at the Pansan Pass (3830m, 1hr; Finaid: Somdan, sheet: 2885 13, ref: 153 165) where locals have built a small gompa.

Descend through rhododendron forest for 1¾ hours, passing through a couple of kharkas, which are potential campsites. However, it is best to continue to the terraced fields of Lawadun or Tipling village (1890m, 1¼hrs), and camp in the school. Nearly all the locals in this region of the Ganesh Himal are friendly Gurung Christians, who have decided to ban all alcohol from their communities.

DAY 5: TIPLING–LAPAGAON 6¾HRS
From Tipling follow the main trail to Sertun (1920m, 100 mins) and on to Boran (1560m, 2½hrs). As you enter Boran there is a stone house on the right-hand side of the trail. Next to this house is a stone staircase that cuts down through the northern edge of the village to the Akhu Khola below. Either camp in the school grounds at the centre of the village, or descend to the river, cross a suspension bridge and camp in a small grassy field beside the Lapa Khola (1285m, 30 mins; Finaid: Somdan, sheet: 2885 13, ref: 030 168). If you choose to camp by the river you will need to post a night guard on your camp as local thieves are not uncommon.

Note: it is possible to descend to the Dhading Besi roadhead in 3 days from Boran by following the main trail to the south.

From just beyond the riverside campsite, cross another suspension bridge to the true right bank and begin the long climb to Lapagaon (1850m, 2hrs), a large Tamang village, where the school grounds would make a good campsite. Unless someone in your group knows the trail ahead it is wise to employ a local guide from this village.

DAY 6: LAPAGAON–NAUBAN KHARKA   6½HRS
A new, steep trail climbs a hillside to the west of the village to a chautara with views back down the valley (2200m, 50 mins). You now enter a section of mixed forest with many trails. After 70 minutes you reach a kharka with a dharamsala (GPS: 2441m, N 28° 10.246' E 084° 59.077'). The trail heads north-west up a gully with a rocky spur to the north. The gully steepens as it nears a ridge and the barely distinct Mangro Pass (2936m, 1¼hrs; GPS: 2782m, N 28° 10.102' E 084° 58.726'), which leads to the first of a series of shallow basins that make the next few hours tricky to navigate.

Descend into and then climb out of the first basin to another minor forested ridge in 45 minutes (GPS: 2728m, N 28° 09.908' E 084° 58.354'). The trail now heads north-west, first through forest and then across an exposed hillside to the large Myangmal Kharka (50 mins, GPS: 2936m, N 28° 09.468' E 084° 57.656'), where there is a dharamsala. However, rather than camp here, ascend an easy trail to a final forested ridge marked with a chorten (2975m, 10 mins, GPS: 2975m, N 28° 09.475' E 084° 57.506'), which the locals call Myangmal

Bhanjyang. Descend a good trail through forest for 25 minutes to Nauban Kharka (GPS: 2750m, N 28° 09.732' E 084° 56.900'), which makes a better campsite.

DAY 7: NAUBAN KHARKA–MACHHAKHOLA   7½HRS

The trail continues to descend, sometimes steeply, through dense forest for 140 minutes to a bridge over the Richel Khola (GPS: 1555m, N 28° 10.729' E 084° 55.522') from where it is less than an hour to Yarsa village (GPS: 1877m, N 28° 10.857' E 084° 54.773'). As you leave the village, the trail swings north-west into the large Budhi Gandaki valley and in 30 minutes you reach a trail junction, right is to Kashigaon, but turn left and descend to the river. Do not go to Kashigaon. In 3 hours reach a bridge to Machhakhola (870m) and the main Manaslu Circuit trail, see pp178-83.

Note: If you miss the descent to the Budhi Gandaki before Kashigaon you will probably have to continue to Kerauja/Rumchet and then make a very difficult descent to another bridge across the river to Tatopani. This route involves rock scrambling and should not be attempted with loaded porters. You should also consider taking a local guide from Rumchet for this section.

DAY 8: MACHHAKHOLA–ARUGHAT   7½HRS

The main trail south following the true right bank of the Budhi Gandaki feels like a super-highway compared the trails of the previous days! It is a short and easy walk to the road-head at Soti Khola (700m, 3hrs), where there are jeeps. The main bus station for Kathmandu and Pokhara is at Arughat (508m, 4½hrs).

OTHER TRAILS IN THE GANESH HIMAL

[See maps opposite inside back cover]   From Timure (the village before Rasuwa, to the north of Syabrubesi) there is a small trail to **Dudh Kund** on the northern slopes of Langtang Lirung. WH Tilman was the first European to trek in Nepal in 1949. This was the first place he tried to reach, but he couldn't find it as the trails were bad; they're not much better today!

From Tatopani in the Chilime valley you can ascend the Chilime Khola to the border with Tibet and then climb a steep rocky hillside to your west (left) to the **Sangjung Kharka** (4-days from Tatopani return trek), a pretty valley that lies beneath Paldor and the Ganesh Himal.

To the west of Paldor is **Kalo Pokhari** ('Black Lake'), the starting point for a technical mountaineering circuit around the trekking peak (4 days).

Gatlang is a good place from which to head up to **Jaisuli Kund** (4-day return trek), to the south of Paldor and another potential route to Sangjung Kharka (a further 2 days). Once in the valleys to the south-west of the Ganesh Himal there are a number of *shikari* (hunter trails) that you could explore to the southern slopes of Pabil, or Ganesh IV (7104m) and Salasungo, or Ganesh III (7043m).

The sacred lakes of **Kalo Tal** and **Seto Tal** and perhaps the best Ganesh Himal viewpoint are north from Sertun. From the centre of the village, descend and cross the Menchet Khola and climb to Hindung (5hrs). A steep climb through forest to Thulo Kharka (6hrs) is followed by an easier gradient to Nochhet Kharka (5hrs). The main viewpoint is on the ridge above the lakes. The return to Sertun along the same route takes 2 days.

If you have a little extra time, access to or from Dhading Besi is best combined with **Sing La**, which connects to Boran, Tipling and Somdang. Sing La has wonderful views of the Ganesh, Langtang and Manaslu Himals.

ROUTE GUIDE

MANASLU CIRCUIT

Few can argue that the Manaslu Circuit is one of the best general treks in the Himalaya and a must-do for any keen walker. The rapid development of both trails and facilities over the last five years reflects both demand and the pride locals have in welcoming visitors to their region.

If you haven't been, it's time to go! There are a number of ways to begin your Manaslu adventure:

● Option 1: Drive to Soti Khola, north of the market town of Arughat, and begin trekking, giving the shortest overall itinerary of 13-14 days.

MANASLU CIRCUIT

Rapidly becoming one of the classic Nepal Himalaya treks, the Manaslu Circuit has it all: stunning mountain vistas, enchanting cultures, some of the most beautiful sections of trail in Nepal, and all around the eighth highest mountain in the world.

GRADE 4

● **Duration & distance**: About 16 days total; days not more than 20km per day
● **Gradient**: Very steep with some arduous climbs
● **Quality of path**: Formed track, some obstacles
● **Quality of markings**: Signs at beginning, end and major intersections
● **Experience required**: Some walking experience required

● **Walking times**: Less than 7 hours per day
● **Steps**: Steps not included in grade
● **Highest point**: 5135m
● **Best season**: Mar-May/Oct-Dec
● **Accommodation**: Camping and teahouses
● **Recommended map**: NP106 GHT Series Manaslu & Ganesh Himals, Himalayan Map House, 2013

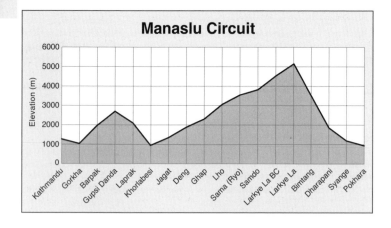

Manaslu Circuit

● Option 2: Drive to Gorkha and hire a jeep to Barpak, then cross the Gupsi Danda to Laprak, and join option 1 at Khorlabesi (on day 4 of the route described). This route adds 3 days to option 1 and is described in full below.

Rupina La is rarely crossed and should only be attempted by experienced and acclimatised trekking groups. Drive to Gorkha and then hire a jeep to Barpak where you begin trekking north up the Daraudi Khola to Rupina La via Jarang. This route adds at least 4 days to option 1, joining at Nya (before Deng).

Manaslu Himal has a long trekking season from early October through to mid-February. It then re-opens, after a brief winter in mid-March, and can be trekked until the monsoon begins in June. However, snow can block Larkye La at any time of year and it can be icy, requiring a rope. Delays occur in all seasons, except monsoon, so you should make sure you can adjust your itinerary if necessary.

DAY 1: KATHMANDU–GORKHA
ALL DAY

It is a good idea to leave Kathmandu early to avoid the traffic gridlock and (all being well) arrive at Gorkha (1060m) by lunchtime (it's roughly a 6-hour bus trip), where there are simple hotels. Towards the top of the town is Tallo Durbar, or lower palace, of Prithvi Narayan Shah who unified Nepal in 1769. This palace is being turned into a museum and is not always open to tourists.

Opposite the palace entrance is a series of stone steps that climb up between traditional Gurung homes to the ridge above. At the top is the World Heritage Listed original palace, Gorkha Durbar (1490m, 1hr) and Gorkha Kalika (temple to the Goddess Kali). Remove all leather garments (including shoes) before entering the temple. The Goddess Kali traditionally represents death and destruction and is supplicated through animal sacrifice. These days she represents time and change, but she is still revered with sacrifices.

DAY 2: GORKHA–BARPAK ALL DAY

Hire a jeep in Gorkha and enjoy bouncing along the new road to Barpak (1950m); make sure you have a scarf to protect against dust. Barpak is one of the largest Gurung villages, where many of the families have at least one male relative in the Royal Gurkha Rifles. There are some teahouses and good campsites close to the treeline above the village with views of the village, Manaslu, Peak 29, and Himal Chuli.

DAY 3: BARPAK–LAPRAK   4½HRS

A main trail climbs up to and then through extensive rhododendron forest above Barpak. The gradient is unrelenting for 2 hours but then eases as you begin to near the top of the Gupsi Danda and a minor pass (2670m, 3hrs from Barpak). There are good views of the entire Manaslu range from here. A broad grazing pasture, or kharka, provides an easy and enjoyable initial descent from the pass.

After 20 minutes the trail steepens and you can see another large Gurung village, Laprak (2100m, 1½hrs), where there is a large school ground to make camp.

DAY 4: LAPRAK–KHORLABESI
5HRS

This section involves some tricky navigation, so it might be a good idea to employ a local guide from Laprak or Singla (see overleaf). Follow the main trail through the village, which then descends directly, for about 300m, to a bridge across the Machha Khola. Over the bridge, the trail climbs roughly 200m before swinging eastwards and traversing the hillside.

There is a large tree with a chautara beside the trail, which marks where the main trail turns towards the north-east. It is important that you continue traversing at this height and do not descend towards the

ROUTE GUIDE

river. There are no teahouses at the village of Singla (2020m, 2hrs), but you can camp in the schoolyard. Continue through the village and be careful not to take some of the smaller tracks that descend towards the Machha Khola. After roughly an hour you will come to a fork where it looks like the right-hand trail begins to descend across unused terraces – do not descend. Instead, take the left trail that climbs for less than 100m. If you or your crew accidentally descend you will find the trail ends in old terraces and you will have to climb back up.

In another 20 minutes there are good views of the Budhi Gandaki river and the main Manaslu Circuit trail, which you will reach in another 1½ hours at Khorlabesi (970m). There is a good campsite at the junction of the Namrung Khola and Budhi Gandaki.

DAY 5: KHORLABESI–JAGAT 5½HRS

The trail from Khorlabesi to Jagat is through a dramatic gorge with lots of waterfalls and some landslides. Follow the broad track on the west bank of the river to Tatopani (990m, 1hr) where the waterspouts make a good washing stop. At the end of the village, cross a suspension bridge to the true left (east) bank and continue through sometimes dense forest to Dobhan (1070m, 80 mins), where there is a fine campsite in the centre of the village.

Continue on a broad trail on the true left bank of the river to Yaruphant (1170m, 1hr), where there are a few teashops on a broad grassy slope. From here, the trail climbs about 200m up what was once an enormous landslide that blocked the Budhi Gandaki. The trail descends a little from the top of the climb to the broad riverbed. In the trekking seasons there are some temporary teashops (80 mins from Yaruphant) at the confluence of the Yara Khola.

Vertical cliffs rise on both sides of the valley as the trail continues on the true left (eastern) bank for 15 minutes to a bridge, which you cross to the true right bank and where the Budhi Gandaki has cut a narrow gorge. After a short climb and descent of 20 minutes you reach a flat area where there is

a teashop and two grassy campsites signposted 'Jagat'. The village is actually 10 minutes further up the trail, behind a rocky spur. As you enter Jagat (1340m) on a good stone-paved trail, there is a community-owned campsite on your left and a couple of basic teahouses before the Manaslu Conservation Area Project (MCAP) and police checkpost. *Jagat* is a common village name in the high mountains as it means 'customs post' and is the traditional tax collection point for trade to and from Tibet.

DAY 6: JAGAT–DENG 6HRS

Beyond the village is the Pangaur Khola, which is crossed using stepping-stones and log bridges. The trail now climbs an easy gradient to a chautara (1hr), where there are good views of Shringi Himal to the north. Descend to Sirdibas (1420m, 40 mins) and turn a sharp left turn at the end of the village to ascend a stream for about 50m before turning sharp right for the main trail. Continue to a suspension bridge, which you cross to the true left bank of the Budhi Gandaki (there is a police checkpost at the bridge) and then climb 200m to the village of Phillim (1570m, 40 mins) and another MCAP checkpost.

This next section of trail is spectacular and well worth the effort of a long day's walk. Ekla Bhatti (1650m) is about 45 minutes from Phillim, but take your time and admire the waterfalls on the west side of the valley. After the monsoon, there is a large waterfall beyond Ekla Bhatti, after which you enter scrubby forest that gives way to large pine trees. Forty minutes from Ekla Bhatti you reach a trail junction, where you turn left (the right-hand trail goes to *Tsum*, see pp184-5). Descend (5 mins) to and cross a bridge, where the trail begins a gradual climb as the valley turns westwards. After the initial climb away from the bridge there is a small trail junction where you turn right (the left trail climbs steeply to Nya).

Another bridge across the Budhi Gandaki is reached in 45 minutes, which you cross to the true left (north) bank to avoid a steep cliff. In another 15 minutes you cross back to the true right (south) bank using a dilapidated wooden suspension bridge, which was scheduled to be replaced in June 2014. In 20 minutes you will reach Pewa and the junction with the high trail from Nya (this is where you join the Circuit trail from Rupina La). It's a good campsite at Deng (1860m), which is now 50 minutes away along a pleasant trail with good views of the narrow gorge cut by the Budhi Gandaki.

DAY 7: DENG–NAMRUNG   5HRS

As the Manaslu Circuit trail turns westwards, the shape of the homes changes to squat, dry-stone structures to reflect the changing demands of climate, and the architectural influences of Tibet. Mani walls, chorten and kani are common along the trail. Rice and wheat are replaced by buckwheat, barley and maize in the fields. The trail descends to a suspension bridge, which you cross to the true left (north) bank of the Budhi Gandaki and then climbs roughly 100m to Rana (1910m, 35 mins).

The trail now climbs an easy gradient beneath the village of Umbaie (above which is Shringi Gompa) before winding through the Shringi Khola gorge to Bhi (1990m, 45 mins). Follow an undulating trail through sparse pine trees and hamlets to a large kani (1½hrs) that marks the entry to the Prok and Ghap communities. The paintings and mani stones on this kani are in good condition. The fierce blue and red characters on the

kani ceiling and walls are protectors who are meant to stop evil spirits from entering the villages beyond. There is a campsite at Prok, only 10 minutes further on.

The trail now gradually swings back to the river, which you cross to the true right bank via a suspension bridge. It's a slight climb to Ghap, where there are a couple of teashops. The valley narrows and you pass through fine broad-leaf forest to a spectacular canyon carved by the river (45 mins), which you re-cross in another 15 minutes on a larger bridge.

Note: the Himal Chuli Base Camp trail veers left here and climbs the Sherang Khola valley.

From the second bridge, the trail climbs more steeply for almost an hour to Namrung (2630m), where there is a campsite and basic teahouse.

DAY 8: NAMRUNG–SAMA (RYO)   5½HRS

Leave Namrung by crossing Therang Khola along an easy trail that passes a waterfall on your left before entering the scattered village of Barchham (20 mins). The trail now climbs a bit less than 300m on an easy gradient to Lihi (2920m, 50 mins), where there is a campsite and teashop at the far end of the village. Descend and cross the Hinan Khola on the far side of the village and ascend an easy trail to Sho (2880m, 45 mins). It is now an easy up-hill gradient to Lho (3180m, 1hr), where there is a campsite and teashop, but

---

❏ **Larke & Siar people**
The high valleys around the back of the Manaslu range, and bordered by Ganesh Himal to the east and Tibet to the north, are called the Larke region. There are two groups of people who live here, the Mongoloid Buddhist people in the Ryo (Sama) and Tsum valleys, and the Siar people of mixed Gurung ancestry who occupy the hills above Gorkha and Dhading.

The people of the high valleys of Larke originally came from Tibet and are therefore enthusiastic followers of Buddhism. The Siar people share many of the habits and traditions of the Gurungs to the south, while still being ardent Tibetan Buddhism practitioners. Their economies are based on agriculture and trade, as their villages lie along two important trade routes to Tibet, which were possibly established by the Sherpas of the Solu-Khumbu. Tibetans exchanged salt and wool for food grains and Nepali merchandise. They are relatively poor, but kind hearted and fun loving, and always ready to share a glass or two of *rakshi* (fire water) or a pot of boiled potatoes.

take your time and enjoy the evolving mountain panorama around you.

Manaslu dominates the skyline at Lho and if you have the time explore the village's mani walls, kani and Ribang Gompa, which sits on a hill above the village. The trail descends to the Thusang Khola and then climbs a steady gradient for 300m to Shyala (80 mins), a community of mainly log cabins where there is another campsite and teashops. Next the trail dips through the Numla Khola before descending slightly and then becoming flat all the way to Sama (Ryo; 3520m, 70 mins), where there are a number of teahouses and campsites to choose from at the far end of the village.

DAY 9: SAMA (RYO)　　　　ALL DAY

It is a good idea to spend a day in Sama (Ryo) exploring the village and/or some of the surrounding viewpoints as part of an acclimatisation programme. One of the most popular places to visit is the Pung Gyen Gumba beneath the east face of Manaslu. To get there, back track on the Shyala trail to a junction before the Numla Khola, where you turn right and begin a long and sometimes steep climb for 2 hours and 20 minutes. Once you have crested the ridge above the river the gradient eases and ahead you will see the small gompa. You will be expected to provide a donation to the gompa if you visit it. Higher still is a cave gompa and hot springs, but relaxing in the grassy kharka near the gompa and enjoying the view of Manaslu is a popular

pastime before returning to Sama in 1½ hours. Alternatively, explore the village and gompas of Sama, or take a local guide to Birendra Kund for reflections of Manaslu and its northern icefall.

DAY 10: SAMA (RYO)–SAMDO
2¼HRS

An easy day to Samdo can be combined with a side trip to Birendra Kund. Leave Sama on a broad trail that runs north from the village across grassy kharkas. Remain on the western side of the valley, following a trail that runs parallel to the Budhi Gandaki. After 45 minutes cross the outflow from Birendra Kund to the summer herding area of Kermo Kharka where there is an excellent view of Manaslu from the impressive mani wall.

The trail continues to climb an easy gradient for an hour before dropping to a bridge over the river. Climb to an impressive kani, which marks the entry to Samdo (3875m, 30 mins). This is a Tibetan refugee settlement of about 40 homes, created after the Chinese occupation of Tibet. The border runs along the top of the hills above Samdo and makes an ideal side-trip.

DAY 11: SAMDO　　　　ALL DAY

It is wise to add a day to your itinerary at this point for acclimatisation: consider climbing Lajyung La, which goes to Tibet (north-east of Samdo), or up the slopes to the north of Samdo for some great view of the entire Manaslu range.

❏ The Ru-Pa people of Samdo

Former residents of Ru, an old Tibetan trading village and home to the famous Taiga Gompa, fled to Samdo after the Chinese occupied their village in Tibet. They had grazed their herds in the fields of the Nubri Valley for centuries, but they left everything, crossed the passes and began a new life. The first group arrived above Sama in spring 1962. They claimed Nepali citizenship, based on a set of copper plates granting them land rights over 600 years before. Villagers petitioned the King of Nepal and received the rights they so desperately needed to remain in Nepal. Since then, there has been an almost constant disagreement with the people of lower villages, such as Sama, over who has the right to these lands. They still maintain many of the Tibetan Buddhist and animist customs their forefathers followed, and live a mostly subsistence life, trading and carrying their goods across high passes on *dzo* (a yak and cattle cross breed).

DAY 12: SAMDO–LARKYE LA DHARAMSALA   3HRS

From Samdo the trail descends to a bridge across the Gyala Khola. Climb the trail on the far side to a large pile of mani stones (40 mins), where you can look down on Larkye Bazaar, a trading ground (there are no buildings as such) where Tibetans sell large herds of goats before the Nepali festival of Dashain in October/November. The trail now climbs an easy gradient with views of Larkye Peak and the north face of Manaslu for 2 hours and 20 minutes to Larkye La dharamsala (4460m), where there is a large emergency shelter and some new teahouses. Take some time to check that you are well prepared to cross the pass tomorrow.

DAY 13: LARKYE LA DHARAMSALA–LARKYE LA–BIMTANG   7HRS

The longest and toughest section of the Manaslu Circuit now awaits, but also the most magnificent views – Himalayan majesty and grandeur all around. It is wise to start before sunrise and climb an ablation valley to views of Cho Danda. Although there are some prayer flags at the top of the ablation valley (4690m, 80 mins) you are not at the top of the pass. The trail now crosses rough undulating moraines for 30 minutes to another dharamsala (4905m). From here the trail begins to climb more steeply to the top of Larkye La (5135m, 1¾hrs), where you will be greeted by magnificent views of the upper Bimtang valley and a roofless dharamsala. Views of Himlung and Cheo Himals, Gyagi Kang, Menjung, Kang Guru and Annapurna II fill the horizon. Descend from the pass down a steep slope, which is often snow covered and icy (and may require a handline), for 1½ hours. Beneath you are three glaciers spotted with numerous turquoise lakes; head for the ablation valley to the left of all the glaciers. An easy gradient then leads down to the campsite at Bimtang (3590m, 2hrs), which is serviced by four competing teashops staffed by pretty Gurung women.

DAY 14: BIMTANG–DHARAPANI   6¾HRS

[See map p187]   Continue to follow the ablation valley south from Bimtang, which soon gives way to lateral moraine after 10 minutes. There are good views of the west face of Manaslu from here. Cross a branch of the glacial melt and then turn left, over some more moraine before crossing the main stream of glacial melt and then climbing a ridge of lateral moraine topped by some prayer flags (20 mins).

The trail descends a little steeply through pine and rhododendron forest for 15 minutes before levelling to a gentle downhill gradient. As you descend towards the Dudh Khola through forest the trail passes through a few kharka. There is a lone teashop at Yak Kharka (aka Sangure Kharka, 3020m, 80 mins) after a copse of mountain pepper trees. From here the trail can be a little difficult to follow across some large landslides and through scrubby forest to the scattered settlement of Kharche (1hr). The trail now climbs an imposing ridge that juts into the centre of the valley before a long descent to the many fields of Goa (2515m, 1½hrs), where there are two teahouses.

It is now a gentle downhill to the large Gurung village of Tilije (2300m, 50 mins), where you cross a bridge and pass a new school. After 20 minutes you come to a trail junction; turn right and descend to Thonje (1965m, 50 mins), which you reach after crossing a long suspension bridge. Once at the village follow a stone-paved trail to a T-junction in front of a teahouse. Turn left onto a dirt track and pass the school; after a short descent, cross a suspension bridge over the Marsyangdi river to Dharapani (1965m, 10 mins), where there is a police checkpost and many comfortable teahouses. Welcome to the Annapurna Circuit!

DAYS 15-16: DHARAPANI–SYANGE–KHUDI–POKHARA   7HRS

Follow the Annapurna trail (see *Naar, Phu & Thorung La*, days 1-3, pp189-90) but in reverse. A road has been built up from Besisahar to Koto, however jeep services normally start/stop at Syange (1150m, 7hrs from Dharapani), and then you can transfer to a bus in Besisahar for services to Pokhara or Kathmandu.

ROUTE GUIDE

OTHER TRAILS IN THE MANASLU HIMAL

[See maps opposite inside back cover] GHT through-hikers have few options in this region. The Ruby Valley trek (pp174-7) is the most obvious and popular route for joining the Manaslu Circuit with the Langtang/Helambu region.

For those wanting to avoid the stunning Manaslu Circuit, the cross-country route from Gorkha to Besisahar (see below) takes 3-4 days and is an enjoyable short trek in its own right.

Gorkha to Arughat

Instead of ascending the Daraudi Khola from Kalika Temple above Gorkha, there is a cross-country route to Arughat via a dirt road to Khanchowk (6hrs) and then descend to Arughat (4½hrs). You can get a jeep or walk along the dirt road to Arkhet Bazaar (2hrs) and continue to Machhakhola (5hrs), which is 30 minutes before Khorlabesi and then begin the *Manaslu Circuit* from day 7, see p181.

Gorkha to Besisahar

Heading west from Gorkha means first crossing the Daraudi Khola and then climbing to either Luitel Bhanjyang or Appipal (one day of 6-8 hours either way). Both routes are similar and lead through mixed farming land broken by patches of shrub forest. The descent to the Marsyangdi Nadi valley will ultimately lead to the Besisahar road. There are a number of places to cross the Marsyangdi, your choice will depend on how quickly you want to get to the accommodation offered in the bazaar towns of Paudi, Sundar (both a 6- to 8-hour day depending on the route) to then arrive at Besisahar (one 6- to 7-hour day following the road) and onward trek options.

Tsum Valley

Tsum Valley (Grade 3) was opened to tourists in 2002 and is becoming a popular side trip to the Manaslu Circuit. The Larke communities here have three gompas all run by nuns.

Warning! Only experienced trekkers should attempt the Thak Khola exit route as it is exposed and extremely dangerous; porters should not be taken.

The Tsum valley is entered via a right (north-east) trail fork after Thangmurmu and before crossing the Chumjet/Nyak bridge over the Budhi Gandaki (1½hrs from Phillim). You first climb through pine forest to the few small fields of Lukuwa (aka Lokpa, 2040m, 1hr), where there are views up the Siyar and Budhi Gandaki valleys. Descend through bamboo jungle to a wooden bridge that crosses the Gumrung Chu (30 mins) – this is a good lunch spot. The valley now swings north and the trail climbs a rough trail through jungle and then on to grassy hillside with stone slabs. Once across the slabs, the trail descends again to a suspension bridge that crosses to the north bank of the Siyar Khola (1½hrs).

The main trail crosses the bridge (rather than going to Ripchet – see *Landan Kharka*, opposite) over the Siyar Khola. You then climb through terraces and scattered stone houses to Tumje (3230m, 1¼hrs), where you can camp in the school grounds. Do not leave anything unattended in this campsite, not even your toilet tent! Locals have a reputation for theft during the night and in all weathers.

A pretty grass-covered trail descends to the Siyar Khola and passes a small gompa run by three nuns who will be glad to offer a cup of Tibetan tea for a donation. Not far beyond the gompa is a bridge over the Sarpu Khola to Kowa (2630m, 1hr). Here the trail forks, the right-hand track leads to Domje (2460m, 20 mins), see *Landan Kharka*, below. Take the left-hand trail that leads through the village and past a row of chorten before climbing at a constant gradient through scrub rhododendron for 450m. A chorten and mani wall at 2970m mark the edge of a broad flat valley and the outskirts of Chokung (3031m, 3hrs) where there is another small gompa and campsite. Continue up the valley on an easy trail to Rachen Gompa, which houses 63 nuns and was established in 1927. Beyond is Mu Gompa, where the valley branches in two; each branch has a trail that leads to Tibet.

It is possible to return to Tumje in 5 hours from Chokung, where you then have to choose your exit route: either retrace your steps to Lukuwa and then join the Manaslu Circuit trail at the bridge to Chumjet, or take the high and difficult route via Thak Khola to Lana.

This route is for experienced trekking groups only; no one with vertigo should attempt the route – it is exposed and very dangerous – and porters should not be taken. Do not stop at Tumje, instead continue for 2 hours to Chumje (3020m), which is a small collection of homes before the Urgin Chu. The following day follow a trail that crosses the Urgin Chu and then climbs out and up to a grassy ridge with three chortens (3150m, 2hrs). The trail now drops steeply before crossing a tricky section of steep ground covered in scrub. Climb another ridge and descend again through bamboo forest. The trail can be hard to find and you must be careful on the slippery log ladders. Beyond the forest, the route again climbs a ridge on a trail that follows a stream. Once on top of the ridge you enter a small village, Durjung Kharka (2570m, 5hrs), where you can camp in the terraces beyond the village. From here, it is only 3 hours down to the main trail at Lana.

Landan Kharka (north face of Ganesh I)
From the trail junction before crossing the Siyar Khola bridge, take the right-hand track to Ripchet (2420m, 1hr) and then on to Domje (2460m, 2hrs). You should check in Domje if the trail to Landan Kharka is accessible; if there have been landslides it might be wise to employ a guide here. From Domje, climb a steepening forest trail on the north bank of the Landan Khola. After 3 hours you will reach a kharka with good views of Ganesh I (aka Yangra, 7422m). The trail continues through forest for another 2 hours before leaving the treeline and reaching an ablation valley on the north side of a nameless glacier. In another hour you reach the final kharka and campsite beneath a natural amphitheatre below the Ganesh Himal.

Annapurna, Naar & Phu

For over 30 years the Annapurna region has been one of Nepal's premier trekking destinations. The recent construction of two roads, one to Manang from Besisahar (completed as far as Koto by mid 2014) and the other to Muktinath and Lo Manthang from Beni (now completed) has changed or diverted many of the traditional trekking routes. However, the famous Annapurna Circuit still attracts many trekkers from around the world and new routes are providing fresh perspectives on what is an amazingly beautiful region. The road network is helping the region re-invent itself and mountain-biking trips abound as well as more pilgrims to Muktinath than ever before.

Nepal's second largest city, Pokhara, is the ideal starting place for exploring the Annapurna region. For many, the early morning viewpoint of Sarangkot provides the first rush of a Himalayan panorama and whets the appetite for more. The Annapurna Himal, to the north of Pokhara, has over 20 major peaks, including Annapurna I (8091m) and the stunning Machhapuchhare, also known as Fish Tail Peak (6997m). To the north of the massive bulk of the Annapurnas is a valley system that leads to Tibet through the villages of Naar and Phu as well as the Mustang region. The airport and road hub of Jomsom is also a major trail junction for routes to the Dhaulagiri and Dolpo regions, so you can design treks of almost any length and difficulty, unlike anywhere else in the Himalaya.

The opening of new areas and increase in the range of facilities throughout the Annapurnas means there is a wide range of trekking-style options. From the comfort and convenience of the teahouses on the main Annapurna Circuit trail (described with Naar and Phu valleys on pp188-93), to camping treks with limited teahouse support, or remote wilderness experiences, there are some truly amazing treks on offer for every type of trekker. For those wanting to indulge in authentic cultures there are Tibetan villages in Naar and Phu, and the famous Manangba, Thakali and Gurung communities of the main trail. Or, for some serious mountain close-ups, consider visiting Tilicho Tal (Tilicho Lake) (summary on p203), or Dhaulagiri and Hidden Valley. For those with limited time, the Annapurna Sanctuary (described in full on pp195-8) offers a wonderful mountain 'fix', and for the novice trekker, the famous sunrise panorama sites of Khopra Ridge (Khopra Danda) and Poon Hill (described in full on pp198-202) are still a must-see.

The Annapurna Conservation Area Project (ACAP) is the largest protected biodiversity area in Nepal. Local community groups are pushing hard for improved services and support from Kathmandu, and have invested heavily in tourism facilities. The more tourists are attracted to the area, the more value local communities will feel their natural environment has to offer, and therefore, the more likely they will help to preserve their region. So use local facilities and services where you can and try to encourage sustainable practices at all times.

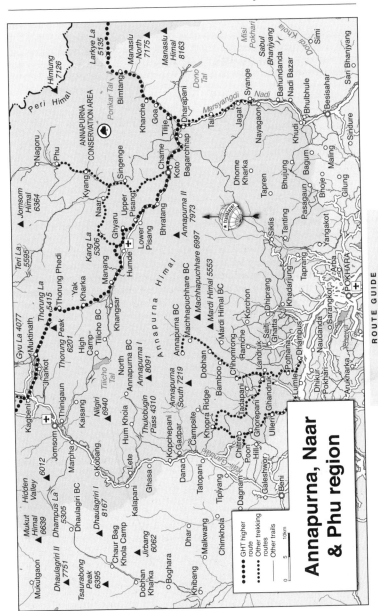

ROUTE GUIDE

Annapurna, Naar & Phu region

As at March 2014, the trekking permit fees for the Manang District areas of Naar, Phu, and northern area of Tilche Village and Thochhe are:
• September to November US$90 per person (pp) per week.
• December to August US$75pp per week.
Plus the Annapurna Conservation Area Project entry fee of Rs2000pp.

NAAR, PHU & THORUNG LA TREK

Opened to tourism in 2003, this trek can be combined with trails to or from Mustang, or via Tilicho Tal to produce some exceptional and challenging itineraries. To assist acclimatisation most people walk in from Syange and then either fly out of Humde (short itinerary) or Jomsom (full itinerary). A new trail from Muktinath through the Kali Gandaki valley provides a trekking route all the way back to Pokhara via Ghorepani (see *Poon Hill and Khopra Ridge*, pp198-202).

The Annapurna Circuit is rarely closed to trekking – only a period from mid-February to early March will see the Thorung La closed. However, large amounts of snow can fall in intense storms throughout the trekking season, so you should always be cautious of impending weather changes.

Lying in the rain-shadow of the Annapurna Circuit, beyond a steep-sided canyon to the north of Koto, the villages of Naar and Phu receive little rain throughout the year. Phu, where there are teahouses, lies just a few kilometres from the Tibetan border, and is a medieval stonewalled village that sits precariously on a rock spur overlooked by Tashi Gompa, famous for the head Lama

❑ **Gurung people**
Gurungs usually live along the southern slopes of the Annapurnas, from Gorkha in the west to Lamjung in the eastern Gandaki zone. They first became famous in Nepal when they formed the bulk of the Shah armies of Gorkha, which conquered the Kathmandu valley in 1768 and united Nepal. This fighting tradition continues to this day, with many young Gurung men in the Gurkha regiments of the British and Indian armies, as well as the Nepal Army and police. Gurungs who are not in the armed forces survive on agriculture and livestock breeding. As many of the older men of a village receive service pensions they tend to hold only small amounts of land; it is always a treat to see an old ex-Gurkha decked out in his neatly pressed uniform in a village in the middle of nowhere!

In April, Gurungs take their sheep or goats to high pastures, where they remain until about September. After the harvest they take their flock to lower altitudes to sell for the important Dasain festival, when every family will have at least one animal for dinner. Gurungs also cross the border to Tibet or India to trade.

The Gurung people are hardworking and fun loving, and the women especially are flirtatious, even with foreigners. Their round faces, bright eyes and broad cheeky smiles are hard to resist. Gurungs traditionally speak a Tibeto-Burman language, though many now speak Nepali. Gurungs uniquely have a system called *rodi* where young boys and girls have sleepovers in a house under supervision, as a method of courting. Couples, once married, do not live together, but remain with their respective parents until a child is born. The girl then finally leaves her parents and lives with the boy and his family.

NAAR, PHU & THORUNG LA TREK

The trek to Naar and Phu represents the future of trekking in the Annapurna region; ancient Tibetan communities combine with the extraordinary alpine views from Kang La and Thorung La, and teahouses throughout – this is a magnificent trek!

GRADE 3

- **Duration & distance**: About 17 days total; days not more than 20km per day
- **Gradient**: Short steep sections
- **Quality of path**: Formed track, some obstacles
- **Quality of markings**: Signs at beginning, end and major intersections
- **Experience required**: Some walking experience required

- **Walking times**: Less than 9 hours a day
- **Steps**: Steps most days
- **Highest point**: 5416m
- **Best season**: Mar-May/Oct-Jan
- **Accommodation**: Camping and teahouses
- **Recommended map**: NP107 GHT Series Annapurna, Naar & Phu, Himalayan Map House, 2013

who is an expert in traditional medicine. Naar is to the south of Phu behind Pisang Peak (6091m), a popular trekking peak, and has teahouses and shops where you can purchase supplies.

DAY 1: POKHARA–BESISAHAR–SYANGE   10HRS' DRIVE
A new road is slowly being built to Manang, and by mid 2014 it had reached Koto (see day 4 of this trek). However, I still recommend walking from Syange through the impressive Kali Gandaki gorge as it is such a wonderful start to the trek.

The village of Syange (1100m) is the current jeep-stop for commercial vehicles; getting here takes about 10 hours from Kathmandu or 6 hours from Pokhara. The drive follows the Marsyangdi river, which you will follow in the days to come. Almost all the villages in this region are Gurung

ROUTE GUIDE

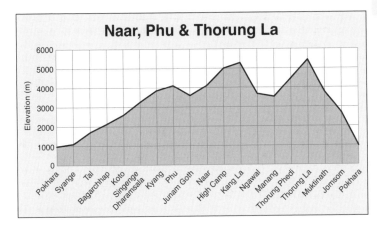

communities, which are noted for their friendliness, jovial spirit and excellent work ethic.

DAY 2: SYANGE–TAL   4HRS

From Syange the Marsyangdi river has cut a gorge, which becomes steeper and steeper as the day goes on. Follow a trail out of the village on the true right (west) bank, heading north; like every riverside trail, it has lots of up and downs. It takes 1½ hours to reach the inviting village of Jagat (1300m), which was once a customs post for the salt trade with Tibet. The trail continues to undulate beside the river, which causes frequent landslides during the monsoon. Beyond the village, cliffs form the far bank and the valley becomes noticeably narrower. It will take an hour to reach Chamje (aka Chyamche, 1430m), where you cross a suspension bridge to the true left (east) bank of the gorge. Climb about 200m to Sattale (1680m), which marks the narrowest section of the valley. A landslide-prone trail then climbs a little to a broad flat-bottom valley and the village of Tal (1700m, 1½hrs), which marks the official entry to Manang District.

DAY 3: TAL–BAGARCHHAP 3¼HRS

Beyond Tal is a short landslide-affected section, which drops down to a suspension bridge to the true right (west) bank of the Marsyangdi river (1½hrs); cross it to Khotro (aka Karte, 1850m). The trail through this section has been blasted from rock to try to reduce the chances of landslide-blockage. Do not re-cross the river for the remainder of the day. In 45 minutes you will reach the beginning of the Gurung village, Dharapani (1860m), which stretches beside the confluence of the Dudh Khola, flowing down from Manaslu. Next, follow the route of the new road to the outskirts of Bagarchhap (2160m, 1hr), which you cut through to rejoin the road on the far side of the village. There was a devastating landslide here in 1995; a memorial in the centre of the village only mentions the tourists who died. At the far end of the village there are good views of the Annapurnas and sections of the Lamjung Himal.

DAY 4: BAGARCHHAP–KOTO 4HRS

From Bagarchhap, continue along the route of the new road to Danakyu (2300m, 35 mins). Beyond the sprawling village, the trail climbs steeply for about 400m through thick pine and fir forest before arriving at Timang (2750m, 85 mins). There are a few teahouses in Timang, any of which make an ideal rest stop with great views of the Lamjung Himal.

Continue along a flat-ish trail to Latamro (2695m, 45 mins), where you descend to and then climb away from a gushing tributary before arriving at Thanchok (2670m, 20 mins). This is a large and often dirty village, but there is a nice teahouse beyond the main settlement, just before re-joining the road for a long and easy descent to Koto (2600m, 50 mins), where there are teahouses and campsites.

Note: To continue on the Annapurna Circuit from Koto takes 1½ days to reach Ngawal if you want to avoid Naar and Phu. The trail follows the road route to Chame and then to Dhikur Pokhari, where you cross to the true left (north) side of the Kali Gandaki and away from the road route. Upper Pisang is not far beyond (total walking time is 6hrs for the day) and the following day it takes 3 hours to reach Ngawal, for more details see *Pokhara/Koto to Manang*, **p204.**

DAY 5: KOTO–SINGENGE   6¼HRS

At the end of Koto village there is a traditional stone doorway and a police checkpost. After registering, descend and cross a suspension bridge to the true left bank and follow a trail into the Naar-Phu Khola gorge, which has been blasted from a sheer rock-face. The gorge quickly narrows and the surrounding pine and fir forest obscure any views.

After 2½ hours, cross a bridge to the true left (east) bank of the Naar-Phu Khola and pass a broad grassy campsite. In less than 30 minutes you will cross a suspension bridge over the Seti Khola tributary. Huge boulders almost obscure the river, which you follow for another 1¼ hours to the second major river obstruction. The trail now becomes steeper and the gorge closes in to form a canyon. The river roars as it crashes against a third and then a fourth series of boulders deposited by ancient landslides. After the last series of boulders cross a wooden bridge (3180m, 30 mins) to the true right (west) bank and follow a trail gouged from a cliff-face. After another 30 minutes re-cross the river to the true left bank and climb through a forested section of trail, then around a cut-away formed by a waterfall over the path before a short final climb to the stone huts of Singenge dharamsala (3230m, 1hr), where there is a small campsite.

DAY 6: SINGENGE–KYANG 5½HRS

The trail remains in the valley bottom for about 30 minutes then crosses a small bridge over a tributary and climbs for about 250m to the seasonal settlement of Meta (3560m, 1hr). As you reach the top of the climb there are good views back down the Naar-Phu Khola to Annapurna II and Lamjung Himal. You can also see a large chorten in the valley bottom near some bridges, which eventually lead to Naar village over a deep gorge – you will take this route on your return from Phu.

The trail now makes an easy traverse of azalea-covered hillside to a broad clearing at Junam Goth (3690m, 2¼hrs). The trail dips down to the Junam Khola and then climbs to the twin villages of Chyako (3720m, 30 mins), which are seasonal settlements shared by both the Naar and Phu villagers. From Upper Chyako, the trail climbs a little before crossing the Mruju Khola, which is the outflow of the Lyapche Glacier above. The trail now climbs and crosses an eroded section of moraine that offers excellent views back down the valley to Pisang Peak and to the north of Kyang (3850m, 1¼hrs), where there is a good campsite.

DAY 7: KYANG–PHU 4¾HRS

The trail enters a narrow gorge that runs due north from Kyang; follow a trail cut away from a large cliff-face before descending to the river. Do not cross a small wooden bridge over the river, instead continue heading north on the true left side

of the river, which swings north-east after 2 hours. The valley now opens up and you pass some derelict chorten, the valley ahead looks completely uninhabitable. Keep watch for blue sheep on the cliff-faces on the far bank. The trail stays beside the river until you can see a large pinnacle of rock standing across the entrance of a gorge. With a little imagination you can see faces in the rock surface, which are said to be evil spirits that have been trapped by the valley guardian. A narrow and steep trail climbs to the right of the rock pinnacle to a doorway and mani wall (4020m, 2hrs), which offers views of the valley ahead.

The trail winds around the eastern hillside above a deep gorge before descending slightly to a series of deserted buildings and large chorten. Cross the bridge to the true right bank to see the chorten, or continue on the true left (eastern) bank to a suspension bridge, which you must cross to reach the village of Phu (4100m, 45 mins).

DAY 8: PHU ALL DAY

The locals say that the dry-stone walled village of Phu has been here for 800 years, which is easy to believe when you start exploring. Take your time and if you are lucky you might be invited into a home for some salt-butter tea. On the far side of the river above Phu is a peninsula of loose rock carved by two rivers. Climb to the top to visit Tashi Gompa and the inspiring *amchi*, traditional Tibetan medicine doctor, Lama Karma. The Lama has many stories to tell and may invite you for a puja ceremony.

Note: A number of trekking/mountaineering groups have crossed from Upper Mustang to Phu via a series of snow plateaus and passes through the Damodhar Himal; it takes 8-10 days and is extremely challenging, involving mountaineering skills, difficult navigation and very high altitudes over 6000m.

DAY 9: PHU–JUNAM GOTH 4½HRS

As today is an easy trek, you might try to organise a morning puja ceremony with Lama Karma. Retrace your steps down the Phu Khola, through Kyang and Chyako to the campsite at Junam Goth.

DAY 10: JUNAM GOTH–NAAR 5HRS

Continue down the same trail to a point where you can see the bridges to Naar. A loose and sometimes steep trail descends towards the bridges, marked by an ancient and derelict tower (3570m, 1¾hrs). You may prefer to cross the 80m deep gorge on the new suspension bridge rather than the original wooden and dry-stone version. From the bridge climb a broad trail, where there are good views of Pisang Peak and Kang Guru. After 2¼ hours you will reach a large chorten and long mani wall where the gradient eases. Continue for less than an hour to Naar village (4110m), built in a natural bowl with many terraced fields beneath. There is an excellent camping area above the village.

Note: The valley behind (to the north) Naar is a route to Tengge in Upper Mustang, via Teri La, see *Teri La – from Naar to Lo Manthang – by Ade Summers*, **pp203-4. This route doesn't offer many water sources, especially in the pre-monsoon months of April and May. You also need a Mustang trekking permit to complete this route to Ghemi (5-6 days), for further information see the** *Mustang* **chapter introduction, p205.**

DAY 11: NAAR–KANG LA PHEDI/ GLACIAL LAKE   2½–5¾HRS

Leave the village on a trail that passes the small hydro plant and then climbs a little to a broad U-shaped valley to the west of Naar. An easy gradient climbs past yak herding pastures and kharka for 2 hours to Kang La Phedi (4530m), where there is a good campsite. This is the largest campsite

before the pass and you should consider staying here if you are in a group of more than 8 trekkers. The trail climbs away from the pastures below and then steepens on a rocky trail, which is often icy. After 2½ hours you will reach a small flat area of loose scree (5020m), where the trail again steepens before arriving at a small glacial lake (5245m, 1¼hrs), where there is a small campsite on scree.

DAY 12: KANG LA PHEDI/GLACIAL LAKE–NGAWAL/HUMDE 4¼-7¾HRS

If you camped at Kang La Phedi it will take less than 4 hours to reach the top of the pass. For those who camped at the glacial lake it will take less than 30 minutes to reach the summit of Kang La (5306m). The pass is about 3 metres wide and decorated with many prayer flags. There are good views from the summit but they improve when you descend a little and can see past the rock wall to your right. Peeking over the ridge joining Annapurna III and IV is the summit of Machhapuchhare (Fish Tail Peak). To the west you can spot Tilicho Peak and the entire Manang valley. The Annapurna Circuit trail lies about 2000m down in the valley below. From the pass, descend steep scree slopes while being careful not to cause rockfall, to roughly 4500m (1½hrs) where the trail becomes firmer underfoot. The trail is easy to follow all the way to azalea and rhododendron bushes, where it then descends a ridge to the village of Ngawal (3660m, 2¼hrs). If you are flying out from Humde (3280m, 1hr), continue down through the village and

---

❏ **Manang-pa (Manang people)**
The inhabitants of the Manang valley are more properly known as Nyeshang. They claim to be Gurung, although the Gurungs don't agree and their language is different from any Tibetan dialect. They farm, cultivate and run successful businesses, both in the mountains and in urban areas. Their houses are usually mud with flat stone roofs, with stables below and living areas above. They are built almost on top of each other up steep slopes, each roof forming the front and base of the next house up. Upper floors are reached using notched wooden ladders. Houses in Manang itself, where there is more flat land, are the traditional mountain homes of stone or wood with storage below and living areas on the upper floor. They follow Tibetan Buddhism, although many gompas have fallen into disrepair over the years.

cross a suspension bridge to the west of the airstrip and the village.

DAY 13: NGAWAL/HUMDE–MANANG
3HRS
Follow any of a number of trails from Ngawal that descend to some large flat fields along the true left (north) bank of the Marsyangdi river. These trails converge as you enter a pretty forest section that leads to Mugji (3330m, 1¾hrs). You are now back on the main Annapurna Circuit road route which leads to the 500-year-old village of Braga (3360m, 30 mins) and then to Manang (3540m, 20 mins), where there are many teahouses and campsites, as well as a maze-like village that dates back hundreds of years. For trekkers on the Annapurna Circuit, Manang is an acclimatisation stop so there are many more services, restaurants and teahouses than you will have come across so far!

DAY 14: MANANG–THORUNG PHEDI
5½HRS
Just beyond Manang is the village of Tangki (3530m, 20 mins), which overlooks the entire community. The trail now swings north and climbs gently to a stone wall with a gate that stops livestock from leaving the high pastures. Do not allow any animals to pass through the gate; if it is locked, use the stone steps to your right. Not much further is Ghusang (3950m, 1hr from Tangki), where you can enjoy some great views of the Chulu Himal, Annapurna III, Gangapurna, Tare Kang (Glacier Dome), Khangsar Kang (Roc Noir) and Tilicho Peak. An easy gradient leads to a suspension bridge over the Ghyanchang Khola, where there are a couple of small teashops (40 mins). In another hour you will reach Yak Kharka (4050m), where there are a few teahouses beneath a slight rise to another teahouse. The trail now climbs fairly constantly at an easy gradient to Ledar (4200m, 40 mins), where there are some simple teahouses, and continues across a hillside covered with many trails. At the first major trail junction take the right, straight route rather than descending to the river. At the next trail junction, take the left-hand straight

route, rather than climbing. After 50 minutes from Ledar the trail descends to a wooden bridge over the Kone Khola, which you cross before climbing to a teashop that is expensive (20 mins). It's now an easy 35 minutes to Thorung Phedi (4450m) where there are extensive teahouses and services.

DAY 15: THORUNG PHEDI–
MUKTINATH 9HRS
It is a good idea to get a pre-dawn start from Thorung Phedi to avoid the strong winds that often affect the pass after 11am. There are 4 large 'steps' up to Thorung La (5415m); the first is a steep climb up scree to Thorung 'Base Camp', a decrepit and expensive teahouse and dirty campsite (4830m, 1hr). The trail now winds through a watercourse before climbing through another, larger gully formed by the melt from a glacier on the eastern side of Thorung Peak. In one hour from 'Base Camp' you reach a well-built dharamsala at 5100m, which also offers a campsite for those wanting a genuine high camp (ensure you are well acclimatised). From here it's 1½ hours across undulating moraine to the top of Thorung La, where there is a teashop in peak trekking season, but expect to pay handsomely for a drink! On a clear day you should be able to see some of the Annapurna range to the south and Mukut Himal bordering Dolpo to the west.

From the pass the trail descends steeply over scree, which gives way to grassy meadows before reaching Muktinath (3760m, 3hrs). This large village is a very important pilgrimage site for Hindus and Buddhists, who live in a sacred compound around an eternal flame-from-water. Take some time to visit the famous Hindu temple with 108 carved spouts from which holy water flows, making a cold shower for the brave!

Note: Muktinath is also a major trail junction to Dhi in Upper Mustang, see South-east of Lo Manthang, pp214-15.

DAYS 16-17: MUKTINATH–KAGBENI–
JOMSOM–POKHARA 4¼HRS
The valley around and beneath Muktinath has five Buddhist gompas and many Hindu shrines. The trail is broad and busy with

four-wheel-drive cars and motorcycles ferrying Hindu pilgrims from Jomsom. From Muktinath, take a trail that descends towards and then through Jharkot (3550m, 30 mins). From here you can avoid the motor road (a 60-min jeep trip to Jomsom, or 40 mins to Kagbeni) by following a small irrigation stream to Khingar (3280m, 20 mins) but from here you will have to take the road route. Make sure you have a scarf or similar to cover your face against dust kicked up by jeeps, or the fierce afternoon wind. Once you reach a broad, flat plateau as you enter the main Kali Gandaki valley there is a shortcut track to Kagbeni (2810m, 70 mins), which avoids the road.

Note: to avoid Kagbeni you can continue on the road route to Jomsom (1½hrs).

Kagbeni is a delightful village that used to be the Nepal/Tibet border, see *Mustang Circuit*, day 2, pp208-9. Kagbeni lies in the bottom of the windswept valley floor of the Kali Gandaki, said to be the deepest river gorge in the world because of the twin 8000m peaks of Annapurna and Dhaulagiri above. The gompa in the middle of the old village is in good condition, and look for the male and female protectors at either end of old boundary wall. The airstrip at Jomsom is 2½ hours (or a 20-minute drive by jeep) to the south, where there are many teahouses and services. There are regular morning flights from Jomsom to Pokhara; the later flights have more potential to be delayed.

Note: If you are delayed because of bad weather in Jomsom, there is an excellent and easy day trip down to Marpha village and back to Jomsom (4hr round trip). Marpha is the centre of the Thakali community and site of a good-quality apple brandy distillery. The locals also make cider and apple pie, both of which are very popular with trekkers!

ROUTE GUIDE

❏ Thakali people

Thakali people come from the high valleys of the Kali Gandaki, about 5 days' walk north-west of Pokhara. Their homeland is called Thak Khola and extends south from Jomsom towards Tatopani. The hospitable Thakali people run most *bhatti*, or trailside teahouses, in the Annapurna region. Their homeland marks the transition between the mainly Hindu lowlands and Buddhist higher areas, although they look more similar to their northern neighbours with regular Mongoloid features of round faces, high cheekbones, flat noses and yellowish skin colour. Thakalis have spread south and east through Nepal, since they were awarded a monopoly over the salt trade with Tibet in the 19th century. Along with the Manangba, these people have evolved into one of the most successful long distance trading groups of Nepal.

Thakali houses generally stand against each other in a line, much like Western terrace houses, are built of stone and have flat roofs for drying grain. The houses are usually spacious inside, and many have an enclosed courtyard for shelter from the wind and keeping livestock, which then leads onto the main living room, with the kitchen off to one side. There are separate sleeping and storage rooms, as well as a family chapel. Thakalis have a financial co-operative system called *dhigur*, where members pay a set amount each year into the 'community chest'. Every year one member is awarded the money, either because of a specific need, or by lottery, which he can use as he pleases. He must repay the principal sum, but keeps any profit and carries any loss he may incur. Dhigur has helped families to build large teahouses, and even businesses in Kathmandu and beyond. Thakali religion is a complex mixture of Jhankrism (a shamanistic religion), Hinduism, Buddhism and Bon. They usually marry by capture where the boyfriend 'abducts' his girlfriend until the families agree to marriage. If no agreement can be made the boy's family must pay a fine, although the couple may elope instead!

ANNAPURNA SANCTUARY

The Annapurna Sanctuary has remained relatively unchanged since the first trekking boom in the mid-1990s, probably because local investment concentrated on the Circuit route and there are limited high trail combination options. It's easy to link this trek with Poon Hill and/or Khopra Ridge (Khopra Danda) via Tadapani, and to the east of Landruk you could connect to the Mardi Himal trails and even go cross country as far as Siklis and the old (and high) monsoon route over the Namun Bhanjyang to Timang.

Lying to the south of the Great Himalaya Range, this region has a typical monsoonal climate: a long rainy season from June/July through to the end of

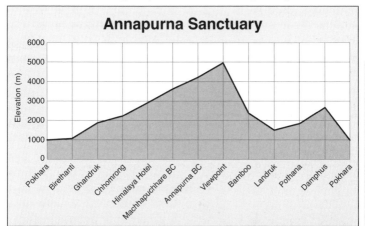

Annapurna Sanctuary

Elevation (m): Pokhara, Birethanti, Ghandruk, Chhomrong, Himalaya Hotel, Machhapuchhare BC, Annapurna BC, Viewpoint, Bamboo, Landruk, Pothana, Damphus, Pokhara

ANNAPURNA SANCTUARY TREK

The Annapurna Sanctuary is a fabulous mountain amphitheatre with magnificent views of the surrounding peaks; en route there are relaxing hot springs, lush forests, fun-loving Gurung communities and many wonderful extension options if you have a little more time.

GRADE 3

- **Duration & distance**: About 10 days total; days not more than 20km per day
- **Gradient**: Short steep sections
- **Quality of path**: Formed track, some obstacles
- **Quality of markings**: Signs at beginning, end and major intersections
- **Experience required**: Some walking experience required
- **Walking times**: Less than 5¾ hours a day

- **Steps**: Steps most days
- **Highest point**: 4234m
- **Best season**: Mar-May/Oct-Jan
- **Accommodation**: Camping and tea-houses
- **Recommended map**: NP107 GHT Series Annapurna, Naar & Phu, Himalayan Map House, 2013

September and then a period of stable weather through to mid-January. Later winter storms frequently fill the Sanctuary with large amounts of snow, often burying the teahouses completely. The spring thaw is in March and the trails soon re-open and remain so even through monsoon.

Excellent teahouse services line the main trail, but exploring further afield requires a full camping kit.

DAY 1: POKHARA–BIRETHANTI–GHANDRUK   6HRS+

There are many taxis plying the new road route from Pokhara to Kimche (3hrs' drive), or you can take a bus to Birethanti (1050m) and begin your trek along the road route (add an extra 4½ hours of walking time).

To begin at Birethanti first cross the metal bridge to the true right bank of the Modi Khola and register at the ACAP checkpost. The trail heads north from Birethanti, up the Modhi Khola valley, following a rough dirt-road route. Currently the road ends at Kimche (1640m) where you then follow an impressive stone-paved trail, climbing all the way to Ghandruk (1940m, 3hrs). This village is an amazing example of stone-work and is worth spending a day exploring. Spread over the entire hillside there are views of the Annapurna range which are best appreciated from one of the many bakery cafés in the village.

Note: It is easy to link Birethanti and Ghandruk with trails to Poon Hill, adding another 2 days to this itinerary, see *Poon Hill and Khopra Ridge* (pp198-202).

DAY 2: GHANDRUK–CHHOMRONG   5HRS

There are a number of route options between Ghandruk and Chhomrong. The fastest and most popular is via Kot Danda and Kimrong. Both the two other routes descend into the Modi Khola valley (via New Bridge and/or Jhinu) and take considerably longer. The New Bridge option is only worth considering if you are not going to return on the Chhomrong–Landruk route (see day 7), which passes the hot springs. To reach Kot Danda, follow the main trail out of the north-western end of the village, which heads to Tadapani. To your north rises the impressive bulk of Annapurna South and the dramatic Machhapuchhare.

Once you leave the village it is easy to see Kot Danda on a ridge across a small valley and the trail route as it branches away from the Tadapani trail. It's a pleasant stroll for 2 hours to Kot Danda where there are some tea shops to sit and enjoy the view. It is a steep downhill to Kimrong (1860m, 45 mins) where groups often stop for lunch. A steady climb for 1¼ hours brings you to Taulung (2180m) and Chhomrong (2170m) is less than an hour further.

DAY 3: CHHOMRONG–HIMALAYA   4¾HRS

Descend a stone stairway and cross a bridge to the true left bank of the Chhomrong Khola and then climb through some small terraces to Tilche (2010m, 40 mins). Beyond the village, enter a bamboo forest and traverse above Bhanuwa and enter the Modhi Khola valley, which forms a striking V shape ahead. The trail climbs to the last permanent settlement of Sinuwa (2360m, 35 mins) and continues through oak and rhododendron forest interspersed with large stands of bamboo.

After another 45 minutes you should reach Kuldhigar (2540m), where there are a few teahouses and an ACAP post. From here onwards, sections of the valley are affected by avalanche debris falling from the flanks of Hiun Chuli; you should check with ACAP staff if the trail is clear and safe. A short climb is followed by a steep descent on a well-prepared paved track to Bamboo (2310m, 30 mins), where the trail now deteriorates with many tree roots and slippery sections forcing your pace to slow. Three small bridges cross tributaries en route to Dobhan (2600m, 1¼hrs), where there are a few teahouses.

From Dobhan the forest becomes more impressive with large rhododendrons covered in Spanish moss and pockets of orchids. The locals believe that the god Baraha protects the Sanctuary. Accidents are frequently explained as the unfortunate outcome of upsetting him by taking meat or eggs beyond a small shrine you'll find opposite a pretty 'weeping waterfall'. In an hour you reach the village of Himalaya (2920m), so named because there was initially a single teahouse here, called Himalaya, and the village sprang up around it once the trek became popular.

DAY 4: HIMALAYA–MACHHAPUCHHARE BASE CAMP (MBC)   3¼HRS

Continue to climb through dense forest to a large rock overhang, called Hinku Cave (3170m, less than an hour), once the site of a teahouse. Deurali (3230m, 45 mins) can be seen ahead, beyond another avalanche-prone area. The valley broadens and a fine birch forest fills the far bank before you pass a small snow cave that has been slowly melting for years. Two obvious rock pillars mark the 'gateway' to the Sanctuary, which suddenly opens out to broad grassy slopes and a series of teahouses at MBC (3700m, 1½hrs).

The last expedition to climb this sacred mountain was in 1957; out of respect, it stopped short of the summit. Many trekkers begin to feel the effects of altitude at MBC, so it is a good idea to initially rest and enjoy the views of Machhapuchhare, Gangapurna and Annapurna South on arrival.

If you are still feeling symptoms of altitude sickness later that evening or the following morning, you should rest for the day or consider descending to Himalaya.

DAY 5: MBC–ANNAPURNA BASE CAMP (ABC)   2HRS

The trail climbs ancient moraine, now covered in grass, to the west of MBC. There are many trails that wind slowly upwards to ABC (4130m, 2hrs), some on the edge of the moraine for views of the Annapurna South Glacier, others towards the lower slopes of Hiun Chuli (giving a better perspective of the Sanctuary).

There are four teahouses at ABC, which was the site for the 1970 British Annapurna Expedition, and a day spent wandering further up the valley or along the edge of the nearby moraine is a great way to absorb the majesty of the Himalaya.

DAY 6: ABC–BAMBOO   5½HRS

Backtrack along the same route to Bamboo (2310m, 4½hrs), or if trail conditions allow continue on to Sinuwa (see below).

DAY 7: BAMBOO–LANDRUK 5¼HRS

Reach Sinuwa (2360m) in one hour from Bamboo and continue to Taulung (2180m, 1½ hours from Sinuwa). At the end of the village the trail forks: the right leads back to Kimrong, but take the left trail, which descends steeply to Jhinu (1780m, 45 mins). Before the track swings sharply west (into

---

❏ **Side trip from Annapurna Base Camp (ABC)**
For those who are acclimatised and have the time, there is an excellent viewpoint on the far side of the Annapurna South Glacier and above the Tent Peak Base Camp. From ABC descend to the glacier and look for a trail marked by cairns, which crosses the glacier to a large gully (beware of rockfall!) cut by a stream through the moraine on the far side of the valley. Climb to the left of the gully to a grassy moraine and head west as a small trail winds around the base of some buttresses.

Before the rim of another deep gully (4350m, 1½hrs), climb straight up the face of a buttress which soon begins to level to a point where you can cross a small stream to the west bank and ascend a broad grassy slope that leads up to a viewpoint (4890m, 2hrs) of the entire western basin of the Sanctuary. To the east is Tent Peak (Tharpu Chuli), to the north-east is Singu Chuli, to the north is Khangsar Kang (Roc Noir) and to the west is the massive face of Annapurna I (8091m). The southern horizon is filled with Annapurna South and Hiun Chuli. Your return to ABC will take 2¼ hours.

the Kimrong Khola valley) there is a small sign for a hot spring about 40 minutes to the north in the Modhi Khola valley. If you don't want a hot bath, continue along the trail as it descends to a bridge, which you cross to the true right bank of the Kimrong Khola and then climb the far bank to Samrung (1750m, 30 mins).

After Samrung, descend to the Modhi Khola on a trail heading towards New Bridge (1340m, 20 mins). Just before the final descent to the bridge there is a sign to another hot springs down a scrambly track to the north of the bridge.

Cross the bridge to the true left bank of the Modhi Khola and pass through some small villages before a short climb to the large Gurung village of Landruk (1565m, 1¼hrs).

DAY 8: LANDRUK–POTHANA–POKHARA　　　　　　　4¼HRS

The trail now climbs an easy gradient sometimes on soft ground and sometimes on stone paving to Pothana (1890m, 2½hrs), which straddles the Manjh Danda ridge. There are fine views of Machhapuchhare and the Annapurnas to the north from along the next section of trail, making this one of the best final days on a trek in Nepal. Descend from Pothana along a large ridge trail to Dhampus (1650m, 1hr), before a final steep descent through forest to the taxi stand and car park at Phedi (1130m, 45 mins), which is only a short drive from Pokhara.

Note: From Landruk and Pothana there are dozens of trails heading east and towards Pokhara that can add a touch of delightful cultural immersion to the end of this itinerary.

POON HILL AND KHOPRA RIDGE TREK

The fantastic mountain views from Poon Hill (note that without Khopra Ridge, this is a Grade 2 trek) attract thousands of trekkers every year and is an ideal introduction to Himalayan trekking. For those who want a closer mountain experience Khopra Ridge (Khopra Danda) and the stunning ridge walk near Bayeli will sate your desire! The Khopra Ridge route is also a complete contrast to the often crowded trails in and around Poon Hill. Once away from Ghorepani you stay at community-owned teahouses, so you are both enjoying the mountains and helping to improve lives. Lying to the south of the Great Himalaya Range, this region has a typical monsoonal climate: a long rainy season from

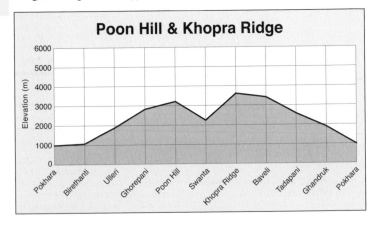

POON HILL AND KHOPRA RIDGE TREK

Poon Hill has been the most popular mountain trekking viewpoint for over 30 years and it still attracts hundreds of trekkers every day! For extra-close views of the Annapurnas and to escape the crowds, Khopra Ridge adds a wonderful contrast and a touch of cultural authenticity.

GRADE 3

- **Duration & distance**: About 7 days total; days not more than 10km per day
- **Gradient**: Short steep sections
- **Quality of path**: Formed track on natural surface
- **Quality of markings**: Signs at beginning, end and at major intersections
- **Experience required**: Some walking experience required
- **Walking times**: Less than 5½ hours per day
- **Steps**: Steps most days
- **Highest point**: 3651m
- **Best season**: Oct-Jun
- **Accommodation**: Camping & teahouses
- **Recommended map**: NP107 GHT Series Annapurna, Naar & Phu, Himalayan Map House, 2013

June/July through to the end of September and then a period of stable weather through to February. Later winter and spring storms frequently obscure the trail until the spring thaw in late March.

Excellent teahouse services line the main trail, but exploring further afield requires full camping kit.

DAY 1: POKHARA–BIRETHANTI–ULLERI   4½HRS

A 3-hour taxi or bus ride from Pokhara brings you to Birethanti (1025m) and the beginning of the trek. First cross the metal bridge to the true right bank of the Modi Khola and register at the ACAP checkpost. From the checkpost climb a few steps that wind between the teahouses of Birethanti to the road just above the village. Follow the road west as it follows the Bhurungdi Khola on the true left bank. You must remain on this bank of this river all the way to Tikhedhungga. It is an easy gradient as you ascend to Lamdawali (1160m), Sudame (1340m), Hile (1430m), and on to Tikhedhungga (1540m, 2½hrs). The trail now steepens to well-made stone steps; apparently there are 3280 of them!

You should reach the Magar village of Ulleri (1960m) in 2 hours, where there are comfy teahouses and views of Annapurna South and Hiun Chuli.

DAY 2: ULLERI–GHOREPANI 3½HRS

The trail continues to climb from Ulleri, leaving behind the cultivated section of the Bhurungdi Khola and heads into oak and rhododendron forest. In less than an hour you should reach Ban Thanti (2210m) and in another 1½ hours, Nangge Thanti (2430m), both of which now have good teahouses and make ideal rest stops. Continue climbing for another hour along the same track to reach Ghorepani (2860m), a large village with a police checkpost at the entry. There are many teahouses all vying to boast the best views of the Annapurnas, which dominate the skyline. To the west is the huge bulk of Dhaulagiri and the unseeable depths of the Kali Gandaki gorge.

DAY 3: GHOREPANI–POON HILL–SWANTA   3½HRS

The panorama of Machhapuchhare, the Annapurna and Dhaulagiri ranges from Poon Hill is one of the classic Himalayan views. It takes about 1¼ hours to reach the

❏ **Magar people**
Magars have Mongoloid features and are more yellow skin-toned than other Nepali people. They speak at least three mutually unintelligible Tibeto-Burman languages, but most speak Nepali as a second language. Magars live in western Nepal, from the high Himalaya to the terai, around the Gorkha District, and in small pockets to the east, past Kathmandu. Many Magars become soldiers, and they are skilled craftsmen and hunters, so they spread across Nepal looking for work. Magars form the largest number of Gurkha soldiers outside Nepal. Their traditional home is a two-storey stone house, covered in whitewash, with thatch or slate roof. In the west, many smaller houses are round or oval and washed in red mud or ochre.

Most Magar villages will have a number of men away on army duties, and many older fellows who have retired from the service. Their marriages are similar to the other hill folk, with most young people choosing their partner to a certain extent. The majority of Magars are Hindu, and the most influential call themselves Thakuris.

top of Poon Hill (3200m) and many trekkers get up early to enjoy the sunrise. There is a wooden viewing tower on the summit but you will need to be early to beat the crowds and get a good vantage point; remember to take water and a snack. The crowds will begin to thin out about an hour after sunrise as people head down to their teahouse for breakfast and prepare for the day's trek.

The Poon Hill–Ghorepani ridge marks a cultural change as well as being a wonderful viewpoint. So far you have been trekking through Gurung communities (see box p188) but now you enter Magar villages. Sometimes, there is a little friction between the two ethnic groups as many of the businesses developed for trekking (teahouse, etc) are controlled by Gurungs. *Annapurna-Dhaulagiri Community Trail*

(see box opposite) is exclusively Magar controlled and it is interesting to see how Nepali people are both proud of their heritage and understand that diversity adds flavour and contrast to mountain tourism.

From the centre of Ghorepani follow the main trail north as it rapidly heads downhill. In an hour you reach the new dirt road at Chitre where you turn left (west) and in a few minutes come to a corner where a small ACAP sign points towards Khopra Ridge.

The trail heads down through scrubby forest and bears left into a tributary gully, which you follow straight down to a bridge over the Ghara Khola (2100m, 30 mins). Cross the river and then a 20-minute climb brings you to the two teahouses in Swanta (2230m), you might need to ask around to find them as road construction has broken

❏ **Direct route to Ghandruk avoiding Khopra Ridge**
Trekking from Ghorepani to Tadapani takes 4 hours and thus reduces the Poon Hill trek to 4 days.

From Ghorepani take the main trail that heads due east from the centre of the village. The trail remains high on a forested ridge, which offers excellent views of Machhapuchhare, Annapurna and Hiun Chuli, especially when you crest a small pass with teashops, which is called Ban Thanti on many maps, after 1½ hours. From here the trail drops steeply through rhododendron forest covered in Spanish moss to a stream, before climbing to a deserted quarry now occupied by teahouses. The trail now traverses to the hamlet of Liui Kharka before heading out on to a broad hillside above the Kimrong Khola and the teahouses of the pretty village, Tadapani (2630m, 2½hrs). You then follow the last day of this itinerary, see day 7.

❏ **Annapurna–Dhaulagiri Community Trail**
The viewpoint of Khopra Ridge, to the north of Poon Hill, was first researched and developed by Mick Chapman in 1978. Over the course of the last ten years the community-trail concept has evolved and is strongly promoted by social entrepreneur, Mahabir Pun. The result is an interesting combination of homestay, community-owned lodges and commercial teahouses.

Each community in the region maintains the community facilities and donates profits to specific schools and health posts. There is no doubt that the system has potential to help development of what are comparatively poor villages when compared to the successful neighbouring Gurung areas. However, a lack of commercial understanding and often competing community interests are hampering further investment. The project needs trekkers to survive and grow, otherwise there is a risk that stronger commercial interests will buy up the key sites and the project could then collapse.

The amazing views from Khopra and Bayeli are more than enough reason to trek this route, and knowing that you are helping education and healthcare in the region provides the icing on the cake!

some of the old trails. You should check here that the lodges ahead will be open. The morning view of Dhaulagiri from this village is very impressive.

DAY 4: SWANTA–KHOPRA RIDGE
5¾HRS
Head through the village school, which is partially funded through a community tourism project, see *Annapurna–Dhaulagiri Community Trail* box above.

The trail gradually climbs north-east into the Dhasta Khore Khola, with occasional loose sections but nothing difficult. Blue and white painted trail markers are obvious along the whole trail and in 1½ hours come to a waterfall beside a small bridge (2348m) over the Khola. Locals claim that they sometimes see tigers drinking here! A short climb brings you to a lovely 'Rest Cottage' (2501m, 15 mins), which makes an excellent snack or lunch stop.

It is now a long climb through rhododendron forest to Chhistibang (aka Dhankharka, 2995m, 1½hrs) where a couple of teahouses can provide lunch. It is worth checking with the locals in Swanta before you leave, just to make sure someone is here! If you want to break the climb into two days, this is the only place to stop.

Continue climbing through rhododendron forest to a major trail junction at 3474m (1½hrs). You will return here

tomorrow, so make sure you familiarise yourself with the trail options. To reach Khopra Ridge you turn left (west) passing between some boulders before climbing across grassy hillside to a ridge. Stay on an obvious trail, which follows the trail to the teahouses at Khopra Ridge (3651m, 1hr). There is normally only one teahouse operating, and again it is worth checking in Swanta that it is open.

The views of Annapurna, Annapurna South and Dhaulagiri are fantastic in both evening and morning light!

Note: Two trail options from Khopra Ridge require camping equipment. The most popular route is to Khayer Barah Kund, a small lake nestled on the north side of the Annapurna South ridge (1 long day). Another lake, on the south side of the ridge takes 2 days to reach and you will need a local guide to then find a rough trail to Chhomrong. There is also a trail heading north and downhill from Khopra Ridge to Narchyang (where there are teahouses, 1510m) beside the Kali Gandaki Nadi (1 long day).

DAY 5: KHOPRA RIDGE–BAYELI
5HRS
After enjoying the great views over breakfast, retrace your steps to yesterday's trail junction (45 mins) and take the trail to Bayeli. This is a small, undulating trail and

ROUTE GUIDE

feels a little exposed at times. There is a very good chance of spotting Bharal (Blue sheep) along this trail as well as many Daphne pheasant. After a long hill-side traverse, you reach a small stream and then climb though rhododendron forest to Bayeli (3405m, 4hrs). The sense of peace and stunning views from the dining room of the pretty teahouse make it hard to believe you are in the most popular trekking region in the Himalaya!

DAY 6: BAYELI–TADAPANI   5½HRS
Today begins with a short climb to the ridge above Bayeli and then a truly fantastic ridge walk. Wildlife is common along this trail so take your time, enjoy the views and spot as many birds and wild sheep as you can!

Dobato has a few teahouses (3376m, 2½hrs) and makes a good lunch stop if you have taken your time. You now trek through pristine forest to Isharu (3087m, 1½hrs)

where there are a few teahouses. The trail becomes easier as you descend about 250m before following an undulating trail through mixed forest. There are a couple of small teahouses being built along this trail and they should be finished in 2014. Entering the extensive village of Tadapani (2655m, 1½hrs) feels like returning to civilisation!

DAY 7: TADAPANI–GHANDRUK–POKHARA   3½HRS
From Tadapani the trail winds through beautiful oak forest with great views of Annapurna South and Macchapuchhare all the way to the large village of Ghandruk (1940m, 2½hrs), where there are plenty of teahouses. Follow a stone paved trail south out of the village towards Kimche (1640m, 1hr) where you can hire a taxi to Pokhara. The walk along the road to Birethanti takes about 4 hours, where there are buses and public vehicles.

OTHER TRAILS IN THE ANNAPURNAS

[See maps opposite inside back cover] GHT through-hikers have many trail options between Besisahar and Beni, which are the two major bus roadheads to the mountains. A few of the more popular options (listed below) can be used in conjunction with the previous treks, but feel free to create your own trek – this is one of the few areas of Nepal where everywhere you go will welcome you with open arms *and* be able to provide good-quality tourist facilities.

Syange to Pokhara
For those returning from the Manaslu Circuit, or beginning the Annapurna Circuit, and have a little extra time this trek is a fabulous option. Often called the **Royal Trek** (Prince Charles from the UK once did a part of it) this trail is hardly trekked and offers a more complete Nepali experience when combined with the major tourist trails. This route description begins from below Syange and heads over to the famous picnic spot of Begnas Tal, which is a short bus ride from Pokhara.

Khudi is a 5-hour walk south from Syange (or a 60-minute jeep drive), and is where you cross the Khudi Khola on a suspension bridge. Next, take a right-hand trail that leads to Sera (870m, 30 mins). From here there is a long series of stone steps that rise above the Boran Khola to Baglungpani (1595m, 3hrs) where there are some great views of Manaslu, Lamjung Himal and the Annapurnas, with the distinctive Macchapuchhare (Fish Tail Peak) standing sentinel. A long ridge descent via Nalma (1240m, 2hrs) brings you to the Midim Khola, a broad valley that leads down to Karputar (490m, 2½hrs). From here it is 1½ hours to Begnas Tal, which is one of Nepal's favourite picnic spots. Catch a bus to Pokhara from here (less than an hour).

Tilicho Tal

For many years visiting Tilicho Tal (Tilicho Lake) was hazardous because of dramatic/unpredictable changes in weather and potential rockfalls. The potential weather danger still exists but a new route bypasses both the rockfall danger and the heavily iced Mesokanto La. The new route (built in 2012 via Mandala Pass) was pioneered by mountain bikers! This camping-based itinerary takes 4-5 days depending on prior acclimatisation and the time you want to spend enjoying Tilicho Tal views. There is a lodge at Tilicho Base Camp for those who are prepared to trek for a very long day to Jomsom, thus making a 3-day itinerary.

It's an easy walk to Khangsar (3734m, 2½hrs) from Manang following the Marsyandi Nadi. Continue following the now nascent Nadi to Tilicho Base Camp (4150m, 4hrs) and then ascend a steep moraine wall for 2 hours to Tilicho Tal Camp (4990m) where the views of the lake and surrounding peaks are sublime. There is a teahouse here but if you want to use it, you should check in Manang and/or Khangsar that it is open. Both old routes around the lake edge are dangerous and prone to rockfall. The safest and fastest route goes behind a minor peak to the north of the lake and crosses 'Eastern Pass' (5340m, 3hrs) before descending to a kharka at the northern end of the lake (4940m, 1hr). The views throughout the day are wonderful. Mandala Pass (aka Donkey pass, 5200m) is a 1½-hour climb away. The trail heads due west and soon rejoins the Mesokanto La route before a long descent to Kaisang (3510m, 3hrs). The steep descent continues to Thinigaon (2840m, 3hrs) and then to Jomsom (2720m, 30 mins).

Teri La – from Naar to Lo Manthang   [by Ade Summers]

This camping-only trek takes 8 days from Naar without acclimatisation time. As well as a Naar–Phu and ACAP permit, you will also require a Mustang controlled area permit; see the *Mustang* chapter introduction, p205.

From Naar, first ascend the Lapse Khola (aka Labse Khola) on a clear but undulating trail to a campsite in 6-7 hours. A good trail continues to follow the Lapse Khola to the next camp in 5 hours. You now cross back and forth over the Lapse Khola to approach the high camp (5225m, 3hrs) before the pass. Contour up the valley, then start gaining height. You can see Teri La on the left (eastern) skyline, and you'll soon see the prayer flags. It is a steep gully ascent to Teri La (5595m, 4hrs) where there are great views of the Dhamodhar Himal, Dhaulagiri, the Annpaurnas and many peaks in Mustang.

It is a steep descent (possibly in snow) into the next valley, where the gradient eases to a good lunch spot beside a river at 5050m (1hr). Follow the valley and then climb a rocky ridge with a small scramble section. Turn right (north) and traverse the ridge to reach a grassy and less rocky ridgeline. Another steep descent brings you to a camp beside the Yak Khola (4730m, 3hrs).

Remain on the true right side of the valley as you continue descending, crossing minor spurs and a landslide area to a possible lunch spot after 3 hours at 4470m. Continue descending to a confluence of two rivers where there is a steep drop on a zig-zag rocky path. Cross the interesting Dhakrung Khola and climb the far ridge. Contour around a second ridge to a minor pass and then turn sharp right and descend into the Samena Khola valley. Cross the river and a short climb to a big wash out area and campsite at Yakpa (4370m).

It's a steep climb passing an old deserted village, Purano Kog. The trail
can be a bit loose and exposed. Ascend a zigzag path up to a ridge for about
500m before the gradient eases across a flat-ish plateau, with amazing views
of Dhaulagiri, Nilgiri and Tilicho. Cross a minor ridge at 4730m before traversing around two ridges and descending into the arid Tengga valley.
Entering the village is an amazing sight, first crossing a long suspension
bridge and then passing the village Kani and Mani walls. There is a campsite
beside the village (3240, 6hrs). Climb about 200m to the plateau behind
Tengge, where there are some incredible eroded rock flutes. Descend to a
lunch spot near the river, where there are more views of Dhaulagiri. After
lunch cross the Dhechyang Khola, which can be tricky and ascend a steep
moraine wall. Once on top traverse across a plateau and then descend to Yara
Gaon (3650m) via a good bridge. An easy walk takes you down the valley to
the valley junction with the Kali Gandaki river, where you cross a good bridge
at Dhi Gaon (3450m, 5hrs). It's then a steep climb to the Lo Manthang trail
(3809m, 6hrs, see *South-east of Lo Manthang*, pp214-15).

Pokhara/Koto to Manang

From Pokhara, follow the same route as described in days 1-4 of *Naar, Phu &
Thorung La* (pp188-90) to Koto, where you should stop for the night.

From Koto: The district centre of Manang is Chame (2675m), 20 minutes up
the road-trail from Koto, where there are many teahouses and tourist services.
Walk through the village on stone paving and cross a suspension bridge to the
true left bank of the Marsyangdi Nadi and a couple of teahouses near some hot
springs. Continue to follow the road route to Talekhu (40 mins), where the valley narrows to steep cliffs on either side. In the middle of the next gorge section
is Bhratang (1hr), where there are a couple of simple teahouses. The trail
descends after the village to a bridge (20 mins), which you cross to the true right
bank of the Marsyangdi Nadi before climbing about 200m through fine pine forest to Dhikur (3060m, 1hr), where there are some extensive teahouses. You have
now walked through a massive bend in the Marsyangdi river and an enormous
concave rock wall rises to your right.

The road route levels and it is a very pleasant trek through sparse pine forest to Lower Pisang (3200m, 50 mins), where there are many teahouses. Look
for a large stuffed yak with lightbulb eyes in an ornately decorated teahouse on
your left as you enter the village. The trail remains flat for 15 minutes or so
before climbing an easy gradient on the dirt road to a minor pass called Deurali
Danda (3470m, 50 mins). The trail descends to another long flat section to
Humde (3280m, 40 mins) where there is an airstrip, police checkpost and teahouses. A lack of shade through this section of trail can make it very hot going
to Mugji (50 mins), where there are a couple of basic teahouses and where you
cross a suspension bridge to the true left bank of the Marsyangdi Nadi. It is now
only 30 minutes to the 500-year-old village of Braga (3360m) and then another
20 minutes to Manang (3540m; see p193).

For details of crossing Thorung La from Manang and then descending to
Muktinath and Jomsom, see *Naar, Phu & Thorung La*, pp188-94.

Mustang

'Mustang is one of the few places in the Himalayan region that has been able to retain its traditional Tibetan culture unmolested... authentic Tibetan culture now survives only in exile and a few places like Mustang, which have had long historical and cultural ties with Tibet.'   **The 14th Dalai Lama**

Closed to foreigners until 1992, the 'Forbidden' Kingdom of Mustang is where today collides with medieval Asia; where a vibrant culture, dating back over a thousand years is coming to terms with the 21st century. Fortunately, the communities and their traditions are resilient, as are their mud-walled towns and monasteries covered in original frescos, for now. A recently built road from Tibet runs through the heart of Mustang to Jomsom and on to Pokhara; it offers unprecedented change to this unique and ageless place. Jeeps and motorcycles have replaced decorated horses, and art experts are assessing the potential dangers of traffic vibrations to fragile artworks. Mustang may not last forever, see it while you can.

Lying to the north-west of the Annapurnas and extending onto the Tibetan Plateau, Upper Mustang is a large mountain-fringed basin home to the headwaters of the Kali Gandaki. The main trail runs north–south from Lo Manthang to Jomsom with some side trips en route, but none that conveniently connects to other trekking routes. So, until some serious trail work is completed there isn't a reliable general route option through Upper Mustang for GHT through-hikers. However, if you have alpine skills, there are a couple of high-altitude routes that are well worth considering. A trail from Ghemi to Upper Dolpo (see p225) is open October to November and the Damodhar Himal offers a spectacular 6000m+ route between Tsarang and Phu.

Mustang is part of the Annapurna Conservation Area Project (ACAP), which is the largest protected biodiversity area in Nepal. Referred to as a Trans-Himalayan Ecosystem (the lower, lush valleys of the mid-hills are linked with the arid Tibetan plateau), this is a culturally and environmentally sensitive and fragile region, which demands the utmost respect and care. Please take all precautions to tread softly and follow the *Great Himalaya Trail Code*, see p12.

In October 2008, King Jigme Palbar Bista's (b 1930) reign over Mustang ended by Nepali Government order, which effectively terminated the monarchic tradition established in AD1350.

As at March 2014, the trekking permit fee for the Mustang District (Upper Mustang beyond Kagbeni) is US$500pp for the first 10 days and after that US$50pp per day. Plus you require the ACAP entry fee of Rs2000pp.

MUSTANG CIRCUIT

The standard return route from Jomsom to Lo Manthang takes 12 days, which works well with the 10-day Upper Mustang permit.

ROUTE GUIDE

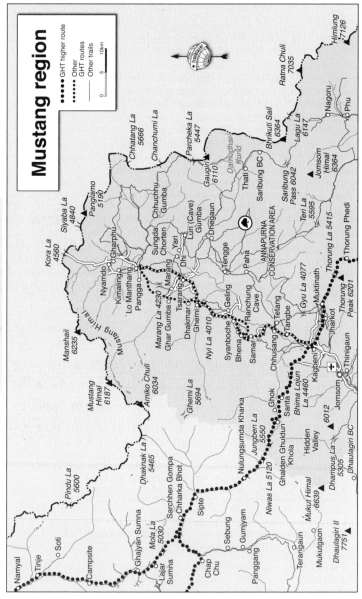

Mustang region

- ●●●●● GHT higher route
- ●●●●● Other GHT routes
- ⋯⋯⋯ Other GHT routes
- —— Other trails

0   5   10km

There are some loop itineraries to the north of Lo Manthang and those with mountaineering experience could try the eastern link via Luri Cave Gumba and the Damodhar Glacier to Phu (7-10 days). The western link, which ascends the Ghemi Khola valley and crosses the Khyaklum Himal to Chharka Bhot, is only open from October to November.

Most routes in Mustang open in late March or early April when the sun is strong enough to melt the large volumes of snow dumped by winter storms. From June, the effect of the monsoon is significantly reduced due to the 'rain-shadow'

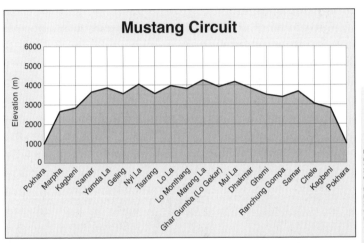

Mustang Circuit

MUSTANG CIRCUIT

Like nowhere else on earth does modern day collide so obviously with the Middle Ages, where life is both booming and threatened by progress. Try to coincide your visit with the Teeji festival to really immerse yourself in a timeless culture set amid dramatic mountain scenery on the 'Plain of Aspirations'.

GRADE 3

- **Duration & distance**: About 12 days total; days not more than 20km per day
- **Gradient**: Short steep sections
- **Quality of path**: Formed track on natural surface
- **Quality of markings**: Signs at beginning, end and major intersections
- **Experience required**: No experience required
- **Walking times**: Less than 7¼ hours per day

- **Steps**: Occasional steps on some days
- **Highest point**: 4170m
- **Best season**: Mar-Nov
- **Accommodation**: Camping and teahouses
- **Recommended map**: NP108 GHT Series Mustang, Himalayan Map House, 2013

effects caused by the Annapurna and Dhaulagiri massifs. This means that trekking routes are pleasant even in the middle of the monsoon, as rainstorms have less intensity than in the rest of the country. After the monsoon has finished, a long period of cold but stable weather interspersed by occasional intense storms continues to early December, when snow accumulates on the passes and the trekking becomes challenging.

Mustang has remained an exclusive trekking destination because of the large trekking permit fee, which is US$500pp for 10 days (Kagbeni to Lo Monthang and return to Kagbeni). To visit the northernmost settlements and valleys above Lo Manthang you must have an extended permit before you arrive in Lo Manthang, without a fully paid extension and a specified route you will not be permitted to trek beyond Lo Manthang.

DAY 1: POKHARA–JOMSOM–MARPHA   ALL DAY

The ascent of the Kali Gandaki valley can cause altitude sickness so it is wise to include acclimatisation periods. One of the most popular first stops is to stay at Marpha (2670m), whether you fly to Jomsom (where you could also rest) and then walk for 2 hours (20 mins by vehicle), or drive up from Beni. Marpha is a picturesque stone-flagged village surrounded by apple orchards, from which the locals produce cider and brandy.

The Kali Gandaki valley is one of the oldest and most important trade routes between Nepal and Tibet. Dating back to the 1400s, the local Thakali people were renowned traders in all goods, especially salt and wool (from Tibet), and grains (from Nepal). This valley is said to be the deepest natural river gorge in the world, as it runs between two 8000m peaks, Annapurna I (8091m) and Dhaulagiri (8167m).

DAY 2: MARPHA–KAGBENI 4½HRS

The trail to Jomsom (2720m, 2hrs) is normally busy with local traffic and can be reached in 50 minutes by vehicle. The town is spread along the road and crosses the Kali Gandaki beyond the Nepal Army barracks. A broad dirt road now follows the east bank of the river to Ekla Bhatti (2740m, 2hrs) where there is a fork: the right track climbs to Muktinath (see day 15 of *Naar, Phu & Thorung La*, pp188-94), but you continue along the valley bottom to Kagbeni (2810m, 30 mins), which can be seen ahead. Your Mustang permit is from Kagbeni onwards so it is important that you arrive here the day before it becomes valid.

Kagbeni, an oasis-like settlement of narrow flagstone-paved paths and flat-roofed homes, is dominated by an old but still functioning Tibetan Buddhist gompa of the Sakyapa sect. The remains of an old fort lie on the northern edge of the village and

---

❏ Baragaunle people

These people live south of Lo Manthang and north of the Thakalis, and usually prefer to be thought of as Gurungs. They are more widely travelled than the Lopa (from Mustang) and the region in which they live is slightly more advanced. Their major villages are Muktinath and Kagbeni, both of which form the border to Mustang, and are often visited by trekkers crossing Thorung La. Their houses are similar to the houses in Lo, built of mud and poorly ventilated. They are, however, quite warm and manage to keep out most of the wind that howls up the valley every day from about 11am. Their clothing, like the Lopa, is Tibetan in style and often brightly coloured. The Baraguan villages used to supply large numbers of bonded servants to rich Thakalis. They follow Tibetan Buddhism with some Bon influences.

would have looked formidable before the local king fell on hard times and his dethroned descendants moved on. A male spirit-protector guards the northern gateway of the village (there is a smaller female protector at the southern entrance) and beyond is a mani wall, next to which is the ACAP registration office and information centre.

Beyond the village there are excellent views of the gompa with Nilgiri, Tilicho, Annapurna and Dhaulagiri rising above.

DAY 3: KAGBENI–SAMAR   6HRS

From Kagbeni the trail continues on the true left (east) bank of the Kali Gandaki, often traversing slopes of loose rock where you might be lucky and find ammonites. The valley narrows and a large cliff-face on your right is dotted with ancient cave dwellings before opening out again at the village of Tangbe (3060m, 2½hrs).

The trail undulates across what looks like moonscape to Chhusang (2980m, 45 mins), where there is a small teahouse. If you have the time, ask one of the locals to guide you to a small but impressive cave gompa dedicated to White Tara (Buddha of Success and Achievement) about 20 minutes from the village. There are also impressive rock formations and some meditation caves in the cliffs on the west bank of the Kali Gandaki. Chhusang is bordered to the north by a broad river, which can be tricky to ford after heavy rain.

The valley ends abruptly at a narrow canyon with more meditation cliffs above and a metal bridge that leads to Chele (3050m, 45 mins) on the true right bank of the Kali Gandaki. There are a few teahouses here and good views back down the valley, with the peaks of Nilgiri and Tilicho in the distance. The trail climbs through the centre of Chele and up a loose rocky slope where the gradient eases. From here you can see the trail enter an eroded valley, on the far side of which is the rarely visited village of Ghyakar. Continue on a track blasted and chiselled from an enormous cliff-face, which eventually leads to a small grassy basin and Dajori La (3735m, 1½hrs) pass with views down to the Samarkyung Khola. Samar (3660m, 30 mins) is a small,

picturesque village surrounded by poplar trees, *chatta* on tall poles, and terraces used for cultivating millet.

DAY 4: SAMAR–GELING   6¼HRS

The trail runs through the centre of the village to an old kani where the track rapidly descends into a heavily eroded watercourse and then climbs a steep trail on the far bank. Cross a short section of flat grassy ground, past an old stupa before reaching another eroded watercourse, which you cross by another switchback trail. Once you reach the top of the far bank the trail forks: the right fork climbs a ridgeline and ultimately leads to Ranchung Cave Gompa, but this is best saved for your return trek, so turn left and continue up towards Bhena La (3838m, 2hrs). The trail dips and then climbs again to Yamda La (3860m, 1hr) and your first expansive views of Upper Mustang. Ahead is range after range of copper, chocolate, grey, ochre and coffee-coloured hills, scarred by deep canyons forming a maze of windswept depths. The trail descends rapidly into a small valley, which you descend on an easy gradient before contouring to the left and around a steep hillside. The trail steepens again as you near Syanboche village (3800m, 45 mins), which is where the Ranchung Cave Gompa trail rejoins the main trail. There are a few teahouses here should you want to rest. On the far side of the village the trail climbs to another pass before descending an easy gradient to a fork marked by a painted cairn. The left trail traverses the upper slopes of the valley, past an enormous stupa at Chhunggar, but the next teahouse is at Ghemi on this route. So turn right at the cairn and descend to a broad flat-bottomed valley and the village of Geling (3570m, 2½hrs).

There are two Ngor-pa sect (an offshoot of the Sakyapa) gompas in the village, which date back to the sect founder Ngorchen Kunga Zangpo in the 15th century. The main gompa is dedicated to Maitreya (the Future Buddha) and contains frescos of the thousand of Buddhas of the Bhadrakalpa (a time when all 1000 Buddhas shall appear). The second, smaller gompa is high on the rocks above the

ROUTE GUIDE

village, and is called the Gonkhang. This is where the village spirit-protectors are stored, and is a very holy and powerful shrine. The resident lama may not be willing to uncover the fierce-looking deities for fear of angering them.

DAY 5: GELING–TSARANG 6¼-7HRS

There are two trail options from Geling; the fastest route climbs a steep hillside above the two gompas before heading due north along a shallow valley to a pass (4025m, 2hrs) with excellent views back towards the Annapurnas. Then descend to the main road route and on to Ghemi (3520m, 1¾hrs). The second, slower trail takes an easier gradient climb up the main Geling valley to the road route over Nyi La (4010m, 2½hrs), which also offers some great views. A long but easy descent brings you to Ghemi (3520m, 1hr), where there are a couple of teahouses. From the centre of Ghemi descend a rough and sometimes-slippery trail next to a stream out-flow from the village. Cross the suspension bridge in the valley bottom to the true left side of the Ghemi Khola, and ascend the far bank to a valley with the longest mani wall in Mustang. Follow the trail beside the mani wall and then swing right into a small valley where the trail climbs another pass, Tsarang La (3870m, 2hrs). Another long, easy descent brings you

to the old capital of Mustang, Tsarang (3560m, 1½hrs), which is dominated by a huge crumbling fort that used to be the royal residence. The extensive gompa and library here has similar but larger frescos and statues to those in Geling's gompa.

DAY 6: TSARANG–LO MANTHANG 4½HRS

The trail from Tsarang drops into the Tsarang Khola ravine to the north of the town; you will need to duck under a metal water pipe as you descend. Cross the bridge and climb the far bank, and ascend to the mouth of the Thulung Khola and the dirt road, which you follow for 2½ hours, past a large stupa, to a broad plateau where there is a lone teashop. In the cliff-face above the teashop you can see more cave dwellings. Continue to follow the road to Lo La (3950m, 1¼hrs), where there are fine views of Lo Manthang (3809m) and northern Mustang. From the pass it is an easy downhill for 45 minutes to the ancient walled capital, which sits upon the 'Plain of Aspiration'.

Only the (ex-) King of Mustang is allowed to ride through the main gateway, all others must walk into the 600-year-old mud-walled city. It is worth spending at least two days exploring Lo Manthang, which is crammed with about 150 homes

---

❏ Lopa people

The Lopa people of Mustang live in mud-brick homes that are whitewashed on the outside and decorated on the inside, much like Tibetan homes. Lo Manthang also boasts the Raja's Palace and many beautiful monasteries, which are being restored by art historians from Italy and other European countries. The land around Lo Manthang is arid and windswept, and not at all conducive to agriculture. The altitude is between 3000m and 3500m. Where there are small streams, however, willows grow and wheat, potatoes and barley are cultivated.

The Lopa traditionally traded with Tibet but in the mid-18th century the Thakalis to the south were granted a monopoly on the salt trade, so the Lopa lost a great deal of income. Local wealth deteriorated further when Tibetans began crossing the border in 1959 and encroached on the small pastures the Lopa used to feed their sheep, yaks, donkeys and mules, causing great hardship. They practise Tibetan Buddhism, and have marriages by parental agreement, capture and elopement. Like many people who live in harsh landscapes, they are kind and generous but also shrewd businessmen. The most famous festival in Lo Manthang is Teeji (see box opposite), which is generally in April/May.

❑ **Teeji festival**

The Teeji (comes from the words 'ten che', meaning the hope of Buddha Dharma) festival is a three-day ritual known as 'The Chasing of the Demons', which centres on a local myth that tells of a deity named Dorje Jono, who must battle against his demon father (Dorje Sonnu) to save the Kingdom of Mustang from destruction. The demon father wreaked havoc on the Kingdom by creating a shortage of water (a precious resource in this very dry land), which caused all sorts of disasters including famine and animal loss. Dorje Jono eventually beats the demon and banishes him from the land, and the community is saved from a plague of misfortunes. Of course, the local population celebrates their salvation, as water will be plentiful again, and the balance and harmony of day-to-day life is restored.

Over three days, the lamas from Chhoede Gompa enact battles and folklore scenes through intricate mask-dances, which culminate in a fireworks and musket-firing melée outside the main gate of the city. Each of the three evenings, there is a cultural programme in the centre of the city, where young and old come to enjoy dance and singing performances. Teeji is a lively, vivid and amusing celebration and reaffirmation of a myth said to have been bought to Mustang by Padmasambhava in the 8th century. Apart from the symbolic ritual of cleansing the Kingdom, Teeji coincides with the end of the dry winter/spring season and ushers in the wetter monsoon season (the growing season in Mustang). So for everyone in Mustang, it is a 'must-see' event, where locals dress up in their finery and have a good time.

ROUTE GUIDE

linked by narrow, twisting alleyways. The flat roofs of each home are used for drying crops during the daytime, and at night young lovers are able to easily climb from roof to roof for liaisons. Established as the capital of Lo by Raja Amapal in the 1380s, the people of Lo Manthang avoid building homes outside of the city walls believing that bad spirits will cause havoc in their households if they do. The Lamas, who circumambulate the city during festivals blessing the walls as they go, perpetuate many such superstitions.

The former Raja, 'Lo Gyelbu', named Jigme Dorje Palbar Bista, fulfils a mainly ceremonial role when in residence although he is loved and respected throughout his Kingdom. It is said that he keeps some of the best horses, Lhasa Apsos, and the most ferocious Tibetan mastiffs in Mustang. The Raja's palace is an imposing 4-storey building in the centre of the city. His wife, the Rani, is from an aristocratic family in Lhasa.

DAY 7: LO MANTHANG   ALL DAY
Apart from the intriguing town itself, there are three major gompas to explore, Jhampa,

Thupchen, and Chhoede, all of which have undergone expert restoration over the last 20 years.

The oldest gompa is Jhampa Lhakang (meaning 'god house'), begun in AD1387 during the reign of King Amapal, and later designed by Ngorchen Kunga Zangpo (who also established Geling and Tsarang gompas). Jhampa is said to contain 1000 hand-painted Yogatantric mandalas of amazing intricacy, as well as a large gilded clay statue of Maitreya (Future Buddha), which is two stories tall. The ground floor is undergoing long overdue restoration, but the second floor is accessible, so too is a third floor sanctum, which leads to a flat roof, which offers excellent views of the city and surrounding countryside.

Nearby is the great gompa of Thupchen, founded in AD1412, which you enter through an entrance hall protected by baroque statues of the four Lokapala, who keep evil spirits at bay. Commissioned by King Chang Chen Tashi Gon, the grandson of Amapal, this is perhaps the most impressive of the three gompas. The main prayer hall has two rows of ornate statues, the larger row against the western wall are Shakyamuni, Avalokiteshwara (Compassion of all Buddhas), Manjushri, and Padmasambhava (Guru Rinpoche), and a lower one with statues including Vajradhara (Primordial Buddha), White Tara, Amitaya, and Hayagriva (the wrathful manifestation of Avalokiteshwara). The walls are adorned with large frescos of Buddhist deity triads, which are flanked by hundreds of minor deities. An antechamber on the northern side of the gompa is under renovation and is likely to be for several years; it was probably dedicated to the protector Mahakali.

The final gompa to visit is Chhoede, the main religious hub of Lo Manthang, and normally guarded by some fierce Tibetan mastiffs, so you are advised to secure the services of a monk to accompany you. Established in AD1757, there are three notable places to visit, the main gompa prayer hall with many bronze, brass and copper statues and the sacred *thanka* of Mahakala and Dorje Sonnu (the evil demon ritually killed during the Teeji festival).

Note: the monks prohibit taking photographs of these statues in an apparent bid to limit interest in them among collectors of stolen art.

In a small building next to the gompa is a large prayer wheel, which almost fills the room. It is said that circumambulation three times while spinning the wheel will drive away any bad dreams. The final spot worth visiting is the monastic school beside the entry to the Chhoede compound, where the students and teachers welcome visitors and are keen to show off their language skills. A large new prayer hall opposite the school is where the monks prepare for their dances at each festival.

DAY 8: LO MANTHANG–LO GEKAR–GHEMI   6HRS

Instead of retracing your steps back towards Tsarang, follow a smaller trail that slowly climbs to the south-west of Lo Manthang to Samduling Kharka (4080m, 1½hrs), where the trail forks. Take the smaller, right-hand trail that crosses the Thulung Khola and then heads towards the hills to the south.

Once on top of the gently curved hill, known as Marang La (4230m, 45 mins) the trail descends a rough but shallow valley formed by a stream running south. The valley gradually steepens, before reaching a relatively flat area with boulders washed down from the mountains to your right.

A bridge crosses the upper Chharang Khola (3820m, 1hr), which has carved a deep gully. Ghar Gumba (3950m, 20 mins) sits in a grove of poplar trees on the hillside above Lo Gekar ('Pure Virtue of Lo').

Note: if you accidentally take the left-hand trail at Samduling Kharka you will cross Marang La and then have to walk up the Tsarang valley, past Lo Gekar to Ghar Gumba.

From Lo Gekar, climb a section that is a bit steep before descending and crossing a tributary of the Chharang Khola. The trail now climbs to another pass, Mui La

---

❑ The legend of Lo Gekar

A local legend says that the Buddhist saint Padmasambhava founded Ghar Gumba in the 8th century, when he came to Mustang to do battle with evil powers out to destroy Buddhism. It is said that he came to Lo Gekar while he was on a journey through Mustang to Samye, where he established the first gompa in Tibet (built AD775-787), thus making Ghar Gumba one of the oldest Tibetan Buddhist gompas in the Himalaya. The main statue in the inner prayer room is said to be a self-emanating image of the saint, flanked by his two principle consorts, Mandarava and Yeshe Tsogyal. Smaller statues of other deities are displayed around the room, which is decorated with some fine frescos. The anteroom is uniquely decorated with hundreds of wooden tablets each with a Buddhist deity painted in vivid colours. A large cavity in the north wall holds a very rare collection of wooden and clay statues, including one of Padmasambhava on a horse prepared for battle against the demons.

(4170m, 1hr), which leads to a broad flat valley. Some prayer flags mark a notch in the hillside on the far side of the valley where the path descends rapidly on loose ground to the red and pink cliffs of Dhakmar (3820m, 1½hrs).

From the centre of Dhakmar follow a trail that first descends the true left-hand (northern) side of the valley before crossing a small river to the true right (southern) bank, then rises slightly to three decorated chorten before rounding the hillside and descending rapidly to Ghemi (3520m, 1hr).

DAY 9: GHEMI–RANCHUNG CAVE GOMPA–SAMAR   7¼HRS

Retrace your steps up to Nyi La (4010m, 1¾hrs) and descend to a trail junction marked by a painted cairn. Take the right-hand trail, which contours across easy ground to the large painted chorten at Chhunggar (3750m, 45 mins).

Continue on a broad easy gradient up to Syanboche La (3850m, 1¼hrs). From the top of the pass you should be able to spot a small trail that heads down the true left side of the valley beneath the village, to Ranchung Cave Gompa (3420m, 1hr).

The trail to the cave is sometimes steep and on loose ground, but for the most part it is easy. As you descend into a canyon formed by a tributary of the Kali Gandaki, you begin to realise how mysterious this place must feel to the locals, who are used to the expansive, windswept plateau above.

The cave is in a cliff wall, about 100m above the junction of two small rivers.

Ranchung chorten means 'the chorten that built itself', or appeared by a miracle. The cave has a large natural pillar, which appears to be supporting the roof of the cave temple. Locals also worship this pillar as a chorten. From the entrance, go to the left of the pillar and climb a few steps into a dark passageway that runs behind the pillar. There are many carvings in the rockface worn smooth by devotees touching them. It is said that the images are predominantly of Padmasambhava (8th century) and Atisa (11th century), the two great teaching lamas who founded what became competing Tibetan Buddhist sects (red hat and yellow hat respectively). However, scholars believe that the cave was of religious importance long before Buddhism arrived in Mustang and was probably a ritual site for an animist belief system.

The trail from the cave crosses a small bridge and then climbs relentlessly to a ridge to the north of Samar (3660m), which you will reach after 2½ hours.

DAYS 10-12: SAMAR–KAGBENI– POKHARA   5½hrs

It will take about an hour to descend to Chele, and a further 4½ hours to Kagbeni (2810m), where you must register at the ACAP office. It is possible to drive to Jomsom and onwards to Pokhara, or take the short flight.

ROUTE GUIDE

SIDE TRIPS FROM LO MANTHANG

[See maps opposite inside back cover] If you have purchased an extended permit for more than 10 days, you are allowed to visit the villages to the north and east of Lo Manthang. However, camping equipment is recommended to explore these areas, as there are few teahouses. In 2007, a team of archaeologists discovered a series of caves in a remote valley in Upper Mustang that had lain untouched for centuries. The team who made the discovery believe that there are more caves waiting to be discovered.

North of Lo Manthang

The heart of Mustang is two broad, fertile valleys that lie to the north of Lo Manthang, and makes an enjoyable two-day trek, or a one-day horse ride. An ancient trade route linking India with Tibet passes through these valleys, which were once much wealthier judging by the many decaying buildings that dot the landscape. If you want to stay in the teahouse in Gharphu you should begin your circuit in the eastern, Chhosar valley. If you are riding, it is probably best to head to Namgyal first to try to see some of the morning puja ceremony.

● **Chhosar Valley including Gharphu, Nyphu and Jhong Cave gompas**
Follow the dirt road from Lo Manthang along the main trade route to Tibet along the true right (west) bank of the Mustang Khola. Nyphu Gompa (3750m, 2hrs) is across the valley, its red walls stand out against the rugged cliff-face above the true left (east) bank of the river.

After another 45 minutes you reach Gharphu (3900m), also on the true left bank of the river. Jhong Cave Gompa (3950m, 30 mins) is further north on the true left bank of the Mustang Khola and is reached by some wooden ladders and tunnels, ask at Gharphu if the gompa is open.

● **Thinggar valley including Namgyal Gompa, Kimaling and Nyamdo**
From the north-west corner of Lo Manthang follow an obvious trail to Namgyal Gompa (Monastery of Victory, at 3910m, 1hr), set on a ridge with excellent views of the walled city, Lo Manthang, in the valley below. Namgyal Thupten Dhargyeling Gompa was founded in AD1310, and continues to be the busiest and most important gompa outside of Lo Manthang. The abbot, or *khenpo*, Ven. Khenpo Tsewan Rigzin, is working hard to maintain both a school and the ancient gompa building, so donations are welcome!

On the far side of the ridge, a trail leads through the village of Namgyal to Thinggar (4025m, 30 mins) where the Raja had his Summer Palace. Phuwa Gompa can be seen on the far side of the valley, about 30 minutes away. Kimaling (4030m) is 45 minutes from Thinggar, and the largest village in the valley. The locals here happily try to sell arts and crafts as well as hand-made rugs. To reach Gharphu, continue up the valley and follow a trail that turns east at the Nyamdo Khola.

South-east of Lo Manthang

● **Dhi, Tashi Kabum Cave Gompa and Luri (Cave) Gumba** From Lo Manthang a small trail descends into the Kali Gandaki valley canyon, which you follow to Surkhang and Dhi (3390m, 6hrs).

Note: this route is only open during the winter months when the river is frozen.

An alternative and easier route involves following the main trail to Tsarang. Just before you leave the Thulung Khola valley, descend to a bridge across the river and climb an easy gradient to a minor pass, which offers good views south. The trail then descends an eroded gully to a bridge over the Kali Gandaki; cross to the campsite at Surkhang (5hrs from Lo Manthang).

Note: you do not actually need to stay at Dhi, which is on the far bank a little upstream. However, when asking for directions, ask for Dhi as it is older and better known than Surkhang.

From Surkhang, ascend the Puyung Khola valley to the campsite at Yara village (3650m, 2hrs), which makes an ideal base to visit Tashi Kabum Cave Gompa (1hr from Yara) and Luri Cave Gumba (2hrs from Yara). Both caves pre-date the main gompas in Lo Manthang by about 100 years and are good examples of Buddhist art before the Tibetan style was fully developed. Employ a local guide from Yara to find both gompas.

OTHER TRAILS IN MUSTANG

GHT through-hikers don't have many options in Mustang, which is currently considered a side-trip to most itineraries. However, if you have alpine skills, there are a couple of high-altitude routes that are well worth considering! A trail from Ghemi to Upper Dolpo (see p225) is open October to November and the Damodhar Himal offers a spectacular 6000m+ route between Tsarang and Phu.

Damodhar Himal is normally accessed from Tsarang (through Dhi) following the Luri Gompa trail and then climb to the sacred source of the Kali Gandaki of Damodhar Kund (4890m, 5 days from Tsarang). Groups often add climbing the trekking peak, Saribung (6328m) to their itinerary as you pass very close to the base camp. The route over Saribung Pass (6042m) is glaciated so alpine skills are necessary. Crossing the pass and a long descent to Phu (see *Naar, Phu and Thorung La*, p191) takes 4-5 days. The total itinerary from Jomsom to Humde would take about 22 days.

An alternative route to the lakes at Damodhar Kund (4890m) is via a high route from Muktinath, which is still used by pilgrims (7-8 days via Tengge, 3240m). The trail crosses Baha La (4400m) and Gyu La (4077m), however, beware that water is scarce along this route especially before the monsoon (April to July).

Also from Tengge is a route to the south-east over **Teri La** (5595m) to Naar, which takes 7 days and has also few water sources, see *Teri La – from Naar to Lo Manthang: trail notes by Ade Summers*, pp203-4.

From Ghemi, there is a trail up the Dhuva Khola heading due west, which eventually leads over a pass to Upper Dolpo. The locals in Ghemi believe that powerful spirits live in the mountains along this route and will not allow anyone to approach the pass between March and September (it's closed during the winter months from December to February) out of fear of losing essential rainfall in the pre-monsoon season.

Dolpo region

Dolpo is remote, wild and considered by many to be one of the most magical and mysterious of places in the Himalaya. Linked for hundreds of years to Tibet, this region lies among the high peaks, on top of the roof of the world. Trekking here is very different from much of Nepal; oasis-like villages dot barren landscapes, scarred by deep canyons, and all beneath velvet blue skies.

Boasting a diverse terrain and extraordinary biodiversity, Dolpo connects the Tibetan plateau with the *pahar* of Nepal, and has some of the highest continuously inhabited settlements on earth along the Thakchu Khola, at 4100m. To

ROUTE GUIDE

Dolpo region

●●●●● GHT higher route

●●●●● Other trekking routes

——— Other trails

0   5   10km

Kanti Himal
6182

Thajuchaur

Takla
Khola

Chyandi
Khola

Chyargo
La 5150

Pung Kharka

Yala La
5414

Danphesail 6109

Palchung Hamga Himal

Khung La 5411

Meng La
5335

SHEY-PHOKSUMDO
NATIONAL PARK

Namlan Khola

Dangerous
Trail

Nyingma Gyanzen
5563

Pho

Yanjer
Gompa

Mai Sundo

Musigaun

Yanan
La
5487

Gautam Himal

Jhonpa La
4835

Yambur
La 4813

Luri

Nisal

Shimen La

Shimen

Kande
Hiunchuli
6627

Nisingyan
La 5097

Bonpo Gompa

Bhijer

Sungjer
Gompa

Khoma

Pu
Gompa

Namyal

Patrali 6450

Kang Nyung
Than 6248

Shyamling
Gompa

Tata

Saldang

Khoma La

Kanjirowa
6289

Namgung

Rapa Gompa

Tinje

Chhonakpo
Tal

Crystal
Mountain

Sela La

Chagaon

Soti

Palta Thumba
6126

She Shikhar
6139

Chhokarbo Tal

Shey Gompa

Darsumana
Dhobhan

Campsite

Nangdala La
5350

Campsite

Dudhkundi
Tal

Kanchauni Lek
6444

Jyanta La
5220

Chhoila La
5051

Lhashamma
6412

Lasa

Phoksumdo
Khola Camp

Phoksumbo Tal

Danigar

Numala BC

Ghajyan
Sumna

Kangmara
Phedi

Ringmo

Bagala La

Tokyu

Dhoro
Gompa

Toijum

Kagmara
La 5115

Sanduwa
Rechi

Temche

Numala La
South

Dho
Tarap

Maran

Lajar
Sumna

Hurikot

Kaigaon

Langa Camp

Chan
La

Chap
Chu

Balangra Lagna
3760

Liku

Tripurakot

Chhepka

Shyanta

Ghyamghar

Lahagaun

Kageni

Nawarpani
(Pibuk)

Tribeni

Juphal

Central
Gompa
(Dunai)

Dunai

Laina Odar

Tarap Khola

Majphal

Taligaun

Lawan

Chhedhul Gompa

Laisicap

Kakkotgaun

Hiunchuli
5916

Dwari Bhanjyang
4715

Swargadwari Lekh

Sun
Tal

Tarakot

Lam Gompa

Jang La 4535

Sisne

the south is a large east–west valley system called Lower Dolpo, and to the west is Mugu, which lies beyond the sacred Crystal Mountain and the Kanjiroba massif. To complete Dolpo's isolation, the Khyaklum and Dhaulagiri Himals create a natural border to Mustang and Annapurna to the east. A combination of ancient animist beliefs, Tibetan Buddhism, and Bon religions predominate throughout the region.

The traditional route to Dolpo was from the south, through the Dhorpatan Hunting Reserve, along a trail that has been used as a salt-trade route for hundreds of years. However, most trekkers enter and exit Dolpo via the dirt airstrip at Juphal in Lower Dolpo. There are several trekking options that run through Dolpo, they are all magnificent and provide some wonderful GHT options. Experienced trekkers could consider some committing routes from Mustang (east) or Mugu (north-west), where trail finding and acclimatisation pose considerable challenges.

Perhaps the most beautiful place in Nepal is Phoksumdo Tal, in the centre of Dolpo, which can be combined with trails to Shey (Crystal Mountain) to access Bhijer, Saldang and the northern villages, or Dho Tarap and the valleys to the south-east. There are also route options that follow the Bharbun Khola, through Chharka Bhot and even to Hidden Valley to the north of Dhaulagiri.

Most of Dolpo and eastern Mugu are protected by the Shey Phoksumdo National Park and Buffer Zone which covers a massive 3555 sq km and is the largest such park in Nepal. Referred to as a Trans-Himalayan Ecosystem (the lower, lush valleys of the mid-hills are linked with the arid Tibetan plateau), this is a culturally and environmentally sensitive and fragile region, which demands the utmost respect and care. Please take all precautions to tread softly and follow the Great Himalaya Trail Code (see p12).

As at March 2014, the trekking permit fees for Dolpa District are:
• Areas of Lower Dolpa, US$10pp per week.
• Areas of Upper Dolpa, US$500pp for the first 10 days; then US$50pp per day.
  Plus the Shey Phoksumdo National Park entry fee of Rs3000pp.

UPPER DOLPO CIRCUIT

There are many trails to and from Upper Dolpo, including the traditional salt-trade route through Dhorpatan to the south of Dunai and Tarakot, from Pokhara and/or Tansen. A less-used route is via Chharka Bhot in eastern Dolpo (see map p206) from Kagbeni in the Annapurna region.

For the really adventurous there are two wild linking trails to Mugu from Pho, in north-west Dolpo, that climb through the Mugu Karnali Nadi valley system to Jumla. Within the region there are several loops that link Upper and Lower Dolpo, but any itinerary should include the stunningly beautiful Phoksumdo Tal (Phoksumdo Lake).

Dolpo has a similar weather pattern to Mustang as it lies in the 'rain-shadow' region behind the Annapurna and Dhaulagiri massifs, meaning the main trekking season is from May to October. Although the high passes are only closed in winter, you will need to brave extreme cold out of season. Large

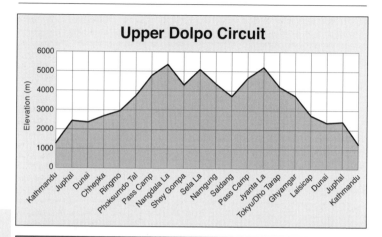

UPPER DOLPO CIRCUIT

Mysterious and spectacular, Dolpo is one of the last genuine examples of traditional Tibetan culture. Add the stunning beauty of Phoksumdo Tal and amazing ecological diversity, and this trek reveals the very best of the Himalaya.

GRADE 4

- **Duration & distance**: About 20 days total; distance per day is not important
- **Gradient**: Very steep with some arduous climbs
- **Quality of path**: Formed and rough track with some obstacles
- **Quality of markings**: Limited signage with occasional markers
- **Experience required**: Experienced walkers require navigation skills

- **Walking times**: Less than 7 hours per day
- **Steps**: Occasional steps on some days
- **Highest point**: 5220m
- **Best season**: Apr-Oct
- **Accommodation**: Camping
- **Recommended map**: NP109 GHT Series Dolpo & Mugu, Himalayan Map House, 2013

storms that dump huge amounts of snow can hit at any time before or after the monsoon so make sure you have some flexibility in your itinerary.

Upper Dolpo was opened for trekking in 1992. However, the substantial permit fee of US$500pp for 10 days has deterred many trekkers from exploring this magnificent corner of Nepal. Those who have braved the expense wholeheartedly say it was worthwhile!

DAY 1: KATHMANDU–NEPALGUNJ
ALL DAY

As the flight from Nepalgunj (150m) to Juphal (see opposite) leaves before any

flights from Kathmandu arrive, you have to overnight in Nepalgunj. There are some hotels in town and a few, more basic places to stay near the airport. Whichever option you choose, it is advisable to book in advance, as they are frequently full. There isn't much to see or do in Nepalgunj so perhaps book a mid-afternoon flight.

DAY 2: NEPALGUNJ–JUPHAL–DUNAI   3HRS

Make an early start to the airport for the 40-minute flight to the dirt airstrip at Juphal (2475m). Once back on the ground there isn't much to see, so make a start downhill on a broad trail, which descends between terraced fields. The trail turns into a shallow gully before once again heading out to terraced fields and descending a bit more steeply. You will clearly see the trail angling down to a small group of buildings beside the Thuli Bheri Khola (2080m), which you should reach in 45 minutes.

At the river, follow the broad dirt track that was built as a service road between the airstrip and the sprawling district headquarters at Dunai (2140m, 2¼hrs), where there are some simple teahouses.

DAY 3: DUNAI–CHHEPKA   5¾HRS

Dunai is the administrative centre for all of Dolpo, as well as the main trading centre. From the centre of the town descend to a suspension bridge and cross the Thuli Bheri Khola to the true right bank and then turn left on a trail that heads upstream along a denuded hillside to the confluence of the Suli Khola. There are two options, a higher, quicker trail that climbs over the lower Palihalna Danda, or the slightly longer riverside route, both of which converge at Sulighat (2282m, 1¾hrs), where you need to register at the National Park office.

The trail up the Suli Khola has little shade and seems to endlessly go up and down, but it is faster and more convenient than taking the old higher route via Rahagaon, which is some 600m above.

From Sulighat continue on the true left (east) bank of the river for 1¼ hours to Raktang (2421m), where there is a teashop and the trail crosses to the true right (west) bank on a suspension bridge. In another hour you will need to re-cross the river at Shyanta, a winter settlement for Ringmo

village. Cross a large tributary, the Ankhe Khola, in 15 minutes, then the trail begins to climb for an hour to Chhepka (2720m), where there are some simple teahouses and a campsite. If you have time, continue to an excellent campsite in a pretty walnut grove 20 minutes beyond Chhepka.

DAY 4: CHHEPKA–JHARINA HOTEL   6HRS

Less than 10 minutes beyond the walnut grove the trail crosses the Suli Khola to the west bank but soon returns to the east bank (70 mins) after avoiding a steep, landslide affected area. The trail continues through dense forest for another hour before crossing a tributary from your right and then climbing a switchback trail for roughly 380m to a broad grassy plateau (80 mins). The enjoyable flat trail does not last long – in 45 minutes you descend to the river. There is a campsite on the far bank at Rechi (2940m, 30 mins) but most trekkers continue from here to Sanduwa (2960m, 1½hrs).

To reach Sanduwa, continue on the true left (east) bank beyond Rechi for an hour to a bridge, which you must cross, near the Tapriza Secondary School and gompa (established by a Swiss ethnology student, Marietta Kind, who spent 1½ years in Ringmo). The teachers and children are always happy to receive guests and please consider giving a generous donation as the school receives very little support from the government. See ⌨ www.tapriza.org for further information.

From the school, continue on the true right (west) bank of the Phoksumdo Khola (previously called the Suli Khola). In 20 minutes you will reach Jharina Hotel and campsite (3020m).

DAY 5: JHARINA HOTEL–RINGMO   4HRS

The trail climbs slightly along the true right (west) bank of the Phoksumdo Khola for 30 minutes to a campsite on the hillside, well above a wooden bridge that leads to Rike and the trail to Dho Tarap. Do not descend to the bridge. Instead, continue climbing through cedar and pine forest on a trail that swings northwards. There is now a long climb past another small winter settlement, called Polam (3400m, 1hr), where there is another checkpost. Continue climbing switchbacks to a ridgeline with excellent views of the turquoise and cobalt blue Phoksumdo Lake, and an enormous waterfall formed by the headwaters of the Phoksumdo Khola (3800m, 80 mins). The trail now descends through birch forest to the clear-running headwaters before climbing an easy gradient towards Ringmo village (3640m, 1hr), where there are some simple teahouses. On the far side of the village, cross a bridge to the National Park office and campsite (10 mins), or you can also camp on the western side of the lake outflow (but it is a little dirty). Ringmo is undergoing transformation into a homestay village so check for details when you arrange your trip.

DAY 6: RINGMO   ALL DAY
Phoksumdo Tal (Phoksumdo Lake) is a RAMSAR-registered wetland (The Convention on Wetlands of International Importance, especially to Waterfowl Habitat) and is Nepal's deepest, and second largest, lake. Perched on the southern shoreline is Ringmo, a traditional Tibetan village, where the locals make a range of handicrafts. About 1.5km away, on the south-eastern edge of the lake, is the Bon tradition Pal Sentan Thason Chholing Gompa. There is much conjecture about the Bon religion, but one well-respected expert David Snellgrove (in 'Himalayan

Pilgrimage', Shambala Publications) asserts that it is contemporary and extremely similar to Tibetan Buddhism. The most important distinction is that all movements are opposite to Tibetan Buddhist practice, so for example, you should pass a mani wall or chorten on your left side, and when walking around or within a gompa, you should walk anti-clockwise.

DAY 7: RINGMO–PHOKSUMDO KHOLA CAMP   5½HRS
This day begins with one of the most spectacular sections of trail in Nepal: from the western side of the lake outflow, head towards the cliffs to your west (left), which you traverse along a precipitous trail. For the first 40 minutes the trail doesn't climb very much but does feel exposed in places, and there are excellent views of the lake and village. After crossing a small stream, the track climbs about 400m steeply before contouring around a rock-face at roughly 4140m (1¼hrs). It is amazing to think that yaks frequently use this trail!

After 80 minutes the trail descends to the floodplain of the Phoksumdo Khola at the northern end of the lake (3630m), where there is an excellent grassy lunch place or campsite. This valley is overgrown in the lower reaches with black caragana bushes, which have needle-like thorns. After 35 minutes cross the river and enter patchy pine forest which is soon replaced by silver birch (the bark of which is often used by Tibetans for writing prayers to

❏ The Legend of Reng
For many locals throughout Dolpo, Phoksumdo Tal is referred to as 'the evil lake of Reng' and the gompa is sited here to keep any bad demons at bay. It is believed that long ago there used to be a village where the lake now is. The valley was flooded by a spiteful demoness who was fleeing from the wrath of the Buddhist sage and magician, Padmasambhava, who was on his way to Tibet to convert the people there to Buddhism. In an effort to confuse the sage, the demoness gave the people in the village a turquoise, making them promise not to tell her pursuer that she had passed that way. But Padmasambhava turned the turquoise into a lump of dung. Thinking the demoness had tricked them the people told the sage where she had gone. In a rage of revenge, she flooded the valley killing everyone before Padmasambhava destroyed her. It is thought her spirit remains in the lake and each year she takes a pack animal from the trail...

leave on passes and important chorten) as the valley narrows. Cross the river via stepping-stones several times as you ascend the valley. After 70 minutes the valley begins to narrow to a cliff-lined gorge and the trail remains on the true left (northern) bank.

You will pass through a few copses of silver birch, which could make a campsite, but continue for 30 minutes to a large copse at the mouth of a tributary gorge of the Tuk Kyaksar Khola (3750m) with a red-pink western (left) cliff line and a dark grey eastern (right) cliff. There are also some cairns beside the small river that flows from this gorge, which mark a rough trail. There is a trail that continues up the main valley at this point so you will need to be vigilant not to miss the gorge and campsite.

DAY 8: PHOKSUMDO KHOLA CAMP–PASS CAMP   5½HRS

From here there are two routes to Shey Gompa: the first, which initially continues up the Phoksumdo Khola, is used by pack animals and takes a little longer. The second route is more direct but rougher and not suitable for pack animals. From the campsite it is only a few minutes to the mouth of the gorge, which is more safely ascended in the morning when the river is lower. The trail winds up the gorge, crossing the river many times. There are many animal tracks in the gorge so take care when routefinding. The sound of the river reverberating from the cliffs makes conversation difficult, so make sure to keep your group together.

The gradient eases after 1½ hours as the gorge widens. In another hour there is a small campsite (4435m) of about eight flat plots scraped out of rocky ground on the true right (western) side of the valley. However, there is a far better camp at the head of the valley where a small waterfall has carved a gully (4717m, 30 mins).

From here you have two choices. If the flow of water through the waterfall is low you should probably camp at this spot, as there will be little or no water higher up. If the flow is strong, such that it fills the bottom of the gully (you might need to climb for about 100m to check), then continue to the higher camp above.

Climb the switchback trail to the true left (east) of the waterfall and after about 100m the gradient eases. You now ascend the upper reaches of the river valley, which gradually broadens, to a large basin. A large scree slope rises on the true right (west) side of the basin and Nangdala La is on the above ridgeline, which is called Churan Lekh. Do not be tempted towards either of the easier-looking saddles to the north and north-east. There are plenty of flat areas in the basin (4810m, 2½hrs from the previous camp), the most popular is at the base of the long curving trail that leads up to the pass.

DAY 9: PASS CAMP–SHEY GOMPA   5HRS

The trail to the pass is over loose slate-scree up an unrelenting gradient for 2 hours and 20 minutes. From the top of Nangdala La (5350m) you can see a broad valley descending to the north carved by a substantial stream, which you should reach in an hour from the pass.

The trail now follows an easy gradient down the valley, crossing the stream a few times depending on your chosen route. This valley is popular with yak and sheep herders so try to buy some fresh yoghurt, butter, or milk as you descend.

In 1½ hours, you will reach the red-painted walls of Shey Gompa (4343m), ringed with mani walls and chorten, set amid a large pasture.

DAY 10: SHEY GOMPA   ALL DAY

It is worth spending a day at Shey to explore both the Kagyupa sect gompa as well as the hermitage at Tsakang. There are many legends surrounding the founder of Shey Gompa and Tsakang, Tsan-zin Ra Pa, who lived in the early 17th century (see David Snellgrove's *Four Lamas of Dolpo*, Himalayan Book Seller), making this one of the most sacred valleys in Dolpo. Locals insist that the killing of any animal is prohibited in or around Shey Gompa; this perhaps explains why it is relatively common to spot blue sheep and snow leopard in the valley.

Perched on the cliffs of Crystal Mountain, about an hour north from Shey,

ROUTE GUIDE

❏ **The legend of Shey**
Shey means crystal, a name derived from Crystal Mountain due west of the gompa, which is streaked with quartz veins.

An annual festival in June/July is based at the gompa and involves circumambulating Crystal Mountain in honour of Drutob Senge Yeshe who defeated a demon and converted Dolpo to Buddhism a thousand years ago. Joel Ziskin, in his *National Geographic* article (see Vol 151, No 4, April 1977), was the first to relate the legend, '*Many years ago, the Buddhist ascetic Drutob Senge Yeshe came to Dolpo and found here a wild people whose supreme god was a fierce mountain spirit. The lama went directly to this mountain and meditated. There he attained enlightenment… A flying snow lion* [a legendary companion of the Snow Leopard] *had served the yogi* [male practitioner of various forms of religious practice] *as a mount. When the mountain god resisted with an army of snake-beings, this loyal lion reproduced itself 108 times and overcame them. Drutob Senge Yeshe then transformed the earth spirit into "a thundering mountain of purest crystal." A white conch shell fell from the sky, and the yogi rose on his lion and pierced a hole in Shey's summit. Rainbows arced across the heavens.*'

is the hermitage of Tsakang. Traditionally the Lama of Shey lived here, although the current incarnate is at school in Kathmandu. However, if you can find the key-holder to let you in, the frescoes here are worth the climb.

See *Shey to Shyamling & Dho Tarap*, pp230-1 for details of other trails from Shey.

DAY 11: SHEY GOMPA–NAMGUNG
6-6¾HRS
From the gompa, head east into the arid Sephu Khola valley, following a trail along the north bank. After 80 minutes, the trail forks where a tributary flows down from the north. Turn left into this tributary valley and climb on loose ground for 2½ hours to Sela La (5095m).

From the pass, descend into a shallow valley, where a number of trails seem to converge from different directions, to an obvious fork in an hour. The right-hand trail descends beside a watercourse to a campsite upstream from the small village of Namgung (4360m, 1hr). Alternatively, take the left-hand fork, which climbs a ridge and then descends a parallel watercourse to the old Kagyupa sect Namgung gompa set high on a cliff-face (1¼hrs), from where you can walk downstream along the Namga Khola to the campsite (less than 30 mins).

DAY 12: NAMGUNG–SALDANG
2¾HRS
From Namgung there's a number of trails that climb over the ridge on the far side of the valley and then descend to Saldang; do not follow any trails that head down the Namga Khola valley. Once over the ridge that forms the northern bank of the Namga Khola (1¾hrs), descend heading north-west towards the Nagon Khola and the commercial and administrative centre of Upper Dolpo, Saldang (3770m, 1hr), where there is a school established by some German trekkers who first came in 1995. A horse-racing festival in July to honour the Black Goat King, who once ruled central Dolpo, begins from the newly decorated gompa in the village.

Trails from all over Dolpo converge at Saldang; to the north are interesting gompas in the Karang valley (2½hrs), Luri (Sunger Gompa) and Nisalgaun (Yangze Gompa, a further 2 hours from Karang). Circling around via Nisalgaun, or crossing Khoma La to the east of Saldang, is the village of Shimen, which leads to a route via Chharka Bhot, Niwas La, and Kagbeni to Jomsom (see *Kagbeni to Chharka Bhot*, pp226-8).

Heading east, over Neng La (Nengla La), is the route to Bhijer, Pho (see *Shey to Pho*, pp230-1) and on to Mugu (see *Pho to*

Gamgadhi, pp231-4). To the south, is the main trading route to Dho Tarap (see *Other Trails in Dolpo*, p226).

DAY 13: SALDANG–CHAGAON
3HRS

The Nagon Khola valley has gently sloping hills on its true right (south-eastern) bank across which runs an easy undulating trail. Settlements merge into one another and provide glimpses of the day-to-day lives of this seemingly inhospitable region. An easy 3 hours from Saldang is Chagaon (3840m), where you can see a gompa beside the river. There is another hermitage gompa, popular with local and Tibetan lamas, high on the ridge above. Camp in or near Chagaon, there are many spots to choose from.

DAY 14: CHAGAON–DARSUMANA
DHOBHAN   6½HRS

As you continue south the valley walls become steeper and the terrain more desolate. A crumbling fort stands as an impotent guard above the river beyond the last village, Chasip (less than 30 mins). Continue along the main trail as it slowly climbs beside the river. After 1½ hours cross the river to the true right (east) bank, and a couple of stone houses at Rakyo Kharka. From here you may need to wade through the river a few times if floods have damaged the trail, but try to remain on the true left

(west) bank. In a further 2 hours a large tributary, the Dachung Khola, flows into the valley from the south as the main valley swings westwards. Cross the Nagon Khola to the true right (east) bank and turn into the Dachung Khola valley. Stay on the true right bank of the Dachung Khola, do not cross the river.

A further 1¾ hours brings you to another major river junction with rivers from the south-east and south-west. Turn right, crossing the Dachung Khola, into a steep-walled valley (the south-west option to your right) and reach a flat grassy campsite at 4700m, in 45 minutes called Darsumana Dhobhan.

DAY 15: DARSUMANA DHOBHAN–
TOKYU   5HRS

A steady gradient climbs about 500m from the campsite to the top of Jyanta La (5220m, 2hrs). Take care when route-finding as there are many trails in the area, it might be easier to try and stay in the middle of the valley to avoid moving off course. Descend into a huge shallow alpine valley, which is boggy (and normally frozen) at the bottom, beside the Jyanta Khola.

The gradient remains gentle on the true left (east) bank of the river until you reach a loose wall of terminal moraine after 1½ hours. Once down the moraine the gradient eases again and you cross the river to the

ROUTE GUIDE

❏ Dolpo people

West of the upper Kali Gandaki, at around 4000m, lies the remote area of Dolpo. Surrounded by mountains over 6000m, this landscape can only be successfully inhabited by tough, hardy people. There are 25 or 30 villages spread over an area of about 1300 square kilometres.

The Dolpo-pa (Dolpo people) are very hospitable and kind, and grow most of the crops they need, as well as keeping yaks, sheep and goats for meat, wool and milk products, or to be sold or traded. Their houses are built of rough stone and all huddled together, as though trying to gain warmth and comfort from each other. This often makes the villages look like forts. Their traditional 'fancy' dress for women includes a striking headdress made of two rectangular brass plates with edges that turn up over the top and back of the head. These headdresses are adorned with coral and turquoise and often represent the wealth of the family. They marry by choice or arrangement, and follow Buddhism and Bon. The 1998 movie *Caravan* (also called *Himalaya*) was shot here and told the tale of the now defunct salt caravans. You can still find locals in villages such as Saldang who appeared in the film.

true right (western) bank. You will pass a series of mani walls and chorten on either side of the valley as it widens. A final descent brings you to the upper reaches of the Dho Tarap valley, and a campsite near to the village of Tokyu (4209m, 1½hrs).

DAY 16: TOKYU–GHYAMGHAR
6HRS

The large, fertile Thakchu Khola valley is home to 10 Magar and Bhotia villages, which almost merge together. This is one of the highest permanent settlements on the planet at an average of 4100m, and a popular place for Tibetan nomads to graze their yak herds. There are both Buddhist and Bon gompas in the valley, although they are not as old as those in Upper Dolpo.

The trail down through the valley is an easy and enjoyable walk past villagers busy with daily life. Some French donors built the Crystal Mountain school towards the end of the valley (where you can camp). It's just before the trail turns south past some large kani and mani walls, and enters Dho Tarap (3950m, 1½hrs), the last village in the valley. If you have time, visit the nunnery of Ribum Gompa and Regu Chorten on the hillside above the village, which has a large and well-preserved statue of Tsong Kharpa. A tributary branches west from Dho Tarap and leads to Chharka Bhot, see *Chharka Bhot to Pho via Dho Tarap, Phoksumdo and Shey*, pp228-30.

From Dho Tarap, continue descending the now narrowing Tarap Khola valley. The trail through this valley can be affected by landslides, which slow your progress. There are few campsites so consider which to use to suit your group's speed. At first, the valley doesn't descend too rapidly as it follows the true left (east) bank of the river. After 2½ hours there is a campsite, called Kama or Langa Kharka (4010m) at the confluence of a tributary, Klang Khola, flowing from the east (left). Cross the Tarap Khola to the true right (west) bank beyond the campsite and descend a rough rocky trail through scrubby patches of forest; it might be a surprise to see and smell trees again after the denuded slopes of Upper Dolpo! The trail descends rapidly to the Sisal

Khola, where woodcutters have made a rough camp. The trail swings back into the Tarap Khola and descends rapidly to a bridge in a narrow gorge, which you cross to the true left (east) bank. You might be able to spot Blue Sheep on the rock-face high above on either bank. Beyond the bridge is a climb of about 200m over a small peninsula in the valley called Ghyamghar (3755m, 2hrs), where there is a small campsite.

DAY 17: GHYAMGHAR–LAISICAP
7HRS

The valley now becomes a sheer-sided canyon with the river in a white rage beneath a bridge, which you cross to the true right (west) bank. The gradient eases to a more gradual descent on an undulating trail for the next 2½ hours to another major tributary junction with the Nawarpani Khola where there is another campsite. The trail then crosses back to the true left (east) bank for a short section before returning to the true right (west) bank at Chhyugar (3440m, 1hr), where locals sometimes camp beneath a large rock overhang.

The trail has been blasted and gouged from rock as it now descends more rapidly to a steep switchback section that drops to a pretty lace-waterfall at Laina Odar (3370m, 2½hrs). The trail descends rapidly again and suddenly the Tarap Khola valley merges with the Thuli Bheri Khola valley. Either camp at an excellent site in a fine pine forest near a deserted police post before the bridge to the true left (south) bank, or continue, crossing the bridge, to a smaller campsite before entering Laisicap village (2775m, 1½hrs).

DAY 18 : LAISICAP–DUNAI   5HRS

After days of descending treacherous trails it is a relief to be walking on a broad thoroughfare beside the Thuli Bheri Khola. However, a lack of shade can make this a hot walk on a sunny day, so have plenty of water and sun cream.

Follow the trail west and about an hour beyond Laisicap is a fine kani at the entrance to Tarakot (2540m), a popular winter settlement for people from Dho

Tarap. Beyond Tarakot the trail crosses to the true right (north) exposed bank of the Thuli Bheri Khola and resumes a typical up and down profile all the way to Dunai (2140m, 4hrs), which you reach by crossing a bridge back to the true left (south) bank of the Thuli Bheri Khola.

DAY 19-20: DUNAI–JUPHAL–NEPALGUNJ–KATHMANDU

Retrace your steps from the first day of trekking to the airstrip at Juphal (2475m, 3½hrs), where you can fly back to Nepalgunj and then catch a late morning or afternoon flight to Kathmandu.

OTHER TRAILS IN THE DOLPO REGION

[See maps opposite inside back cover] Great Himalaya Trail options abound throughout Dolpo and the first decision is where to start: to take a high route from Kagbeni or Ghemi in Mustang, or to take a lower route via Dunai? Either way, you will need to cross a major dividing ridge system running north from Dhaulagiri to Tibet. The entire region is a very remote area where it is a rare but pleasant surprise to bump into a wandering nomad. Whichever route you choose, your destination is likely to be the Far West trading hubs of Jumla or Gamgadhi, near Rara Lake.

One note of caution, the locals in Ghemi are very superstitious and will only allow trekking groups to cross Ghemi La in October and November. They believe that the mountain spirits will be offended and prevent rain from falling on their fields if anyone disturbs the pass between December and September. They have been known to violently defend this belief.

The highest trail across Dolpo is from Kagbeni to Chharka Bhot via Santa and Ghok and is open throughout the main trekking seasons and is described on pp226-8. You could also approach Chharka Bhot from Marpha, Dhampus La and Hidden Valley and then connect to the main trail near Ghok. This route is easily closed by small amounts of snow so be sure to check weather forecasts. Note that the Dhaulagiri Circuit also offers a longer but spectacular route to Hidden Valley from Beni.

Trails from the Kali Gandaki valley converge at Chharka Bhot and then head north and west. Running parallel with the Tibetan border is an old trade route to Shimen and the Saldang valley, before it then heads north-west to the remotest village in Dolpo, Pho.

Heading west and then north from Chharka Bhot are trails to Dho Tarap, Phoksumdo Tal and Shey Gompa, which also lead to Pho (all described on pp228-31).

It is also possible to head south from Chharka Bhot and wind around the Thuli Bheri Khola through Lower Dolpo to eventually arrive at Jumla. Of the first two options, the route via Dho Tarap and Ringmo is longer than the Saldang route but it visits some 'unmissable' highlights of Dolpo. For the trails from Pho to Mugu and the Namlan Khola, see *Pho to Gamgadhi*, pp231-4.

● **Dhorpatan** – offers a lower route option to Lower Dolpo from Beni. The trail isn't fully serviced with teahouses so you will need to camp for one or two nights. Dhorpatan Hunting Reserve is rarely visited by trekkers despite offering some fantastic views of the Dhaulagiri and Kanjiroba massifs.

ROUTE GUIDE

Typical itineraries from Beni to Dunai take 10 days via Darbang, Lamsung, Jaljala La, Thakur, Jang La (4535m), Guibang and Purpang. For complete trail notes by Linda Bezemer, see *Great Himalaya Trail Low Route application*, Apple iBook.

● The low route between **Dunai and Jumla** is an excellent option for those wanting to avoid the wilderness and navigation challenges of Upper Dolpo to Mugu. The trek follows a still-used trade route and normally takes 4-5 days. From Dunai follow the main trail along the true left bank of the Thuli Bheri Nadi, which you cross at Tripurakot (4hrs).

The trail climbs a little and then traverses the hillside before reaching Balangchaur (7hrs). You then begin a constant gradient climb over Khome La and descending to Majhgaon (7½hrs). It is a long winding trail that climbs to Nauli Ghot (7hrs) before crossing the Maure Lagna and a long descent to Kudigaun (8½hrs). A final push of 6 hours brings you to Jumla.

● **Lower Dolpo Circuit** from Ringmo (see *Upper Dolpo Circuit*, day 6, p220) descend to the Maduwa Khola valley and head eastwards to Bagala La (5210m, 2 days). Cross the pass and camp again at or near Danigar (4631m, 1 day), which is a popular herding pasture.

From Danigar, it is a long day up and over Numala La South (aka Numa La South, 5238m, see *Chharka Bhot to Pho via Dho Tarap, Phoksumdo and Shey*, pp228-30) to the upper reaches of the Dho Tarap valley, where you will rejoin the *Upper Dolpo Circuit* on day 16, see p224. The Lower Dolpo Circuit is typically a trek of 10-12 days in total and does not require the US$500pp trekking permit, only the Lower Dolpo US$10pp per week permit.

● **Shey to Shyamling & Dho Tarap** – From Shey (see *Upper Dolpo Circuit*, day 10, pp221-2) there are several route options. To the north is a high ridge-top trail to another important gompa complex at Shyamling (aka Samling, 2 days via Tata). This route can be linked with a long and difficult trek from Pho, the remotest village in Upper Dolpo, to the Namlan Khola system in Mugu and then on to Jumla (12-16 days from Shey). This is a hazardous and challenging route even for experienced groups and you will need to employ local guides (you need at least two for safety reasons); see *Pho to Gamgadhi*, pp231-4, for further details.

The Sephu Khola behind Shey Gompa leads to a major trail junction, the right-hand fork leads over two high passes (Lanmuse La and Numala La North, Numa La North) to the Dho Tarap valley (3 days).

There are not many good tourist maps of the entire Dolpo region, so rather than quoting Finaid map references, GPS coordinates are used for places that could be hard to locate.

Kagbeni to Chharka Bhot

Wind through the southern end of Kagbeni (2810m) village to a suspension bridge behind the school. From the far bank there are two trail options, a steep switchback climb or the longer, easier route up the Kali Gandaki valley to Tirigaon (1hr). If you take the steep route take the right fork after about 250m, which leads to a grassy plateau (40 mins). The trail from Tirigaon forks just before the village, take the left trail and climb an easier gradient to a small gully where there is a slight scramble up to the grassy plateau (1hr). Once on the plateau there is a main trail that leads to a kharka (3478m, 1hr), where there is a water source in a deep gully to your left.

From the kharka ascend to a saddle to the north (3810m, 50 mins), where the trail then climbs the hillside to the west; do not descend. The gradient increases as you enter a gully and pass some caves frequently used by locals as a bivouac. The trail follows the watercourse in the gully for about 50m before switchbacking again. At 4050m you meet the larger main trail from Phalyak and turn west (right) and continue to climb on a much-easier gradient to a ridgetop pass (4306m, 1½hrs). From here the trail continues west and contours through two basins before climbing a little more to Bhima Lojun La (4460m, 1hr). Now make an undulating traverse for the next 1½ hours to a small spur. Head down into a large ravine where some camping groups have cleared tent platforms.

From here the trail contours across a loose scree-covered hillside to a flat point on a ridge marked by chorten. Take the left, slightly higher trail at the first chorten and then descend steeply to the compact village of Santa (3777m, 1¼hrs) where there are some stone-walled fields to camp in that belong to an old man called Wangyel.

From the western end of the village follow a trail that heads through two gullies before reaching a switchback climb to Jhansye (4195m, 2hrs). The trail now stays relatively flat as it crosses steep hillside for an hour before a steep and loose descent to the Kyalunpa Khola (25 mins). There used to be a river trail to the west but it has been cut by landslides and the locals no longer use it. Instead, cross a simple wooden bridge to the true left (north) bank and climb the trail to Ghok, but when you reach a grassy plateau before the village turn west (left) and continue to climb towards a narrow gully. Do not go to Ghok.

The trail climbs up though the steep gully made by the Ghalden Ghuldun Khola before reaching a campsite among juniper trees and scrub (110 mins, GPS: 4247m, N 28° 54.813' E 083° 37.259'). There is another potential campsite in 20 minutes (4380m) but it has less shade and shelter from the afternoon winds. From here it is a continual climb to the Gharchak Chuksa Danda and Jungbenley La (5122m, 2¾hrs), which is finally reached via a rocky gully. Descend into a shallow valley on the far side of the pass before climbing very slightly to a potential campsite at 5140m beside the Lhanimar Khola (45 mins). Jungben La (5550m, 1½hrs) is on the ridge to your west and once at the top you'll have excellent views of Hidden Valley (south) beyond which the summit of Dhaulagiri can be seen. The Annapurnas are on the horizon to the south-east, and to your west is the Kanjiroba range.

Descend on an easy trail from the pass to the large plateau of Niwas La (5120m), where a cairn marks the highpoint, in 80 minutes. From here it is an easy descent for 30 minutes to the Nulungsumda Kharka (4987m) campsite at the confluence of the Malun and Thasan Kholas.

Note: if you are trekking this route in the opposite direction, it is essential you do not descend into the valley on the eastern side of Niwas La

plateaux. **Instead follow the obvious trail that climbs a ridge extending north-east from the plateaux.**

From the Nulungsumda Kharka, follow the Thasan Khola along the true right (northern) bank to another good camping spot, where a river joins from the north (right), in 40 minutes. There is another campsite, where the Yalku Khola joins from the south (left), in another 80 minutes. The trail does not cross the river at this point. Instead it climbs for 40 minutes to avoid a landslide area before a long descent to the end of the valley where it joins the Chharka Tulsi Khola (4380m, 2hrs and 20 mins). Walk along the top of the long peninsula that divides the two rivers. Continue to the very end and then descend to your left to a suspension bridge (15 mins), which you cross to the true left (south) bank of the river. Do not descend to the right on an old trail that crosses to the true right (north) bank of the Chharka Tulsi Khola.

Note: the true right (north) bank crossing of the Chharka Tulsi Khola is the route to Ghemi La and on to Ghemi in Upper Mustang (4 days).

Climb an easy gradient for about 15 minutes before following an easy trail for one hour to a rigid metal bridge to the true right (north) bank of the Chharka Tulsi Khola. The large village of Chharka Bhot (4302m) is now only 20 minutes away. Many groups take a rest day here and explore the ancient village and Bon gompas. It is also a good place to restock food staples such as rice and flour.

Chharka Bhot to Pho via Dho Tarap, Phoksumdo and Shey

The main trail to Dho Tarap takes a southerly route around the craggy peaks that dominate the western end of the valley from Chharka Bhot. However, the route requires many river wades and would be difficult in, or soon after, rain. There is a northerly route that crosses two passes but you will need a local guide as trail finding is very difficult before the second pass, and you should avoid taking pack animals as the descent from the second pass is difficult.

● **Northern route** Take the main trail west out of Chharka Bhot to an old chorten, which marks a trail junction (40 mins), turn right and then climb a steady gradient for 2 hours to Mola La (5030m). On the far side is a large plateau and the Myantikti Khola which you should follow to the confluence with the Pandi Ladum Khola (2hrs) where many nomads camp.

Ascend this river valley to the Jhyarkoi Bhanjyang (5360m, 3hrs), where the trail descends on a steep cliff-face trail, which is usually not suitable for pack animals. Descend the Maran Khola to Maran (4350m, 2hrs), where you meet the southern route.

● **Southern route** Take the main trail west out of Chharka Bhot to an old chorten, which marks a trail junction (40 mins), turn left and descend an easy gradient to a small confluence with the Chuchen Khola (roughly 4300m, 20 mins). Descend the Chharka Tulsi Khola for 10 minutes on the true right (west) bank before wading to the true left (east) bank which you follow for 15 minutes before wading back to the true right bank.

In another 35 minutes cross again to the true left bank for 10 minutes before crossing back for the final time to the true right bank. Then climb for a short section before descending to a minor tributary from the west, which is crossed by stepping-stones. The trail then climbs for 45 minutes to a small lake, Chap Chu (4320m), where there is a campsite. Continue up the valley on a trail that frequently crosses back and forth over a small watercourse for 2¼ hours to a gully that leads to a basin and an easy gradient to Chan La (5378m, 45 mins). The trail descends switchbacks to a small valley before ascending about 100m to follow a ridge above the Sheru Khola, which is to your south (left), and the Tarpi Khola to your north (right). At a chorten (50 mins) on the ridge, head down into the Tarpi Khola valley on the true left hillside, cross back and forth over the river a few times to eventually end up on the true right (east) to reach Maran (4350m, 110 mins), where you meet the northern route.

From Maran it is an easy hour to Dho Tarap (3944m), which is a large trading village and a good re-stocking point.

Note: you can descend the Tarap Khola to Laisicap (2 days) and thence to Juphal (2 days), see *Upper Dolpo Circuit*, days 18-19, pp224-5.

Above the village of Dho Tarap is the nunnery of Ribum Gompa and Regu Chorten, which is well worth a visit. The Tarap valley makes for an enjoyable and easy walk as you slowly climb past small villages to Tokyu (4209m, 1hr), where there is a major trail junction. To the north (right) is the main trail to Saldang, see *Other Routes to Pho*, p231, whereas, this GHT route heads west (left) to Ringmo and Phoksumdo Lake.

Continue up the Tarap valley for another hour to a point where a valley enters from your south (left) and there is a monastery perched on the hillside to your north (right). Do not cross the small stream flowing out of the valley, instead climb into the valley's mouth to a campsite marked by a small, roofless dharamsala (4440m, 25 mins), which can be used as a kitchen. Follow a trail on the true right (south-east) bank of the river to a point where the valley bends and climbs sharply to the south (left). Instead of following the river, cross it and climb a small stream from the west (right).

The trail soon emerges onto grassy slopes and the gradient eases as it rounds into a basin dominated by snow-covered craggy peaks to the south (left). From the melt-water stream in the centre of the basin, ascend the north-western (right) side of a gully between two obvious peaks for about 300m to what the locals confusingly call Numala La/Numa La South (3¼hrs, GPS: 5309m, N 29° 10.542' E 083° 05.965'). There are three points to cross the Numala ridge, including this southern pass, the other two are: a pass to the north which is an alternative route to Saldang, and a central pass that is marked on many tourist maps as the southerly route but is very rarely used.

Descend steeply from the pass for roughly 800m of altitude to the Gyampo Khola, which you follow to a trail junction (1¾hrs), where you should take the left fork.

Note: the right fork is a long route to both the central and northern Numala passes.

The trail now climbs 200m as it rounds a craggy ridge and then descends to the picturesque campsite at Danigar (4512m, 1hr), which is dominated by

Norbung Kang (6085m) at the head of the valley. From the campsite, cross the Panklanga Khola and climb a switchback trail for 1¼ hours before the gradient eases to a long traversing ascent to Bagala La (5210m, 1hr).

On the far side of the pass is a steep rocky descent to a flat-bottomed valley (4686m, 1hr), which is the high camp for groups coming the other way. Another steep descent brings you to Temche (3995m, 50 mins), a large grassy kharka that trekking companies refer to as the Bagala La Base Camp. In another 40 minutes is the even larger Yak Kharka (3860m). As many animals are kept here it is frequently dirty. The trail now traverses a steep and craggy hillside for 70 minutes on the true right (north) bank of the Maduwa Khola before a couple of short climbs high above the confluence with the Phoksumdo Khola. The views down the valley from here are very pretty. The trail now swings north into pine forest, where you should look for views of a spectacular cascade on the far hillside, and in 40 minutes reach the village of Ringmo (3640m), where there are a few teahouses and campsites, see p220. One of the most beautiful places in Nepal, Phoksumdo Lake, is a few minutes beyond the village. There is a National Park office on the foreshore where you should register.

See *Upper Dolpo Circuit*, days 7-10, pp220-1, for route and additional information to Shey Gompa.

Shey Gompa to Pho

From Shey Gompa, take a trail that climbs up from the campsite for about 400m (70 mins) before swinging into a small valley. The trail descends slightly to the stream, which you cross, before climbing the far hillside for another 100m or so (35 mins) to a ridge (4860m) with views of the Tartan Khola and Tsankang Gompa opposite. Traverse the broad hillside before dropping into the Den Khola valley, where there is a kharka of the same name (4553m, 1hr).

The trail then heads back up to a minor ridge (1hr) before traversing past some monsoon kharkas to another ridge (4810m, 30 mins). A final undulating traverse brings you to the last minor pass of the day (4840m, 25 mins), which is decorated with prayer flags and chorten.

An easy descent leads to the large kharka of Tora (1hr) where there are three trails. The most northerly (right) trail climbs rapidly to the ridge above, the middle takes an easier gradient to a point further along the ridge and the more westerly (left) descends to the village of Tata and on to Shyamling (aka Samling). Do not take the path on your right. If you have the time, visit Shyamling Gompa (2hrs) and then take the round-about trail to Bhijer (1½hrs).

The direct route to Bhijer (3850m, 1¾hrs) is the middle trail that makes an easy ascent of the ridge before a sometimes steep descent to the village where there is a campsite. The lama at the gompa in Bhijer is also an *amchi* (a Tibetan medicine doctor) and he tells an intriguing tale of the first settlement of the village (see box opposite).

Wind through the village to a trail that climbs to some chorten to the north. Switchbacks ascend a ridge, where there is a cairn and some prayer flags (4605m, 2¼hrs). You now enter a basin beneath the rocky Yambur Peak. Traverse the rocky trail for 40 minutes to the base of the final steep climb to

❏ **Bhijer folktale**
Long ago, a lama came from Tibet on the Saldang trail and when he was on the pass
he saw a large Blue Sheep, which he followed to a big valley. The lama became
thirsty so he dug into the ground and a river came forth. Deeper in the valley, he saw
a giant rat which attacked him. In defence, he killed it with an arrow through the
heart. The arrow struck the ground and he left it there. Sometime later an apricot tree
grew where the arrow lay and when donations are made at the gompa the tree bears
fruit. The locals have never cut the tree, which stands in the gompa forecourt.

Yambur La (4813m, 30 mins). Descend a steep trail on the far side of the pass
to a large kharka, which makes a good lunch spot (4030m, 1¼hrs). The next
section of trail has had some extensive maintenance but is still steep and slippery in places. Descend into the Tora Khola canyon on a trail carved from cliff-
faces to a large wooden cantilever bridge (roughly 3400m, 70 mins). The crisp,
clear water here makes it an excellent site for a cool swim! The trail winds
around some craggy cliffs before ascending a steep gully via switchbacks to the
terraces of Pho (4087m, 2¾hrs), where there are a couple of campsites.
    If you haven't already employed a local guide you will definitely need to
get one here at Pho. The next section to Mugu is one of the toughest parts of the
GHT.

Other routes to Pho
● **Via Dho Tarap and Saldang** From Tokyu take the northern trail via Jyanta
La to the Saldang valley (3 days). From Saldang there are trails direct to Shey
and Bhijer (both 2 days).
● **Via Shimen and Saldang** From the large kharka after the Mola Bhanjyang
(from Chharka Bhot) head north along the Kehein Khola for 2 days to Tinje. It
is then a long day to Shimen. There is a cross-country trail to Saldang (2 days)
as well as a round-about route (3 days) via Nisalgaun. From Nisalgaun there is
a high route to Pho over two rarely used passes, which the locals believe to be
the homes of dangerous spirits.

PHO TO GAMGADHI

[See maps opposite inside back cover] There are two route options from Pho in
Dolpo to Gamgadhi, the district centre of Mugu; both are very challenging:
    The highest, most northern route can be trekked in either direction;
employ a guide either in Pho or Mugugaon. This route is described in detail on
pp232-4.
    There is another 'northern route', which is only accessible when trekking
from west to east as the only local guides who know it live in Dolphu (the last
village on the Mugu Karnali Nadi). If you want to try this route all your party
should have rock-climbing experience and equipment as there are three difficult
rock sections plus two wire-rope river crossings that require pulleys, etc. A summary of this route is provided on pp234-5.

ROUTE GUIDE

Pho to Gamgadhi – the higher Northern Route

From the top of the village climb to a painted chorten (10 mins) where the northern and southern trails diverge. Take the right fork and climb switchbacks across scrubby slopes to the first ridgeline at 4645m (1½hrs; Finaid: Phophagau, sheet: 2982 04, ref: 889 675), from where there are good views back down to Pho. The trail then climbs at an easy gradient though a basin to a major ridge, the Gyallo Raud Lekh, that descends from the large rocky peak above you to the south (left). The ridge has a large cairn and prayer flags at which you should turn north (right) and follow a gradually ascending ridgeline.

The trail rounds a rocky hill to then follow a sharp and craggy ridgeline, which steepens considerably to Nyingma Gyanzen La (5563m, 2hrs 50 mins; Finaid: Phophagau, sheet: 2982 04, ref: 857 714). This pass sits in the very centre of the Great Himalaya Range, with Kanjiroba Himal to your south and a line of slightly lower snowy peaks along the Tibet border to your north. It is like no other place in the Himalaya and makes you feel as if you are walking along the spine of the planet.

Descend a steep trail that continues to follow the craggy ridgeline down to a notch marked by a large triangular rock and prayer flags (5450m, 20 mins). Cross through the notch and continue to descend steep ground into the valley to the north-east of the pass. The trail winds down the centre of the valley, but stays in the central scrubby vegetation rather than on the left or right side. After about 900m of descent you will reach the end of the valley (100 mins) but do not continue to the river confluence. Instead, follow a track that winds beneath a cliff line to your north (left).

Note: if you are trekking this route in reverse, it is critical that you do not head further downstream than 4440m; Finaid: Phophagau, sheet: 2982 04, ref: 876 737. Beyond this point the river valley becomes extremely dangerous.

The trail then slowly descends to the Swaksa Khola (4440m), where there are a few tent platforms scraped out by nomads. However, there is a far better site on the eastern (right) side of the valley on the grassy Pung Kharka (4650m, 55 mins). In another hour, pass a river that flows down from the west (left) through a huge kharka area of grassy hillocks. There are some small caves on the east (right) bank opposite the river confluence; just beyond them cross to the west bank. Continue to follow the Swaksa Khola up a valley that becomes flatter as you reach another large kharka and potential campsite (4820m, 50 mins).

Note: Locals have established two Yala pass options, the safer one of which is not marked on the Finaid map. The not-so-safe Yala La is prone to rockfall and is slightly to the south of the route described below. Note also that the not-so-safe Yala La is the pass marked on the Finaid map, so try to follow the trail to the more northerly and safer Yala La.

The safer Yala La (5414m, 2¼hrs from the kharka; Finaid: Phophagau, sheet: 2982 04, ref: 866 817) is an obvious saddle to the north of the Yala La marked on the map and is reached by climbing a trail up steep grassy hillside which then traverses beneath a rock band to a small basin of red and orange rocks. Climb through the basin towards the rocky ridge above, where a series of large cairns and chorten can easily be seen from below. There is a steep descent on the far side to a shallow basin before another steep descent into the large grass-covered valley of the Chyandi Khola (4830m, 1¼hrs). Snowy mountains surround you; as there are no settlements for miles around, the sense of wilderness is palpable. There are many potential campsites in the valley for the next 40 minutes. The trail follows the northern bank of the river before moving right next to the water's edge. You may need a 20m hand line in places as the trail can be a bit tricky. Approaching some forest, the trail suddenly starts to climb and descend steeply to avoid a series of landslides.

A final slippery descent brings you to a confluence with a small river entering from the north (3995m, 2hrs 50 mins; Finaid: Mugu, sheet: 2982 07, ref: 778 828). All the river names on the Finaid maps differ from those used by guides, who also disagree with each other!

Cross the simple log bridge over the river and climb a steep switchback trail straight up a shallow gully to a ridgeline at 4365m (1¼hrs; Finaid: Mugu, sheet: 2982 07, ref: 775 832), which is marked by a chorten. The trail now traverses a broad hillside, with great views of the valleys to the south. A final rocky scramble brings you to a last ridge marked by four large cairns (4495m, 1hr), before a steep descent through silver birch forest to the Takla Khola (3785m, 2hrs), where a few small logs to act as a bridge. There is a good campsite on the far bank in a grove of silver birch (Finaid: Mugu, sheet: 2982 07, ref: 737 836).

Leave camp by following a trail up the forested river valley to your west (rather than the larger river to your north). After 40 minutes pass a tributary that flows down from the north (called Chhyugulden Khola on the Finaid map).

Continue on an easy gradient ascending ancient moraine and landslide debris for about an hour to a small lake, after which the trail slowly crosses a boulder-filled watercourse to the beginning of the pass-climb (4410m, 15 mins from the lake). Follow switchbacks that climb a grass- and wildflower-covered slope to a scree-filled basin. The trail climbs the left-hand side of the basin across rocky ground to the cairn-covered Chyargo La (5150m, 2½hrs).

A good trail descends from the top of the pass and at roughly 4600m (1¼hrs) there is a potential campsite. Follow the ancient moraine on the north (right) side of the valley down to an enormous flat-bottomed valley called Thajuchaur (4050m, 1¼hrs).

Note: if you are trekking this route in reverse look for a black rock with a large white cairn that marks the route up to the moraine.

The trail now descends into a V-shaped valley and frequently climbs away from and descends back to the Chham Khola. There are many trail junctions, at each one follow the largest or freshest route. After 30 minutes the trail crosses to the middle of the river and then back to the northern (right-hand) bank to avoid a landslide.

In another hour you reach a large flat, pine-forested area that makes an excellent campsite (roughly 3500m; Finaid: Mugu, sheet: 2982 07, ref: 599 818). From here, cliffs rise on both sides but a good trail leads down to the end of the valley. There used to be a both a cantilever and log bridge to the south bank of the Chham Khola but ignore them all. Instead, scramble over some boulders to the very end of the valley along the northern bank. Once you have reached the Mugu Khola (1hr), turn north (right) and follow an easy trail for 30 minutes to a bridge that crosses to the west bank of this much larger river. It is not necessary to go all the way to Mugu. Instead, turn south (left) and head downstream through the Shilenchaura Kharka (2945m, 20 mins), opposite the Chham Khola confluence and a good campsite. In fact, for the next 3 hours there is a series of riverside glades that would all make a good campsite. The river performs a massive S-bend and on the second curve a tributary joins from the north (right) and is crossed by a rigid metal bridge. After 3 hours from Shilenchaura the valley narrows and in 45 minutes you reach another major confluence, at Tiyar, with the Namlan Khola, which the locals also call the Karnali Nadi. Just before the confluence, cross a wooden bridge to the west bank of the Mugu Khola and climb a dusty trail to some large chortens. Just beyond the chorten is a gompa with a grassy forecourt that makes an excellent campsite (2418m). Padma Dundul Choling Gompa was used as an 'education' camp by the Maoists but is now being restored by the resident lama.

Retrace your steps past the chorten and cross back to the north bank of the Mugu Karnali Nadi. Once on the far bank, turn west (left) and climb an easy gradient to the main trail, which you follow for 3¼ hours to a large blue suspension bridge.

Note: there is a small shop just before the bridge, which sells rice and flour.

Cross the bridge and continue heading west (right) for 30 minutes to a major bend in the river where there might be a small water source near a large bank of river stones. In another hour is a campsite in a small copse beside the Mugu Karnali Nadi (Lhumsa) and there is a small shop in another hour. Continue on the south (left-hand) bank all the way to the end of the valley, marked by a small school with a large stele in the forecourt (2hrs). There are more of them behind the school and they either declare land rights, or mark the old border between Tibet and the Khas Kingdom. The trail swings south (left) and descends into a smaller valley. At a large trail junction, take the left, higher fork, then descend to and cross the Gam Gad river via a small wooden bridge (15 mins). It is a 40-minute climb up a hillside where a few pine trees offer some shade to the large bazaar of Gamgadhi (2095m). There is a teahouse as you enter the village but no campsite.

Dolphu to Pho – the slightly lower Northern Route

The trail that connects Dolphu with Pho mainly follows the Namlan Khola, also called the Mugu Karnali Nadi by locals. This route is difficult and requires rock-climbing skills and equipment as well as two local guides from Dolphu. Locals in Pho neither have the equipment nor trail knowledge to guide this route. From Dolphu expect the route to take 6-8 days, depending on the group size, as the climbs and wire-rope river crossings slow progress considerably.

Dolphu is a day from Padma Dundul Choling Gompa (see opposite), where there is a trail that follows the north bank of the Namlan Khola before coming to a large gully. Climb through the gully on a trail that scrambles up the far wall and then traverse through terraced fields to Dolphu. You can camp by the gompa and it will take at least a day to find, and then negotiate with, local guides.

From Dolphu the trail descends to the Namlan Khola to a wire-way. If you have made an early start you should cross the wire, but normally locals camp in a scrubby campsite before crossing. You need pulleys (the local guides should have some home-made pulleys) and about 60m of rope, plus harnesses. Once on the far side the trail climbs to a cliff line, which you need to climb. On top, cross a flat grassy area before descending a very steep rock section, requiring a handline; on the far side is a good campsite. This was the base camp location for the first snow leopard survey in 1981.

For the next couple of days negotiate three more rock sections of varying difficulty before arriving at a large grassy area as the river swings north. Climb the hillside to the west of the campsite past ancient juniper trees to a deep gully. Ascend the gully to a point where the cliff line on the far side (north or left) runs out and you should see some log ladders. Camp here, in the gully, as there are no more sites on this side of the pass. Ascend the ladders and the sloping rock-face above and continue up the ridgeline towards an obvious saddle on the ridge above. The approach to the pass is beneath the north (left) cliff line. From the top of the pass the gradient steepens, descending rapidly to a gully and then climb a short section, before again gradually descending back to the Namlan Khola. You have just cut through a huge curve in the river.

Once again, cross a wire-way to a campsite on the far bank. The trail is now hard to find as it ascends the loose scree slope to the east of the campsite. Climb to a minor rock band and then traverse eastwards (right). The trail climbs a little to a small flat area on a ridge above a confluence with a small river that flows down from the north (left). Follow the cliff line around to the north (left) to a large rock overhang just before a final descent to the river. This is the best place to camp before the next passes.

Cross the river and climb up through forest to a minor ridge where the trail turns south-east and ascend another ridge line (4790m; Finaid: Bhijer, sheet: 2982 12, ref: 852 616). Swinging due north the trail now climbs around another ridgeline before crossing a spectacular saddle to a kharka, but there is no water here for much of the year. From the kharka, climb switchbacks to another ridgeline to your north-east (right). Once on the ridge turn east (right) again to climb towards a minor peak (shown as point 5096m on Finaid: Bhijer, sheet: 2982 12, ref: 874 643) before traversing north-east (left). There are amazing views of northern Dolpo and the Kanjiroba Himal. There is a tricky section of loose fine scree beneath a black cliff line before a long steep descent to the village of Pho.

ROUTE GUIDE

The Far West

The Far West districts of Nepal have remained isolated and untouched while the rest of the country has been developing. Poor infrastructure, scarce resources, and marginalised ethnic groups are among many issues that have held the region back in years past. However, since 2008 a massive effort has been under-way to develop and promote this region, which is considered by many to be a future adventure-tourism 'hotspot'. If you are looking for an authentic trekking experience in pristine mountain scenery interlaced with legend and folklore, look no further, this region is for you!

Covering about 25% of Nepal's Great Himalaya Range, the Far West is massive compared to the other trekking regions, but despite its size there are few recognised trekking routes. Dividing the region in two is the Karnali Nadi, one of the great Himalayan rivers. To the east, are Kanjiroba Himal and the mountains of Dolpo, to the west are the Api and Saipal Himals and the border with India. The second largest district in Nepal, Humla, fills the entire northern boundary with Tibet, and the southern districts of Darchula, Bajura and Bajhang lead to the pahar. Villages are largely subsistence based, so don't rely on pur-chasing many foodstuffs; accommodation is frequently limited to finding a flat bit of pasture. The entire experience is similar to that of the first trekkers to Nepal in the 1950s, when the country first opened up. And that is part of the wonder and joy of visiting the region; the logistical effort in reaching these dis-tricts is far outweighed by the welcome you will receive and the feeling of won-der that every day brings.

Trekking is in its infancy throughout all these districts, trails can be rough and take an unrelenting approach to ascent and descent. There are two routes through Mugu from Pho in Dolpo and they are both very tough and wild trails. Rara Lake National Park, near Jumla, receives some trekkers, as does the Yari valley (near Simikot, popular with groups trekking to Mt Kailash) and Khaptad National Park. Mountaineering groups have explored both Api and Saipal Peaks, but trekkers here are extremely rare. No doubt, things will change.

The two smallest National Parks in Nepal, Rara and Khaptad, and the newly formed Api-Nampa Conservation Area are the only protected mountain areas in the Far West (other than Bardia National Parks, Sukla Phanta Wildlife Reserve and the Blackbuck Conservation Area on the terai). However, controlled area trekking permits are required to visit all districts. Maps are hard to find, espe-cially for the areas around the Api and Saipal Himals. This region will benefit enormously from tourism in the years to come; as one of the first to trek here, it is important that you lead by example. Please follow the Great Himalaya Trail Code (see p12) in every respect and help make a positive difference to a region that desperately needs all the help it can get.

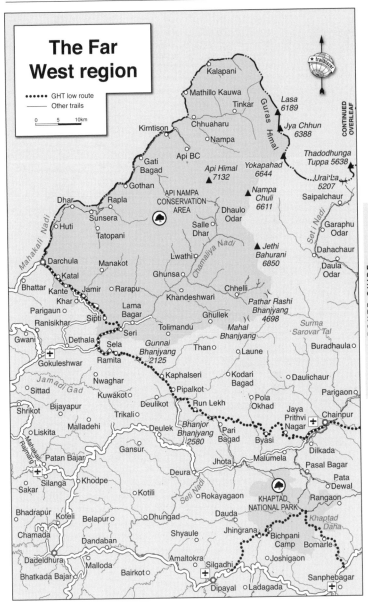

CONTINUED OVERLEAF

Changwathang 6130

Tholing
Dzang
Takchhe

Halji
Limi Khola

Talun (Limi) Khola

Hilsa (Yulsa)
Manepeme
Tiljung

Chhúmgo Daha

Numuche Tuppa 5250

Tarkesya Nadi

Nyalu La 5001

Humla Karnali Nadi

Sarpe La 5008
Nara La 4560
Yarig (Yari)

Khyúnggar Daha

Chhunaso Daha

Chima La 5092

Ustan
Nim

Tumkot

Salli Khola

Kui La

Mota Gompa

Taplun

Sechi La 4530

Urai La 5207
Thadodhunga Tuppa 5638

Muchu

Purya

Sangrak Kermi

Chyaduk

Saipalchaur

Saipal Himal

Sumjumkharka

Dharapori

Syada
Ralling Gompa

Garaphu Odar

Siyanban Khola
Syang Tal

Sakya La 4709

Simikot
Kharpunath

Dahachaur

Phirankoph Chuli 6730

Chhipra

Daula Odar
Dhuli

Saipal Chuli 7030

Tharagikharka

Lali

Sapdule Dobhan

Lampato

Balaudi
Kada
Kangarkot

Ghat Khola

Gumba

Bhedali

Kawadi Khola

Khada Lek

Buradhaula

Lokanda

Budhinanda Nijar

Chogariu Goth

Kakhe

Parigaon
Talkot

Masta Daha

Bichchhya

Thapagaon

Budheli

Thulagaon

Rokaya Bada
Paudali

Dhaulpura Daha

Chainpur

Bateli Bhanjyang 3236

Pokhara

Bugaidaya

Rugin

Dhaina

Boldhik
Hyanglu

Dilkada
Kaudakot

Dadagiri 3309

Kolti
Chhepi

Rolgaon

Sukhadhik
Khatye

Pasal Bagar
Kotgaon
Martadi
Dharamsala
Wai

Pata Dewal
Dogadi
Jadanga

Sintaba
Porakhe Bhanjyang 2702

Luma

Bhateda

Rangaon

Bramhatola

Mahati
Supana

Khaptad Daha
Dewalsain
Kailashmandau

Khin

Bomarle

Budhiganga Khola

Mumra
Phukot

Badki

Sanphebagar
Durbagaon
Rupsha
Bindadasini
Syuna
Sirkun

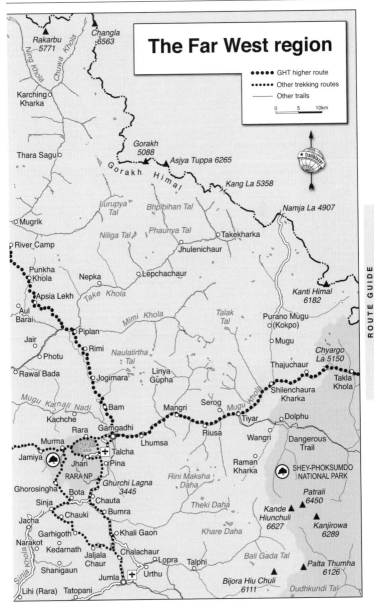

The Far West region

●●●●● GHT higher route
●●●●● Other trekking routes
—— Other trails

0   5   10km

ROUTE GUIDE

Rakarbu 5771
Changla 6563
Ning Khola
Chuwa Khola
Karching Kharka
Thara Sagu
Gorakh 5088
Asjya Tuppa 6265
Gorakh Himal
Kang La 5358
Namja La 4907
Lurupya Tal
Bhplbihan Tal
Niliga Tal
Phaunya Tal
Takekharka
Mugrik
River Camp
Jhulenichaur
Punkha Khola
Nepka
Lepchachaur
Apsia Lekh
Take Khola
Kanti Himal 6182
Aul Barai
Mimi Khola
Talak Tal
Purano Mugu (Kokpo)
Piplan
Jair
Rimi
Naulatirtha Tal
Mugu
Chyargo La 5150
Photu
Linya Gupha
Thajuchaur
Takla Khola
Rawal Bada
Jogimara
Mugu Karnali Nadi
Bam
Mangri
Serog
Mugu Khola
Shilenchaura Kharka
Kachche
Rara
Gamgadhi
Lhumsa
Riusa
Tiyar
Dolphu
Murma
Rara Lake
Talcha
Wangri
Dangerous Trail
Jamiya
Jhari
Pina
Raman Kharka
SHEY-PHOKSUMDO NATIONAL PARK
RARA NP
Ghurchi Lagna 3445
Rini Maksha Daha
Ghorosingha
Bota
Chauta
Patrali 6450
Sinja
Chauki
Bumra
Theki Daha
Kande Hiunchuli 6627
Kanjirowa 6289
Jacha
Garhigoth
Khali Gaon
Khare Daha
Narakot
Kedarnath
Jaljala Chaur
Chalachaur
Lopra
Talphi
Bali Gada Tal
Shanigaun
Jumla
Urthu
Palta Thumha 6126
Lihi (Rara)
Tatopani
Bijora Hiu Chuli 6111
Dudhkundi Tal
Sinja Khola

Trekking permits are a little complicated in the Far West of Nepal, as at March 2014, the trekking permit fees are:

● **Humla District (Simikot and Yari)**: For the first 7 days US$50 per person (pp) and after that US$7pp per day.

● **Areas of Limi and Muchu (as well as areas to Tibet via Tangekhola and Darma)**: For the first 7 days US$50pp and after that US$7pp per day.

● **Mugu District**: Areas of Mugu, Dolpu, Pulu and Bhangri, for the first 7 days US$90pp and after that US$15pp per day.

● **Bajhang District:** Areas of Kanda, Saipal, Dhuli, for the first 7 days US$90pp and after that US$15pp per day.

● **Darchula District**: Areas of Byas for the first 7 days US$90pp and after that US$15pp per day.

Plus National Park entry fees for Rara Lake and Khaptad of Rs3000pp – whereas Api Nampa Conservation Area is only Rs2000pp.

RARA LAKE CIRCUIT

[See map p239] This loop trek from Jumla can be done in either direction, but is slightly easier if you start via Sinja. Connecting trails to Simikot (north, 5 days), Mugu (north-east, 3 days), Dhorpatan and Lower Dolpo (south-east, 10-12 days) and Khaptad (west, 6 days) mean you can link to many other trekking routes, including to Mt Kailash, and Saipal and Api Himals.

A new dirt road runs from Jumla to Surkhet to the south if you want to explore the wild mid-hills of west Nepal. There are only a few basic teahouses along the Jumla–Bumra–Pina–Rara Lake route, so to complete this circular trek you will require camping equipment. For those who want to stay in teahouses, you must follow the same route to and from Rara and Jumla via Bumra.

ROUTE GUIDE

RARA LAKE CIRCUIT TREK

Rara Lake is an idyllic place; the astoundingly clear water surrounded by protected forest is a nature-lover's dream. Add some medieval history and Chhetri and Khas culture and you have a pearl of a trek in remote west Nepal.

GRADE 3

● **Duration & distance**: About 13 days total; days not more than 20km per day
● **Gradient**: Short steep sections
● **Quality of path**: Formed and rough track with some obstacles
● **Quality of markings**: Signs at beginning, end and major instersections
● **Experience required**: No experience required
● **Walking times**: Less than 6¼ hours per day

● **Steps**: Occasional steps on some days
● **Highest point**: 3804m
● **Best season**: Apr-May/Oct-Dec
● **Accommodation**: Camping and basic teahouses
● **Recommended maps**: NP110 GHT Series Far-West and NP109 GHT Series Dolpo & Mugu, Himalayan Map House, 2013

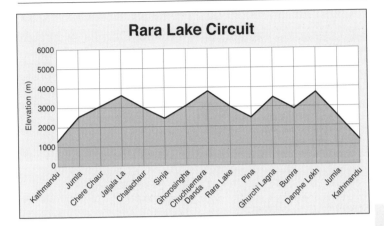

Nepal's largest lake is at its prettiest during spring when wild flowers cover the forest floor. The monsoon is very unpredictable with extremely heavy rains, causing serious flooding, mixed with weeklong periods of relatively light rain. From October through to January, cold temperatures accompany clear skies for great photography. Migratory birds are common at the lake throughout the year, and there are some spotting-towers near the Park headquarters.

When the Park was established in 1976, the only two villages within the Park were resettled to Bardia on the terai, a decision that is still controversial to this day. The nearby town of Gamgadhi is the only place where you could purchase supplies in any quantity, but even here food is scarce. Your group should therefore be completely self-sufficient, which probably means bringing supplies from Nepalgunj to either Jumla (daily flights) or Talcha (near Gamgadhi, weekly flights).

DAY 1: KATHMANDU–NEPALGUNJ
ALL DAY

As the flight from Nepalgunj (150m) to Jumla (2540m) leaves before any flights from Kathmandu arrive, you will have to overnight in Nepalgunj. There are some hotels in town and a few, more basic places to stay near the airport. Whichever option you choose it is advisable to book in advance, as they are frequently busy. There isn't much to see or do in Nepalgunj so most airlines recommend that you book a mid-afternoon flight.

DAY 2: NEPALGUNJ–JUMLA

As if to make up for the inconvenience of having to overnight in Nepalgunj, the flight to Jumla (2540m) is terrific. First you cross the Nepali terai, covered in dense jungle, before climbing over the pahar of west Nepal. Vast forests pass under the wings; this is one of the least densely populated areas of the Himalaya, aside from the very highest mountain regions. The approach to Jumla involves a diving 180° turn over a forested ridge to the airstrip; it's quite a thrill!

Once outside the airport, there are a couple of teahouse-style hotels, or you can head into the main bazaar where there is more accommodation. To get to the main bazaar, head west (turn right out of the gate) and follow a large, dusty trail to

Jumla, which is about 15 minutes away. The centre of town, called Khalanga Bazaar, is paved in large flagstones and is a busy trading post for the region. Beyond the many shops are two interesting Hindu temples, Chandan Nath, which commemorates the yogi who introduced rice farming to the valley some 900 years ago and is dedicated to Vishnu, and Bhairavnath, a newer temple dedicated to Shiva. These temples were built at the beginning of the Malla Empire, a Khas dynasty that dominated western Nepal, Tibet, Ladakh and Kashmir for centuries, see *Khas People*, below.

A strong wind blows through the valley in the afternoons, so if you arrive early enough it is a good idea to complete tomorrow's trek.

DAY 3: JUMLA–CHERE CHAUR
4½HRS

Head due north from Khalanga Bazaar, following a large trail into a shallow valley and towards Karnali Technical College.

The trail is lined by buildings for the first hour and remains on the true right (west) side of the valley. When you reach a section of trail with fields on either side you will come to a bridge to the true left (east) bank. Cross the bridge, turn left and continue towards a large tank of water before the technical college (30 mins). The trail winds around the college and then begins to climb an easy gradient on a trail with little shade for 3 hours to Chere Chaur (3055m). This is a large, grassy plateau and makes an excellent campsite with views back down the valley to Jumla.

DAY 4: CHERE CHAUR–
CHALACHAUR   5HRS

At the northern end of the plateau the trail forks; you need to turn left and enter a pine forest.

Note: the right fork enters a short section of forest before climbing an exposed hillside to Danphe Lekh pass (3685m), which you will cross on the return to Jumla.

❏ Khas people

Khas people are found in the remote valleys of the western hills of Nepal, mainly in Mugu District. Known as Khasas, they have traditionally been illiterate, backward people who originally followed Tibetan Buddhism, until Indian Brahmans, fleeing the Islamic invasion of India (9th-14th centuries), arrived here and converted them to Hinduism. Since then they have had very limited access to education or opportunities. Most modern Khas people will not refer to themselves as Khas (they consider it to be humiliating), instead calling themselves Chhetri, or Thakuris, after the caste that converted them.

The Khasas were a warlike tribe who built three capitals over time: Taklakot in Tibet, and Sinja and Dullu in Nepal. From the 11th century, their powerful kingdom, known as the Malla Empire (not related to the Malla kingdoms of Kathmandu Valley), grew, covering much of west Nepal, Ladakh, Kashmir and western Tibet. As the Empire fell apart from the 14th century, many of the ruling families migrated throughout Nepal, so today many common Nepali surnames (Thapa, Basnet, Bista and Bhandari), as well as the national language, have their roots in the ancient and once proud Khas kingdom.

Most of the men can speak Nepali; however, women, who generally do not leave the village, can only speak the Khas language. Their houses are built of stone and mud with flat roofs of mud or thatch depending on their altitude. They are dark and poorly ventilated and not usually kept very clean. Ground floors are usually for livestock and a notched wooden ladder provides access to the first floor and wooden veranda. Most marriages are arranged when the child is still young. The Khas continue to worship their shamanic mountain deities, and rarely adhere to traditional Hindu rituals.

Having turned left, the trail climbs steadily as it contours around the top of a small river basin to a couple of buildings at Chor Khola (3170m, 45 mins). From here, the trail climbs steeply through forest to the upper pastures of the Dori Lekh and Jaljala La (3585m, 2½hrs). An easy descent on the north side of the pass soon brings you to a broad grassy pasture, Jaljala Chaur (3420m, 30 mins). To reach the few buildings on the far side of the pasture continue along the northern treeline to a trail that crosses a small bridge over a stream. If you take any of the earlier, direct routes, you will have to wade a number of small streams and cross boggy ground. Camp on a patch of cleared ground in front of the buildings should you want to stay here.

From the buildings the trail descends rapidly through forest into the Jaljala Khola valley, where there is a good campsite at Chalachaur (2980m, 1¼hrs).

DAY 5: CHALACHAUR–SINJA
4½HRS

You are now in a fine deciduous forest with the sparkling Jaljala Khola leading the way. Cross the river several times, over bridges with traditional carvings on the handrail supports. After 45 minutes a large tributary valley merges from the right and the first small plots of farmland appear. The trail now remains on the true left (south) side of the valley, and climbs a small spur before continuing to descend an easy gradient. As the valley broadens the terraces of small-holdings appear and you pass through the scattered settlement of Garhigoth (2740m, 2hrs). The next settlement, Chauki (2500m, 1hr), is a larger Thakuri village with its distinctive red- and white-painted homes. Walking through the village you are able to see the end of the valley ahead, and a rocky promontory with commanding views. The trail winds around the southern base of the promontory and then drops to a bridge across the outflow of the Jaljala Khola to a peninsula with the Sinja Khola on the far side. Camp on the peninsula next to the health post (2405m, 45 mins), the main part of the village is on the far side of the valley and can be reached by another bridge.

DAY 6: SINJA
ALL DAY

The promontory that you passed the previous day is a very important site in medieval Nepali history. The western hills of Nepal were once the centre of the largest kingdom ever seen in the Himalaya, prior to the unification of Nepal: the first Malla Empire, and the winter capital was here, at Sinja. The only remains are some ruins of the royal palace and the ancient Hindu Kankasundri Temple on top of the promontory, called Lamathada. Two large stone lions at the entry of the temple are certainly from the right period, but identifying other artefacts within the temple is impossible. Throughout the region are many stone pillars, or stele, that declare land ownership changes, or places of historical interest, but they nearly all date from the 17th century onwards. From the top of Lamathada you look down into a deep ravine to the west, and some caves on the far bank, where the 5th Dalai Lama is said to have meditated. The old border with Tibet is not far away, in the Mugu Karnali Nadi valley, and local legends tell of a time when Sinja was the most important place in the Himalaya ranges. To the south-east, about 5 hours' walk away is a large cave, where locals believe the five Pandava brothers (from the Hindu epic, the *Mahabharata*) were exiled. An annual horse race, in July, is held from Lamathada to the cave and back.

The local people call themselves Thakuri, a noble Chhetri caste, which means you will probably not be invited into homes.

DAY 7: SINJA–GHOROSINGHA
4HRS

From the campsite, cross the suspension bridge to Sinja village but turn right (not left to the village) and follow a dirt trail that climbs a little as it heads through the gorge behind Lamathada. From the gorge it is easy to see why Lamathada was such an obvious choice for a fort palace, any attacker from here would have no chance of success. Continue on the north bank of the Sinja Khola along a trail that continues to climb, do not take any smaller routes that descend to the riverside. After 1½ hours you should reach the outlying homes of Bhota at the entrance of the Ghatta Khola valley (2600m). Unless you want to detour to the main part of the village stay on the true right (west) bank of the river. A detour to the village, which is on the true left (east) bank of the river, will add 45-60 minutes to your day. At the trail junction to Bhota take the left hand, smaller track and begin ascending the Ghatta Khola.

The valley soon narrows and climbs steeply up an exposed trail that passes many grinding wheels. At the top of the ancient moraine wall (3050m, 2½hrs) you are greeted with a meandering stream flowing through a broad grassy valley, and perhaps one of the most inviting campsites you will ever come across, Ghorosingha.

DAY 8: GHOROSINGHA–RARA LAKE   6¼HRS

The trail now winds through beech and pine forest as it continues to ascend the valley. After 40 minutes you will pass some derelict buildings. Climbing further the valley forms a grassy basin and then the river turns sharply to the north-west (right) into a much narrower gorge. Continue along the true right (north) side of the boulder-filled valley to the bottom of a steep switchback trail that climbs to a saddle on the Chuchuemara Danda (3804m, 2¼hrs). Traverse the northern slope to your right on a small but defined trail to a ridge (3756m, 30 mins) overlooking Rara Lake, which makes an ideal lunch spot if the weather is clear. The trail now descends, slowly at first, but more steeply once you enter rhododendron forest for 1½ hours to the main track along the Khatyar Khola (2965m). Cross a wooden bridge to the true right bank of the river, where you turn right to Murma and then ascend an easy gradient to the western end of Rara Lake (3010m, 30 mins). The main campsite (45 mins) is beside the National Park office on the northern shore of the lake, you will have to register here as well.

DAY 9: RARA LAKE   ALL DAY

Rara Lake is an idyllic place; the astoundingly clear water surrounded by protected forest is a nature-lover's dream. A walk around the rim of the lake (13km, 5½hrs) is really worth the effort – see if you can spot the stele marking the cardinal points, nobody knows how or why they are here.

On the north-eastern bank is Rara Mahadev Temple, decorated with woodcarvings of elephant, peacock and people. On the full moon in July/August locals gather here to honour the god Thakur, who, legend says, created the lake by firing an arrow at the western shore and then built the eastern bank by stamping down the earth. Swirling rock formations at the eastern end of the lake are said to be his footprints. There are some old canoes near the army camp that you might be able to use. The lake water is extremely clear for swimming, but cold, and Park rules stipulate that you must use buoyancy aids.

DAY 10: RARA LAKE–PINA   4¾HRS

Take the lakeside trail back to the western end of the lake and the bridge over the outflowing Khatyar Khola. Cross the bridge and continue around the lake to a trail junction in the south-western corner, the left-hand trail continues around the lake, but this time take the southern (right) fork and climb an easy gradient through forest. Crest the grass-covered ridge (3060m) to the south of the lake in 2½ hours from camp. Descend through a fine cedar forest to Jhari (2550m, 1¼hrs) and to a trail junction.

There is a newer trail that avoids Pina and takes an almost direct route south to Ghurchi Lagna, which is reached in 6 hours. You need local knowledge to follow this route, which is committing as the first campsite is in the valley on the far side of the pass. Alternatively, the older route descends to Pina where there is a good campsite; to take this route descend to the small river in the valley, which you should cross to the true right bank. Keep descending for another 20 minutes before a slight climb to a grinding mill, beyond which are the cultivated fields of Pina (2440m, 30 mins). Do not descend through the village, instead contour through the upper parts of the village to a campsite next to a teahouse (10 mins).

Note: if you want to take an extra day to reduce daily trekking hours, it is possible to break the return trek to: Rara Lake to Jhari (day 10), then to Chauta (day 11), then Padmara (day 12), Jumla (day 13) and fly to Kathmandu on day 14.

DAY 11: PINA–BUMRA   7¼HRS

To the south of Pina a valley climbs up towards Ghurchi Lagna (3445m) to the south. The trail follows a stream through forest and some rocky spurs; it takes 3½ hours to reach the pass. From the top of the pass there are good views of Kanjiroba Himal. Descend to a small valley which joins another from your left, take the larger, downstream (south-westerly) route that continues to descend. The valley then curves westward and another tributary joins from your left, again continue downstream (south-west) and descend. Once you reach about 3100m the valley turns to the south and enters forest; pass the National Park office and enter Chauta (2745m, 1¾hrs from the pass). Descend through the village to a trail junction turn south (left) and contour about 150m above the Sinja Khola. It is now 2 hours to Bumra (2850m) where you can camp, but if you have the time, continue for another 20 minutes or so to some better campsites beside the river.

DAY 12: BUMRA–JUMLA   7HRS

If you camped in Bumra, descend to the Sinja Khola and follow the true left (south) bank along a broad trail to a bridge (2720m, 1hr), which you cross. The trail now climbs an unrelenting gradient through birch forest for 3½ hours to some pastures where there is a trail junction (3520m). The left-hand fork, which continues across the meadows, leads to Padmara (3060m, 2½hrs) and will add an extra day to the return to Jumla. A smaller trail branches right towards a tree line; you might have to scout around for this if the meadow is overgrown. Climb through the forest, which soon ends, and emerge onto another grassy pasture that leads up towards the Danphe Lekh pass (3685m, 30 mins). From the top you can see the broad meadow of Chere Chaur, where you camped the first night out of Jumla, descend to it (40 mins) and continue on the same trail back to Jumla (1½hrs).

DAY 13: JUMLA–NEPALGUNJ–KATHMANDU

Reconfirm your flights as soon as you arrive in Jumla. Depending on schedules you should be able to fly to Nepalgunj in the morning and then catch one of many afternoon flights to Kathmandu the same day.

ROUTE GUIDE

KHAPTAD NATIONAL PARK

[See map p237] Lying on the junction of four districts Bajhang, Doti, Achham and Bajura, in the Far West of Nepal, is the small and thoroughly picturesque Khaptad National Park. The Park covers a large plateau thrust up from amid the pahar, just to the south of the Great Himalaya Range. Trails criss-cross the region to the remote district of Darchula (12 days), the Saipal and Api Himals (8 days), Rara Lake (6 days) and dozens of sites throughout the mid-hills.

Since it was established in 1984, the Park has received roughly 350 registered visitors, an amazing contrast to the thousands of pilgrims who come on the full moon each August (during the monsoon) for a *mela* and to honour a famous yogi. However, the monsoon rains are unpredictable, with sudden heavy downpours closing roads and infrastructure for weeks at a time. Winter snow closes the Park from late December to the end of February before the spring sun brings life back to *patans* (grassy meadows) and forests. The post-monsoon period has clear skies for landscape photography, whereas spring is famous for perhaps the best wildflower and medicinal plant display in Nepal.

From Kathmandu you can drive or fly to Nepalgunj and from there drive to the road-head town of Silgadhi and the main trail to the Park headquarters. Alternatively, you could charter a flight to Chainpur (Bajura District), Dipayal (Doti District), Kolti (Bajura District) or Sanphebagar (Accham District) and take one of the many minor trails to the Park.

This itinerary starts at Silgadhi and ends at Sanphebagar, although the most popular route is to return to Silgadhi on the same trail.

DAY 1: KATHMANDU–NEPALGUNJ/ BARDIA   ALL DAY

Whether flying or driving to Khaptad National Park you will probably overnight in Nepalgunj. If you drive the entire way from Kathmandu you could combine your trip with a few days at the beautiful nature

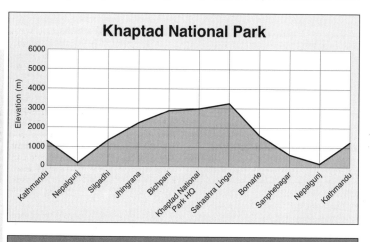

Khaptad National Park

KHAPTAD NATIONAL PARK TREK

This is an idyllic Nepal trekking experience interlaced with intriguing history, sacred pilgrimage sites, pristine forests filled with wildlife and an unbeatable 300km panorama of the Himalaya!

GRADE 3

- **Duration & distance**: About 9 days total; days not more than 20km per day
- **Gradient**: Short steep sections
- **Quality of path**: Formed and rough track with some obstacles
- **Quality of markings**: Signs at beginning, end and major intersections
- **Experience required**: No experience required
- **Walking times**: Less than 7¼ hours per day
- **Steps**: Occasional steps on some days
- **Highest point**: 3276m
- **Best season**: Mar-May/Oct-Dec
- **Accommodation**: Camping
- **Recommended map**: NP110 GHT Series Far-West, Himalayan Map House, 2013

reserves at Bardia or Suklephanta National Park to break the journey.

DAY 2: NEPALGUNJ–SILGADHI
ALL DAY

A 9- to -10-hour drive from Nepalgunj (7-8hrs from Bardia) along a relatively low traffic volume road brings you to Silgadhi (1340m), which is a sprawling town perched on a south-facing ridge. Saileshori Temple, in the centre of the town, is surrounded by a large stone-paved square and is one of Nepal's most important pilgrimage sites. The temple is dedicated to the combined manifestation of Shiva and Parvati, who, it is believed, honeymooned in the picturesque forests and grassy patans at the centre of the Park, as mentioned in the Hindu epic, the *Mahabharata*.

The local market cannot be relied on for a comprehensive range of provisions so stock up in Kathmandu, Nepalgunj, or along the Mahendra Rajmarg (Mahendra Highway though literally Mahendra Kingsway).

DAY 3: SILGADHI–JHINGRANA
6HRS

Climb through the village to the main ridge above the town, then turn north (right) and follow a large dirt trail, which climbs steadily. You can see an aerial mast next to an army camp (1570m, 1hr) not far ahead, where you register before continuing.

The trail climbs an easy gradient past some small farms before steepening on an exposed dirt trail to a viewpoint at 1860m (80 mins). The trail is now predominantly through rhododendron and beech forest as it continues to climb to a small teashop beside an apple orchard (2100m, 1hr), where you can camp. However, it is better to continue along a flat ridgetop trail heading due north before contouring around the head of a small valley to an intersecting ridge, cresting at 2500m in 1½ hours.

Pass a small Shiva temple and follow the ridge past a pond, which used to provide water to the temple. This area would make a good campsite if there was a reliable water supply as it has excellent views both east and west. The trail climbs slightly as it traverses beneath another ridgeline before

descending slightly to a saddle and the National Park entry at Jhingrana (2250m, 1hr). There is a good campsite here, beyond the Park entry post and the army camp.

DAY 4: JHINGRANA–BICHPANI
4½HRS

Just past the army camp, at the edge of the forest, is a trail junction. A sign proclaims that the left-hand trail is only for humans, whereas livestock can be taken up the right trail. If you are a strong walker and enjoy steep, muddy climbs take the left trail, everyone else should go right.

The 'only for humans' (left) track takes a direct route to a shallow valley (2760m, 3½hrs), where it climbs again for 120m to join the main trail that has wound around the eastern side of the same hill (4½hrs). You are now at Bichpani (2905m) where there is a teashop and campsite.

DAY 5: BICHPANI–NATIONAL PARK
HEADQUARTERS (HQ)   4¼HRS

From the campsite the trail climbs about 100m before heading east along an undulating ridgeline that forms the southern edge of the Khaptad plateau. Pass a small deserted building in 1½ hours near to a small stream and a popular place for herders to rest their flocks.

The first patan you come to is Suketa (3070m, 1¼hrs), where a dharamsala was built in memory of some soldiers who died of exposure in a sudden storm. From the end of the valley are views of Api Himal to the north. The dharamsala also marks a trail junction; to reach the National Park HQ, head right and climb a little into forest. Do not take the smaller trail that descends at the end of the valley. After a short climb through some beautiful woodland descend to a large patan and follow the main trail which swings right and descends to a small temple; from here Tribeni (3010m, 1hr) can be seen ahead.

Tribeni marks the confluence of three rivers and is the site of a Shiva temple. Some old statues and stele line the walls inside the temple, which is the focal point of the *dashara mela* held during Jestha Purnima (August full moon). The empty buildings near Tribeni are shelters for the pilgrims who attend the mela. From Tribeni, continue north-east along a main trail that follows a stream. In 5-10 minutes pass a large boulder where offerings have been made. The valley curves to the east and the National Park office and army camp can be seen ahead; camp in a saddle between the two (3020m, 20 mins).

DAY 6: NATIONAL PARK HQ
ALL DAY
Geologists believe that a massive geographic distortion has elevated the sandy plateau that forms much of Khaptad National Park. The excellent drainage and fertile earth here mean that 400 of the 700 medicinal plants found in Nepal can be seen in a single day's walk across the rolling hills of grassland fringed by rhododendron and birch forests. If you have some time, explore the patans that form a giant diamond shape and are home to wild cat, fox, bear and musk deer.

From the centre of the park there are several interesting things to do: a visit to the famous Khaptad Baba's Ashram (also referred to as Khaptad Swami locally, 1½hrs' return trip) should be high on your list. Khaptad Daha (lake) offers some sublime reflections and is another pilgrimage site, as locals believe that Shiva bathed here. The lake lies beside the trail to Kolti (Bajura District, 3 days). Sahashra Linga (3276m) is the highest point in the park and a favourite pilgrimage spot (5hrs' return walk). The views from a grassy hillock near to the National Park office are also excellent. In clear weather you can see from the Kumaon Himal in India to the west, the Saipal and Api Himals to the north, the

ranges of Dolpa to the north-east, and finally, shimmering on the eastern horizon, the massive bulk of Dhaulagiri and the Annapurnas. That's a 300km panorama of the Himalaya that anyone can appreciate!

DAY 7: NATIONAL PARK HQ–
BOMARLE   7½HRS
The other trails in and out of Khaptad are not as well defined as the one from Silgadhi. The route described here takes 2 days to Sanphebagar, where there is a dirt airstrip, and is perhaps the toughest of the alternative routes.

Note: you may need a local guide from the trail junction to the ridge.

From the National Park HQ head towards the viewpoint, but before you get to the end of the patan take the small left-hand fork that leads to Sahashra Linga. Follow this trail for an hour to a trail junction; turn left (right goes to the Linga) and traverse through scrubby woodland to a ridge that emanates from the Linga viewpoint (3030m, 45 mins).

Descend a sometimes-steep trail to a series of kharkas, each of which has many small trails. However, do not deviate more than a few metres from the ridgeline for the next hour. You then reach a junction where a small trail continues along the ridge and a larger track descends south-west through woodland (2815m, 1hr). Take the larger track, which descends steeply through oak and rhododendron forest to about 2600m at the top of a small watercourse (1hr). Descend the watercourse but before reaching the valley floor swing left onto the hillside and traverse a recent landslide. Once past the landslide the trail gradient eases and you traverse to a small, dirty village

---

❏ **Khaptad Baba**
The yogi, Sachidanda Saraswati Khaptad Baba, spent 50 years meditating and administering herbal remedies from his cave hermitage using the incredible range of local medicinal plants. Legend says that the Baba was once a doctor in India, but his life before he started living in a cave, deep in the forest, is largely a mystery. During the 1950s, locals built a simple shelter before the buildings were expanded to the current size by order of King Birendra, who became a follower of the Baba, who died in 1996. A statue of the yogi sits on the south-facing porch, where visitors can leave donations.

(2010m, 2½hrs), where you can camp in the school at the bottom of the village.

If you have the time, it is better to continue to the upper reaches of Bomarle village (1605m) in 1¼ hours. Camp in the school grounds at the top of the village.

DAYS 8-9: BOMARLE–SANPHEBAGAR–SILGADHI/NEPALGUNJ–KATHMANDU
5¼HRS' TREKKING/ALL DAY DRIVE
Descend directly through Bomarle to the river, crossed by a small wooden log bridge (1220m, 45 mins).

Note: if the river is high you have to cross by a suspension bridge a little upstream from the village.

Climb to a main trail on the far bank (1400m, 1hr) through dense jungle. The gradient now eases as you follow a trail that links a series of villages, each with a pretty Shiva shrine, until you round the valley end and head west into the Budhiganga valley (1200m, 2½hrs). There are trails from each subsequent village that descend to the dirt road in the valley bottom (1hr), where you can get a lift on a tractor trailer to Sanphebagar (620m, 1½hrs by tractor).

At the centre of Sanphebagar is a bus park with regular services to Silgadhi (2½hrs) and Nepalgunj (10hrs). There is a dirt airstrip outside Sanphebagar that will accept charter flights. Flights operate throughout the day from Nepalgunj to Kathmandu, but instead of heading straight back to Kathmandu, take a day or two and enjoy animal-spotting in Bardia National Park, where there is an excellent chance of seeing tiger, rhino, elephant and many other animals.

KARNALI CORRIDOR TREK: RARA LAKE TO SIMIKOT

[See map pp238-9] The Karnali Nadi is one of the mightiest rivers in the Himalaya and bisects the entire range linking the forested pahar with the Tibetan plateau. This trek follows the Karnali Corridor between the Kanjiroba range that forms the western border of Dolpo and Mugu and the Saipal Himal to the east. A new road is being built beside the river, but this trek takes higher trails that provide great views and a unique insight to some of Nepal's remotest and least-developed regions.

Rara is Nepal's largest lake and is at its prettiest during spring when wild flowers cover the forest floor. The monsoon is very unpredictable with extremely heavy rains, causing serious flooding, mixed with week-long periods of relatively light rain. From October to January cold temperatures accompany clear skies for great photography; for more information see *Rara Lake Circuit*, pp240-5.

This trek can be walked in either direction, although your choice of campsite will vary. If you start in Simikot there are lots of supplies in the bazaar but they are expensive. Alternatively, beginning in Rara means doing some shopping in the nearby town of Gamgadhi where the range of supplies is limited. Your group should therefore be self-sufficient, which probably means bringing supplies from Nepalgunj to either Simikot (daily flights) or Talcha (near Gamgadhi, daily flights).

To complete this trek you will need a Rara Lake National Park entry permit (Rs3000), a Mugu District controlled area permit (US$90pp per week) and a Simikot/Humla controlled area permit (US$90pp per week).

It is possible to connect this route with other treks in the region. Add 4 days to start from Jumla, see *Rara Lake Circuit*, p242, or you can connect with the *Limi Valley Trek via Hilsa (Yulsa)*, see pp253-9, and you could connect with *Darchula to Rara Lake*, see pp259-67.

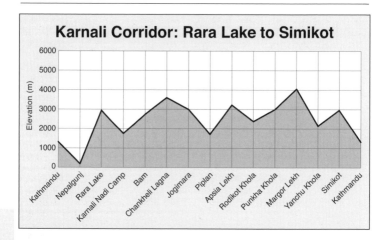

Karnali Corridor: Rara Lake to Simikot

KARNALI CORRIDOR TREK: RARA LAKE TO SIMIKOT

A wonderful insight to the beauty and cultures of Far West Nepal. From Rara Lake you pass through forests, over passes, enjoy great mountain views and end at Simikot, a gateway to Tibet.

GRADE 4

- **Duration & distance**: About 12 days total; days not more than 20km per day
- **Gradient**: Very steep sections with some arduous days
- **Quality of path**: Formed and rough track with some obstacles
- **Quality of markings**: Limited signage
- **Experience required**: Experienced walkers require navigation skills

- **Walking times**: Less than 6¾ hours per day
- **Steps**: Occasional steps on some days
- **Highest point**: 4037m
- **Best season**: Apr-May/Oct-Dec
- **Accommodation**: Camping
- **Recommended map**: NP110 GHT Series Far-West, Himalayan Map House, 2013

DAY 1: KATHMANDU–NEPALGUNJ
ALL DAY

As the flight from Nepalgunj (150m) to Talcha leaves before any flights from Kathmandu arrive, you will have to overnight in Nepalgunj.

There are some hotels in town and a few, more basic places to stay near the airport. Whichever option you choose it is advisable to book in advance, as they are frequently busy. There isn't much to see or

do in Nepalgunj so most airlines recommend that you book a mid-afternoon flight.

DAY 2: NEPALGUNJ–TALCHA–
RARA LAKE   3¼HRS

The flight to Talcha airport (2740m) is magnificent and thrilling! First you fly over the Nepali terai, covered in dense jungle, before climbing over the pahar of west Nepal. Vast forests pass under the wings;

this is one of the least densely populated areas of the Himalaya, aside from the very highest mountain regions. You then follow the Karnali Nadi and the final approach to Talcha involves a diving 180° turn in the valley to the airstrip; it's quite a thrill!

You climb up and through the rapidly growing village of Talcha straight into the National Park. Take your time as the sudden altitude gain can cause mild altitude symptoms. Once in forest the gradient eases and 2 hours after landing you reach the edge of Rara Lake (2980m).

You then walk around the lakeshore (where there are plenty of views of the surrounding hills) for 1¼ hours to the National Park office, where there is a campsite, teahouse and registration post.

DAY 3: RARA LAKE   ALL DAY

Rara Lake is an idyllic place; the astoundingly clear water surrounded by protected forest is a nature-lover's dream. It is a good idea to have an acclimatisation day here as there will be some steep climbs during the trek and getting used to the altitude now will be useful in the days ahead.

A walk around the rim of the lake (13km, 5½hrs) is really worth the effort – see if you can spot the stele marking the cardinal points; nobody knows how or why they are here. On the north-eastern bank is Rara Mahadev Temple, decorated with woodcarvings of elephant, peacock and people. On the full moon in July/August locals gather here to honour the god Thakur, who, legend says, created the lake by firing an arrow at the western shore and then built the eastern bank by stamping down the earth. The swirling rock formations at the eastern end of the lake are said to be his footprints.

There are some old canoes near the army camp that you might be able to use. The lake water is extremely clear for swimming, but cold; Park rules stipulate that you must use buoyancy aids.

DAY 4: RARA LAKE–KARNALI NADI CAMP   2½HRS

Walk to the eastern end of the lake and take the left fork, signposted Gamgadhi (2095m,

1½hrs) and descend to the sprawling district centre of Mugu. The trail is easy to follow the entire way, the last section is on a road that links to Talcha.

The main bazaar, which runs along the ridge, is a good place to buy simple supplies. There are a few very basic teahouses in the town and after looking around it's a good idea to head down to the campsite.

Take the trail from the top of the bazaar at the western end of the town – you will have passed it on your way into Gamgadhi. Descend at a constant gradient for an hour to the Karnali Nadi, where there is a campsite (1740m) before the suspension bridge. Note that the constant passing traffic could pose a security issue for your group so don't leave things lying around.

DAY 5: KARNALI NADI CAMP–BAM   5HRS

Cross the suspension bridge and ascend a steep rocky trail, turning left at 1920m and again at 2046m to crest a ridge at 2180m (1½hrs). Descend to a small river and then climb to Luma (2073m, 30 mins).

The trail climbs steadily from here through fields and then pine forest to another ridge (2600m, 2hrs). Take your time to look at the stele about 20 minutes from the top of the ridge, they are similar to those at Rara Lake.

It's then an easy traverse to Bam (2700m, 40 mins) before a slight climb to the school where you can camp. There is also a simple *dhaba* (eating place) here.

DAY 6: BAM–JOGIMARA   6½HRS

A contouring trail leads to a stream near Ghachaur (2650m, 1hr) where the climb to today's pass begins.

First ascend steep switchbacks before entering forest; it will take about 3½ hours to reach Chankheli Lagna (3594m), where there are some good views of the Kanjiroba range to the south-east and endless hills to the north. It is then a very pleasant 10-minute descent to a great campsite beside the Rauli Khola (3005m) and another 15 minutes to the teashop at Jogimara, where you can sleep in their loft.

DAY 7: JOGIMARA–PIPLAN 6HRS

It is an easy ascent for about 100m to round a hill-spur at 3120m before descending about 500m to the Milchham Khola (110 mins). Then another small climb that involves crossing a landslide, which is still close to another ridge (2717m, 30 mins) with views of the lower valley and Rimi village, where there is a teashop (2552m, 1hr). If you are trekking this route in reverse, you might want to camp here to break this day into two stages and then continue to Jogimara tomorrow.

It is a long traverse to Deuri (70 mins), where you pass a large school before a slight descent to Darma (30 mins). Head through the village to the helipad on the far side and then descend steep switchbacks to the main riverside trail, which winds around to a suspension bridge over Humla Karnali.

Cross the bridge and then it's a short climb to Piplan (1700m, 1hr) where you can camp in the school.

DAY 8: PIPLAN–APSIA LEKH 6¾HRS

Pass through the village to the helipad where a trail turns right and begins to climb slightly before steepening to switchbacks to Nimagaon (1980m, 1½hrs).

Continue up through the village for another 1½ hours to crest a ridge and where the rail starts to traverse through a shallow basin to another ridge (2724m, 20 mins) beneath Korka village. You do not need to enter Korka. An easy descent for 30 minutes brings you to a stream, which would make a good lunch spot.

The trail then climbs again but not as steeply to Puma (2805m, 70 mins) where you could camp in the small school grounds. Just beyond the school the trail forks, turn right and climb switchbacks through pine forest for 1¾ hours to Apsia Lekh (3195m), a broad grassy ridge makes a great campsite. There are great views of Saipal Himal towering over the depths of the Karnali Nadi valley. There is a good water source about 100m downhill on the eastern side of the ridge.

DAY 9: APSIA LEKH–PUNKHA KHOLA 4¼HRS

After yesterday's strenuous walk, today is much easier so take your time and enjoy the morning views! The day begins with a lovely contouring trail and great views of Saipal Himal and the surrounding valleys to Kallas (45 mins) where there is a teashop. Then descend to Nunyapani Khola and ascend an easy trail to a ridge before another easy descent past Phuche to Rodikot Khola (2386m, 2hrs). The trail then climbs an easy gradient for the next 1½ hours to a campsite beside Punkha Khola (3010m) and the base of tomorrow's climb.

DAY 10: PUNKHA–YANCHU KHOLA 6¼HRS

Ascend steep switchbacks through forest for roughly 500m before the gradient eases a little. There is a kharka at 3512m, which could be used as a campsite but water is another 30 minutes beyond. Steep switchbacks lead to the Margor Lekh Bhangjyang (4037m, 3½hrs) with great views north to the Simikot valley, Saipal Himal and endless ranges to the south. The trail descends slightly as it traverses steep hillside to the Bhigauda Dada (30 mins) before becoming very steep and switchbacking down to the Yanchu Khola (2100m, 2hrs).

There are several campsite options in this valley, your choice will depend on the time taken to cross the pass and the number of herders and livestock at each place. There is a kharka about 10 minutes before the Yanchu Khola, or a site in a forest on the far bank or, if dry, one of the grassy sections beside the river a little further downstream (10 mins).

DAY 11: RIVER CAMP–SIMIKOT 6½HRS

Descend the true right bank of the river for about 15 minutes before a gradual climb to Durpa village where the trail then contours past the school.

Beyond the village wind around open hillside and then begin the long, dusty descent to the pilgrimage site of Kharpunath (2100m, 3hrs) where there are a few teashops. This is not a very secure campsite and if you need to stay here you will have to be very careful of your possessions. A better option is to walk up the true left bank of the Humla Karnali for 30 minutes to another collection of teashops before turning right into the Kudila Khola valley, where there are more camping options.

If you have the energy, continue to the comfortable hotels and teahouses of Simikot. From the Kudila Khola, head upstream, crossing small tributaries for 45 minutes or so to a few teashops and a rigid metal bridge, which you cross and then start the long switchback trail to Simikot (2985m, 2hrs 20 mins). You enter the large bazaar town from the south and most of the teahouses and hotels are near the airport entry on the far side of the village, but the opportunity for a shower and a comfy bed are great motivators!

DAY 12: SIMIKOT–NEPALGUNJ–KATHMANDU
There are daily flights from Simikot to Nepalgunj and you should try to book seats on the first flight so that you can connect easily to Kathmandu the same day.

LIMI VALLEY TREK VIA HILSA (YULSA)

[See map p238] Much of this trek follows ancient trade routes that connect Tibet, Nepal and India. A constant flow of mule, dzo and goat trains ply the route and a new road-building programme throughout the region is aimed at increasing prosperity in one of Nepal's poorest districts. Much of this trek follows the road as the old trails take the only feasible route through what would otherwise be impassable terrain. But following the road doesn't reduce the surrounding beauty, nor the fascinating local history and cultures, the highlight of which is Halji's magnificent gompa.

Most trekkers visit Humla during the monsoon period as part of a visit to the holy Mt Kailash but good weather continues from April to the end of November. Away from the warm summer months (June-Sep) you are unlikely to see many (if any) trekkers on the trail. Logistics can be problematic in the summer months when local porters ask for high rates of pay assuming they will

---

LIMI VALLEY TREK VIA HILSA (YULSA)

Fascinating local history and cultures, dramatic trans-Himalayan scenery, an ancient monastery at Halji all combine to make this a great Himalayan trek.

GRADE 3

- **Duration & distance**: About 17 days total; days not more than 20km per day
- **Gradient**: Short steep sections
- **Quality of path**: Formed and rough track with some obstacles
- **Quality of markings**: Signposted at beginning, end and major intersections
- **Experience required**: Some walking experience required

- **Walking times**: Less than 6 hours per day
- **Steps**: Occasional steps on some days
- **Highest point**: 5001m
- **Best season**: Apr-May/Sep-Nov
- **Accommodation**: Camping
- **Recommended map**: NP110 GHT Series Far-West, Himalayan Map House, 2013

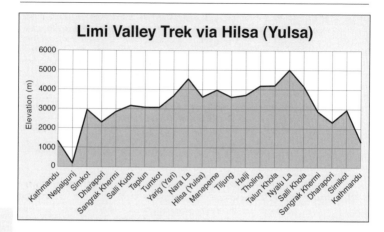

only be employed to Hilsa (Yulsa), as most Mt Kailash treks then exit via Lhasa back to Kathmandu. Purchasing rations can be expensive in Simikot (daily flights in the morning) so you might want to take more valuable items with you from Nepalgunj. However, you will have to balance the cost of excess baggage with the potential saving of buying local produce.

There are no protected areas in Humla, but you do need a controlled area permit to trek anywhere in the district (US$90pp per week). This trek can be combined with *Rara Lake to Simikot*, see pp249-53.

DAY 1: KATHMANDU–NEPALGUNJ
ALL DAY

As the flight from Nepalgunj (150m) to Simikot (2985m) leaves before any flights from Kathmandu arrive, you will have to overnight in Nepalgunj. There are some hotels in town and a few, more basic places to stay near the airport. Whichever option you choose it is advisable to book in advance, as they are frequently busy.

There isn't much to see or do in Nepalgunj so most airlines recommend that you book a mid-afternoon flight.

DAY 2: NEPALJUNG–SIMIKOT
ALL DAY

The flight to Simikot (2985m) offers some great views of the Kanjiroba and Saipal Himals as you follow the Karnali valley north. The airstrip in Simikot has a new surface so the landing is not as bumpy as it used to be. Many groups decide to spend a

night in Simikot both to aid acclimatisation and to organise supplies and/or crew. There are many teahouses in and around the town and an extensive bazaar area that attracts locals from all over the region.

DAY 3: SIMIKOT–DHARAPORI
4½HRS

A substantial trail winds westwards uphill and away from the village centre. It's an easy climb for about 300m (3270m, 1hr from the airstrip) to the top where there are a couple of teashops. Then steep switchbacks down through pine forest and then more open hillside as you pass a few homes and another teashop (1hr).

From here continue down but do not go all the way to Dharaphaya, which you can see below. From above the village the main trail heads up the Humla Karnali valley on the true left bank and continues to descend towards the river. In an hour pass through Manjgaon, where there is a teashop and where the trail levels out somewhat about 150m above the Karnali. A final short descent to the campsites at Dharapori (2360m) is in another 1½ hours. There is a small campsite beside the trail as you pass a grove of walnut trees, and two larger, grassy sites after you cross a small bridge over the Hepka Khola. The main village is less than 10 minutes further along the trail.

DAY 4: DHARAPORI–SANGRAK KERMI   4¾HRS
Follow the main trail passing Dharapori village and in about 40 minutes come to a few large rocks at a trail junction, take the left fork where the route descends a little into a gorge section of valley. The Humla Karnali valley turns left into a steep-sided gorge where there is a series of waterfalls called Chaya Chahara (2hrs), which is a popular lunch spot. From here climb some switch-

backs to Dhar Kermi (aka Dhad Kermi, 1hr) and then an easier gradient all the way to Sangrak Kermi (2860m). There are some good trailside campsites beneath the village of Sangrak Kermi which is about 1 hour above the main trail.

In the narrow valley beside the village is a hot spring (30 mins from campsites) that fills a knee-deep concrete pool. There is a short-cut trail which is best used on your return to camp as it is a little confusing in dense scrub at a few points. The main route to the hot springs goes through the village.

DAY 5: SANGRAK KERMI–TAPLUN (YALWANG)   4½HRS
Begin with a long easy ascent on a trail with little shade for an hour to Okharthala, then patchy pine forest for another hour to Salli Kudh (3143m), a minor pass with prayer flags and views back down the valley. The pass is atop a peninsula around

❏ Humla Bhotia
The lower valley areas throughout Humla are inhabited by a mix of Khas, Newar and Chhetri people. The higher regions, however, are home to people who are an amalgum of traders, horse and yak breeders and farmers who have arrived in successive waves of migrations from central and western Tibet over the last 1200-1400 years. The largest communities are Baragaon and the villages of the Limi valley who all refer to themselves as Bhotia (people from Tibet). These two regions intermarry and they believe they share a similar ancestry. Polyandry is practised, though becoming less common, and weddings are formal agreements that may be made when the children are very young or at birth. The ceremony generally takes 2-3 days and is attended by everyone in the village.

Trade is a vital income with many men going to India during the winter months to purchase metal items, wood to make high quality and sought-after bowls and, it is alleged, animal parts especially rare species. Salt and general goods are bought from Tibet during the summer using mule, dzo and large herds of goats as pack animals.

Losar, the New Year festival, is celebrated for 15 days but the community is separated into groups – men for the first 3 days, women over 40 for the next 3 days, younger women for the 3 days after that, then school children for the next 3 days, and the final 3 days is for monks and gompa attendants.

Saga Dawa, a festival to celebrate Buddha's Enlightenment, is a large feast at which all of the 36 gompa lamas plus a guest lama must be present. If anyone is missing the host (each year a household) must pay a large fine to the village and gompa.

Rimche, the main village festival includes lama dancing and is celebrated on the February-March full moon for 3 days (one is for preparation and cleansing). The festival celebrates the victory of Buddhism over minor faiths and features a victorious Padmasambhava mask dance.

which massive cliffs rise from the turquoise Humla Karnali. Descend for 30 minutes (en route pass a flat area with an unreliable water supply) to the Salli Khola, which you cross on a long suspension bridge to a flat area that makes a good lunch spot. Follow the road/trail to a large flat area beside the river – a popular halt for mule trains – in another hour. Then it is a gradual climb to Taplun (Yalwang, 3060m, 1hr), a scattered community on a large south-facing hillside. On the far side of the village is a gompa and school where you can camp in the grounds.

DAY 6: TAPLUN–TUMKOT   5HRS

The trail winds around a rocky ridge before descending to Yalbang village (30 mins), a pretty Buddhist settlement at the entrance to another gorge section of the Humla Karnali. Sheer rock walls rise from the rushing turquoise river that is said to pre-date the Himalaya. Occasional glimpses of snow-capped mountains dwarf the minor ups and downs as the trail undulates to avoid rocky bluffs.

In 1¾ hours from Yalbang reach a small copse near the end of the gorge section. In another 30 minutes cross a wooden bridge to the true right (south) bank then it's a gradual climb to Muchu village (30 mins) where the valley is considerably wider. Cross a small watercourse to Chhuigan village and then descend gradually to Tumkot Khola and a good campsite (3073m, 45 mins). On the pointy hill above is a Sakya gompa, ask locals if the key holder is around before going.

DAY 7: TUMKOT–YARIG (YARI)
                                     4¼HRS

From the end of the campsite, the trail enters a small gorge and climbs switch-backs for about 400m (3467m, 1½hrs) to a minor pass marked by a cairn and prayer flags called Pathalna by locals. Here the gradient eases and continues to follow the under-construction road to Palbang (3472m, 1hr) where there are a couple of shabby teashops. Then a gradual ascent to the Yari valley where the trail flattens to a cluster of homes (3663m, 1¾hrs) where there are normally fallow fields to camp on.

Note the old village is in the valley below (10 mins) but campsites are very limited.

NOTE: The route via Nim (aka Nyam) to Kit (via Sarpe La) is now closed as it was a smuggling route. The trail is closed 1km before Kit and any pack animals must be accompanied by a Nepali with a passport as they have to take a trail on the Chinese side of the border – the trail on the Nepal side is only for humans and not accessible for pack animals. Chinese patrol the entire border region and are discouraging locals from yarsagungha hunting and grazing.

NOTE: There is a potential high route from Ustan/Nim to Saipal Khola, which locals say is open from May to September. For more information, contact Changchok Lama (from Ustan) who takes yaks to Saipal to trade. He says there are 3 route options over Saipal Dada depending on snow conditions. The first pass (main ridge) is very steep on the Saipal side, cut across the headwaters of the Thado Khola, then easy ascent and descent direct to Saipal Khola. It is important to note that crossing to Tinkar from Saipal not allowed by Chinese who patrol the area as it has a disputed border with India.

DAY 8: YARIG (YARI)–HILSA (YULSA)   6HRS

The trail descends a little past the main Yari village area (10 mins) before beginning the climb up an easy gradient to Jogi Odar (4052m, 1½hrs) where there is a series of tent platforms carved beside the new road route and a couple of teashops.

The gradient steepens a little before entering a shallow valley called Shiv Shiv (aka Sip Sip) and has a couple of disused kharka and a potential campsite full of broken bottles. The last section is a steep ascent to Nara La (4560m, 2hrs) with views of Saipal and Muztagh Ata ranges. Descend crossing the road a few times before following it on a long gradual descent across barren hillside. Come to a point where the main trail descends rapidly down scree or you can continue on the longer road route.

If you take the scree shortcut, you will arrive in Hilsa (Yulsa) (3647m) in 2½ hours from the pass; the road route takes another 45 minutes. There are no good campsites in Hilsa (Yulsa), but there are two local tea-houses and another new one is being built. The sealed road to Taklakot and the Chinese border post are on the far side of the river, so don't be surprised if you see the occasional Chinese tourists in town!

DAY 9: HILSA (YULSA)–MANEPEME 4½HRS

Cross the squeaky suspension bridge, but avoid the border area and climb the scree slope on the far bank for about 320m (1½hrs) to the main trail from Taklakot to Halji. Locals in Hilsa (Yulsa) ask for dona-tions from tourists, saying they want to spend the money to improve the almost non-existent trail up the scree slope.

Once on the main trail turn right (east) and continue to climb more gradually for an hour to a high point marked by prayer flags. From here the trail undulates between 3950m and 4080m for 2½ hours to a short descent on switchbacks soon followed by the campsite at Manepeme (3950m) so called because of a large boulder engraved with the Buddhist prayer, *Om Mani Padmi Hum*.

DAY 10: MANEPEME–TILJUNG (TIL KHOLA) 5½HRS

Take your time along the easy trail and see if you can spot Himalayan Griffon and Lammergeyer cruising on thermals first thing in the morning. It will take about an hour to reach the beginning of today's climb at a point where the cliffs rise 2000m from the distant rumbling of the Karnali below. You don't have to climb to the top of them as the trail traverses across rocky

bluffs and it makes for some great views throughout the day. After 1½ hours you come to a slight basin (4050m) where the main donkey trail climbs switchbacks and another 'human' trail traverses right, around cliffs. It is actually not very exposed but those with vertigo should avoid this route. In 30 minutes round a rocky bluff high above the confluence of the Limi Khola and Karnali, and find the remains of a hermitage. There are the remains of a few buildings, some chorten and frescoes nes-tled against an immense cliff-face, called Chay Gompa. This is a great lunch spot.

After a short traverse away from the hermitage, climb switchbacks to a minor pass, Jhonbo La (4230m, 30 mins). In another 20 minutes you join the main trail, which becomes an undulating route to the Til valley. The main ridge into the valley is marked by some chorten, mani stones, yak skulls and horns with *Om Mani Padme Hum* carved on them.

Descend easy switchbacks to some ter-races and more chorten where you then turn right and descend to the Til Khola to where it joins the main Limi Khola. There is a large dusty campsite called Tiljung (3577m, 100 mins) at the confluence.

DAY 11: TILJUNG–HALJI 2HRS

Cross the upstream bridge, which you can see a little upstream from the campsite, to the true left (south) bank of the Limi Khola and follow an easy trail. Reach another campsite (3627m, 40 mins) surrounded by a wall at the base of vertical canyon walls. The easy trail continues for another hour to a bridge back to the true right (north) bank of the Limi Khola and the outskirts of Halji village (3741m, 20 mins from bridge). The campsite is on the far side of terraced fields away from the village, near the health post.

❏ Til's Yeti
Long ago a woman went to light candles in Til gompa. On the way she was chased by a yeti and only just made it to the gompa. As the yeti was almost upon her she acci-dentally spilt yak butter on herself and as she tried to rub it off the yeti started mim-icking her. As the yeti smeared butter on its face the woman quickly lit a match and set light to the yeti's hair, which sent it screaming to the hills never to be seen again.

❏ Rincheling Gompa

Rincheling Gompa is the centre of Halji village and belongs to the Drepung Kagyupa sect that is linked to gompas throughout Ladakh. The first building contains a large prayer wheel and statues of Avolkishwara, Sakyatua, Chenrisig and Guru Rinpoche.

On the ground floor of the west room is a 4m-high wooden statue of the 4-cardinal-point Buddhas surrounded by 12 more Buddhas. All are wooden and said to be 1050 years old. Locals believe they were created at the time when the Ladakhi-based Lama Lotsarinchen Sanu Polanamo, the 'Great Translator', consecrated this and 107 other gompas that he built in his lifetime.

The shrine room above contains many masks for the Rimche Festival and two statues of Chesuda (one seated on a horse and one standing).

DAY 12: HALJI–THOLING   6HRS

The trail out of the eastern side of the village winds up a rocky valley with occasional grazing areas for 2 hours, before you reach Sunkarni, where a new police post is being built.

The craggy canyon continues for another 2 hours to Dzang (aka Jang, 3990m) where there is a large gompa and pretty houses. Immediately after the village the trail climbs and in 30 minutes you reach new road construction and a large alpine valley where there is a small hot springs at 4063m.

Continue along the impressive flat-bottomed valley for 1½ hours to a couple of buildings called Tholing (4152m), which is a convenient and comfortable campsite.

DAY 13: THOLING–TALUN (LIMI) KHOLA   5½HRS

The valley broadens before Takchhe where there is another hot spring bubbling beside the river; however, it is not possible to bathe here. There are many deserted buildings in this section of the valley, which was the first settlement in the region.

The surrounding hills and large moraine deposits make this feel like a dead end, but to your south what may look like patches of snow on moraine is in fact a massive sand dune over which you must climb to a large shallow lake (1½hrs). If the lake waters have receded, head straight for a trail that climbs above the eastern shoreline. Otherwise it is quite a long walk around boggy ground to meet the trail. The trail doesn't climb much above the shoreline and

❏ Ghost riders

Long ago Lama Palme (maybe this is the local name of Lotsarinchen Sanu Polanamo?) arrived in the Limi valley at Takchhe. At the time the residents were fighting each other (there is a long history of feuding in the Limi valley) and the community at Takchhe was the largest and most violent. The locals killed all the Lama's pack animals and in fear of his life he retreated to a meditation cave. He chanted and threw his prayer beads into the air. As they hit the ground all the locals who had committed crimes died.

The Lama led the remaining faithful down to Halji where they were haunted by ghost riders each night. As the ghosts would not leave the residents alone the Lama chanted in a sunny place above the village (some chorten mark the spot below a cliff line) and impeached Chesuda to protect them and the ghost riders went away.

To this day it is believed that every family must pray to Chesuda each day otherwise the ghost riders will return. Even villagers who now live in Kathmandu or overseas still pay their respects to Chesuda.

ROUTE GUIDE

eventually descends at the far end of the lake to some scattered kharka (4173m, 1½hrs). Ahead, the Talun Khola valley rises in a series of moraine steps created by intersecting glaciers, which have long gone. Each is an easy climb to a flat section of valley and in 2 hours you reach some rocks painted with 'Limi Campsite' but, if you have the energy and time available, continue for another 30 minutes to a slightly higher camp at 4380m.

DAY 14: TALUN (LIMI) KHOLA–SALLI KHOLA   4HRS

Get an early start for the short walk to the bottom of a long series of switchbacks that climbs to a cairn (4834m, 1¾hrs) where there are great views of the Talun valley and Lubuchela Himal. Here the gradient eases as you wind through some lumpy moraine to the base of the final climb to Nyalu La (5001m, 45 mins). Descend past the Selima Dada, a pretty turquoise lake, to a small moraine lip at its southern end (4565m, 45 mins). A steep and rocky descent into a large flat-bottomed valley and potential campsite (4100m) takes 45 minutes. If you want to catch good views of the Saipal Himal, it's best to camp here rather than continuing down the valley.

DAY 15: SALLI KHOLA–SANGRAK KERMI   5½HRS

Follow a section of road that heads down the true left (east) side of the valley floor before descending through pine forest to

another potential campsite beside the Salli Khola (3811m, 1hr). It is now a delightful descent through silver birch and pine forest with views of the Saipal Himal to your south. After 1½ hours, pass another potential campsite (3387m) beside the trail. From here there are occasional steeper sections as the valley gradually narrows.

At 3109m (45 mins) cross a wooden bridge to the true right (west) bank and descend a little further before climbing to the Salli Khad pass (3144m, 35 mins), which you crossed on day 5 of this trek and where you rejoin the main trail to Simikot. It is an easy 1½-hour descent to the campsites at Sangrak Kermi (2860m).

DAY 16: SANGRAK KERMI–SIMIKOT   6½HRS

You may choose to break today into two short sections but if you have the energy it is not too far to get to Simikot by the afternoon. Follow the main trail as you descend past the waterfalls at Chaya Chahara (1¾hrs) and then on to Dharapori (1hr).

From here it's all up to the minor pass above Simikot (3hrs) before the final 30-minute downhill to the teahouses and airstrip.

DAY 17: SIMIKOT–NEPALGUNJ–KATHMANDU   ALL DAY

There are daily flights from Simikot to Nepalgunj and you should try to book seats on the first flight so that you can connect easily to Kathmandu the same day.

FAR WEST DISCOVERY: DARCHULA TO RARA LAKE

[See map pp237-9] The Far West districts of Nepal that border or include mountain areas, Darchula, Bajura and Baghang, are a trekking heaven. Locals are unbelievably friendly and welcoming, the trails are generally good with plenty of views and places of interest. It is hard to understand how this region hasn't seen more trekkers, but for many years logistics and permit restrictions prevented normal trekking. Now the region is open it feels as if you are trekking back in time, although the rapid pace of development will see many changes in the years ahead.

Lying to the south of Api-Nampa Conservation Area, this region has countless trails rarely, or never, trekked by tourists. The trek described here can be completed by any trekker and is a great introduction to the Far West. If you want more challenges there are plenty to keep you busy, with high routes between Darchula, Chainpur and Kolti.

ROUTE GUIDE

The best time to trek is between mid-April and June and from September to the end of October. Supplies are available in all the main bazaar towns and dhabas are commonplace along routes that have been used by travelling locals for centuries. This area is easy on the legs and pocket as well as being a lot of fun!

If you want to visit Api-Nampa Conservation Area you will need an entry permit (Rs3000) and a similar permit for Rara Lake National Park. However, you do have to buy a controlled area permit to trek anywhere in Darchula, Baghang, Bajura and Mugu (if you exit via Jumla) districts (US$90 each district per week). This trek can be combined with *Rara Lake to Simikot*, see pp249-53 and you can walk out from Rara Lake to Jumla, more information is in *Rara Lake Circuit*, see pp240-5.

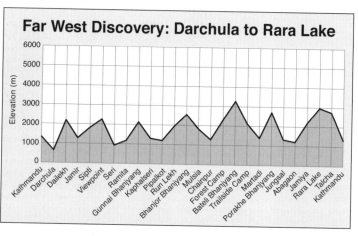

Far West Discovery: Darchula to Rara Lake

Elevation (m) / Kathmandu, Darchula, Dailekh, Jamir, Sipti, Viewpoint, Seri, Ramita, Gunnai Bhanjyang, Kaphalseri, Pipalkot, Run Lekh, Bhanjior Bhanjiyang, Mulsia, Chanpur, Forest Camp, Bateli Bhaniyang, Trailside Camp, Martadi, Porakhe Bhanjyang, Jungsal, Abagaon, Jamiya, Rara Lake, Talcha, Kathmandu

FAR WEST DISCOVERY TREK: DARCHULA TO RARA LAKE

An amazing adventure that includes wild road trips, unbelievable hospitality, gorgeous landscapes and the sublime beauty of Rara Lake – this is a cultural trekking experience second to none in the Himalaya!

GRADE 4

- **Duration & distance**: About 20 days total; days not more than 20km per day
- **Gradient**: Short steep sections
- **Quality of path**: Formed and rough track with some obstacles
- **Quality of markings**: Limited signage
- **Experience required**: Some walking experience required

- **Walking times**: Less than 8 hours per day
- **Steps**: Occasional steps on some days
- **Highest point**: 3236m
- **Best season**: Mar-Jun/Sep-Dec
- **Accommodation**: Camping
- **Recommended map**: NP110 GHT Series Far-West, Himalayan Map House, 2013

DAY 1: KATHMANDU–DHANGADHI
ALL DAY

There isn't much to do in Dhangadhi beyond exploring the bazaar area, so it's a good idea to take the afternoon flight (70 mins). Tucked in a remote south-western corner of Nepal there aren't many hotel options either, but Hotel Shree Jagadamba (📧 jagadambadgd@wlink.com.np, ☎ +977 (0)91-523590, 520390, 526090) is pleasant and the manager (Bishnu Raj Bhatt) can organise a four-wheel drive to Darchula.

DAY 2: DHANGADHI–DARCHULA
ALL DAY

It is a long drive to Darchula (expect it to take 14-16 hours), so a 4-5am start is advisable. The first section to Dadeldhura takes about 3½ hours and Hotel Sunrise is a good place to stop for breakfast.

Not far beyond the town centre is the Darchula/Baitadi and Chainpur road junction where there are great views of Api and Saipal Himals. Sealed road continues for another 3 hours to Gokuleshwar (where there is a charter-flight-only airport), then you are on a very slow dirt road to Darchula (680m, 9hrs with many delays). You cannot drive into the centre of Darchula as the 'road' is more like an alleyway. A couple of simple hotels are near the centre of town; both offer Nepali food.

The suspension bridge across the Mahakali is not an international border crossing for tourists, although locals can cross with ease. It makes sense to shop for provisions on both sides of the river as prices vary dramatically and the quality of fuel in India is much better.

DAY 3: DARCHULA–DAILEKH 5HRS

From the centre of Darchula, walk north through the town, passing the main market area. At a fork take the right-hand trail that climbs very slightly (the left goes down towards the river) and follow as it enters a tributary valley from the right. The trail is now a jeep track, which goes as far as Sela (the road is expected to be finished to Sipti in 2014) and involves a short climb to Kante (1332m, 1½hrs), where there are some dhabas. In another 30 minutes on an easy gradient, you reach Sela, where there are more dhabas and the current road-head. A good trail leaves the road construction heading up the true left (south) bank of the river. You pass through some friendly villages as you gradually climb to Maiakohli (1825m, 1½hrs). A further 1½ hours brings you to the top of the valley, a minor pass called Dailekh (2166m). There are some dhabas and basic 'hotels' on the pass and it is possible to camp on some unused terraces on the far (east) side.

DAY 4: DAILEKH–SIPTI 4½HRS

The descent from the pass on the true left (north) hillside is on an easy gradient at first, passing through a couple of hamlets that have the same name as the large village, Khar, which is on the other side of the valley. When you reach an old hydro-feeder pipe take the steep shortcut downhill to the riverside. Follow the true left bank and cross a suspension bridge (1400m, 100 mins) to a couple of teashops, and then some larger dhabas at Jamir (10 mins, 1380m).

Beyond Jamir the trail becomes almost as large as a dirt road; no doubt cars will arrive from Gokuleshwar and Darchula in the next year or two. Continue descending beside the river on the true right bank and cross two bridges, the second (1292m, 30 mins) marks the low point before the climb to Sipti.

Ascend steep switchbacks to 1511m (40 mins) where the gradient then eases. The trail gradually climbs across rocky hillside and has many small ups and downs. There is a short final climb of about 100m to Sipti (1842m, 1¼hrs) where there is a basic hotel with accommodation; ask the hotel owner if he can make his excellent smoked fish curry!

DAY 5: SIPTI–SERI 3¾HRS

To make the day more interesting it's a good idea to wake early and climb to the viewpoint above Sipti, where you can see a building on top of a hill to the east of the village.

Walk through the village to the police post and shortly after take a left-hand fork

ROUTE GUIDE

that climbs past some houses and then through forest. After 40 minutes the trail forks again, take the left trail, which heads north towards a saddle.

In 15 minutes reach the saddle and then follow small tracks up the ridge to your right. Sometimes you have to push through scrubby bushes but it only takes 20 minutes or so to reach the telephone repeater tower on top of the hill (2232m, 1¼hrs from Sipti). From here, there are good views of Api and Nampa Himals, although not a full panorama.

Leave the summit on an obvious track that leads down the southern ridge to another saddle and the main trail to Seri. It's a long descent and there are many shortcuts, some of which are very steep, so choose your trail carefully! On your descent take a little time to identify a suspension bridge below, and perhaps stop for a cup of tea at the hamlet of Ninta (1730m, 45 mins).

Once at the bottom of the climb turn downstream (right, on the true right bank) to a hamlet where you then have to wind between paddies to the suspension bridge. Cross the bridge and turn upstream (on the true left bank) and walk along the newly built road to Seri (939m, 1¾hrs from Ninta) where there are several dhabas. Ask locals for a place to camp as there are some fields near to the river.

DAY 6: SERI–RAMITA   5HRS
Follow the dirt road as it descends slightly to Nala Bugara (971m, 1¾hrs) where there are a few teashops and a good view of Api Himal. In another 45 minutes you pass the new hydro-electric power project and remain on the true left (east) bank of the river. In another 45 minutes you reach the current road-head of Gunna (868m) where buses frequently depart to most major west Nepal towns, including Dhangadhi.

❏ **Optional side trip from Seri**
Following is a 2- to 3-day side trip from Seri to Khandeshwari and back; note that from Lama Bagar to Khandeshwari is a long and tiring day.

Alternatively, from Khandeshwari, you could attempt a high route that heads north-west back to the Mahakali river, or head east over a high route towards Chainpur. Both of the high routes are only open May-October.

1-2 days: To Markarkot Temple, before Khandeshwari Bazaar   6hrs
Remain on the road to Lattenatia (1054m, 1¼hrs), and then register at the police checkpost at Lama Bagar in another 20 minutes. About 5 minutes beyond the checkpost is a stone-walled campsite (1066m) on your right.

Continue following the new road to Dharamgaon (1hr) where it ends at the base of a rock-face. As the valley narrows there are plenty of ups and downs, some up to 200m, which can be tiring. There is very little drinking water beside the trail, so the dhaba at Chauki Bagar (1210m, 1¾hrs) is a welcome sight. The trail is easier from here but still up and down to Makari Gad (1479m, 1½hrs). From the collection of dhabas you look straight up a steep rock and grass-covered face to a ridge where two pine trees stand against the skyline, 1000m above – they mark Makarkot Temple! The switchbacks are mostly on an easy gradient but there are steeper runs closer to the top.

Once you crest the ridge there is a small teashop and a little higher above the teashop is a small campsite (2222m, 2hrs). Further up this ridge are excellent views of Api and Nampa Himals and in the shallow basin below is the large trading village of Khandeshwari. If you have the time, continue to Khandeshwari, where there is a basic teahouse and campsite. There are fine views of Api from above the village and there is plenty of local life to see!

Retrace your steps the following day and as much is downhill it is an easier 6½ hours to Lama Bagar.

From Gunna, head east, up a pretty tributary and in 1¼ hours reach the teashops of Sela Tada (1150m). There is a school here where you can camp if you are running short of time. If you continue onwards look for potential campsites beside the river, there is a small island in the river near Ramita (1148m, 30 mins) that makes a nice campsite.

DAY 7: RAMITA–KAPHALSERI
5¾HRS

The trail climbs very slightly for the next 20 minutes before descending to a wooden bridge over a small gorge. There is a pretty waterfall and plunge pool here but the place rarely gets sunlight so it's a bit slippery. The trail climbs steadily up switchbacks for the next 2¼ hours to Gunnai Bhangjyang (2125m) where there are pleasant valley views, but not of mountains.

From the Bhanjyang, head true right (south-east) into the next valley. The trail is flat at first but then becomes a steep descent into a small valley. It will take about an hour to reach the river beside which there are many pleasant places to lunch – unfortunately there are no dhabas here. The gradient is easy downhill again to a new bridge, which you cross to the true left bank. An easy trail winds between cultivated fields and pretty villages to Kaphalseri (1350m, 2¼hrs), where there is a good campsite before crossing the suspension bridge at the start of the village.

DAY 8: KAPHALSERI–RUN LEKH
4¾HRS

The easy trail continues to Pipalkot (1208m, 1½hrs) where there is a police checkpost where you must register. Soon after the village, turn left (uphill) at a trail junction. After a short climb the trail levels and traverses open hillside to a village that sits on top of a small peninsula of land created by the confluence of a major valley, the Paudi Khola, to your left.

Pass through the village and descend to a bridge over the Paudi Khola (1228m, 30 mins), which you cross. Turn left on the true left bank (east) following a small trail that along the valley floor for about 20 min-

utes and then climb steep switchbacks to Bubir Gaon (1535m, 1hr from bridge). From above Bubir the gradient eases for 30 minutes before another steep switchback section to Khollekh Gaon (30 mins) and just beyond the village, the ridge of Run Lekh (1982m, 20 mins). It is possible to camp before and after Run Lekh or near to Khollekh; search around for the best spot.

DAY 9: RUN LEKH–MULSIA   5HRS

From the small teashops on Run Lekh, turn left (north-east) on an open trail across scrubby hillside to a minor ridge (2275m, 40 mins). The gradient eases but continues to climb towards Kadachaud. Just before the final ascent to the village there is a small and very friendly teashop. Beyond Kadachaud is Bhanjor Bhanjyang (2580m, 2hrs), which does not have any teashops or shelter. Here you have two choices:

● **Option 1:** Continue traversing hillside to your left on good trails that take 2 days towards Chainpur. There are many trails to choose from but none actually reaches Chainpur as the new road follows the final 10km of old trail to the town.

● **Option 2:** Descend into the valley below and then continue down to the road the following morning. Note that this route is also ideal for those wanting to trek to Khaptad National Park. This route is described (see pp245-9).

There are not many campsites in the valley below Bhanjor Bhanjyang. There are a few flat spots after descending for about 30 minutes, when you then cross to a main trail on the true left of the valley and descend to Mulsia (1845m, 2hrs) where there is excellent spring water. It is a good idea to find a local guide in the village for the following morning as the trails are very confusing.

DAY 10: MULSIA–CHAINPUR   3HRS

Descend to Mulsia but stay on a trail that stays to the true left (east) of the village – do not go through the village! There are now many trails between compact villages so keep your group close together. The trail eventually reaches the riverside beneath some cliffs (2hrs 20 mins) and you now

ROUTE GUIDE

have to cross many streams along the
riverbed to reach the road (20 mins) and the
Seti Nadi valley. The village of Jhote is
about 20 minutes north (left) along the
road, where there are dhabas and frequent
passing vehicles to Chainpur (1296m, 2hr
drive). There are a few 'hotels' in Chainpur
and some good dhabas, but the highlight is
the local doughnut shop!! You must register
at the police post and expect a small
squadron of government officials who will
want to see your documents as a pretext for
a boring chat.

If you are continuing to walk,
Chainpur has a good market where you can
restock almost all supplies. There are frequent buses to Dadeldhura and Dhangadhi
throughout the day.

**NOTE: From Chainpur there are
two routes to Martadi. The main trade
route takes 4-5 days and heads back
down the Seti Nadi valley on the true left
bank before turning left at
Khairadagaon into a tributary valley.
You then pass through Pasal Bagar,
Gadraya and Dogadi en route to
Martadi. However, this route is long,
congested with donkeys and the likely
route of a road-construction project.**

**The alternative route is faster (3-4
days), considerably more challenging
and offers some great views of the Api
and Saipal Himal; this route is described
here.**

DAY 11: CHAINPUR–FOREST CAMP
6½HRS

Today is a tough day, so get an early start.
Cross the suspension bridge at the northern
end of Chainpur to the true left bank of the
Seti Nadi. Then wind between fields and
pass a hamlet before beginning a gradual
ascent on open hillside. The gradient eases
after 30 minutes and you cross a minor
ridge into the Pandhirabis Khola. Continue
on an easy traversing trail on the true right
side of the valley, passing small villages to
Khetkot (1675m, 2hrs). You can camp in
the school here if you had a late start from
Chainpur.

Descend to the river at the far end of
the village and cross a small bridge. The

trail gradually climbs the true right bank,
again passing through small villages. The
last village is Thanatholi (2105m, 2½hrs),
which is very friendly and you might want
to ask for a local guide here to take you to
the pass or beyond. The trail now climbs
through forest to a kharka (2365m, 1½hrs),
which is a good place to stop before
attempting the pass tomorrow.

DAY 12: FOREST CAMP–TRAILSIDE CAMP
8HRS

The trail remains on the forested true right
side of the valley the entire way to the pass.
For most of the way it is easy to follow but
there are a few tricky navigation sections
when enclosed by bushes. After 1½ hours
the gradient begins to increase and eventually becomes switchbacks before a final
short traverse to Bateli Bhanjyang (3236m,
3hrs) where there are some great views of
Api and Saipal Himals.

Beyond the pass is a steep switchback
descent to a small kharka and then steep
again to the Gwani Gad. Just before reaching the river there is a campsite on your left
behind some trees (2050m, 3hrs) but you'll
have to use the river water. If you have
some energy, there is another small campsite in 30 minutes. It's about 80m down to
the river, which you cross and follow an
easy trail that gradually climbs the true left
bank.

After leaving the forest you round a
prominent ridge, where there is a slightly
sloping grassy campsite (2062m, 30 mins).
There is a small spring water source a little
further along the trail and the small village
of Kotgaon, another 20 minutes on, where
you can buy very basic supplies.

**NOTE: There is another trail option
between Kotgaon and Kolti, which is
best done in reverse for navigation reason. See *Other Routes: Kolti to Kotgaon*,
pp267-8.**

DAY 13: TRAILSIDE CAMP– MARTADI
5HRS

Passing through Kotgaon, the trail then
begins a long gradual descent to the river
and there is a dhaba at Manakot (1548m,
1½hrs). Less than 10 minutes further, cross

a suspension bridge to the true right bank and then follow a good trail that gradually climbs away from the river. At each trail junction, take the larger, more used route and do not descend to the river. The valley turns sharply south (right) and there is a good water source at Satera (1519m, 1hr) if you are feeling hot. Another short traversing section is followed by a descent to the river and suspension bridge at Jugadakot (1302m, 1¼hrs).

Cross the bridge to Gumti (yes, the villages on either side of the river have different names) and follow a very worn trail up a small side valley, which becomes switchbacks in about 15 minutes. This last section up to Melkha Bhanjyang (1583m, 30 mins) can feel much tougher than it is, but there are some teashops at the top.

Follow the dirt road and you will soon see Martadi on the far side of the valley. There are some excellent campsites (1410m, 20 mins) beside the river; it is another 20 minutes to the main bazaar if you want to explore and buy rations or stay in a teahouse.

DAY 14: MARTADI–FOREST CAMP
5HRS

If you have camped by the river, you will have to cross it to follow the road (under construction) heading east. If you stayed in Martadi head east from the town and descend to the road. You soon come to a suspension bridge where the river has cut a gorge, cross the bridge and a short climb brings you back to the road (1685m, 1hr). Continue along the road, which is the quickest route. If you want to avoid the road you can take trails in the valley bottom, but it will add an extra hour or so to the day.

At Rajatholi (1946m, 1¾hrs) there are some dirty dhabas at the entry to the village, and a much nicer dhaba at the far end of the village where they have excellent buffalo curd and ginger and lemon tea. Continue along the road but take the occasional shortcut to avoid long U-bend corners. After an hour you pass the last village and leave the road to follow a trail through open forest. The road building is continuing

through this forest so it is easy to navigate. There are some excellent grassy areas to camp and some derelict buildings that offer very basic shelter at 2569m (2¼hrs from Rajatholi).

DAY 15: FOREST CAMP–JUNGSAL
4¼HRS

The pass of Porakhe Bhanjyang (2702m) is only 20 minutes away, where there are a couple of small teashops. A large and well-used trail descends through open forest with views of distant peaks to take your mind away from the endless donkey trains. In 20 minutes pass the ramshackle collection of dhabas popular with donkey drivers, called Dharamsala on most maps. It's a constant descending gradient on a loose trail for the next 2 hours and there are a few teashops beside the trail. In another hour you reach Kolti, and in another 30 minutes pass the airstrip (daily flights to Nepalgunj).

The hotels in Kolti are expensive and not very pleasant, so continue for another 30 minutes to Jungsal (1344m) where there are some good campsites to your right about 100m from the trail. The locals here are very welcoming and there is a small shop for basics.

DAY 16: JUNGSAL–ABAGAON
5½HRS

Today will be a hot walk so get an early start! Continue down the main trail to the end of the Kolti valley. A chautara (1106m, 1¼hrs) beneath a huge Bodhi tree marks the point where you head north into the Karnali Nadi valley. The trail remains on the true right bank of the Karnali Nadi, it's a hot walk! Every 20-30 minutes there is a teashop or dhaba, so refreshments are close at hand.

After 2 hours you pass a couple of small dhabas and the trail climbs exposed hillside. On the far side of the hill the Karnali Nadi has cut a deep gorge and the trail forks. The main trail, which heads uphill (left) is the longer donkey route. The right-hand, smaller trail, is only for humans; do not attempt it if you suffer from vertigo! The smaller trail is much faster but

ROUTE GUIDE

does involve some ups and downs on exposed rock, for most people the walk is exhilarating!

Beyond the final rocky section descend to a trail beside the Karnali Nadi – it is not necessary to go through Boldhik village. Head for a long suspension bridge (1131m, 1hr), which you cross and then turn north (left) to follow a flat trail that winds around into the Kateri Khola valley. Enter the valley and remain on the true left (south) bank trail – do not cross the river! The trail soon climbs switchbacks for about 100m and then levels again.

There are no organised campsites near here, so it is best to identify a field and ask locals for permission to camp. There are some friendly locals in Abagaon (1283m, 1¼hrs) and the locals have some basic provisions to sell.

DAY 17: ABAGAON–JAMIYA 5½HRS

The valley twists and turns and it feels like you are making slow progress, but the villages are pretty and there are many distractions along the trail. Reach Matichaur (aka Tallibagar or Takbagar, 1795m) in 3¼ hours, where there are a few dhabas.

The valley now straightens and you make rapid progress along a route that the locals prepared as a road a few years ago but there was never enough money to build a bridge over the Karnali Nadi. As you head up the valley the houses become smaller – a clear reflection of the smaller plots of farmable land.

In about 2 hours you reach Jamiya (2170m) where locals will tell you there is a campsite beside the old trail about 100m above. If you are a small group ignore the advice and continue along the main trail to where the valley narrows considerably; there are some grinding wheels beside the river (below you) and a small campsite among boulders (2179m, 20 mins).

DAY 18: JAMIYA–RARA LAKE 4¼HRS

You are now walking through a delightful mixed forest to Baunpani (2431m, 1¼hrs), the last village before Rara Lake National

Park. There are a few teashops and dhabas here. Beyond, there are some lovely campsites, the first is at Karmasi (30 mins). The gradient increases and there can be some muddy sections after heavy rain, but the trail is great for most of the time.

The only community inside the National Park is Murma (2900m, 2¼hrs) where there are a few dhabas. In another 40 minutes you reach Rara Lake; walk around to the National Park centre and campsite (2983m) where you need to register. In clear weather the views of and around the lake are magnificent and it is worth spending a whole day walking around.

DAY 19: RARA LAKE ALL DAY

Rara Lake is an idyllic place; the astoundingly clear water surrounded by protected forest is a nature-lover's dream.

A walk around the rim of the lake (13km, 5½hrs) is really worth the effort – see if you can spot the stele marking the cardinal points, nobody knows how or why they are here. On the north-eastern bank is Rara Mahadev Temple, decorated with woodcarvings of elephant, peacock and people. On the full moon in July/August locals gather here to honour the god Thakur, who, legend says, created the lake by firing an arrow at the western shore and then built the eastern bank by stamping down the earth. Swirling rock formations at the eastern end of the lake are said to be his footprints.

There are some old canoes near the army camp that you might be able to use. The lake water is extremely clear for swimming, but cold, and Park rules stipulate that you must use buoyancy aids.

DAY 20: RARA LAKE–TALCHA– NEPALGUNJ–KATHMANDU 2½HRS' WALK/ALL DAY

Follow the trail east around the northern edge of the lake and at a junction turn right (the left trail goes to Gamgadhi) and continue following the lake shore.

After 1¼ hours you come to a small landing beach used by the army to ferry supplies and VIPs across the lake. The trail now heads straight into forest before turning right (south) and descending. There are some confusing trail junctions but there are always many villagers in the forest cutting firewood who can provide directions.

The trail comes out of the forest above Talcha airport (2740m, 1¼hrs), which you descend to on a steep trail. The village is growing rapidly and there are a couple of teashops and a teahouse.

The flight out of Talcha is magnificent and thrilling! First you fly over Rara Lake before turning south and flying over some of route you trekked over the last few days. Then the forests of the pahar and terrai pass beneath the wings before landing in Nepalgunj (150m).

GAMGADHI/JUMLA TO HILSA (YULSA) OR DARCHULA

[See maps opposite inside back cover] From Gamgadhi, there are two established route options in the Far West of Nepal for GHT through-hikers:

From Gamgadhi to Simikot and the Yari valley to the Tibetan border at Hilsa (Yulsa)

This route is appealing as it follows the route of the Humla Karnali river across the Great Himalaya Range to the Tibetan plateau, but it ends here as you cannot cross the border, nor can you trek to the further Indian border. So as far as a continuous trans-Himalayan trail is concerned this route is a picturesque dead-end. There is a route from Simikot to the north side of Saipal Himal and then trek to Darchula via a series of high passes. This route has only been completed by a lightweight mountaineering group and is currently not a viable option for trekkers. For trail notes see *The Karnali Corridor*, pp249-53 and *Limi Valley Trek via Hilsa (Yulsa)*, pp253-9.

From Gamgadhi to Darchula via Rara Lake, Kolti and thence to Chainpur, see *Far West Discovery: Darchula to Rara*, pp259-67. This route has the appeal of providing a continuous route to the Indian border, but runs across the southern flanks of both the Saipal and Api Himals so doesn't offer as many mountain views. The Kolti to Kotgaon trail described below is an alternative route to Chainpur for those wanting a wilderness challenge.

Kolti to Kotgaon

This trail is notoriously difficult to find and the only reliable guides are found in or near Kolti. The route is described in detail, but you will need a local guide. The best person to talk to in Kolti is Pradeep Kumar Giri who has a large house near the centre of the village. He will probably find a guide from a nearby village, which will take a day or two.

Take a path to the left of Pradeep's house that climbs through the village and then through a small gully. The trail stays on the north (right) side of the Kunda Khola and passes through small villages to a point where the river forks. However, before you get to the confluence look for a shortcut log bridge to a large grassy area. The trail then winds around scrubby hillside, past the suspension bridge to the villages of Jagar and Ghodakot (2½hrs from Kolti). Turn left in the village to a trail that climbs steep hillside to Tari (2170m, 1hr).

Walk through the village and slowly descend about 100m to a small river (40 mins) that flows down from the south (left). On the far bank the trail climbs through scrubby forest but be careful, there are many tracks here and you should stay close to the ridge on your right. There are many trails all the way up this ridge and your local guide should be familiar with a small forest campsite about 5 minutes away from the main route (2750m, 2hrs 20 mins from the small river; Finaid: Kolti, sheet: 2981 07, ref: 554 650). After 30 minutes there is a kharka at the top of which there is another potential campsite.

Continue to climb on an easier gradient on a trail, which has more and more traversing sections as you head towards the main ridge. In 45 minutes you reach the main ridge, which you follow north (right) for another 30 minutes to a small pass marked by a decorated cairn, Dadagiri (3309m; Finaid: Kolti, sheet: 2981 07, ref: 540 654). After a short traverse descend to the large Shingtua Kharka (3148m, 30 mins).

Ascend a trail to the north-west up a scrub and grass-covered hillside to the small village of Bugaidaya (3460m, 45 mins; Finaid: Kolti, sheet: 2981 07, ref: 524 658), where the trail climbs a little more to the final pass across the main ridge (3565m, 20 mins). Descend along the top of a spur from the ridge before branching right, down a *shikari* (hunter's) trail, which is both difficult and dangerous, for 4 hours to a small river. There is a campsite (2170m; Finaid: Kolti, sheet: 2981 07, ref: 493 661) just after the confluence with the larger Madi Khola, about 5 minutes downstream.

From the camp, head downstream; you will have to cross a few times before finally meeting a trail that climbs the north (right) bank in 15 minutes. The trail climbs an easy gradient for 20 minutes to Madigaon village (2300m). Head through the village on a trail that continues to climb to a ridge line offering views of the surrounding valleys and the lower snow-covered peaks of the Api range.

Follow the ridge to a stinging nettle-choked village called Pokhara (2290m) where the trail then descends rapidly to a bridge over the Buriganga Khola at Sim (1636m, 2hrs 50 mins). The trail climbs the west (right) bank of the Buriganga Khola for about 200m before traversing to the village of Dahakot. Walk through the village on the main trail to a bridge beneath the school, which makes a good campsite (1662m, 1¼hrs). There are in fact two trails from here to Chainpur, a direct route on a small track leads up the valley from Dokot to cross the Binayak Dada via Dhalkada (estimated time 5-6hrs). This trail then descends a long, forested ridge to Chainpur (7-8hrs).

Alternatively, take the main trail, which is both easier to follow and a little faster. Ascend the switchbacks beyond the bridge to a saddle on Mel Lekh (2233m, 1½hrs) before descending to Kaudakot (2197m, 30 mins; Finaid: Martadi, sheet: 2981 10, ref: 398 624). The trail then traverses scrubby hillside for 45 minutes to Manakot and on to Kotgaon (1hr). From here you cross Bateli Bhanjyang to Chainpur, see *Far West Discovery: Darchula to Rara*, pp259-67 for details (but in reverse).

APPENDIX A: BIBLIOGRAPHY

Adhikary, Surya Mani – *The Khasa Kingdom* Nirala Publications, 1988

Bezemer, Linda – *Great Himalaya Trail Low Route*, Apple iBooks, 2014

Bista, Dor Bahadur – *People of Nepal* Ratna Pustak Bhandar, 2004; *Fatalism and Development* Orient Longman, 2001

Blum, Arlene – *Breaking Trail* Mariner Books, reprint edition 2007

Chorlton, Windsor – *Cloud-dwellers of the Himalaya* Time-Life Books, 1982

Crane, Richard and Adrian – *Running the Himalayas* Hodder & Stoughton Ltd, 1984

Dingle, Graeme & Hillary, Peter – *First Across the Roof of the World* Hodder & Stoughton, reprint edition 1982

Doig, Desmond/Bhagat, Dubby – *Down History's Narrow Lanes: Sketches and Myths of the Kathmandu Valley* Braaten Books, 2009

Drs Duff, Jim & Gormly, Peter – *Pocket First Aid and Wilderness Medicine* Cicerone, 2007

Jest, Corneille – *Tales of The Turquoise. A Pilgrimage in Dolpo* Mandala Book Point, 1993

McGuinness, Jamie – *Trekking in the Everest Region* Trailblazer, 2009

Poirier, Bruno – *Himalaya: Courir le Ciel* VO2, 1995

Poussin, Alexandre & Tesson, Sylvain – *La Marche dans le Ciel* Robert Laffont, 1999

Rogers, Clint – *Secrets of Manang* and *Where Rivers Meet* Mandala Publications, 2004 and 2008

Schaller, George B – *Stones of Silence. Journeys in the Himalaya* Bantam Books, 1982

Shaha, Rishikesh – *Ancient and Medieval Nepal* Manohar Publishers, 2001

Shakya, Sujeev – *Unleashing Nepal* Penguin Books, 2009

Snellgrove, David L – *Himalayan Pilgrimage* Shambala Publications 1989; *Four Lamas of Dolpo* Himalayan Book Seller, 1967

Stiller, Ludwig F – *Nepal Growth of a Nation* Human Resources Development Research Centre (HRD), 1999; *The Rise of the House of Gorkha* Human Resources Development Research Centre (HRD), 1995

Thomas, Bryn – *Trekking in the Annapurna Region* Trailblazer

Toffin, Gerard – *Man and his house in the Himalayas* Sterling Publishers, 1991

Tucci, Giuseppe – *Journey To Mustang* Bibliotheca Himalayica, 2003; *Nepal: The Discovery of the Malla* E P Dutton & Co, 1962

Wilby, Sorrell – *Across the Top* Sun Books 1992

Wright, Daniel – *History of Nepal with an introductory sketch of the country and people of Nepal* Asian Eductional Services, 2003

Ziskin, Joel F – *Trek to Nepal's Sacred Crystal Mountain* National Geographic magazine Vol 151, No 4, April 1977

APPENDIX B: GLOSSARY

Ablation valley – an often shallow valley created by snow and/or ice melt from a glacier

Amchi – a traditional doctor in Tibetan medicine

Amrit – mystical water of immortality

Bato – Nepali word meaning path, track or trail

Bazaar/Bazar – trading place or town

Bergschrund – a deep crevasse between a glacier and mountainside

Bhanjyang – a pass and the ridge around it, see also *Deurali* and *La*

Bhatti – trailside teashop of simple lodging, see also *Teahouse*

Cairn – pile of stones marking a route ('stone men')

Chang – fermented beer made from millet, barley or other grain

Chatta – vertical prayer flag normally mounted on a bamboo pole

Chautara – a resting place beside the trail, often shaded by two giant trees

Chu – Tibetan word meaning running water, often used for stream or small river, see also *Gandaki, Khola, Kosi and Nadi*

Chorten – Buddhist memorial or decorated cairn built on passes, ridges, or other significant spots

Crampons – spikes that strap on to boots that aid walking on ice

Crevasse – dangerous crack in a glacier

Danda – ridge

Deurali – minor pass, see also *La* and *Bhanjyang*

Dhaba – a local eating place

Dhal bhat – Nepal's national dish of rice, vegetable curry, lentil soup and some pickle

Dharamsala – emergency shelter usually without windows or doors

Dhigur – Thakali financial co-operative system where members pay a set amount each year in to the 'community chest'

Dhokos – woven baskets of various sizes used to carry goods throughout the Himalaya

Dorje – also known as a *vajra*, this is a symbolic short metal weapon that represents a diamond that can cut any substance but not be cut itself as well as being a thunderbolt (irresistible force)

Dzee stone – precious stone found in the Himalaya often believed to be a fossilised caterpillar

Dzo – infertile male yak/cow crossbreed; see also *Dzum*

Dzum – fertile female yak/cow crossbreed; see also *Dzo*

Gandaki – a sacred tributary network of seven rivers that flow from Nepal to the Ganges. They include the Daraudi [Khola], Seti [Khola], Madi [Khola], Kali [Gandaki], Marsyangdi [river], Budhi [Gandaki] and Trisuli [river]; see also *Chu, Khola, Kosi* and *Nadi*

Gaon/Gaun – Nepali word for village (the 'n' is barely pronounced)

Gompa/Gumba – Buddhist temple (literally: 'meditation')

Gurkhas – one of a number of fierce army regiments in the British Army (Royal Gurkha Rifles) and Indian Army (6 regiments of Gurkha Rifles), which were first established by recruiting soldiers from the Gorkha Kingdom, most notably after the Gurkha War in 1815

Guru – Hindu or Buddhist sage or holy man, although the term is widely used for 'teacher'; see also *Khenpo, Lama, Sadhu* and *Yogi*

Guthi – (pronounced Goot-hee) Newar club or association that comes together for religious services, social events and public services

Himal – snowy mountain range

Himalaya – the 'eternal snows'

Jagat – a common village name in the high mountains that means 'customs post'; a traditional tax-collection point for trade to and from Tibet

Kang – Tibetan origin word meaning 'mountain'

Kani – entrance gateway to Buddhist communities to cleanse evil spirits

Khadag/khata – Buddhist prayer/blessing scarf made of silk

Kharka – summer grazing pasture

Khola – river or stream, see also *Chu, Gandaki, Kosi* and *Nadi*

Khenpo – Tibetan Buddhist Abbot or highly respected meditation practitioner; see also *Guru, Lama, Sadhu* and *Yogi*

Khukuri – traditional mountain knife common in Nepal

Kosi – alternative name for river; see also *Chu, Gandaki, Khola,* and *Nadi*

Kund – lake; see also *Tal, Pokhari* and *Tsho*

La – a pass; see also *Bhanjyang* and *Deurali*

Lama – Buddhist priest, and a surname in some ethnic groups; see also *Guru, Khenpo, Sadhu, Yogi*

Lhakang – Lopa word from Mustang meaning 'god house'

Linga – a stone pillar representing the Hindu god Shiva's fertility

Lumdar –prayer flags strung together

Mani/Mati stone or wall – carved prayer stones often mounted on a wall structure

Mantra – Tibetan Buddhist prayer

Mela – Hindu religious festival

Mitai – any form of sweet treat

Nadi – very large river; see also *Khola, Kosi, Gandaki, Chu*

Namlo – often referred to as the 'Nepali passport', it is the sling used to carry loads, mainly *Dhokos*

-pa – people

Pahar – the mid-hills or Central Himalaya ranges

Patans – grassy meadows

Pokhari – lake or large pond, see also *Kund, Tal, Tsho*

Puja – Hindu or Buddhist prayer(s) ceremony

Rakshi – crudely distilled 'fire-water' from almost any grain or root vegetable

Rodi – traditional Gurung method of courting where young boys and girls have sleepovers in a house under supervision

Sadhu – Hindu holy man who has taken a vow of renunciation and is respected as a mystic, an ascetic, practitioner of yoga and/or wandering monk. See also *Guru, Khenpo, Lama* and Y*ogi*

Shikari bato – Nepali phrase meaning 'hunter trail'

Sirdar – Nepali guide or the person in charge of the trekking crew (literal meaning 'trail finder')

Tal – small lake or pond; see also *Kund, Pokhari* and *Tsho*

Teahouse – what Nepali people call a mountain lodge or basic hotel, normally owned and operated by a family. Distinct from teashops, which are common throughout the hills, teahouses are normally only found on regular trade and tourist routes; see also *Bhatti*

Terai/tarai – the plains area, once covered in dense jungle, which forms the southern border to India

Thanka/thangka – traditional Tibetan Buddhist painting on paper or cloth, often displayed in *gompas*

Tongba – drink made from fermented millet, barley or other grain and drunk from a bamboo flask, or plastic jug, which is refilled with hot water

Tsho – word of Tibetan origin meaning lake or pond; see also *Kund, Pokhari* and *Tal*

Yogi/yogini – male/female practitioner of various forms of religious practice; see also *Guru, Khenpo, Lama* and *Sadhu*

APPENDIX C: THE WORLD'S 8000m+ PEAKS

Rank	Mountain	Location	Height (m)	Height (ft)	First ascent
1	Mount Everest/ Sagarmatha/Chomolungma	Nepal	8848	29,028	1953
2	K2/Qogir/Godwin Austen	Pakistan	8611	28,251	1954
3	Kanchenjunga	Nepal	8586	28,169	1955
4	Lhotse	Nepal	8516	27,940	1956
5	Makalu	Nepal	8485	27,838	1955
6	Cho Oyu	Nepal	8188	26,864	1954
7	Dhaulagiri I	Nepal	8167	26,795	1960
8	Manaslu	Nepal	8163	26,781	1956
9	Nanga Parbat	Pakistan	8126	26,660	1953
10	Annapurna I	Nepal	8091	26,545	1950
11	Gasherbrum I	Pakistan	8080	26,509	1958
12	Broad Peak	Pakistan	8051	26,414	1957
13	Gasherbrum II	Pakistan	8034	26,362	1956
14	Shishapangma	China	8027	26,335	1964

APPENDIX D: WIND CHILL CHART

Temperature °C

Wind speed km/h	5	0	-5	-10	-15	-20	-25	-30	-35	-40	-45	-50
5	4	-2	-7	-13	-19	-24	-30	-30	-41	-47	-53	-58
10	3	-3	-9	-15	-21	-27	-33	-39	-45	-51	-57	-63
15	2	-4	-12	-17	-23	-29	-35	-41	-48	-54	-60	-66
20	1	-5	-12	-18	-24	-30	-37	-43	-49	-56	-62	-68
25	1	-6	-12	-19	-25	-32	-38	-44	-51	-57	-64	-70
30	0	-6	-13	-20	-26	-33	-39	-45	-52	-59	-65	-72
35	0	-7	-14	-20	-27	-33	-40	-47	-53	-60	-66	-73
40	-1	-7	-14	-21	-27	-34	-41	-48	-54	-61	-68	-74
45	-1	-8	-15	-21	-28	-35	-42	-48	-55	-62	-69	-75
50	-1	-8	-15	-22	-29	-35	-42	-48	-56	-63	-69	-76
55	-2	-8	-15	-22	-29	-36	-43	-50	-57	-63	-70	-77
60	-2	-9	-16	-23	-30	-36	-43	-50	-57	-64	-71	-78
65	-2	-9	-16	-23	-30	-37	-44	-51	-58	-65	-72	-79
70	-2	-9	-16	-23	-30	-37	-44	-51	-58	-65	-72	-80
75	-3	-10	-17	-24	-31	-38	-45	-52	-59	-66	-73	-80
80	-3	-10	-17	-24	-31	-38	-45	-52	-60	-67	-74	-81

Risk of frostbite in prolonged exposure: -25 to -34

Frostbite possible in ten minutes if warm skin is suddenly exposed. Shorter time if skin is cool at the start: -35 to -59

Frostbite possible in two minutes if warm skin is suddenly exposed. Shorter time if skin is cool at the start: -60 and below

APPENDIX E: HEAT INDEX CHART

Temperature versus Relative Humidity

	90%	80%	70%	60%	50%	40%	30%	20%	10%
18°C	19	18	18	17	17	16	16	15	15
21°C	22	22	21	20	20	19	19	18	18
24°C	27	25	24	24	23	23	22	22	21
27°C	31	30	29	28	28	27	26	25	25
29°C	39	36	34	32	31	30	29	28	26
32°C	49	44	41	38	36	34	32	30	29
35°C	61	55	50	45	42	38	36	33	32
38°C	76	68	61	54	49	44	40	37	35
41°C	93	83	73	65	57	51	45	41	38
43°C	113	100	87	76	67	58	51	45	41
46°C	135	119	103	90	77	67	58	50	44
49°C	160	140	121	104	89	76	65	55	48

Source: www.crh.noaa.gov/pub/heat.htm

Note: Exposure to direct sunlight can increase the HI by up to 9°C

27°C – 32°C	Fatigue possible with prolonged exposure and physical activity
32°C – 41°C	Sunstroke, heat cramps and heat exhaustion possible
41°C – 54°C	Sunstroke, heat cramps and heat exhaustion likely; heat stroke likely
54°C or more	Heat stroke highly likely with continued exposure

APPENDIX F: SAMPLE GHT HIGHER ROUTE ITINERARY

DAY	HOURS	PLACE	HEIGHT (METRES)	SECTION
Eastern Himalaya				
1		Kathmandu (KTM)	1300	**Kanchenjunga**
2	flight	KTM–Biratnagar (BIR)	2420	
3	flight	BIR–Suketar/Taplejung	2420	
4	4	Phurumbu	1542	
5	6	Chiruwa	1270	
6	5.5	Sukathum	1576	
7	6	Amjilosa	2308	
8	5	Gyabla	2730	
9	4.5	Ghunsa	3595	
10	REST	Ghunsa	3595	
11	5.5	Khangpachen	4050	
12	REST	Khangpachen	4050	
13	5	Lhonak	4780	

Day	Hours	Place	Height (metres)	Section
Eastern Himalaya *(cont'd)*				
14	REST	Lhonak	4780	
15	4	Kanchenjunga BC	5143	
16	REST	Kanchenjunga BC	5143	
17	4	Khangpachen	4050	
18	3	Ghunsa	3595	
19	5.5	Nango La camp	4776	
20	5	Yangma Khola	3430	
21	4	Olangchun Gola	3191	
22	REST	Olangchun Gola	3191	
23	6.5	Pass Camp	4453	**Makalu–Everest**
24	7	Thudam	3556	
25	6.5	Kharka	2700	
26	5	Chyamtang	2187	
27	REST	Chyamtang	2187	
28	5	Hongon or high camp	2323	
29	3.5	Bakim Kharka or high camp	3020	
30	4	Molun Pokhari	3954	
31	5	Saldim Khola	2980	
32	3.5	Cave shelter	3115	
33	5	kharka	3870	
34	5	kharka	4097	
35	4	Yangla/Yanghri Kharka	3557	
36	REST	Yangla/Yanghri Kharka	3557	
37	4	Langmale Kharka	4410	
38	4	Makalu Base Camp (MBC)	4870	
39	4	Swiss Base Camp	5150	
40	5	Sherpani Col (Base Camp)	5688	
41	7	Baruntse High Camp	6050	
42	4	Honku Basin	5500	
43	5	Amphu Labsta Base Camp	5527	
44	9	Chhukung	4730	
45	3	Dingboche/rest in Loboche	4410	
46	3.5	Loboche	4910	
47	5.5	Gorak Shep–Kala Patthar	5140	
48	6.5	Everest Base Camp (EBC)–Loboche	4910	
49	4	Dzongla	4830	
50	6.5	Dragnag–Gokyo	4790	
51	REST	Gokyo–Gokyo Ri	4790	
52	REST	Gokyo–5th Lake	4790	
53	6.5	Lumde	4368	
54	3	Thame	3820	
55	6.5	Parchemuche Tsho	4780	**Rolwaling**
56	5.5	Cave Camp	5665	
57	7.5	Trakarding Glacier	4735	
58	4.5	Kabug	4820	
59	5	Beding	3740	
60	REST	Beding	3740	
61	4.5	Dokhang	2791	
62	5	Simigaon	2036	

DAY	HOURS	PLACE	HEIGHT (METRES)	SECTION
Eastern Himalaya *(cont'd)*				
63	7	Orangdanda	2029	
64	6.5	Loting	1768	
65	4	Bigu Gompa	2516	
66	5.5	Sano Jyandan	3127	
67	5.5	The Last Resort/KTM/REST	1170	
Central Himalaya				
68	REST	The Last Resort	1170	**Langtang**
69	4	Listi	2260	
70	5	Bagam	2705	
71	4	Chogomogor Kharka	3924	
72	4	Bhairav Kund	4050	
73	6	Sumsur Danda	2820	
74	4.5	Balephi Khola Camp	1460	
75	5.5	Jhulkedanda	2480	
76	5	Pauwa Bas	3000	
77	5	Hille Bhanjyang	3600	
78	4.5	Panch Pokhari	4074	
79	3.5	intemediary camp	4100	
80	4	Tin Pokhari	4255	
81	4.25	High Camp – south	4867	
82	6.5	High Camp – north	4720	
83	6.5	Kyangjin Gompa	3830	
84	5	Ghoratabela	3030	
85	4	Syabrubesi	1503	
86	REST	Syabrubesi	1503	
87	4.5	Gatlang	2238	**Ganesh, Manaslu, Annapurna**
88	6	Somdang	3258	
89	7	Tipling	1890	
90	5.5	Lapa Khola	1285	
91	7	Nauban Kharka	2750	
92	7.5	Kerauja	2074	
93	6.5	Jagat	1340	
94	3	Phillim	1570	
95	5	Deng	1860	
96	5	Namrung	2630	
97	5.5	Sama (Ryo)	3520	
98	2.25	Samdo	3875	
99	REST	Samdo	3875	
100	3	Larkya Base Camp	4460	
101	7	Bimtang	3590	
102	6.75	Dharapani	1860	
103	5	Chame	2675	
104	4	Upper Pisang	3320	
105	4.5	Manang	3540	
106	3.5	Yak Kharka	4050	
107	3	Thorung Phedi	4450	
108	9	Muktinath	3760	
109	3.5	Kagbeni	2810	
110	REST	Kagbeni	2810	

Day	Hours	Place	Height (metres)	Section
Western Himalaya				
111	4	Kharka	3478	**Dolpo**
112	6	Santa	3777	
113	REST	Santa	3778	
114	5.5	Ghalden Ghuldun Khola camp	4247	
115	7.5	Nulungsumda Kharka	4987	
116	7.5	Chharka Bhot	4302	
117	REST	Chharka Bhot	4302	
118	5.5	Chap Chu	4320	
119	5.5	Maran	4350	
120	3	Dharamsala	4440	
121	6.5	Danigar	4512	
122	5	Temche	3995	
123	3.5	Ringmo	3641	
124	REST	Ringmo	3641	
125	7.5	Pung Kharka	4650	
126	4.5	Chyandi Khola	4830	
127	7.75	Takla Khola	3785	
128	7	Thajuchaur	4050	
129	6.5	Tiyar	2418	
130	7.5	Gamgadhi	2095	
131	2.5	Rara Lake	3010	
Far West				
132	REST	Rara Lake	3010	
133	2.5	Gamgadhi	2095	
134		Shumla	unknown	
135		Forest Camp	unknown	
136		Darma	unknown	
137		Puma	unknown	
138		Syala	unknown	
139		Durpa	unknown	
140		Simikot	2910	
141	5.5	Dharapori	2300	
142	5	Salli Khola	2700	
143	7	Muchu	2920	
144	7	Yarig (Yari)	3663	
145	REST	Yarig (Yari)	3663	
146	5.5	Muchu	2920	
147	5.5	Salli Khola	2700	
148	7.5	Simikot	2910	
149	flight	Nepalgunj–KTM	1300	
150		Kathmandu	1300	

APPENDIX G: TREKKING OPERATORS

There are more than 1800 registered trekking companies in Nepal, so choosing one can be very time consuming. Unfortunately, registration with the Trekking Agents Association of Nepal (TAAN; 🖥 www.taan.org.np) is no guarantee of quality service or operation.

To help you identify the good from the bad, we have developed the GHT Alliance and the GHT Code of Conduct (see 🖥 www.greathimalayatrail.com and the country-specific trekking operator pages). The website also encourages you to provide feedback about your trek and the quality of service and operations you received.

Companies that adopt and promote the GHT Alliance Code of Conduct are voluntarily setting a standard in responsible tourism. If you are a trekking company committed to the principles of responsible tourism and you would like to join the GHT Alliance, please contact us through 🖥 www.greathimalayatrail.com and we will add you to the relevant trekking locations.

The agencies listed below are members of the GHT Alliance.

Nepal-based operators

Adventure Connexion
Contact: Kulendra Baral
🖥 info@adventureconnexion.com
🖥 www.adventureconnexion.com

Adventure Karnali
Contact: Topden Lama
🖥 karnali@topden.wlink.com.np
🖥 www.trekkinginhimalaya.com

Adventure Mountain Club Treks
Contact: Deepak Raman Dhakal
🖥 deepak@mountainclub.com.np
🖥 www.adventuremountainclub.com

Beauty Nepal Adventure
Contact: Bijay Rai
🖥 info@beautynepaladventure.com
🖥 www.beautynepaladventure.com

Beyond the Limits Treks & Expedition
Contact: Saroj Neupane
🖥 blimits@ntc.net.np
🖥 www.treksinnepal.com

Eco Holiday Asia
Contact: Ashok Dhamala
🖥 info@ecoholidayasia.com
🖥 ecoholidayasia.com

Funny Nepal Treks and Expeditions
Contact: Fanindra Dhamala
🖥 faninepal@yahoo.com
🖥 www.trekkingfun.com

Himalaya Alpine Guides
Contact: Luke Smithwick
🖥 luke@himalaya-alpine.com
🖥 himalaya-alpine.com

Himalayan Dream Team
Contact: Indira Khatiwoda
🖥 info@himalayandreamteam.com
🖥 himalayandreamteam.com

Himalayan Leaders
Contact: Jagat Dahal
🖥 info@himalayanleaders.com
🖥 himalayanleaders.com

Kamzang Treks & Expeditions
Contact: Kim Bannister
🖥 kim@kamzang.com
🖥 www.kamzang.com

Karnali Excursions
Contact: Hira Dhamala
🖥 karnaliexcursions@gmail.com
🖥 www.trekkinginnepal.com

Nature Adventure Trekking
Contact: Lakhbir Rai
🖥 natrekking@gmail.com
🖥 natureadventuretrekking.com

Off the Wall Trekking
Contact: Ian Wall
🖥 info@offthewalltrekking.com
🖥 www.offthewalltrekking.com

Nepal-based operators *(cont'd)*
Pema Trek & Expedition
Contact: Pema Tshiri Sherpa
📧 info@pematrek.com/pema_te
📧 www.pematrek.com

Project Himalaya
Contact: Jamie McGuinness
📧 jamie@project-himalaya.com
📧 www.project-himalaya.com

Shambhala Holidays
Contact: Mr Sonam Lama
📧 info@shambhalaholidays.com
📧 www.shambhalaholidays.com

Social Tours
Contact: Raj Gyawali
📧 info@socialtours.com
📧 www.socialtours.com

Tibet Holidays
Contact: Pema Tsering
📧 info@tibetholidays.com
📧 tibetholidays.com

Wild Stone Adventure
Contact: Tika Adhikari
📧 info@trekintonepal.com
📧 trekintonepal.com

Operators based elsewhere
Eco Holiday Asia (see p277)
(Australia, India and USA)

Hauser Exkursionen
(Germany, Austria & Switzerland)
Contact: Barbara Mittlmeier
📧 info@hauser-exkursionen.de
📧 www.hauser-exkursionen.de

Operators based elsewhere
Himalayan Leaders (see p277)
(websites in German and Dutch)

Karnali Excursions (see pp277)
(USA)

Lost Earth Adventures
(UK)
Contact: Richard Goodey
📧 info@lostearthadventures.co.uk
📧 www.lostearthadventures.co.uk

Mountain Adventures
(India)
Contact: Percy Fernandez
📧 percy@mountainadventures.in
📧 www.mountainadventures.in

Sherpa Tours
(Australia)
Contact: Pramod Khatiwada
📧 pramod@sherpatours.com.au
📧 sherpatours.com.au

The Mountain Company
(UK)
Contact: Roland Hunter
📧 roland@themountaincompany.co.uk
📧 www.themountaincompany.co.uk

World Expeditions
(Australia, Canada, New Zealand, UK, USA)
📧 info@worldexpeditions.com.au
📧 www.worldexpeditions.com

Xplore the Himalaya
(Belgium)
Contact: Rik Van Belle
📧 info@xplorethehimalaya.be
📧 www.xplorethehimalaya.be

INDEX

Page references in **bold** type refer to maps

TRAILBLAZER TREKKING GUIDES
Europe
British Walking Guides – 14-title series
Corsica Trekking – GR20
Dolomites Trekking – AV1 & AV2
Scottish Highlands – The Hillwalking Guide
Tour du Mont Blanc
Walker's Haute Route: Mt Blanc – Matterhorn

Australasia
New Zealand – The Great Walks

South America
Inca Trail, Cusco & Machu Picchu
Peru's Cordilleras Blanca & Huayhuash

Africa
Kilimanjaro
Moroccan Atlas – The Trekking Guide

Asia
Nepal Trekking & The Great Himalaya Trail
Sinai – the trekking guide
Trekking in the Everest Region

Peru's Cordilleras Blanca & Huayhuash
The Hiking & Biking Guide
Neil & Harriet Pike, 1st edn, £15.99
ISBN 978-1-905864-63-8, 242pp, 50 maps, 40 colour photos
This region, in northern Peru, boasts some of the most spectacular scenery in the Andes, and most accessible high mountain trekking and biking in the world. This new practical guide contains 60 detailed route maps and descriptions covering 20 hiking trails and more than 30 days of paved and dirt road cycling.

Kilimanjaro – the trekking guide
Henry Stedman, 4th edn, £13.99
ISBN 978-1-905864-54-6, 376pp, 40 maps, 50 colour photos
At 5895m (19,340ft) Kilimanjaro is the world's tallest freestanding mountain and one of the most popular destinations for hikers visiting Africa. Route guides & maps – the 6 major routes. City guides – Nairobi, Dar-Es-Salaam, Arusha, Moshi & Marangu.

Sinai – the trekking guide *Ben Hoffler,* 1st edn, £14.99
ISBN 978-1-905864-41-6, 288pp, 74 maps, 30 colour photos
Trek with the Bedouin and their camels and discover one of the most exciting new trekking destinations. The best routes in the High Mountain Region (St. Katherine), Wadi Feiran and the Muzeina deserts. Once you finish on trail there are the nearby coastal resorts of Sharm el Sheikh, Dahab and Nuweiba to enjoy.

Inca Trail, Cusco & Machu Picchu
Alexander Stewart, 5th edn, £13.99
ISBN 978-1-905864-55-3, 320pp, 65 maps, 35 photos
The Inca Trail from Cusco to Machu Picchu is South America's most popular trek. Practical guide with detailed trail maps, plans of Inca sites, guides to Lima, Cusco and Machu Picchu. Includes the Santa Teresa Trek, the Choquequirao Trail and the Vilcabamba Trail. With a history of the Incas by Hugh Thomson.

Trekking in the Everest Region
Jamie McGuinness 5th edn, £12.99
ISBN 978-1-873756-99-7, 322pp, 79 maps, 30 colour photos
Fifth edition of this popular guide to the world's most famous trekking region. Covers not only the classic treks but also the wild routes. Written by a Nepal-based trek and mountaineering leader. Includes: 27 detailed route maps and 52 village plans. Plus: Kathmandu city guide

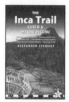

TRAILBLAZER TITLE LIST

For more information about Trailblazer and our
expanding range of guides, for guidebook updates or
for credit card mail order sales visit our website:

www.trailblazer-guides.com

Far West

POKHARA ● ● KATHMANDU

N

0   10km   20km

▦▦▦▦▦ Great Himalaya Trail – high routes
▦▦▦▦▦ Great Himalaya Trail – low route
▦▦▦▦▦ Other trekking routes

Kalapani
Mathillo Kauwa
Tinkar
Lasa 6189
Chhuaharu
Jya Chhun 6388
Kimtison
Nampa
Yokapaha 6644
Api B.C.
API NAMPA
CONSERVATION
AREA
Saipal
Gati Bagad
Gothan
Api Himal ▲7132
Rapla
Nampa Chuli 6611
Dhar
Dhaulo
Odar
Suhsera
Salle Dhar
Huti
Tatopani
Jethi Bahurani ▲6850
Lwathi
Manakot
4696
Dahachaur
Ghunsa
Pathar Rashi
Bhanjyang
Darchula
Khandeshwari
Chhelli
Katai
Kente
Jamir
Rarapu
Ghullek
Surma
Sarovar Tal
Khare
Sipti
Lama Bagar
Tolimandu
Mahal
Bhanjyang
Malikarjun
Otlekh
Panjgaun
Dethala
Sela
Seri
Than
Laune
Banisikhar
Ramita
2125
Kaphalseri
Kodari
Bagad
Darulchaur
Gwani
Gokuleshwar
Gunna
Bhanjyang
Lali
Makholi
Sittad
Nwaghar
Pipalkot
Shrikot
Kuwakot
Deulikot
Run Lekh
Pola Okhad
Baitadi
Bijayapuri
Trikali
Bhanjor
Bijula
Jiskita
Malladehi
Deulek
Bhanjyang
2580
Byasi
Patan
Gansur
Ipan Bagad
Dili
Patano
Jhota
Malumela
Salena
Sakar
Patan Bajar
Pasal B
Aanpchaur
Silanga
Khodpe
Kotili
Deura
Pata Dewal
Melauli
Rokayagaon
Bilashpure
Bhadrapur
Belapur
Dhungad
Dauda
KHAPTAD NATIONAL
PARK
Sarmali
Koteli
Khaptad
Daha
Chamada
Damdaban
Shyaule
Jhingrand
Comp
Bichpani
Bagarkot
Amaltokra
Silgadhi
Boma
Rupal
Dadeldhura
Malloda
Joshigaon
Dhursan
Bhatkada Bajar
Bairkot
DIPAYAL
Gankhet
Asigram
Sikhar
Ladagada
Simkhet
Mahabharat
Buhargaon
Bayalp
Rangun
Khola
Jinga
Gaira
Lekh
Kapalleki
Siudi
Mang
Baseni
Jogbuda
Maurikhet
Rawatkatte
Balaban
Gaguda
Lestigg
Sidhanathsthan
Shahisawan
Budar Bajar
Khahada
Kapadi
Lana Kedareswor
Tanakpur
Betkot
Asfadi
Sahajpur
Maljol
Kanachaur
Hich
dachauk
Chow
MAHENDRANAGAR
Palandigaun
Mauri
Nigal
Chyuri
Sim
Balata
Daiji
Bhamarbhoj
Kachan
Thuli Gad
Kapra
Simle
Atri
Nayagaun
Jhalari
Khairala
Golabilar
Pandaur
Betan
rsnanagar
Kipaladi
Krishnapur
SHUKLAPHANT
WILDLIFE RESERVE
Rani Tal
Dekhaltbhuli
Malakheti
Ramsikhar Jhala
Ratnapur
Shankarpur
Attariya
Bichhawa
Chaumala
Urma
Sukhad Chosal
Sadepani
Gogonpani
Meld
Shreepur
Belaedivipur
Dhangadhi
Gadariya

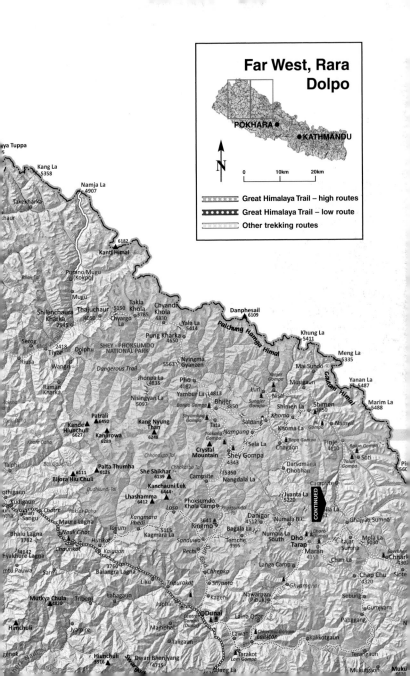

Far West, Rara Dolpo

POKHARA ● ●KATHMANDU

N

| | 0 | 10km | 20km |

Great Himalaya Trail – high routes
Great Himalaya Trail – low route
Other trekking routes

...ya Tuppa
5

Kang La
5358

Takekharka

Namja La
4907

...haur

6182
Kanti Himal

Purano Mugu
(Kokpo)

Tilak Tal

Mugu

Shilenchaura
Kharka
2945

Thajuchaur
4050

5150
Chyargo
La

Takla
Khola
3785

Chyandi
Khola
4830

Danphesail
6109

Yala La
5414

Palchung Hamga Himal

Khung La
5411

Serog

2418
Tiyar

Dolphu

Pung Kharka
4650

SHEY – PHOKSUMDO
NATIONAL PARK

Meng La
5335

Riusa

Wangri

Dangerous Trail

5563
Nyingma
Gyanzen

Mai Sundo

Yanan La
5487

Raman
Kharka

Thuli Bheri

Jhonpa La
4835

Pho
4087

Yambur La
4813

Lurb

Yenjer
Gompa

Musigaun

Marim La
5488

Nisingyan La
5097

Bongo Gompa

Bhijer
3850

Sunjer
Gompa

Nisal

Shimen La

Shimen
3850

Gandaki Himal

Kande
Hiunchuli
6627

Patrali
6450

Kang Nyung
Than

Shyamling
Gompa

Tata

Saldang

Khoma

Namyal

Kanjirowa
6289

6248

Tsakang Gompa

Namgung
4343

Khoma La

Lo
Gompa

Khore Dhola

Chhonakpo Tal

Crystal
Mountain

Sela La

Ropa Gompa

Tinje
4110

Baiun Gompa

Talphi

Bali Gade Tal

Palta Thumha
6126

6111
Bijora Hiu Chuli

She Shikhar
6139

Shey Gompa
4343

Chagaan

Darsumana
Ohobhari

Soti

Talun
Gompa

Pi
56...

Dudhkundi Tal

Kanchauni Lek
6444

Chhokarbo Tal

5350

Campsite

Nangdala La

Jyanta La
5220

Campsite

Lhashamma
6412

Phoksumdo
Khola Camp

Kangmara
Phedi

Raksu Daha

Lasa

Phoksumdo
Tal

Danigar
4512

Numala South

Dho
Tarap

Choro
Gompa

Lajar
Sumna

la L...
6...

Ghajyan Sumna

Mola La
5030

Serchhen
4302

Bhalu Lagna
3782

Maure Lagna

Nauli Ghot

Hurikot

5115
Kagmara La

Sanduwa

Temche
3995

Numala B.C.

CONTINUED

Marah
4350

Chan La

Chhark...

Siote

hyakhure Lagna

4142

Chaurikot

Kaigaon

Rechi

Langa Camp

Chap Chu
4320

mtu Pauwa

Sarmi

3760
Balangra Lagna

Tolium

Liku

Tripurakot

Chhepka

Shyanta

Gyamghar

Sebung

Gumjyam

Mutkya Chula
4820

Triben

Lahagaun

Juphal

Kageni

Nawarpani
(Pibuk)

Pangganj

N

Himchuli

Jyamire

Majhphal

Central
Gompa
(Dunai)

Dunai

Laina Odar

Lawan

Chhachuli Gompa
Laisicap

Kaikotgaun

Terangaun

genok

Suli Gad

Hiunchuli
3916

Dwari Bhanjyang
4715

Taligaun

Tarakot
Lam Gompa

Lang La

Mukutgaun

Muku
55...

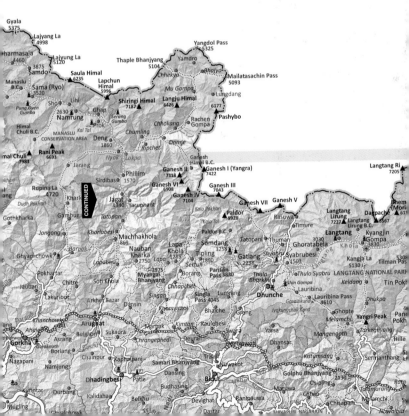

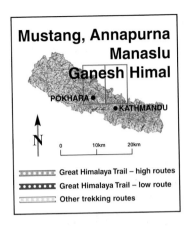

Mustang, Annapurna Manaslu Ganesh Himal

POKHARA ● ●KATHMANDU

N

0   10km   20km

░░░░░░ Great Himalaya Trail – high routes
▓▓▓▓▓▓ Great Himalaya Trail – low route
░░░░░░ Other trekking routes

Gyala
5375
Lajyang La
4998
Dharmasala
4460
Laiyung La
5120
Samdo
3875
Manaslu
B.C.
Sama (Ryo)
3520
Saula Himal
6235
Lapchun
Himal
5996
Thaple Bhanjyang
5104
Yangdol Pass
5325
Yamdro
Chhekya
Bhajyo
Mailatasachin Pass
5093
Mu Gompa
Lungdang
Sho
Lihi
Shiringi Himal
7187
Langju Himal
6426
6177
Pung Gyen
Gumba
2630
Namrung
Ghap
Prok
Serang
Gumba
Chhokang
Rachen
Gompa
Pashybo
Himal
Chuli B.C.
MANASLU
CONSERVATION AREA
Deng
1860
Kal Tal
Chumling
Ripchet
Domje
Ghanal Chuli
7985
Rani Peak
6693
Nyak
Lokpa
Ganesh
Himal B.C.
Langtang Ri
7205
Jarang
Sirdibas
1570
Phillim
Ganesh II
7118
Ganesh I (Yangra)
7422
Khani
Khola
Rupina La
4720
Kharka
Ganesh VI
6908
Ganesh IV
7104
Ganesh III
7043
Bhem
(Mori
619
Dapcache
6567
Dudh Pokhari
Gothkharka
Gambu
Jagat
1340
Yaruphant
Tatopani
Paldor
5928
Ganesh VII
Ganesh V
Langtang
Lirung
7227
Langtang
Lirung B.C.
Jongong
Khorlabesi
Machhakhola
869
Paldor B.C.
Kala Tal
Rasuwa
Timure
Kyangjin
Gompa
Ghyachchowk
Barpak
Nauban
Kharka
2750
Lapa
Khola
Lapa
1285
Somdang
3258
Tatopani
Thuman
Ghoratabela
3030
Langtang
3430
Kangja La
5130
Tilman Pas
530
Pokhartar
2975
Myangal
Bhanjyang
Tipling
1890
Sertung
Gatlang
2238
Shyabru
Syabrubesi
1503
Thulo Syabru
LANGTANG NATIONAL PARK
Jaubari
Chitre
Soti Khola
Borang
Chhapchet
Pansan
Pass 3830
Thulo
Bharkhu
Shin Gompa
Keldang
Tin Pokh
Lakuribot
Arkhet Bazar
Dansin
Singan
Singla
Pass 4045
Lumrang
Lauribina
Dhunche
Gosainkunda
Lauribina Pass
4610
Dhukpa
Ghorwa
Ahiale
Khanchowk
Gorkha
Belghari
Sukaura
Arughat
Marbak
Khorsyattol
Kimtan
Kaulebesi
Bhalche
Grang
Jyagkungchiok Kund
Ghopte
Melamchi
Yangri Peak
Pani
Pokh
Nagapani
Asrang
Borlang
Chrangephedi
Deurali
Yarsa
Dhansar
Mangengoth
Tarkeghyang
Hille
Kunintar
Chainpur
Kaphalpani
Samari Bhanjyang
Trisul
Nuwakot
Kutumsang
Sermanthang
Ghaprang
Namjung
Dhadingbesi
Patle
Dansing
Budhasing
Bidur
Golphu Bhanjyang
2130
Chipling
Thadarang
Rato
Durbang
Kalidaha
Belkhu
Devighat
Ranipauwa
Chhap
Chisapani
Melamchi
Nowalpul
Mugling
Ghaialchowk
Dastar
SHIVAPURI NAGARJUN

CONTINUED

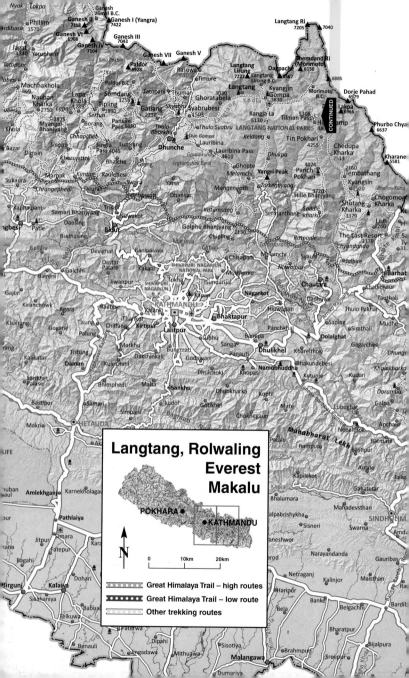

Langtang, Rolwaling
Everest
Makalu

POKHARA
KATHMANDU

0   10km   20km

░░░░░░ Great Himalaya Trail – high routes
●●●●●● Great Himalaya Trail – low route
░░░░░░ Other trekking routes

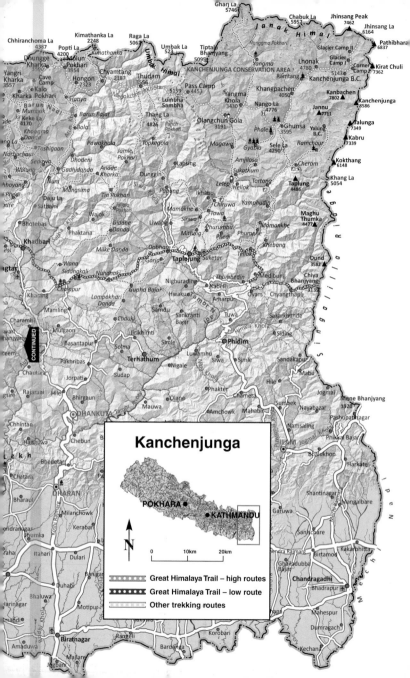

Kanchenjunga

POKHARA

KATHMANDU

N

0   10km   20km

∷∷∷∷∷ Great Himalaya Trail – high routes

▪▪▪▪▪ Great Himalaya Trail – low route

∷∷∷∷∷ Other trekking routes